Self-Determination, International Law and Post-Conflict Reconstruction

The right to self-determination has played a crucial role in the process of assisting oppressed people to put an end to colonial domination. Outside of the decolonisation context, however, its relevance and application has constantly been challenged and debated. This book examines the role played by self-determination in international law with regard to post-conflict state building. It discusses the question of whether self-determination protects local populations from the intervention of international state-builders in domestic affairs. With a focus on the right as it applies to the people of an independent state, it explores how self-determination concerns that arise in the post-conflict period play out in relation to the reconstruction process. The book analyses the situation in Somalia as a means of drawing out the impact and significance of the legal principle of self-determination in the process of rebuilding post-conflict institutions. In so doing, it seeks to highlight how the relevance of self-determination is often overlooked in this context.

Dr Manuela Melandri's research interests lie at the intersection of international law and post-conflict justice issues. She has published journal articles on the complementarity system of the International Criminal Court, gender justice in post-war settings, just war theory and the ethics of post-conflict reconstruction as well as on the topic of self-determination. She holds a PhD in Law from University College London.

Post-Conflict Law and Justice
Series Editors: James A. Sweeney
Lancaster University
and
Matthew Saul
University of Oslo

International law has great relevance in post-conflict contexts, but the complexity of its role, both as a supporting and restraining factor, can be underestimated. This series explores the role of law, and in particular international law, in securing 'justice' in post-conflict contexts. The remit of the series extends to matters of law connected to, for example: post-conflict legal reforms and the development of constitutions; the establishment of the rule of law; the place of international organizations in post-conflict; peace-keeping; transitional justice mechanisms (including criminal justice); and discussion of jus post bellum. It also seeks self-reflexive works on notions of post-conflict justice, transitional justice, and similar.

Available titles in this series include:

International Law and Post-Conflict Reconstruction Policy
Matthew Saul and James A. Sweeney

Silenced Victims of Wartime Sexual Violence
Olivera Simic

Sexualized Crimes, Armed Conflict and the Law
The International Criminal Court and the Definitions of Rape and Forced Marriage
Hannah Baumeister

Self-Determination, International Law and Post-Conflict Reconstruction
A Right in Abeyance
Manuela Melandri

For more information about this series, please visit: www.routledge.com/Post-Conflict-Law-and-Justice/book-series/POSTCONLAW

Self-Determination, International Law and Post-Conflict Reconstruction

A Right in Abeyance

Manuela Melandri

Routledge
Taylor & Francis Group
LONDON AND NEW YORK

First published 2019
by Routledge
2 Park Square, Milton Park, Abingdon, Oxon OX14 4RN

and by Routledge
52 Vanderbilt Avenue, New York, NY 10017, USA

First issued in paperback 2020

Routledge is an imprint of the Taylor & Francis Group, an informa business

British Library Cataloguing-in-Publication Data
A catalogue record for this book is available from the British Library

Library of Congress Cataloging-in-Publication Data
Names: Melandri, Manuela, author.
Title: Self-determination, international law and post-conflict reconstruction : a right in abeyance / Manuela Melandri.
Description: Post-conflict law and justice. | Abingdon, Oxon ; New York, NY : Routledge, 2018. | Based on author's thesis (doctoral – University College London, 2016) issued under title: Self-determination and state-building in international law : a right in abeyance. | Includes bibliographical references and index.
Identifiers: LCCN 2018020303 | ISBN 9781138609280 (hardback)
Subjects: LCSH: Self-determination, National. | Postwar reconstruction—Law and legislation. | Nation-building. | Somalia—International status. | Somalia—Politics and government—1991–
Classification: LCC KZ1268 .M45 2018 | DDC 341.26—dc23
LC record available at https://lccn.loc.gov/2018020303

ISBN 13: 978-0-367-58655-3 (pbk)
ISBN 13: 978-1-138-60928-0 (hbk)

Typeset in Galliard
by Apex CoVantage, LLC

The right to self-determination of peoples
should be proclaimed in such a way
as to prevent weak peoples from
being dominated by strong peoples.[1]

(Mr A Waheed, Pakistan General Assembly Delegate, 1952)

1 Commission on Human Rights, Summary Record of the 253rd Meeting, UN Doc E/CN.4/SR.253 (15 April 1952) 13.

Contents

Figures and table

Figures

Table

Table of cases

International Court of Justice Judgments and Advisory Opinions

Legal Consequences for States of the Continued Presence of South Africa in Namibia (South West Africa) Notwithstanding Security Council Resolution 276 (1970) (Advisory Opinion) [1971]

Namibia (South West Africa) (Advisory Opinion) [1971]

Western Sahara (Advisory Opinion) [1975]

Military and Paramilitary Activities in and against Nicaragua (Nicaragua v. United States of America) (Merits) [1986]

Case concerning the Frontier Dispute (Burkina Faso v. Mali) (Judgment) [1986]

Case concerning questions of interpretation and application of the 1971 Montreal Convention arising from the aerial incident at Lockerbie (Libya v. United States) [1992]

Case concerning East Timor (Portugal v. Australia) [1995]

Legal Consequences of the Construction of a Wall in the Occupied Palestinian Territories (Advisory Opinion) [2004]

Accordance with International Law of the Unilateral Declaration of Independence in Respect of Kosovo (Advisory Opinion) [2010]

European Courts

Case T 315/01 *Kadi v Council of the European Union and Commission of the European Communities* Court of First Instance ECLI:EU:T:2005:332

App No 71412/01 *Agim Behrami and Bekir Behrami v France* and App. No 78166/01 *Ruzhdi Saramati v France, Germany and Norway*, European Court of Human Rights [2007].

Case C-402/05 P and C-415/05, *P. Kadi and Al Barakaat International Foundation v Council and Commission* European Court of Justice [2008] ECR I-6351

Decisions of the African Commission on Human and People's Rights

African Commission on Human and People's Rights, *Jawara v The Gambia* (2000) AHRLR 107

Supreme Court of Canada

Supreme Court of Canada, *Re Secession of Quebec* (1997) DLR 161 (1998) 4th Series, 385

Other courts and bodies

Aaland Islands Case (1920) League of Nations Official Journal Special Supplement 3

'The Aaland Islands Question' (1921) 1 *League of Nations Official Journal* 691

Islands of Palmas Case (1928) Case (or Miangas), *United States v. Netherlands*, Award, (1928) II RIAA 829, ICGJ 392 (PCA 1928), 4 April 1928, Permanent Court of Arbitration [PCA]

Conference on Yugoslavia, Arbitration Commission, Opinion No 2, 31 ILM (1992) 1494

Conference on Yugoslavia, Arbitration Commission, Opinion No 3, 31 ILM (1992) 1497

Gillot et al v. France, Human Rights Committee, Communication n. 932/2000 of 26 July 2002, UN Doc CCPR/C/75/D/932/2000.

Table of legislation

Declaration on Principles of International Law concerning Friendly Relations and Co-operation among States in Accordance with the Charter of the United Nations, GA/RES/2625 (XXV), adopted 24 October 1970, UN Doc A/RES/25/265

European Convention for the Protection of Fundamental Rights and Freedoms, *as amended by Protocols Nos 11 and 14*, 4 November 1950, ETS 5

Final Act of the Conference on Security and Cooperation in Europe, 1 August 1975, 14 ILM 1292

Geneva Convention relative to the Protection of Civilians Persons in Times of War (GCIV),12 August1949, 6 UST 3516, 75 UNTS 287
 Article 47
 Article 64

Hague Convention Respecting the Laws and Customs of War on Land, Annex, 18 October 1907, 36 Stat 277
 Article 43

International Covenant on Civil and Political Rights, 16 December 1966, 999 UNTS 171
 Article 1
 Article 4
 Article 25
 Article 27
 Article 47

International Covenant on Economic, Social and Cultural Rights, 16 December 1966, 993 UNTS 3
 Article 1
 Article 5

Montevideo Convention on the Rights and Duties of States, 26 December 1933, 165 LNTS 19
 Article 1

Optional Protocol to the International Covenant on Civil and Political Rights, 19 December 1966, 999 UNTS 171

Protocol Additional to the Geneva Conventions of 12 August 1949, and relating to the Protection of Victims of International Armed Conflicts (Protocol I), 8 June 1977, 1125 UNTS 3
 Article 1(4)

Protocol to the African Charter on Human and People's Rights on the Establishment of an African Court on Human and People's Rights, adopted June 9, 1998, OAU Doc OAU/LEG/EXP/AFCHPR/PROT (III)

United Nations World Conference on Human Rights, Vienna Declaration and Programme of Action, 25 June 1993, 32 *ILM* (1993) 1661

Vienna Convention on the Law of Treaties, 23 May 1969, 1155 UNTS 331
 Article 31
 Article 32
 Article 53

Peace agreements and related documents

Somalia

Agreement between the Federal Government of Somalia and the Government of Puntland State of Somalia of 4 April 2016

Agreement between the President of the Transitional Federal Government of Somalia and the Speaker of the Transitional Federal Parliament of Somalia (The Kampala Accord), done in Kampala, Uganda, 9 June 2011

Agreement between the Transition Federal Government of Somalia (TFG) and the Alliance for the Re-liberation of Somalia (ARS), done in Djibouti, 9 June 2008

Constitution of the Somali Republic (1961)

Declaration on Cessation of Hostilities, Structures and Principles of the Somalia National Reconciliation Process, UN Doc S/2002/1359, done at Eldoret, Kenya, 27 October 2002

- Article 1

Garowe Principles on the Finalization and Adoption of the Constitution and the End of the Transition, adopted at the Somalia National Consultative Constitutional Conference, held in Garowe, Puntland, Somalia, 21–23 December 2012

- Principle 1(b)
- Principle 1(d)

Protocol Establishing the Somali National Constituent Assembly, done in Nairobi, 22 June 2012

- Article 3(1)
- Article 4(1)
- Article 4(2)

Provisional Constitution of the Federal Republic of Somalia, adopted in Mogadishu, Somalia, 1 August 2012

- Article 135

Roadmap on Ending the Transition, adopted in Mogadishu, 6 September 2011

- Benchmark 2

Transitional Federal Charter of the Somali Republic, adopted in February 2004

- Article 11
- Article 49

Somali National Leaders Forum, Communiqué on the Electoral Model for 2016, of 27 January 2016

Acknowledgements

This book was conceived in light of a genuine curiosity to understand whether and how the principle of self-determination could be invoked by local populations as a shield against external actors imposing a reconstruction agenda in post-conflict settings. The book ended up raising more questions than it set out to answer; but this is an authentic luxury that one can afford when engaged in academic research, and one from which I have benefited enormously.

My interest in this topic started with a dissertation that I completed in 2008 as part of my LLM studies at Lancaster University. As a doctoral student at University College London, I benefited from the generous financial support of a Faculty of Laws Research Scholarship and from the unconditional freedom to design, direct and shape my research so that it has developed into this book. Special thanks are owed to the various supervisors who have been involved at different stages of the research: Alex Mills, Douglas Guilfoyle, Basak Cali and Tobias Lock. Without their constant encouragement and support, my project would have derailed many times, many years ago. As a PhD student I held a Visiting Researcher position at the National University of Singapore (NUS) Faculty of Law, and a Visiting Fellowship jointly hosted by the Johns Hopkins University and the Centre for Constitutional Studies and Democratic Development (CCSDD) in Bologna. Thanks are due to Simon Chesterman at NUS for useful feedback and insight. I am also grateful to my *viva voce* examiners, Roger O'Keefe and James Summers, and to the editors of the Routledge Series on Post-conflict Law and Justice for improvement suggestions.

At home, I owe my warmest thanks to my father and to Riccardo. The book is dedicated to my mother, who would have been truly happy to see me complete this project.

Abbreviations

AMISOM	African Union Mission in Somalia
ARS	Alliance for the Liberation and Reconstruction of Somalia
ASWJ	Ahlu Sunna Wal Jama'a
AU	African Union
CPA	Coalition Provisional Authority
EU	European Union
GA	General Assembly
GAOR	General Assembly Official Records
GA Res	General Assembly Resolution
GCIV	Fourth Geneva Convention
GOE	Government of Ethiopia
FCC	Federal Constitution Committee
ICCPR	International Covenant on Civil and Political Rights
ICG	International Crisis Group
ICJ	International Court of Justice
ICESCR	International Covenant on Economic, Social and Cultural Rights
IGAD	Inter-Governmental Authority on Development
IGASOM	IGAD Peace Support Mission to Somalia
ITA	International Territorial Administration
NCA	National Constitution Assembly
OAU	Organization of African Union
SC	Security Council
SC Res	Security Council Resolution
SFG	Somali Federal Government
SRRC	Somalia Reconciliation and Reconstruction Council
TFC	Transitional Federal Charter
TFI	Transitional Federal Institutions
TFP	Transitional Federal Parliament
TNC	Transitional National Charter
TNG	Transitional National Government
TNP	Transitional National Parliament
UIC	Union of Islamic Courts
UK	United Kingdom

UN	United Nations
UNCIO	United Nations Conference on International Organization
UNDPKO	United Nations Department of Peacekeeping Operations
US	United States
USSR	Union of Soviet Socialist Republics

Introduction

1 Background and issues

The creation of a legal principle of self-determination was one of the most important normative developments of the twentieth century. Commonly understood as the right of a people to control its own destiny,[1] in the 1950s and 1960s the norm came to play a crucial role as a legal instrument for oppressed people to put an end to colonial subjugation and obtain independence at the international level. In essence, self-determination worked for colonial peoples as a right to choose their own political organisation, including independent statehood, and as reinforcement to independence claims in case of ineffectiveness of the units seeking independence.[2]

Notorious for its vagueness and indeterminacy, the right of self-determination has seen its relevance and application outside the context of decolonisation being constantly challenged and debated. At some point, its very existence outside of this specific context was altogether challenged.[3] This book takes issue with the role played by self-determination, as a legal principle, in contemporary international law. It does so by drawing together two important topics in international law research: self-determination and state-building. State-building is defined here as extended international involvement in war-torn states 'directed at constructing or reconstructing institutions of governance capable of providing citizens with physical and economic security'.[4]

Over the last 25 years, states and international organisations have engaged heavily in the reconstruction of post-conflict states, so that, today, state-building is an established policy for post-war recovery. The basis of international

1 Nathaniel Berman, 'Sovereignty in Abeyance: Self-determination and International Law' (1988) 7 *Wisconsin Journal of International Law* 51, 52.

2 James Crawford, *The Creation of States in International Law* (2nd edn, OUP 2006) 128.

3 Prakash Sinha, 'Is Self-Determination Passé?' (1973) 12 *Columbia Journal of Transnational Law* 260.

4 Simon Chesterman, *You, The People: The United Nations, Transitional Administration and State-Building* (OUP 2004) 5. The same definition is used also by David Chandler in his *Empire in Denial: The Politics of State-Building* (Pluto 2006) 1.

involvement in post-conflict settings has to do with the ineffectiveness of war-torn states, and with the threats that ineffective states can pose for international security.[5] This extensive use of international assistance in post-conflict states has gradually led to the emergence of a scholarly debate on the role of international law in regulating the process.[6] This book seeks to contribute to this debate by exploring the role of self-determination, as one of the fundamental principles of international law, in this specific context.

2 Argument and contribution

The book explores the significance and impact of the principle of self-determination in current international law by focusing on its use in state-building practice, as a means to ground the discussion on self-determination in a clearly defined realm of practice. The nature of state-building efforts brings in self-determination concerns because rebuilding a state often requires a radical re-structuring of the state. This process may include also the need to make and implement decisions with respect to certain fundamental constitutional and economic arrangements. Such exercises are generally supposed to be made by the people but are frequently designed, orchestrated and possibly also influenced by international state-builders. Does the right to self-determination protect local populations from the intervention of international state-builders in domestic affairs? And if so, how and in which ways?

The main argument set out in this book is that international law on self-determination is not irrelevant in this context, but its significance and impact remain still largely unknown in legal scholarship. As a result, self-determination runs the risk of remaining, in many respects, a right in abeyance. To overcome this risk, and in order to fill the existing knowledge gap, this book proposes to adopt a new way to study the relevance of self-determination in relation to this specific context. To do so, first it identifies a specific aspect of self-determination that applies in relation to state-building – namely, the right as it attaches to the people of an independent state. Secondly, it provides the first systemic account of this aspect of the norm, setting forward an original interpretation of the scope, meaning and character of this right. In so doing, this book makes a contribution to the study of self-determination by setting out the contours of a little-analysed dimension of the principle. Thirdly, it approaches the study of practice in state-building through the lens of the normative account thus

5 See generally Ashraf Ghani and Clare Lockhart, *Fixing Failed States: A Framework for Rebuilding a Fractured World* (OUP 2009).

6 See Brett Bowden, Hilary Charlesworth and Jeremy Farrall (eds), *The Role of International Law in Rebuilding Societies after Conflict: Great Expectations* (CUP 2009); Ray Murphy (ed), *Post-Conflict Rebuilding and International Law* (Routledge 2016); Matthew Saul and James Sweeney (eds), *International Law and Post-Conflict Reconstruction Policy* (Routledge 2015); Jane Stromseth, David Wippman and Rosa Brooks, *Can Might Make Rights? Building the Rule of Law after Military Interventions* (CUP 2006).

developed, aiming to explore the contribution of state practice in the development and attribution of meaning to the norm.

The study demonstrates that there is a contradiction between what the law requires and what practice shows. This contradiction can be interpreted in two ways. Either practice is a violation of the law; or practice should be seen as an interpretive exercise and should be analysed in order to see whether it can tell us something novel about the law. By adopting this second perspective, this study opens up a number of key questions that only a greater research project could aim to answer. A further goal of this book is therefore to inspire a richer debate on the meaning and significance of self-determination in contemporary international law, and to point to the need to generate a set of practice-based analyses to answer some of the key questions raised by this research project.

3 Methodological approach

This book looks at self-determination in the context of state-building and aims to understand the significance and impact of self-determination on state practice. To this end, first we must get a strong grasp of the concept of self-determination and of what it means in the context under examination. The book is a qualitative literary study and its methodological approach builds on a three-fold structure.

First, I provide a literature review in which I critically approach the way in which self-determination was studied so far and raise a set of objections that a new approach needs to overcome. Secondly, I develop a normative account of the norm in question, that starts with a first-hand analysis of the sources of international law and retraces the development of the principle from its appearance in the United Nations Charter to its inclusion in treaty law and crystallisation in international customary law. This is the doctrinal part of the book. In this part, I adopt a positivist approach to the identification of international law on self-determination. Thirdly, I delve into a study of practice, in order to ground my analysis on self-determination in a detailed contextual analysis. I employ a case study to expose the way self-determination was used and the role it played in the process of reconstructing state institutions after conflict. The use of a case-study method was chosen as a means to elucidate exactly when and how self-determination issues are at stake during the process of state-building; as well as to understand what impact and significance self-determination standards can have in the various stages of the reconstruction. In order to do this, the choice of a single case study was preferred in order to allow the necessary space to dig into the details of a complex conflict situation.

4 Structure

The book is composed of five chapters and a conclusion. Chapter 1 aims to understand the phenomenon of state-building from the perspective of international law. It provides a legal conceptualisation of the phenomenon of state-building and sets out to identify the overarching framework through which international law should approach state-building processes. In so doing, the chapter introduces the discourse on self-determination, and underlines the need to understand what we do and do not know about the role of self-determination in relation to state-building. Chapter 2 digs deeper into this issue and offers a review of the literature that explores and explains what is known about the role played by self-determination in the context of state-building. The chapter takes a critical approach to the existing literature and sets forward a number of objections in relation to how self-determination was studied so far. It argues that if we want to know more about the significance and impact of the principle of self-determination then a different approach should be used, and proposes a conceptual framework for a new approach.

Chapter 3 builds on this conceptual framework and provides an in-depth, first-hand analysis of the meaning and content one specific dimension of self-determination, namely the right as it attaches to the people of independent states. This dimension of the right has often been overlooked in existing literature because it is considered essentially uncontroversial due to its strong overlap with the concept of state sovereignty. This chapter provides the first systemic account of this specific aspect of self-determination. It examines its origins and development in legal instruments and custom, and finds a core legal meaning attached to it.

Chapter 4 is dedicated to study the character of the norm as presented in Chapter 3, and offers a conceptualisation of self-determination that is complex and multi-faceted. It provides an original interpretation of this norm that revisits existing conceptualisations of self-determination set forward in the existing literature. In so doing, the chapter proposes an alternative way of thinking about self-determination as the right that attaches to the people of independent states.

Chapter 5 tests the application of the normative model elaborated in Chapters 3 and 4 through a study of practice. It studies the state-building process in Somalia with the purpose of exploring whether practice reflects, expands, further details or maybe contradicts the interpretation of the norm set forward earlier. In so doing, the chapter aims to understand what the Somali state-building process can tell us more generally about the role and impact of self-determination in shaping the state-building process in a situation of power vacuum.

Finally, the concluding remarks bring together the key features of the argument developed throughout the book and offer some critical reflections on the implications stemming from the main findings of this study. The conclusion also highlights some of the future challenges that international law research on self-determination has to consider if it aims to develop a fuller understanding of this norm.

1 Statehood, state failure and state-building in international law

1.1 Introduction

International state-building has developed as a strategy for conflict resolution as part of the evolution undergone by UN peacekeeping in the 1990s. Whilst the main function of traditional peacekeeping missions was to monitor borders, supervise ceasefires or reestablish buffer zones, post-Cold War peacekeeping mandates became more complex and far-reaching. Complexity is reflected both in the breadth of mandates and range of tasks that such operations set out to perform, and size – including whether there is a civilian presence in addition to the military component. Multidimensional peacekeeping operations indeed include a number of components such as 'military, civilian police, political, civil affairs, rule of law, human rights, humanitarian, reconstruction, public information and gender units'.[1]

In particular, state-building components play a central role of multidimensional peace operations and the deployment of both resources and people (civilians or troops) with a state-building mandate has by now become a constituting feature of the responses elaborated by the international community to address the needs of states recovering from conflict. As a result, state-building programmes are by now a routinised practice in international public policy and a recurrent aspect of post-conflict reconstruction. This systematic use of state-building programmes to assist states in transition from conflict to peace was matched by increasing scholarly attention, so that the literature on this topic is by now conspicuous and cross-disciplinary.

This introductory chapter aims to ground the discussion on post-conflict state-building from the perspective of international law. In a review essay, Chesterman identified the existence of four main trends in state-building literature: a first set of works focuses on what happened; a second on how we can do this better (best-practices type of studies); a third looks at what this phenomenon means for sovereignty; and a fourth examines the legal questions that arise in

1 UNDPKO Best Practices Unit, *Handbook on United Nations Multidimensional Peacekeeping Operations* (UNDPKO 2003) 1.

this context.[2] This chapter focuses on the fourth set of literature, and aims to identify what are the key principles of international law to regulate state-building.

The chapter proceeds in two steps. Section 2 briefly explains how international law scholars have approached the issue and sets forward the idea that state-building is not about 'building' or creating states in a legal sense. Instead, it is about preserving existing states by restoring an effective government where government is missing or dysfunctional. In so doing, it is argued that failed states, likewise functioning states, are protected by international law applicable in times of peace because the lack of a central government does not question a state's existence in the legal sense. Section 3 sets out to outline the key structure of the overarching framework of protection afforded by failed states under international law, and points to the limits and unresolved issues that international law scholarship has to grapple with in dealing with state-building practice. Ultimately, the chapter concludes by identifying the need to better explore the role of self-determination in the area of state-building research.

1.2 Recovering from conflict in international law

In legal scholarship there is an ongoing discussion regarding the law applied and applicable to state-building. This section offers a synthetic overview of this current debate and provides a fresh suggestion for how we should think about state-building in international law at a very basic level. The argument advanced here is that only looking at this phenomenon from an appropriate conceptual framework can lead us to identify what are the key legal principles that regulate this practice. These principles, in their turn, will constitute the sources of limits for state-builders' actions and will therefore guide our interpretation of what state-builders are and are not allowed to do in facilitating transitions.

In the existing debate on how international law deals with state-building, I have identified three different methodological approaches through which current scholarship examines the role(s) played by international law in dealing with transitions from conflict to peace and will briefly discuss them in turn. There is a first set of works which uses an 'inductive approach', whereby scholars look at practical examples of state-building with an eye to identifying legal patterns that can document the current status of the law on this matter. Works adopting this approach study in depth a single case or, alternatively, more cases in a comparative perspective, with a view to establishing the significance of examined practice for general international law and for the development of the discipline.[3]

2 Simon Chesterman, 'International Territorial Administration and the Limits of Law' (2010) 23 *Leiden Journal of International Law* 437, 439–40.

3 The most notable examples of this approach are Eric De Brabandere, *Post-conflict Administrations in International Law: International Territorial Administration, Transitional Authority and Foreign Occupation in Theory and Practice* (Martinus Nijhoff 2009); Gregory H Fox, *Humanitarian Occupation* (CUP 2008); Bernard Knoll, *The Legal Status of Territories Subject to Administration by International Organizations* (CUP 2008) and Carsten Stahn, *The Law and Practice of International Territorial Administration: Versailles to Iraq and Beyond* (CUP 2008).

Of this set of works, the vast majority so far has focused on one specific model of state-building assistance: transitional administration.[4] Scarce, less systemic analysis is available on other forms of post-conflict assistance such as the so-called 'light footprint' or 'assistance model'.[5]

A second set of works adopts a 'deductive approach', whose animating question is the extent to which international law can serve as a framework to shape state-building activities. Scholars using this approach aim to identify what direct role international law can play in local contexts, exploring what are the applicable international norms in a variety of practical post-conflict situations. This kind of approach has been widely used in studies dealing with justice reform, attempts at (re-)establishing the rule of law, efforts to elaborate codes of criminal procedure and the designing of post-conflict constitutions.[6] In general, it is widely recognised that state-builders are expected to at least act in compliance with international norms such as customary human rights law, hence the real issue is how to promote these norms effectively.[7] A general aim of these studies is indeed to identify lessons learnt to be applied to other contexts: they aim to spell out the advantages of using universal principles of law and to identify the risks and limits of adapting them to culturally and politically specific contexts.

Finally, a third set of literature considers the issue of state-building in a more overarching sense, and fundamentally questions the way international law approaches state-building. In this view, post-conflict reconstruction is seen

4 For a list of articles, books and reports that discuss UN transitional administrations in Bosnia, East Timor, Eastern Slavonia and Kosovo, see Beth di Felice, 'International Transitional Administration: The United Nations in East Timor, Bosnia-Herzegovina, Eastern Slavonia, and Kosovo – a Bibliography' (2007) 35 *International Journal of Legal Information* 63.

5 One notable exception is the work of Matthew Saul. See his works: 'From Haiti to Somalia: The Assistance Model and the Paradox of State Reconstruction in International Law' (2009) 11 *International Community Law Review* 119 and *Popular Governance of Post-conflict Reconstruction: The Role of International Law* (CUP 2014). In some instances, the cases of Iraq and Afghanistan have been treated together with international administration cases, although international actors have not exercised full administrative control in Afghanistan. For instance, De Brabandere speaks of 'post-conflict administrations' as a category which includes both internationally led and national interim administrations. See De Brabandere (n 3).

6 See eg Brett Bowden, Hilary Charlesworth and Jeremy Farrall (eds), *The Role of International Law in Rebuilding Societies after Conflict: Great Expectations* (CUP 2009); Vivienne O'Connor, 'Traversing the Rocky Road of Law Reform in Conflict and Post-Conflict States: Model Codes for Post-Conflict Criminal Justice as a Tool of Assistance' (2005) 16 *Criminal Law Forum* 231; Office of the United Nations High Commissioner for Human Rights (OHCHR), *Rule-of-Law Tools for Post-Conflict States* (9 volumes, OHCHR 2006); Naomi Roth-Arriaza and Javier Mariezcurrena (eds), *Transitional Justice in the Twenty-First Century: Beyond Truth versus Justice* (CUP 2006); Kirsti Samuels, 'Post-Conflict Constitutions and Constitution-Making' (2006) 6 *Chicago Journal of International Law* 663; Jane Stromseth, David Wippman and Rosa Brooks, *Can Might Make Rights? Building the Rule of Law after Military Interventions* (CUP 2006); and Chiara Giorgetti, 'Using International Law in Somalia's Post-conflict Reconstruction' (2014) 53 *Columbia Journal of Transnational Law* 48.

7 Christian Lotz, 'International Norms in Statebuilding: Finding a Pragmatic Approach' (2010) 16 *Global Governance* 219, 228.

as a stand-alone phenomenon that is, at present, primarily regulated through ad hoc regimes which develop specifically for each and every situation.[8] In the case of UN-mandated engagements, the applicable regimes are created by one or more UN Security Council resolutions, where each resolution is designed to apply to a specific situation taken in a concretely defined time-framework.[9] The resolutions apply together with other general principles of law, at the intersection of various branches of law, and of customary and treaty law provisions that are normally applicable to post-conflict settings.[10] All together, the combination of these instruments, norms, principles and provisions constitute the legal framework though which state-builders are allowed to operate.

Proponents of a holistic approach deem that this fragmented legal regime is inappropriate to regulate reconstruction and state-building efforts, and suggest the need to elaborate a specific legal regime capable of applying to transitions from conflict to peace. As Christine Bell put it,

> Lawyers dislike 'quasi' legal regimes, laws that do not contemplate or fit the facts, and radical legal pluralism, whereby it is constantly unclear which legal regime applies and has precedence. From this dislike derives an instinct to codify a *jus post bellum* that would regulate post-conflict dilemmas more clearly and more appropriately. If international law is now a law of regimes, and the post-conflict environment has no specific or appropriate regime, then, the argument runs, it now needs one.[11]

From this debate has indeed sprung the idea of creating a *jus post bellum.* The term itself is borrowed by Just War theorists,[12] but it is understood in the legal

8 See Carsten Stahn and Jan K Kleffner, *Jus Post Bellum: Towards a Law of Transition from Conflict to Peace* (TMC Asser 2008) and the follow-up book by Carsten Stahn, Jennifer S Easterday and Jens Iverson (eds), *Jus Post Bellum: Mapping the Normative Foundations* (OUP 2014).

9 Generally, resolutions envisage mandates for 6 to 12 months, subject to review by the Security Council. One exception is SC Res 1244 (1999), 10 June 1999, for which the civil and security presences are to continue unless the Security Council decides otherwise. See UN Doc S/S/Res/1244 (para 19).

10 These international law principles and norms are scattered throughout different sources of law and treaties: international customary law, international humanitarian law, international criminal law, human rights law, refugee law, domestic laws, etc. For a brief discussion see Vincent Chetail, 'Introduction: Post-Conflict Peacebuilding – Ambiguity and Identity' in Vincent Chetail (ed), *Post-Conflict Peacebuilding: A Lexicon* (OUP 2009); and Carsten Stahn, '*Jus ad Bellum*, *Jus in Bello* ... *Jus Post Bellum*? Rethinking the Conception of the Law of Armed Force' (2006) 17 *European Journal of International Law* 921.

11 Christine Bell, 'Peace Settlements and International Law: From *Lex Pacificatoria* to *Jus Post Bellum*' in Nigel D White and Christian Henderson (eds), *Research Handbook on International Conflict and Security Law:* Jus ad Bellum, Jus in Bello *and* Jus Post Bellum (Edward Elgar Publishing 2013) 542.

12 On the concept of *jus post bellum* in Just War Theory see Gary J Bass, 'Jus Post Bellum' (2004) 32 *Philosophy & Public Affairs* 384; Alex J Bellamy, 'The Responsibilities of

sense as 'a framework to deal with [the] challenges of state-building and transformation after intervention'.[13] The debate on *jus post bellum* is still at an early stage, with academics discussing very basic aspects of this concept such as its general meaning, content and operation – and with some questioning the usefulness of *jus post bellum* altogether.[14] Given the relative novelty of the discourse, there is potential for innovative thinking in this area, or at least wide scope for igniting academic discussion. Such potential is clearly shown in the fast-growing interest that the debate on *jus post bellum* has witnessed in legal scholarship over the past 10 years.[15] Many international law scholars seem indeed keen on supporting the development of a body of law which assigns international law a clearer role in guiding transitions from conflict to peace.

Victory: Jus Post Bellum and the Just War' (2008) 34 *Review of International Studies* 601; Richard P DiMeglio, 'The Evolution of the Just War Tradition: Defining Jus Post Bellum' (2005) 186 *Military Law Review* 140; Brian Orend, 'Just Post Bellum: The Perspective of a Just-War Theorist' (2007) 20 *Leiden Journal of International Law* 573. The first contemporary Just War theorist to use the term was theologian Michael Schuck in his brief article 'When the Shooting Stops: Missing Elements in Just War Theory' (1994) 111 *Christian Century* 982, 984. For a critical perspective on the concept of *jus post bellum* in moral theory literature see Manuela Melandri, 'The State, Human Rights and the Ethics of War Termination: A Critical Appraisal' (2011) 7 *Global Ethics* 241.

13 Carsten Stahn, '*Jus Post Bellum*: Mapping the Discipline(s)' in Stahn and Kleffner (eds), *Jus Post Bellum* (n 8) 98. Other proponents of *jus post bellum* as a legal notion are: Kristen Boon, 'Obligations of the New Occupier: The Contours of a *Jus Post Bellum*' (2005) 31 *Loyola of Los Angeles International & Comparative Law Reveiw* 101; Jean L Cohen, 'The Role of International Law in Post-Conflict Constitution-Making: Toward a *Jus Post Bellum* for "Interim Occupation"' (2006) 51 *New York Law School Law Review* 497; Inger Osterdahl and Esther van Zadel, 'What Will Jus Post Bellum Mean? Of New Wine and Old Bottles' (2009) 14 *Journal of Conflict and Security Law* 175.

14 For critical views on the notion of *jus post bellum* see Nehal Bhuta, 'New Modes and Orders: The Difficulties of a *Jus Post Bellum* of Constitutional Transformation' (2010) 60 *University of Toronto Law Journal* 799; Eric De Brabandere, 'Responsibility for Post-Conflict Reforms: A Critical Assessment of Jus Post Bellum as a Legal Concept' (2010) 43 *Vanderbilt Journal of Transnational Law* 119; and 'The Concept of Jus Post Bellum in International Law: A Normative Critique' in Stahn, Easterday and Iverson (eds), *Jus Post Bellum* (n 8) 123–41; Christine Bell, 'Peace Settlements and International Law: From *Lex Pacificatoria* to *Jus Post Bellum*' Edinburgh School of Law Research Paper No 2012/16 (18 May 2012) https://ssrn.com/abstract=2061706 (last accessed 15 May 2018); Nigel D White, *Advanced Introduction to International Conflict and Security Law* (Edward Elgar Publishing 2014) 104–106; Robert Cryer, 'Law and the *Jus Post Bellum*: Counseling Caution' in Larry May and Andrew T Forcehimes (eds), *Morality, Jus Post Bellum and International Law* (CUP 2012).

15 See works cited above in notes 8–14, as well as newer developments: Antonia Chayes, 'Chapter VII½: Is *Jus Post Bellum* Possible?' (2013) 24 *European Journal of International Law* 291; Jens Iverson, 'Transitional Justice, *Jus Post Bellum* and International Criminal Law: Differentiating the Usages, History and Dynamics' (2013) 7 *International Journal of Transitional Justice* 413; James Pattison, '*Jus post Bellum* and the Responsibility to Rebuild' (2015) 45 *British Journal of Political Science* 635; Ruti Teitel, 'Rethinking *Jus Post Bellum* in an Age of Global Transitional Justice: Engaging with Michael Walzer and Terry May' (2013) 24 *European Journal of International Law* 335.

In the present work I do not aim to add substance to the debate on *jus post bellum*. I concede, however, that *jus post bellum* is particularly useful as a tool for drawing attention to the need to study the operation of international law in the context of post-conflict reconstruction.[16] The discourse on *jus post bellum*, indeed, does not exempt international lawyers from questioning what current international law applies to state-building and how this regime functions. In fact it would be inappropriate to think that a *jus post bellum* needs to be created from scratch in order to respond to a legal void.[17] Rather, *jus post bellum* should be seen as 'a call to identify the law that is applicable in the post-conflict setting, to assess its relevance, and to think about its scope for adaptation through new law'.[18] Legal scholarship is therefore called upon first to understand what is the legal framework that applies to state-building and to investigate how it operates. Having done this, we might then be able to discern what aspects of the currently applicable law are suitable to guide transitions from conflict to peace, and what aspects would instead need to be modified in order to guarantee that transitions are better implemented.

The remaining part of this section is thus dedicated to identifying the international legal framework which applies to the phenomenon of post-conflict state-building at the macro-level. To do so, we must put forward a conceptual framework that enables us to make sense of state-building as a stand-alone phenomenon in the perspective of international law. Doing so will enable us to identify a set of key principles whose functioning can lead to a definition of what are the scope and limits of action of international state-builders. In order to move the discourse on state-building forward, international law scholarship – be it concerned with a specific situation or with a more general discourse – must tackle the crucial issue of what international actors are and are not allowed to do to rebuild war-torn states. The issue of limits to action is important because state-building tasks require decision-making authority in areas that were traditionally conceived to be of exclusive concern to domestic governments as matters for internal sovereignty – such as designing institutional, economic and security sector reforms.

Starting with international state-building programmes conducted under the auspices of the United Nations, it is possible to observe that limits to action

16 A similar approach is adopted also by Saul and Sweeney. See Matthew Saul and James Sweeney, 'Introduction' in Matthew Saul and James Sweeney (eds), *International Law and Post-Conflict Reconstruction Policy* (Routledge 2015) 9.

17 Some put forward the idea that exists an alleged 'legal gap of enormous proportions and of enormous consequences when it comes to rules designed to regulate the post-conflict phase'. See Osterdahl and Van Zadel (n 13) 182. A more nuanced view is set out by Stahn, who argues that the creation of a *jus post bellum* can fill a normative gap, and help international lawyers to assess which rules apply in a certain setting and how possible conflicts between such rules can be resolved. See Stahn, '*Jus Post Bellum*: Mapping the Discipline(s)' (n 13). For a contrary view see De Brabandere, 'Responsibility for Post-Conflict Reforms' (n 14).

18 Saul and Sweeney (n 16) 9.

would come from three main sources. In the first place, for every situation in which state-building programmes are implemented there are specific limits that originate from the reconstruction mandates themselves. Such limits draw the contours of the single, ad hoc mandates designed to rebuild war-torn states (typically included in a Security Council resolution), restrict the scope of action of engaged state-builders and are specific to the situation for which they were created.

Secondly, in a more overarching sense, UN-led state-building is also subjected to Charter law and procedures. In virtue of Article 24(1) of the Charter, the Security Council is vested with primary responsibility to maintain international peace and security. In this respect, it is therefore worth at least briefly to recall what limits the Charter imposes on the activity of the Security Council's powers under Chapter VII – given that many important decisions concerning the reconstruction of conflict-affected states are taken pursuant to Security Council decisions. Thirdly, it must be seen whether there are any rules from general international law that could provide limits for the Council's authority under Chapter VII.[19]

Chapter VII of the Charter gives the Security Council enforcement powers with respect to threats to the peace, breaches of the peace and acts of aggression. With such powers comes also little restraint, as the Charter allows the possibility for the Council to derogate from existing rights and obligations. Article 24(2) provides that in discharging its duties to maintain peace and security, the Council shall act in accordance with the Purposes and Principles of the United Nations. However, the Purposes and Principles set forward in Articles 1 and 2 of the Charter are framed in such a vague formula that some commentators have been led to argue that this limit is equivalent to no limit at all.[20] In drafting the Charter there was indeed a clear intent not to restrain the actions of the Council when taking collective measures for the prevention or removal of threats to the peace.[21] To this end, at San Francisco draft Article 1(1) of the Charter was purposely amended as to make clear that the Security Council should have the power to decide on matters related to the maintenance of international peace and security without considering issues of justice and international law.[22]

19 See David Schweigman, *The Authority of the Security Council under Chapter VII of the UN Charter: Legal Limits and the Role of the International Court of Justice* (Kluwer Law 2001) 165.

20 Fox, *Humanitarian Occupation* (n 3) 202.

21 T D Gill, 'Legal and Some Political Limitations on the Power of the UN Security Council to Exercise its Enforcement Powers under Chapter VII of the Charter' (1995) 26 *Netherland Yearbook of International Law* 33, 65–67.

22 Rudiger Wolfrum, 'Chapter 1: Purposes and Principles' in Bruno Simma et al. (eds), *The Charter of the United Nations: A Commentary, Vol II* (2nd edn, OUP 2002) 43. Article 1(1) in relation to the first purpose of the United Nations reads: 'To maintain international peace and security, and to that end: to take effective collective measures for the prevention and removal of threats to the peace, and for the suppression of acts of aggression or other

As Gill notes, this does not mean that the Council is above the law or that legal considerations play no part in the Council's determinations; it is to say, however, that the Council, when taking effective collective measures for the prevention and removal of threats to the peace, and for the suppression of breaches of the peace 'need not base its determinations upon considerations of international law [. . .] in determining that enforcement measures are warranted in relation to a particular situation'.[23] Conversely, the wording of Article 1(1) specifies that in carrying out its functions aimed at the peaceful settlement of disputes, the Council remains subject to the constraints of international law and justice.

In short, in the architecture of the Charter there is a hierarchy between the Purposes, with priority being given to the maintenance of international peace and security. But the loose provisions of the Charter, however, do not mean that the Council is absolutely unbound by law when taking enforcement measures under Chapter VII powers. In this respect we may look to the concept of hierarchy of norms in international law.

Article 103 of the Charter provides that, in the event of a conflict, UN member states' obligations under the Charter prevail over any other international agreement. This applies to decisions and enforcement measures taken by the Security Council under Chapter VII, in virtue of the fact that member states are bound by Article 25 of the Charter 'to accept and carry out the decisions of the Security Council in accordance with the present Charter'. Despite the fact that the article only mentions treaty obligations, it is widely accepted that superiority of Charter obligations exists over both treaty and customary law (the latter at least arguably on the basis of the *lex specialis* principle), and that these include also binding decisions made by UN bodies, amongst which is the Security Council.[24] The higher normative status of UN Charter obligations under Article 103 raises the question of whether the Security Council may trump *jus cogens* norms when acting under Chapter VII. But by definition a peremptory norm is 'a norm accepted and recognized by the international community of states

breaches of the peace, and to bring about by peaceful means, and in conformity with the principles of justice and international law, adjustment or settlement of international disputes or situations which might lead to a breach of the peace'. It therefore appears from the final version of this article that the requirement to act 'in conformity with the principles of justice and international law' applies only in relation to the part of the article which follows the words 'and to bring about by peaceful means'.

23 Gill (n 21) 62.

24 Report of the Study Group of the International Law Commission, 'Fragmentation of International Law: Difficulties Arising from the Diversification and Expansion of International Law', UN Doc A/CN.4/L.682/Add.1 of 2 May 2006, para 33–43. See also Tzanakopoulos, who argues that in mainstream scholarship Article 103 is overwhelmingly considered to constitute a rule of hierarchy and to allow Security Council measures to superseded other obligations whether under treaty or customary law. Antonios Tzanakopoulos, 'Human Rights and United Nations Security Council Measures' in Erika de Wet and Jure Vidmar (eds), *Norm Conflicts in Public International Law: The Place of Human Rights* (OUP 2012).

as a whole as a norm from which no derogation is permitted',[25] and therefore it seems insupportable that states, through the Security Council, could enjoy a legal authority collectively that they cannot enjoy individually. As a result, the only limits that can effectively be set to the application of Article 103 come from norms of *jus cogens*, or (to use an alternative formulation) norms that have acquired a peremptory status.[26]

Overall, it appears that whenever state-building programmes are authorised by the Security Council under Chapter VII powers, international law has essentially no say in terms of limits to action, except for *jus cogens* concerns. In order to understand how international law, more generally, deals with the phenomenon of post-war reconstruction, the next sections will move beyond the role of the Security Council and its powers under Chapter VII of the Charter in designing state-building programmes. In so doing, I aim to make sense of state-building from the perspective of international law and to draw out what are the key principles that form the basis to understand state-building as a legal phenomenon.

1.2.1 What state-building is about: building states or fixing failed ones?

Here I set forward a view on how legal scholarship should conceive what state-building *is*, as a legal phenomenon. We have seen above that, according to *jus post bellum* proponents, peace-making (and state-building with it) is a phenomenon situated in-between peace and conflict which does not currently find a place in the dualist architecture of international law founded upon a distinction between the states of war and peace.[27] On the contrary, I argue that the concept of state-building does have its place in the architecture of international law, and that a dedicated legal regime for it is already in place in the rules governing peace.[28] I concede, however, that a certain level of indeterminacy is affecting this regime because the regime itself is presently evolving through the practice of post-conflict reconstruction, and as such many aspects of it still need to be thoroughly studied and explored.

At a very basic level, I set forward that a key starting point to understand the concept of state-building must embrace the idea that conflict-affected states are 'rebuilt' by (re)building effective governments and institutions. This means that state-builders 'build' states in an institutional, not in a legal sense. Moreover, they also do not work on creating the conditions for the post-conflict

25 Vienna Convention on the Law of Treaties, Articles 53.

26 On this point see also Vera Gowlland-Debbas, 'The Relationship between the International Court of Justice and the Security Council in the Light of the *Lockerbie* Case', 88 *American Journal of International Law* (1994) 643, 667.

27 See Stahn, '*Jus ad Bellum*, *Jus in Bello* ... *Jus Post Bellum* (n 10).

28 Exceptions to this would include situations of occupation, where the rules governing war would apply.

State to become a state in the legal sense.[29] Legally speaking, indeed, the states in which contemporary state-builders operate were already independent before witnessing conflict and have never ceased to be states throughout. In the post-decolonisation world, state-building is to be understood as a form of international intervention in shattered states to restore (or sometimes create) effective governments so that the newly created governmental entities can regain control over state territory.

Framed in this way, the concept of state-building in international law essentially boils down to an idea of 'government-building' or 'government-assistance'. With this in mind, I argue that the discussion on state-building, under international law, does not need to be about a standalone legal category allegedly in need of a dedicated regime. Rather, in order to make sense of this phenomenon there is a need to explore and to understand what makes an ineffective state still a state, and how the United Nations Charter and the principles governing the friendly relations and co-operation between states applies to states with ineffective governments.[30]

1.2.2 State failure in international law

The presence of an effective government enables a state to exercise its capacity to enter into relations with other states; it allows the exercising of authority with respect to persons and territory; and, finally, it confers on States the capacity to be independent – which is, to be able to exercise such control externally, or in relation to other states. Hence, there are a number of legal consequences of government ineffectiveness under international law, given that the lack of an effective government affects a state's ability to exercise its sovereign rights and duties at the international level. Despite this, international law does not have specific provisions for states with ineffective governments. In the last three decades, new terminology has been created to describe States that are in a situation of governmental turmoil. By now, we are used to refer to states without an effective government as 'weak',[31] 'failed'[32] or 'collapsed' states.[33] Such terms, however, do not have proper standing in international law. The terms belong to the language of international relations but have no value in the lexicon of

29 With two notable exceptions: the cases of East Timor and Kosovo.

30 Declaration on Principles of International Law concerning Friendly Relations and Co-operation among States in Accordance with the Charter of the United Nations, GA/RES/2625 (XXV), adopted 24 October 1970, UN Doc A/RES/25/265.

31 Francis Fukuyama, *State Building: Governance and World Order in the Twenty-First Century* (Cornell University Press 2004).

32 Gerald B Helman and Steven R Ratner, 'Saving Failed States' (1992–93) 89 *Foreign Policy* 3.

33 I William Zartman (ed), *Collapsed States: The Disintegration and Restoration of Legitimate Authority* (Lynne Rienner 1995) 5. These terms have at times been used interchangeably, while at other times they pointed at differentiating State's abilities, from weak to collapsed, along a spectrum of ineffectiveness. For a discussion of all three see ch 1 in Robert I Rotberg, *When States Fail: Causes and Consequences* (Princeton University Press 2004).

international law. The question of whether they should, or whether international law should pay special attention to states without an effective government is one open to debate.

Several reasons have been adduced to why international law should have specific provisions for so-called *failed* states. For instance, in the 2005 report of the High Level Panel on Threats, Challenges and Change, *A More Secure World: Our Shared Responsibility*, the UN recognised that the existence of weak states poses risks to collective security.[34] In addition, it is generally acknowledged that weak/failed states with ineffective governments are likely to have internal consequences as they may not be able to protect and promote human rights or provide for the basic needs of its population on its territory.[35] Some have noted that state failure also has a negative impact on representation in bilateral and intra-state *fora*, because the absence of an effective government affects consular relations between states as well as states' representation in the UN General Assembly and other specialised UN agencies.[36] Brooks further notes that there are certain specifically legal challenges posed by ineffective states: 'they [failed states] cannot enter into or abide by treaties, they cannot participate in the increasingly dense network of international trade, environmental or human rights agreements or institutions'.[37] Essentially, a situation whereby a failed state is incapable of acting as a subject of international law leads to the exclusion of the people of the failed state from international interaction.[38] In this respect, Giorgetti adds that failed states are problematic for international legal order not only because they unable to fully perform their obligations towards their citizens, but also because they are unable to live up to their obligations towards the international community as a whole. She writes:

> The increased inter-independence of States and the augmenting normative structure of the international community place obligations upon each State, as it must perform numerous actions in favor of other States and the international community. This is not just a legal requirement; it is a necessity

34 UN High-level Panel of Threats, Challenges, and Change, A More Secure World: Our Shared Responsibility, UN Doc A/59/565 (2004), 14. The report also emphasises the connection between terrorism and the existence of weak states.

35 For a brief overview of the problems posed by failed states see Ashraf Ghani and Clare Lockhart, *Fixing Failed States: A Framework for Rebuilding a Fractured World* (OUP 2009) 3–5.

36 Neyre Akpinarli, *The Fragility of the 'Failed State' Paradigm: A Different International Law Perception of the Absence of Effective Government* (Martinus Nijhoff 2010) 26.

37 Rosa Ehrenreich Brooks, 'Failed States, or the State as Failure?' (2005) 72 *University of Chicago Law Review* 1159, 1162. The same argument is made also in Daniel Thürer, 'The "Failed State" in International Law' (1999) 81 *International Review of the Red Cross* 731, who writes that failed States, 'though retaining legal capacity, [have] for all practical purposes, lost the ability to exercise it'.

38 Riikka Koskenmaki, 'Legal Implications Resulting from State Failure in Light of the Case of Somalia' (2004) 73 *Nordic Journal of International Law* 1.

> of the international community. When a State does not perform the actions that each State has come to expect, the entire system becomes unstable.[39]

On this basis, Giorgetti argues that international law should confront state failure as a matter of stability that affects the international legal system as such, and for this purpose it should adopt a set of principles to guide actions in situations of state failure.[40]

Other scholars remain sceptical about this approach and raise questions concerning the possible consequences of distinguishing effective from ineffective states from a legal-policy perspective. For instance, Wilde argues that the label of 'failed state' is not only inappropriate but is actually misleading, as it suggests that failure is to be attributed to the local players – the state's people and its leaders.[41] This, he suggests, is not simply a misunderstanding but a misinterpretation that has practical consequences in terms of what policy solutions are elaborated in response to a situation perceived as problematic. Policy responses have indeed been designed, he argues, with a view to resolving the local causes of failure – for instance by focusing on capacity-building for local governance.[42] Such an approach, however, is inherently limited because it ignores the role played by external actors and multilateral dynamics in producing failure.

The same point was also raised by Chopra in his disillusioned analysis of state failure in East Timor, which he largely attributes to the international presence.[43] Failure and lack of success, he argues, is due to a number of factors linked to the presence of internationally-led state-building missions, including the work of individuals[44] and the undermining of indigenous forms of political legitimacy, to

39 Chiara Giorgetti, 'Why Should International Law Be Concerned about State Failure?' (2009–10) 16 *ILSA J Int'l & Comp L* 469, 473.

40 Chiara Giorgetti, *A Principled Approach to State Failure: International Community Actions in Emergency Situations* (Martinus Nijhoff 2010).

41 Ralph Wilde, 'The Skewed Responsibility Narrative of the "Failed States" Concept' (2003) 9 *ILSA Journal of International & Comparative Law* 425. A similar point is made by Crawford, who argues that 'the talk of States as "failed" sounds suspiciously like blaming the victims'. James Crawford, *The Creation of States in International Law* (2nd edn, OUP 2006) 722.

42 Wilde, 'The Skewed Responsibility Narrative of the "Failed States" Concept' (n 41) 427. A similar point is made in Shahar Hameiri, 'Capacity and its Fallacies: International State Building as State Transformation' (2009) 38 *Millennium* 55 and 'Failed States or a Failed Paradigm? State Capacity and the Limits of Institutionalism' (2007) 10 *Journal of International Relations and Development* 122; Alexandros Yannis, 'State Collapse and its Implications for Peacebuilding and Reconstruction' (2002) 33 *Development and Change* 817, 818.

43 Jarat Chopra, 'Building State Failure in East Timor' (2002) 33 *Development and Change* 979. On a similar level, Chandler has noticed how the idea that non-Western people can be governed better 'with support from external experts and capacity-builders highlights the diminished view of the importance of politics'. See David Chandler, *Empire in Denial: The Politics of State-Building* (Pluto 2006) 7.

44 This point is shared also by Simon Chesterman, *You, The People: The United Nations, Transitional Administrations, and State-Building* (OUP 2004).

the extent that 'such missions can contribute to outcomes more negative than if they had not intervened at all'.[45] Even more drastically, some have called into question the very idea of building *states*, rather than other forms of political organisation, as an appropriate response to state failure.[46] This view stems from the fact that places commonly regarded as failed states, such as Sierra Leone, Somalia and Afghanistan, can hardly be considered failed states because 'they never really were states to begin with'.[47] For this reason, it is added, the efforts to fix failed states by rebuilding functioning institutions are simply a cure based on an erroneous set of initial assumptions.[48]

As things stand at present, in situations of transition it is often the case that states are left without a functioning government for a more or less prolonged period of time. Whenever this is the case, there is a formal authority vacuum that jeopardises the basis for inter-state relations and, with it, the possibility for a state to exercise control over its territory and of its territory against other states. However, as a matter of law, failed states remain states. There are indeed several examples in general practice of States that have been left without a functioning government and yet have not ceased to exist, with the state of Somalia being the paradigm case.[49] This is due to a number of legal principles that do not cease to apply and give rise to a right of states to continued existence, even in absence of a functioning government. Crawford noticed that: 'There is a strong presumption that the State continues to exist, with its rights and obligations, despite revolutionary changes in government, or despite a period in which there is no, or no effective, government'.[50]

In sum, failed states may be left without a government and/or present a reduced (or suspended) capacity to enter into relations with others, but nonetheless their statehood and independent status is not questioned. In order to become a state, international law requires an aspiring state to possess certain

45 Chopra (n 43) 995.

46 Brooks (n 37). On a similar standing see Outi Korhonen, 'The 'state-building enterprise': Legal doctrine, progress narratives and managerial governance' in Brett Bowden, Hilary Charlesworth and Jeremy Farrall (eds), *The Role of International Law in Rebuilding Societies after Conflict: Great Expectations* (CUP 2009).

47 Brooks (n 37) 1169.

48 ibid 1175. In her article, Brooks also moves a bold critique on the institution of the state more generally, questioning whether one would want to replicate the state as a structure at the global level, given its violent and unsuccessful historical record, and argues that the populations of many failed states could be better off living in 'non-state societies' rather than in a dysfunctional state.

49 For a discussion of state failure in Somalia see Yemi Osinbajo, 'Legality in a Collapsed State: The Somali Experience' (1996) 45 *International and Comparative Law Quarterly* 910. On the legal implications of Somalia's failure see generally Koskenmaki (n 38) and Giorgetti, 'Using International Law in Somalia's Post-conflict Reconstruction' (n 6) and *A Principled Approach to State Failure* (n 40).

50 Crawford (n 41) 34. See ibid at 25 for an overview of International Courts' positions on this matter. On the same point see also David Raic, *Statehood and the Law of Self-Determination* (Kluwer Law 2002) 67–72.

legal criteria.[51] Once a state is created, however, international law sets out to protect its independent statehood notwithstanding the continued possession of these criteria. The following section will therefore illustrate how international law sets out to protect the continued existence of ineffective states, notwithstanding their protracted absence of governmental effectiveness.

1.3 If a failed state remains a state: the legal consequences of state failure

This section explores the way in which international law relates to state failure. The aim is to sketch out an overarching legal framework to approach state failure and the regulation of post-conflict reconstruction. It is set forward that international law regulating the friendly relations between states grants a three-fold system of protection to failed states. First, it safeguards failed states' territorial integrity; secondly, their independence; thirdly, their permanent population. In relation to the first, we will see how its legal effects are relatively well established. In relation to the other two, instead, things are more blurred, and the matter is more open to interpretation.

1.3.1 Territory and the principle of territorial integrity

States are territorial entities and thus territory is an essential element of their nature as states. In order to come into existence, a state must indeed have a defined territory. Once a state is created, international law prohibits other states from any use of force against its territorial integrity, and this guarantees a state's existence as an exclusive spatial zone within its territorial boundaries.[52] First enshrined in Article 2(4) of the UN Charter, the principle of territorial integrity was reiterated by the General Assembly in Resolution 2625 (XXV) as well as in the Final Act of the Helsinki Conference on Security and Co-operation in Europe.[53] According to the ICJ, the principle is to be understood as an interstate principle governing the use of force, hence as a means of protection of a state's territorial boundaries against

51 The criteria are laid out in Article 1 of the Montevideo Convention on the Rights and Duties of States, which reads: 'The state as a person of international law should possess the following qualifications: (a) a permanent population; (b) a defined territory; (c) government; and (d) capacity to enter into relations with other states' and (e) independence. See Montevideo Convention on the Rights and Duties of States (26 December 1933) 165 LNTS 19 (Montevideo Convention) art 1. For an overview of the declaratory theory see Raic (n 50) 38.

52 Christian Marxsen, 'The Concept of Territorial Integrity in International Law: What are the Implications for Crimea?' Zeitschrift für ausländisches öffentliches Recht und Völkerrecht (*Heidelberg Journal of International Law*) (2015) http://ssrn.com/abstract=2515911 (last accessed 15 April 2018).

53 The resolution has been recognised by the ICJ as declaratory of customary international law. GA Res 2625 (XXV) of 24 October 1970, UN Doc A/RES/25/2625; Final Act of the Helsinki Conference on Security and Co-operation in Europe, 14 *ILM* 1293 (1975).

forceful intervention by other states.[54] Furthermore, a state's territorial integrity is also protected by the customary rule of the inadmissibility of the acquisition of territory by war, established by the General Assembly in Resolution 2625 (XXV).[55] This provision makes annexation of territories, including occupied territories, illegal under international law. Conceptually, the prohibition flows as a consequence of the ban on the use of force and fits squarely with the overall structure and purpose of occupation law.[56] As a consequence, under international law state borders are safeguarded against forceful change and this remains the same also in situations of state failure, despite the lack of effective control over territory and thus despite the lack of capacity on behalf of the state to defend its territorial integrity.

Overall, the legal consequences of territorial integrity for failed states are thus relatively straight forward. First, a failed state preserves its territorial boundaries despite its lack of control over territory. The continued existence of failed states as independent states with unchanged borders is in itself a proof of this rule. Second, other states cannot use force against a failed state and cannot claim to annex the territory of a failed state as a result of the use of force or occupation. The continued existence of the state of Iraq during the 2003 occupation is a clear example of the existence of this rule.

1.3.2 Independence and the principle of non-intervention

Another essential criterion for the creation of a state is independence. In fact, independence is so fundamental that it is often employed as a synonym for statehood.[57] In international law, independence means that a state must be independent from other legal orders, so that any outside interference by other states

54 *Accordance with International Law of the Unilateral Declaration of Independence in Respect of Kosovo* (Advisory Opinion) [2010] ICJ Rep 403, para 80.

55 'The territory of a State shall not be the object of acquisition by another State resulting from the threat or use of force. No territorial acquisition resulting from the threat or use of force shall be recognized as legal'. GA Res 2625 (n 53); *Legal Consequences of the Construction of a Wall in the Occupied Palestinian Territories* (Advisory Opinion) [2004] ICJ Rep 136, paras 87 and 117.

56 The protection of the occupied state and of its institutions is a key purpose of the law of occupation and the rationale which underpins its 'no change rule' is enshrined in Article 43 of the Hague Regulations. On this point, Roberts rightly observes how rules of customary law which prohibit unilateral annexation of territory are 'a necessary foundation for the whole idea that occupation is subject to a distinct regulatory framework'. Adam Roberts, 'Transformative Military Occupation: Applying the Laws of War and Human Rights' (2006) 100 *American Journal of International Law* 580, 582. See also Convention (IV) Respecting the Laws and Customs of War on Land and its Annex: Regulations Concerning the Laws and Customs of War on Land (adopted 18 October 1907, entered into force 26 January 1910) 205 CTS 277 (Hague Regulations) art 43.

57 See Crawford (n 41) 62 and Ian Brownlie, *Principles of Public International Law* (7th edn, OUP 2008) 71–72.

or international agency must be based on a title of international law.[58] Non-intervention, or the obligation not to interfere coercively, is an established principle of customary international law according to which states have a fundamental duty not to intervene in the 'internal affairs' of another state, meaning matters on which the state must remain free to decide without interference.[59] The law further affirms a state's independence through Article 2(7) of the UN Charter, which prohibits intervention by the United Nations in matters which are essentially within the domestic jurisdiction of any state. However, the Article introduces also a limitation to this principle, creating an exception to the rule for measures adopted under Chapter VII of the Charter.[60] Chapter VII provides for a set of exceptional measures which can be adopted if the Security Council determines that a situation creates a threat to or breach of international peace and security.[61] In conflict-affected situations, Article 2(7) therefore provides the legal grounds for allowing the United Nations to exercise a certain degree of intrusiveness into a state's internal affairs for the purposes of collective security.

Here, it is important to understand that the practice of state-building, and in particular of UN-led state-building, raises thorny questions about interference, given that reconstruction programmes require decision-making authority in domains that are normally of exclusive concern to domestic governments, and generally at times that are of concern to international security interests. As a result, there is often a clear tension between what successful state-building requires and the limits posed by the principle of non-intervention in a state's internal affairs.[62] In his study on the creation of states, Crawford observed that the debate on so-called 'failed states' has more to do with issues of security and intervention rather than with sovereignty.[63]

58 Brownlie (n 57) 72. Also, Crawford cites the words of Judge Huber in the *Island of Palmas* arbitration, who wrote that 'Independence in regard to a portion of the globe is the right to exercise therein, to the exclusion of any other State, the functions of a State'. See *Island of Palmas Case* (1928) 2 RIIAA 829, at 838; cited by Crawford (n 41) 62.

59 *Military and Paramilitary Activities in and against Nicaragua (Nicaragua v. United States of America)*, Merits, Judgment, ICJ Reports 1986, p 14, para 202–205.

60 Article 2(7) of the UN Charter and *Additional Protocol Related to Non-Intervention* (23 December 1936).

61 Article 2(7) of the UN Charter reads: 'Nothing contained in the present Charter shall authorize the United Nations to intervene in matters which are essentially within the domestic jurisdiction of any state or shall require the Members to Submit such matters to settlement under the present Charter; but this principle shall not prejudice the application of enforcement measures under Chapter VII'.

62 Here, I use the terms 'interference' and 'intervention' interchangeably, to indicate a form of coercive interference into a state's internal affairs which may or may not include the use of force.

63 Crawford (n 41) 719. The view according to which state- and/or peace-building is exploited by Western states to justify an interventionist agenda is shared also by other scholars, see on this point Chandler (n 43); Michael Ignatieff, *Empire Lite: Nation-Building in Bosnia, Kosovo and Afghanistan* (Vintage 2003); Michael Pugh, 'Peacekeeping and Critical Theory' (2004) 11 *International Peacekeeping* 39; Oliver P Richmond, 'UN Peace Operations and the Dilemmas of the Peacebuilding Consensus' (2004) 11 *International Peacekeeping* 83.

Amongst academics there is an open debate concerning what should be the appropriate level of intrusiveness to be afforded by international actors involved in state-building efforts. Here I focus on three major recent works that consider how international law should understand and respond to transitional administration, arguably the most intrusive form of state-building enterprise. The works by Fox, Stahn and Wilde reflect upon these issues in quite some depth, coming to very different conclusions in their analyses of practice.[64] They all have the common aim of comprehensively making sense of international territorial administration as a recurring strategy,[65] but their approaches and overall findings are different and representative of a broader debate. More comprehensive analyses of these works, of their similarities and differences in various aspects, have been offered elsewhere.[66] Here, my aim is to analyse the ways in which they approach invasive state-building reforms within the domain of international territorial administration. Furthermore, the positions of these authors on intervention are of particular interest because they can be located along a spectrum of receptiveness towards intervention. Whilst Fox and Stahn seem to be more open about the legitimacy of state-building efforts, Wilde remains more sceptical about invasive and externally-led reforms. I will show, however, that middle-ground positions also exist.

In his book *Humanitarian Occupation*, Fox examines four examples of international administrations: Bosnia-Herzegovina, Eastern Slavonia, Kosovo and East Timor. He defines these initiatives as 'humanitarian occupations', in an attempt to create an expression which encompasses both the means (i.e. direct administration, which resembles the *de facto* authority exercised by a belligerent occupier) and the aims of these projects (i.e. creating a liberal democratic order).[67] Indeed, Fox argues that these missions have not only sought to manage conflict by means of temporarily administering territory, but that they did so by rebuilding states according to a specific set of values and by adhering to previously set territorial borders.[68]

64 Fox (n 3) 12; Stahn, *The Law and Practice of International Territorial Administration* (n 3); Ralph Wilde, *International Territorial Administration: How the Trusteeship and Civilizing Mission Never Went Away* (OUP 2008).

65 Stahn describes it as a 'device'; Wilde argues that it is a 'policy institution' – ie an established practice used for common purposes. Stahn, *The Law and Practice of International Territorial Administration* (n 3) 155; Wilde, *International Territorial Administration* (n 64) 192.

66 See Lindsey Cameron and Rebecca Everly, 'Conceptualizing the Administration of Territory by International Actors' (2010) 21 *European Journal of International Law* 221; Chesterman, 'International Territorial Administration and the Limits of Law' (n 2); Anne Orford, 'International Territorial Administration and the Management of Decolonization' (2010) 59 *International and Comparative Law Quarterly* 227.

67 Fox (n 3) 3–4.

68 Fox is aware that developments in relation to the status of Kosovo can undermine his argument, but he claims to have demonstrated that the practice supporting the statehood model is 'sufficiently broad and deep to withstand an arguably contrary case'. See ibid 13.

The view according to which state-building missions are laid out to serve a certain liberal-democratic agenda is, in fact, not novel. Also, Buchan used a similar argument to explain why the occupation of Iraq had witnessed the occupiers aggressively pursuing a liberal-democratic agenda, notwithstanding the dubious legality of such acts under applicable international law.[69] In his view, practice in Iraq indicates that the international community regards liberal values as 'absolute normative supremacy' and sees their pursuit as 'justified irrespective that a clear basis for its conduct may be absent'.[70] Also, Roland Paris was amongst the most influential voices to argue that peace operations in general (as opposed to international administrations in particular) are vehicles for the promotion of a particular set of domestic governance norms. Paris argued that, first, peace operations aim to reconstruct war-torn states as Westphalian states, and secondly as liberal market democracies. In his words, peace-building is not 'merely a tool of conflict management, but a new phase in the ongoing and evolving relationship between the core and the periphery of the international system, with the core continuing to define the standards of acceptable behavior, and international peacebuilding agencies serving as 'transmission belts' that convey these standards to the periphery'.[71]

In this perspective, peace-building missions represent a distinctive type of globalisation process that involves the promulgation of liberal values and institutions, and they set out to promote a specific idea of the state itself.[72] For these reasons, Paris argues that peacebuilding missions should be perceived as a modern version of colonial-era *mission civilisatrice*. He therefore concludes – with his famous catchphrase 'institutionalization before liberalization' – that there is a need to have functioning public institutions before democratic politics and capitalist economics can be functioning.[73] This means, he adds, that peace-builders need to commit time and resources to restoring functioning governments and their institutions, sometimes starting from scratch.[74] Such an approach clearly requires a great deal of intervention and long-term agenda commitments, but Paris seems to justify such intervention in the name of the noble ends which peace-builders are there to pursue.

Although Fox's position is not new, the value of his research rests on the depth of its analysis and on his capacity to translate, in a way, Paris' statements into the language of international legal analysis. In *Humanitarian Occupation*, Fox's central legal argument is that the traditional legal justifications that are employed to justify humanitarian occupations face significant challenges and are

69 See Russell Buchan, 'International Community and the Occupation of Iraq' (2007) 12 *Journal of Conflict & Security Law* 37.

70 ibid 61.

71 Roland Paris, 'International Peacebuilding and the *mission civilisatrice*' (2002) 28 *Review of International Studies* 637, 653–54.

72 ibid 656.

73 See Roland Paris, *At War's End: Building Peace after Civil Conflict* (CUP 2004) 205–206.

74 ibid.

inadequate to explain the character and nature of these projects.[75] Such justifications are the consent of the hosting state, the existence of a Chapter VII mandate and the restrictions that would be imposed by the law of occupation. Indeed, whenever these justifications have been closely scrutinised – although this has not been done very often, he acknowledges – they became problematic.[76] The main point, for Fox, is that these justifications fall short of humanitarian occupation because they are inappropriate to explain such a practice. International law is a regime made up of rules created by and for states. As such, the principle of non-intervention was conceived to duly protect states from unilateral intervention. The subject to be regulated in designing humanitarian occupations is, however, the Security Council and not individual states themselves. The Council embodies the collective interests of the international community and, as such, its activity is not suitable to be judged by state-centric norms but should rather be judged by different legal standards.[77] Ultimately, according to Fox, in state-building, the ends legally justify the interventionist means: temporarily suspending a state's autonomy is appropriate when a liberal and autonomously self-sustaining state is the evident goal.[78]

In what is the most comprehensive study on international territorial administration to date, Carsten Stahn reads this phenomenon somewhat similarly, understanding it as an expression of a process of change in the international legal order towards the communitarisation of international law.[79] He argues that the exercise of administrative authority on behalf of international actors over a designated territory is something that goes beyond the mere administration of a common space. International administration, according to Stahn, is a form of governance (i) aimed at benefiting the people of the administered territory,[80] and (ii) which determines the relation between a state, its people and the international community.[81] International territorial administration projects are driven by global interests and not by specific national or sectarian ones. In this sense, Stahn sees international administration as a method of management in conformity with the cosmopolitan project of a world law.[82] For these reasons, he argues that a new

75 Fox (n 3) 8–12.

76 The point is raised also by Stahn in his analysis of the legal basis for territorial administration. See Stahn, *The Law and Practice of International Territorial Administration* (n 3) ch 11.

77 Fox (n 3) ch 8.

78 ibid 308.

79 Stahn, *The Law and Practice of International Territorial Administration* (n 3) 31.

80 ibid 44–45.

81 ibid 32–41.

82 ibid 40. A similar argument from a non-legal perspective was put forward by Yannis, who views the international preoccupation towards failed and collapsed states as evidence of the gradual shift from the traditional concept of the international system as a society of antagonistic states to the idea of international society as a community of states sharing and pursuing common interests and values. Alexandros Yannis, 'State Collapse and Its Indications for Peacebuilding and Reconstruction' (2002) 33 *Development & Change* 817, 828.

system should be elaborated to regulate territorial governance; a system which departs from traditional approaches in that it would impose limits on international authority keeping in mind the specific nature of such projects.[83] It is not surprising, therefore, to see that Stahn is one of the most authoritative advocates of *jus post bellum*, given his reading of international administration as a special type of project that should be ruled by legal standards accordingly conceived.

The works by Fox and Stahn bring a noteworthy contribution to our understanding of state-building. Political scientist Lemay-Hérbert identified two principal schools of thought in the study of state-building: the 'institutional approach' and the 'social legitimacy approach'.[84] Fox and Stahn further elaborate on this division. Lemay-Hérbert believes that these two approaches deal in different ways with the interventionist character of state-building activities. First, the institutional approach sees state-building as mainly aimed at strengthening government institutions and downplays its intrusive character, depicting it as a scientific, technical and administrative process.[85] In this view, it is believed that nation-building and state-building are two different things and the latter can be conducted without the former – thus keeping the process neutral and less politically-sensitive.[86] Secondly, the legitimacy approach emphasises instead the value and role of politics in this process and sees the establishment of institutions as but one part of a bigger picture. Authors adopting a legitimacy approach do indeed maintain the importance of institution-building but bring an additional dimension to the study of state-building: the concept of the state as an idea common to a group of people. Thus, how to build a state which creates ideological content among its people is a specific concern of the legitimacy approach.[87]

83 Stahn, *The Law and Practice of International Territorial Administration* (n 3) ch 18.

84 Nicolas Lemay-Hérbert, 'The Semantics of Statebuilding and Nationbuilding: Looking beyond neo-Weberian Approaches' in Nicolas Lemay-Hérbert, Nicholas Onuf, Vojin Rakić and Petar Bojanić (eds), *Semantics of Statebuilding: Language, meanings and Sovereignty* (Routledge 2013).

85 Examples of this school of thought include the views of Paris and Fukuyama. See Paris, *At War's End* (n 73) and Fukuyama (n 31).

86 Nicolas Lemay-Hérbert, 'Statebuilding without Nationbuilding? Legitimacy, State-Failure and the Limits of the Institutional Approach' (2009) 3 *Journal of Intervention and Statebuilding* 21. On this point see, for instance, Stahn, *The Law and Practice of International Territorial Administration* (n 3) 404. Nation-building is generally defined as the creation and strengthening of a shared national identity, based on a common idea of history and culture.

87 Authors who could be said to use the legitimacy approach are Hameiri, (n 42), Korhonen (n 46), Lemay-Hérbert, 'Statebuilding without Nation-building?' (n 86); William Maley, 'Democracy and legitimation: Challenges in the reconstitution of political processes in Afghanistan' in Brett Bowden, Hilary Charlesworth and Jeremy Farrall (eds), *The Role of International Law in Rebuilding Societies after Conflict: Great Expectations* (CUP 2009). Korhonen states: 'The state is not a tool and locus of this governance, is not a neutral structure, which the classic and the formalist doctrines of state constitution seem to assume. And, there is no prototype, no universally applicable model to benchmark 'good governance'. There is no consensus on the 'good' without qualifying 'for whom and for what' (at 27, footnotes omitted).

The discourses initiated by Stahn and Fox take Hérbert's binary discussion one step further in the domain of international legal discourse. Their views seem to reconcile this dualism by providing a technical and legal reason for why state-building is legitimate in pursuing an agenda that is essentially political. This is because such an agenda upholds a set of values that are an expression of the will of the international community. In other words, what we are witnessing, according to them, is an historical moment of constitutional transformation for the international society, exemplified through the practice of state-building and bearing consequences on how international law treats this phenomenon. A similar, more nuanced argument was made by Buchan, who argues that post-Cold War peacekeeping operations are a conflict resolution mechanism employed by the international community at the international level for the purposes of promoting liberal democracy to non-liberal states.[88]

Other scholars are willing to accept a great deal of intervention by virtue of the supposed 'exceptional' status of failed states and as a means for 'saving, developing or securing the Other'.[89] Giorgetti for instance states very clearly that 'the principle of non-intervention in internal affairs is of limited applicability in the context of state failure because it needs to be balanced with the general interest of States in upholding peace and security and enforcing international law' and that, for this reason, 'any activity to fulfill international obligations in fragile and failed states should be framed as included in this exception'.[90] Such a position not only accepts various kinds of external interference into a failed state's internal affairs, understanding such actions as aimed at promoting international peace and security, but also supports various types of interference because of the fragile conditions of states themselves. For a mix of these reasons, intervention in failed states is considered to be legitimate under international law.[91]

Whilst we could call the above pro-intervention positions, the approach of most writers has generally been more cautious. In his landmark study of transitional administrations, Chesterman has chosen the middle ground in justifying international intervention. His discussion on state-building focuses on the effects of a certain structural approach to intervention and the legitimacy discourse is drawn from there. His research starts with a question: 'is it possible to establish the conditions for legitimate and sustainable national governance through a

88 Russell Buchan, *International Law and the Construction of the Liberal* Peace (Hart Publishing 2013), 220–22.

89 For an overview of works elaborating such a position see David Chandler, 'The Uncritical Critique of 'Liberal Peace'' (2010) 36 *Review of International Studies* 137, quoting Mark Duffield, *Development, Security and Unending War: Governing the World of Peoples* (Polity 2007).

90 Giorgetti, 'Why Should International Law Be Concerned about State Failure?' (n 39) 486.

91 See also Mario Silva, *State Legitimacy and Failure in International Law* (Brill 2014). For a critical view, instead see Nehal Bhuta, 'Democratization, State-building and Politics as Technology' in Brett Bowden, Hilary Charlesworth and Jeremy Farrall (eds), *The Role of International Law in Rebuilding Societies after Conflict: Great Expectations* (CUP 2009) 46.

period of benevolent foreign autocracy?'[92] In answering this question, he tries to make sense of the contradiction that exists between the ends and the means of state-building. More specifically, he identifies a set of three such contradictions: that the means are inconsistent with the ends; inadequate to the ends; and in many situations inappropriate for the ends.[93] These aspects of the state-building enterprise, he argues, are dangerous as they may undermine the outcome of state-building operations. In other words, Chesterman's concerns on the appropriateness of 'benevolent autocracy' are raised in relation to its effectiveness in delivering successful results, rather than in relation to its appropriateness as a means, per se. Like Chesterman, others recognise and accept that peace-builders may need to act illiberally in the earliest phases of post-conflict reconstruction in order to establish the conditions for full local ownership, which is to be achieved at a later time.[94] This type of work is generally aimed at offering insights and 'lessons learned' on how state-building can be done in the best, most skilful and most effective way, so as to minimise the way and the time-frame in which liberal autocratic administrations are kept in place.

Finally, there are a number of voices that consider with suspicion the idea that 'benevolent autocracy' may be justified in view of its ends.[95] These voices speak less about effectiveness (or at least they do so with a view to more long-term horizons of evaluation) and more about international norms and principles. Such principles and norms can be the same as those used by their more pro-interventionist counterparts, but used and/or understood in a different way. Both discourses employ the language of human rights and democratisation, but while one focuses more on standards and outcomes, the other focuses on who are the subjects of those rights and what are their entitlements. In addition, these works tend to contextualise contemporary state-building efforts within a wider historical perspective and to see significant linkages between state-building and colonialism.[96] This approach leads to an attitude less prone to accepting interventionism as a necessity. It rather leads authors to be more sceptical about benevolent autocratic projects for reconstruction. As a consequence, in these

92 Chesterman, *You, the People* (n 44) 1.

93 Simon Chesterman, 'From State Failure to State-Building: Problems and Prospects for a United Nations Peacebuilding Commission' (2007) 2 *Journal of International Law and International Relations* 155, 159.

94 Also, Paris accepts such a possibility. See Paris, *At War's End* (n 73) 209 and Chesterman, *You, the People* (n 44) 9.

95 See generally works cited in this chapter by Chandler, Chopra, Korhonen and Bhuta, who approach the issue of post-conflict state-building through a 'legitimacy approach'. In addition, see Joel C Beauvais, 'Benevolent Despotism: A Critique of UN State-Building in East-Timor' (2001) 33 *NYU Journal of International Law & Politics* 1101 and Oliver P Richmond, 'The Problem of Peace: Understanding the "Liberal Peace"' (2006) 6 *Conflict, Security & Development* 291.

96 Nehal Bhuta, 'Democratization, State-building and Politics as Technology' (n 6); Nehal Bhuta, 'Against State-building' (2008) 15 *Constellations* 517; David Chandler, *Bosnia: Faking Democracy After Dayton* (London 2000).

works the basis for intrusiveness is likely to be seriously questioned and often seriously challenged.

The most exemplificative work of this current is Wilde's *International Territorial Administration*.[97] In the book, Wilde analyses territorial administration projects since the 1920s, aiming to identify commonalities of purpose between contemporary forms of international post-conflict administrations and other forms of trusteeship – including League of Nations projects, occupations, protectorates, Mandates and Trusteeship systems. In doing so, he attempts to foreground the normative basis for international administrations arguing that, to be justified, international administration 'must be able to resist the fundamental critique of trusteeship [...]: that exercising control over people from outside is inherently unjust'.[98] The book provides a lucid analysis of how and why international territorial administration is considered different from colonialism and trusteeship. However, it does not provide a concluding answer to the issue of whether international administration is legitimate because it really is different. Wilde identifies four main legitimating logics that are commonly invoked to differentiate international administration from other trusteeships. He does not directly challenge such rationales but rather he aims to illuminate their logic. In doing so, he nevertheless offers a somewhat problematic reading of these rationales, from which we understand that he maintains a critical view about their validity.[99]

The arguments that he identifies as being recurrently put forward by commentators are four in number. The first is that the projects have been legally authorised – either through the rhetoric of humanitarian intervention, the responsibility to protect or as 'just war', as well as through particular legal mandates, hence state consent and/or a Security Council Resolution.[100] The second argument is that the policies that are implemented reflect principles of international law. The idea of sovereignty as an entitlement of 'liberal' states, which brings about the idea of a gradual attainment of sovereignty for countries in transition, legitimises international administration whereas it is associated with objectives such as democratisation, human rights, rule of law and a free market.[101] The third reason is because of the identity of the administrators. The projects that Wilde considers in his book are conducted by international organisations, which are seen as serving the interests of the international community as a whole. As such their aims are seen to be humanitarian, not exploitative.[102] Fourthly, the projects are 'temporary' and, being so, they are deemed not to impinge on the right to self-determination, even though Wilde contests that

97 Wilde, *International Territorial Administration* (n 64).
98 ibid 444.
99 This point was noted also by Cameron and Everly (n 66) 227.
100 Wilde, *International Territorial Administration* (n 64) 400–408.
101 ibid 408–13.
102 ibid 413–17.

the idea of 'state-building does not in and of itself suggest a short duration'.[103] Overall, because international administration is conducted 'on a legitimate basis, for legitimate polices, by legitimate actors and with a temporary nature', it is generally perceived to be different from colonialism.[104]

To sum up, external interference into a state's internal affairs for state-building purposes has divided commentators in relation to extent to which intervention is legitimate or justifiable. International lawyers who support the liberal peace theory and communitarianism are found to explain the balance shift in the international normative order from non-intervention to externally-led interventionism by saying that what we are witnessing is a constitutional moment in history. Intervention is thus justified in principle and should be justified legally in the name of the values that it sets out to uphold – which are considered to be an expression of the will of the international community. More nuanced positions would, instead, see intervention as a 'necessary evil', a momentum which needs to be carefully balanced but which is justified because of its effectiveness in bringing about peace and security. Finally, sceptical voices bring into question the legitimacy of intervention by recalling similarities between state-building and the colonial enterprise. The great normative conquest of decolonisation is exemplified in the principle of self-determination, which grants an entitlement to all peoples to decide about their own future free from external interference and colonial domination.[105] Sceptical works hence beg the question of where this principle stands now, in a context in which interventionist agendas seem to have simply changed their masks from the colonial past to the post-conflict state-building of present times.

1.3.3 A permanent population and the principle of self-determination

However small, a permanent population as an aggregate of individuals is a necessary criterion for statehood.[106] Once a state is constituted as an independent state its population becomes a people in the language of international law and, as such, it gains an entitlement to self-determination. The right to self-determination is an instrument through which international law is said to protect a people from alien domination.[107] What this means and how this right applies in situations of state failure is something that needs to be investigated. As a legal right, self-determination certainly has a role to play in relation to statehood. In the first place, it gives non-independent people the right to determine their status – including the possibility of acquiring independence as a state. Secondly, it is argued that, in certain circumstances, self-determination supersedes

103 ibid 419–22.
104 ibid 418.
105 Antonio Cassese, *Self-Determination of Peoples: A Legal Reappraisal* (CUP 1995) 55.
106 Crawford (n 41) 52–53.
107 Hurst Hannum, 'Legal Aspects of Self-Determination' *The Princeton Encyclopedia of Self-Determination* https://pesd.princeton.edu/?q=node/254 (last accessed 15 April 2018).

the criterion of effectiveness. In the colonial context, this has meant that self-determination allowed states with ineffective governments to nonetheless become states.[108] More generally, it provides that an effective government set up in violation of the right to self-determination does not have a valid claim to its existence.[109]

The hierarchical relationship between self-determination and governmental effectiveness is said to exist in view of the higher normative status acquired by self-determination in international law, where it is considered as one of the few norms which may have achieved *jus cogens* status.[110] In the discourse on failed states, it is crucial therefore to deepen our understanding of this alleged hierarchical relationship between self-determination and effectiveness in relation to established states. Koskenniemi argued that '[t]he need to look behind states – into self-determination – however, becomes necessary when statehood itself is or becomes uncertain'.[111] Here I contend that there is a need to look into self-determination also when statehood is not under discussion, as a means to understand whether and how international law protects the people of a state against the consequences of ineffectiveness and state failure, hence in situations where a state is incapable of autonomously protecting its people.

If state-builders set out to assist ineffective states in restoring effectiveness by rebuilding government institutions, it is important to understand how they should act to be in accordance with the people's right to self-determination. What this notion means and what it may entail are questions open to research and in need of detailed analysis. The role played by self-determination in the context of state-building has received surprisingly limited attention from international law scholarship and, as a consequence, the impact and significance of this norm in the context examined here are still largely under-explored. The next chapter will offer a detailed literature review on this matter, explaining what has been said in existing literature about the role of self-determination in relation to state-building and what, instead, is still under-addressed.

1.4 Conclusions

This introductory chapter has set out a conceptualisation of the established phenomenon of post-conflict state-building from the perspective of international

108 See Raic (n 50) chs 7 and 8.

109 According to Crawford, this is exemplified in the case of Southern Rhodesia, where a minority government unilaterally declared independence in 1965. The act was condemned both by the General Assembly and by the Security Council, which called on states not to recognise this illegal racist minority regime. See Crawford (n 41) 129–31, and SC Res 216 (1965), 12 November 1065, para 2. See also Brownlie (n 57) 71.

110 See Hector Gros Espiell, 'Self-determination as *Jus Cogens*' in Antonio Cassese (ed), *United Nations, Fundamental Rights: Two Topics in International Law* (Sijthoff and Noordhoff International 1979) 167–74 and 'Article 40: Commentary, Report of the International Law Commission' (2001) 56 GAOR Supplement No 10 (A/56/10) 284.

111 Martti Koskenniemi, 'National Self-Determination Today: Problems of Legal Theory and Practice' (1994) 43 *International and Comparative Human Rights Quarterly* 241, 245.

law. Engaging with literature on so-called failed states, the chapter submitted that state-building, like state failure, from the perspective of international law must be operated within the framework of the law which regulates the friendly relations and co-operation between states. Starting from these premises, I set up an analytical structure for identifying a basic legal framework to regulate this practice in international law. I found that there are a set of applicable principles that guarantee the continued existence of states in need of state-building programmes, and that, under the current system of international law, this regime gives rise to a number of provisions that apply to failed states in the same way as they apply to functioning states.

First, international law prohibits states from using force against the territorial integrity of any state, including states with a failed government. Moreover, it is illegal for the territory of a state to be annexed by other states by forceful means, even when a state cannot defend its territory for a prolonged period of time. Secondly, failed states retain their independent status. This means that they enjoy a certain level of protection against outside interference. This level of protection is modified by international security concerns, which are often called into question in the context of post-conflict reconstruction. The chapter has shown that the extent to which the principle of non-intervention in internal affairs can be set aside in state-building is not clearly defined. Legal scholarship is deeply divided about how it should approach this issue. Whilst some have welcomed deep levels of intrusiveness in UN-mandated operations as an expression of changing values that shape the international legal system, others remain deeply sceptical of such changes. Drawing a parallel with colonialism, the latter works have raised questions over the legitimacy of state-building as an interventionist phenomenon which recalls earlier forms of colonial trusteeship. Thirdly, it was submitted that the there is a need to further explore the role of the right to self-determination in the context of state-building. Given the impressive amount of literature that already exists on state-building, this trend of research remains, somewhat surprisingly, under-analysed. The next chapter sets out to present what is being said about self-determination in relation to state-building, with a view to highlighting gaps and identifying fertile grounds for more in-depth analysis that will be developed throughout this study.

2 Self-determination and state-building in international law*

2.1 Introduction

Chapter 1 set out to identify the basic legal framework to accommodate state-building practice in international law. In so doing, it was found that there is a need to further explore the role of the right to self-determination in this context. This chapter takes a close look at the body of literature which analyses the role of self-determination in the context of post-conflict state-building, with a view to critically assessing its contribution in developing our understanding of the legal significance of this principle. In doing so, I offer a critical appraisal of the current debate on the role of self-determination in a specific domain of practice and highlight the limits and gaps of the ongoing discourse.

It is remarkable that international law scholarship devoted to post-conflict transitions and state-building issues, which is by now voluminous, has dedicated little space to discussing the role of self-determination. The topic was considered by several authors in relation to occupation, at the time when this body of law was revisited and reinterpreted to regulate the rebuilding of Iraq. Beyond occupation, however, the issue was essentially left at the periphery of the state-building discourse. When considered, self-determination was approached rather superficially and generally introduced a secondary concern. This lack of devoted attention means that the legal significance borne by this fundamental principle of international law in the context of post-war transitions remains still under-explored. A full-length study on its application, for instance, is yet to appear.

This chapter constitutes a first step towards filling this gap. It starts by looking at what contribution existing literature has made in advancing our knowledge of the matter and it critically analyses the value of this contribution from the perspective of international law. The key argument set out is that if we aim to understand the role and significance of self-determination in international law fully, a new interpretative framework should be used to study this principle. The discussion will proceed in two steps. Section 2.2 takes issue with

* This is an updated version of the article which appeared in the *Journal of Conflict and Security Law*, Volume 20, Issue 1 (2015) with the title: 'Self-determination and State-building in International Law: The Need for a New Research Approach'.

how self-determination was studied so far. It identifies a common framework through which the issue has been approached, defines the main characteristics of the approach used and critically examines the bases on which authors carry out their studies of self-determination. Section 2.3 advocates for a new way of thinking about self-determination. It points to the need for a new interpretative framework to approach the issue; it suggests what the new approach should look like and highlights the potential advantages of adopting a new perspective for studying self-determination in the context of post-conflict state-building.

2.2 The common framework of analysis

In this section I attempt to make sense of the existing discussion about self-determination and state-building by offering an overview of the main trends, views and issues raised by authors who worked at the intersection of these two areas of scholarship. In doing so, I identify a set of key features that characterise the existing studies on this topic and assess their value to enhancing our understanding of the significance of self-determination as a norm of international law.

This section is organized along the three main features which define the common framework of analysis. First, there is an issue of approach. I establish that a common trait in the majority of studies on self-determination and state-building is the adoption of an evaluative approach. By this I mean the tendency on behalf of scholars to conceive and use self-determination in their work as an evaluative yardstick, through which the legality and legitimacy of state-building practice can be assessed and evaluated. In discussing the evaluative approach, I will focus on how authors proceed in setting up a framework for their evaluations, rather than on their substantial views on whether a violation occurred, with the aim of assessing the limits and the usefulness of adopting such an approach. Secondly, there is an issue of method. I find that evaluations conducted by the authors often rely on hasty accounts of the law of self-determination, drawn from secondary literature rather than from first-hand interpretations of primary sources of international law, and often also quickly dismissive of the much wider debates that concern virtually all aspects of the law in question. Thirdly, there is an issue of interpretation.

Self-determination is a legal principle (or right) with many faces. Its content, application and significance changes greatly, depending on what it is taken to mean but, most importantly, depending on which self it is taken to apply to. The multi-dimensional character of this principle is often overlooked by authors claiming to discuss 'the' right to self-determination, without duly acknowledging how their discussions are in fact operating selectively in interpreting the right. The following paragraphs will discuss these three methodological aspects in turn.

2.2.1 *The evaluative approach*

I argued above that one of the main traits which bring together existing scholarship on state-building and self-determination is what I called the 'evaluative approach'. By virtue of this, the way authors approach the topic of self-determination is by seeking to establish whether state-building practice has or has not violated the norm. In order to carry out their evaluations, I found that most authors apply a similar method. First, they set out to define what they mean by self-determination in international law. Secondly, using this definition, an attempt is made to identify what limits the principle imposes on state-builders and whether the situation provides for exceptions to the rules they have identified. Thirdly, an assessment is made on whether such limits were respected in the situation(s) at stake and, hence, whether the practice respected self-determination standards or not. If violations are found, authors would then suggest ways in which compliance can be achieved in the future for violations not to be repeated.

Here, I critically examine how different writers have carried out their evaluative studies. How were the assessments made? How did authors define self-determination? From what they identified as law, how did they extrapolate the limits posed by self-determination to state-builders and how and when did they argue that exceptions played a role? In answering these questions, I will group literature in relation to the context in which scholars carry out their analyses: international territorial administration, occupation, and light-footprint approach models.

2.2.1.1 Developing the means and methods for evaluation

2.2.1.1.1 INTERNATIONAL TERRITORIAL ADMINISTRATION

To explore the status of the debate on self-determination in the context of international territorial administration (ITA), I will start by looking at look at how Carsten Stahn, one of the leading experts in the field, deals with self-determination in his monograph.[1] Although he dedicates limited space to discussing this topic, for Stahn it is beyond doubt that standards of self-determination apply to transitional UN and multinational administrations because this right is a right of the people. In virtue of its object and purpose, the right is attached to and can be exercised by the people independently of the nature of the public ruler.[2] Starting from these assumptions, Stahn is concerned about determining how the right applies and what it means for the conduct of international administrators.

He sees self-determination as a 'state-people device', which regulates the relationship between a people and a (state-like) international administration.[3] By definition, the right includes two dimensions and it applies both as a defence (external) and participatory (internal) right.[4] More precisely, in inter-state relations, as in the context of ITA, the right applies both as 'the right of a people to organize its own state free from foreign oppression (external self-determination)

1 Carsten Stahn, *International Territorial Administration: Versailles to Iraq and Beyond* (CUP 2008).
2 ibid 459.
3 Stahn (n 1) 458.
4 ibid 458–60.

and the right of a people to adequate political representation within the constitutional structure of its own state (internal self-determination)'.[5] Stahn also affirms that in the context of ITA the right is mostly relevant in its form as internal right: the 'defence' right of the people to decide about their own form of government and a participatory right between the people and its provisional territorial ruler.[6]

On this basis, he then sets out to define the regulatory role played by self-determination in the context of international administrations. He proceeds in two steps. First, he sheds light on what limits self-determination imposes to the exercise of governmental powers by international administrators. Once the limits are established, he identifies exceptions to these rules and defines under what circumstances foreign actors may be afforded a greater scope for action that would not amount to a violation of the right. In carrying out his analysis, Stahn follows the twofold structure by which he defined self-determination: the external/defence component and the internal/participatory one.

In virtue of its first component, self-determination prohibits the imposition of a form of government over the administered people. As a consequence, self-determination forces international administrators to 'refrain from instituting long-term structures of governance and large-scale constitutional reforms which cannot be reversed by the population of the administered territories after the period of transitional administration'.[7] The existence of this general rule is confirmed by other writers and is widely accepted amongst international lawyers (both in and out of the ITA context).[8] Similarly, Kinderlen, in his study of the legal framework of international administrations, notes the existence of a prohibition on UN administrations to 'unilaterally decide on lasting measures which cannot be easily reversed after the administration has ended'.[9] In a slightly more nuanced version of the same rule, Erika de Wet argues that self-determination rules out 'any outside pressure designed to enforce the installation of a particular government or the maintenance of a certain form of government'.[10] This

5 ibid 457–58.
6 ibid 458.
7 ibid 461.
8 See Boris Kondoch, 'The United Nations Administration of East Timor' (2001) 6 *Journal of Conflict and Security Law* 245; Lisa Mardikian, 'Economic Self-determination in Post Conflict Reconstruction: the Case Study of Timor-Leste' in Matthew Saul and James A Sweeney (eds), *International Law and Post-Conflict Reconstruction Policy* (Routledge 2015) and T D Gill, 'Legal and Some Political Limitations on the Power of the UN Security Council to Exercise Its Enforcement Powers under Chapter VII of the Charter' (1995) 26 *Netherlands Yearbook of International Law* 33.
9 Hans F Kinderlen, *Von Triest nach Osttimor: Der völkerrechtliche Rahmen für die Verwaltung von Krisengebieten durch die Vereinten Nationen* [*From Trieste to East Timor. The Legal Framework for the Administration of Areas of Conflict by the United Nations*] (Springer 2008) 449.
10 Erika de Wet, *The Chapter VII Powers of the United Nations Security Council* (Hart Publishing 2004) 327.

includes also a prohibition for the Security Council, in designing ITA mandates, to authorise unilateral secession.[11]

In virtue of its second component, self-determination involves an entitlement to political participation on behalf of the people subjected to transitional administration.[12] In principle, this rule would constitute a significant challenge to the authority of international administrations, that often see an exclusive participation of foreign actors in the running of public affairs. As Wilde put it, international territorial administration, in order to be justified, must be able to resist the fundamental critique of trusteeship, developed through the concept of self-determination: 'that exercising control over people from outside is inherently unjust'.[13] In line with other commentators, Stahn responds to this challenge by arguing that the lack of local participation in the administration of public affairs can be reconciled with a right to participation because exceptions exist to the full realisation of the participatory element of the right.

First, the temporary character of ITAs is highlighted as a fundamental characteristic to ensure compliance with self-determination.[14] Secondly, Stahn argues that the right to access to government is a 'variable concept', whose application is to be assessed in the light of the circumstances and shall take into account security concerns. More precisely, the situation on the ground may require temporary suspension of the people's participatory rights, particularly in the early stages of a mission, in order to better allow the development of stable and representative governance institutions.[15] This view also finds wide support among scholars, who view the entitlement to participate as a right to be progressively realised, depending on the circumstances.[16] Erika de Wet argues that a United Nations civil administration authorised under Chapter VII of the Charter would be 'reconcilable with the right to internal self-determination, if and to the extent that it *consistently* and *progressively* involves all peoples within the territory in all aspects of the governmental process'.[17] On the same line, others

11 ibid 327.

12 Stahn (n 1) 462.

13 Ralph Wilde, *International Territorial Administration: How Trusteeship and the Civilizing Mission Never Went Away* (OUP 2008) 444. The same issue is raised also by Orford in Anne Orford, *Reading Humanitarian Intervention: Human Rights and the Use of Force in International Law* (CUP 2003) 128–29.

14 This position is supported by virtually all commentators, with rare exceptions.

15 Stahn (n 1) 462–63. On participatory legitimacy as a legitimising factor for ITA that must be tailored upon the context see also Carsten Stahn, 'Governance beyond the State: Issues of Legitimacy in International Territorial Administration' (2005) 2 *International Organizations Law Review* 9.

16 See L von Carlowitz, 'UNMIK Lawmaking between Effective Peace Support and Internal Self-Determination' (2003) 41 *Archiv des Völkerrech* 336; Kristen Daglish and Hitoshi Nasu, 'Towards a True Incarnation of the Rule of Law in War-Torn Territories: Centring Peacebuilding in the Will of the People' (2007) *LIV Netherlands International Law Review* 81; and Mardikian (n 8).

17 See de Wet (n 10) 329 (emphasis added).

argue that, where democratic legitimation is not possible as a means to express popular consent due to the security circumstances, international administrators should aim to create representative authorities to balance self-determination and security imperatives.[18]

The realisation of a true participatory entitlement, therefore, can be delayed in the context of ITA without this constituting a violation of the right to self-determination. Two arguments are brought to justify such position. First, there is no violation because democratic participation is the ultimate aim of a transitional administration. International administrations are set up with the purpose of creating functioning democratic institutions; they are designed to make the participatory right a reality and aimed at delegating governmental functions to the local population.[19] Therefore, in a context of governmental paralysis or collapse, external intervention in the form of an ITA aimed at creating and developing effective governance structures is not a violation of but a precondition for the exercise of internal self-determination.[20] Secondly, a delay in participation is allowed in the name of concerns about the political climate, the adequacy of local institutions and depending on the overall fragility of the state.[21]

This second argument relies on the idea that the participatory component of the right to self-determination is a right to which, under certain circumstances, derogation is permitted and its application may be fully or partially suspended. Those who understand self-determination as a right from which derogation is permitted argue that this is so because, outside of the colonial context, this norm cannot be assumed to have the character of *jus cogens*. As such, the right is not absolute and it can and must be balanced against others.

The implications of conceiving self-determination as a derogable right are wide-ranging. On the one hand, it means that both international administrators as managers of ITAs and the Security Council in designing ITA mandates are allowed to balance self-determination rights with the interests of international peace and security.[22] On the other, it means that evaluating balancing exercises can be a complex task, and scholars seem to have adopted certain lenience towards actions undertaken by international administrators. For instance, both Fox and De Brabandere acknowledge that international administrators might have gone beyond the rule against imposing long-term economic policies on

18 Daglish and Nasu (n 16) 108.

19 Eric De Brabandere, *Post-conflict Administrations in International Law* (Martinus Nijhoff 2009) 73.

20 See von Carlowitz (n 16) 365–66.

21 See e Wet (n 10) 334–35.

22 Rudiger Wolfrum, 'International Administrations in Post-Conflict Situations by the United Nations and Other International Actors' (2005) 9 *Max Planck Yearbook of United Nations Law* 649, 679–80. See also Kinderlen (n 9). For a critical stance on the willingness on behalf of the international community to favour the interests of peace negotiations over the interests of self-determination see Catriona Drew, 'The East Timor Story: International Law on Trial' (2001) 12 *European Journal of International Law* 651.

an administered territory (particularly in Kosovo and East Timor); yet invasive practice is justified by virtue of the derogable nature of self-determination.[23]

Overall, conceptualising self-determination as a qualified right calls for a careful scrutiny on the conditions under which derogation is permitted in order to avoid usurpations of this right. Excessive indeterminacy about when and where balances can be struck may lead down a slippery slope where compromises concerning the implementation of the right are easily accepted and remain highly subjective. In this respect, von Carlowitz observes that: '[i]t is not easy to find the legitimate degree of intervention in domestic affairs for the purposes of peace maintenance, and that finding the right balance between competing demands of international responsibilities and local self-determination rests on the shoulder of the international lawmakers and depends to a good extent on the personal style of the administrator'.[24]

Summing up, this discussion of how legal scholars have considered self-determination in relation to ITA revealed a number of important findings concerning existing views on the nature of the right and on how it operates in practice. I have identified three main limits imposed by the right to self-determination on the conduct of international administrators:

(i) a substantive limitation not to impose a certain form of government and/or long-lasting structures of governance
(ii) a procedural obligation to include the local population in all aspects of the governmental process
(iii) a temporal limitation – intrinsic to both points (i) and (ii) above – for the exercise of public authority on behalf of the people concerned.

The dominant view, however, considers that these limits can be subject to derogation. Indeed, in the context of ITA self-determination is not considered to be an absolute right but a right from which derogation is permitted in selected circumstances. In relation to point (i), in some cases long-lasting economic reforms have been imposed on administered territories, and this practice was justified as measures to ensure stability and, with it, to help the maintenance of peace and security. In relation to point (ii), at least three circumstances are proposed to justify a delay in the full application of self-determination's participatory rights: a) the security situation; b) the fragility of the state; c) the

23 See De Brabandere (n 19) 73–74 and Gregory H Fox, *Humanitarian Occupation* (CUP 2008) 205–10.
24 See von Carlowitz (n 16) 388. Talking about East Timor, Fox says that to mandate for the participation of the East Timorese in political decision-making at all costs one would need to link their exclusion to future substantive harms and 'this is ha difficult hurdle, since there appears to be no a priori reason why UNTAET could not wholly exclude the Timorese from its administration and still fully respect and preserve future substantive rights. A benevolent despotism to be sure, but the law of self-determination has little history of criticizing such arrangements'. Fox (n 23) 105.

adequacy of local institutions. In relation to point (iii), the 'temporary clause' is always left vague, used to indicate a chunk of time conceived in abstract terms and is also subjected to contextual factors, amongst which the security situation.

2.2.1.1.2 OCCUPATION

In 2003, following the invasion of Iraq by a coalition of states, the law of occupation was dusted off to be applied in the modern context. The application of its 'no change' rule – also known as 'the conservationist principle', set out in Article 43 of the century-old Hague Regulations – proved to be particularly challenging as it provides relatively little scope for changes to the laws in force in the occupied territory.[25] Occupation law was indeed not designed to accommodate state-building and does not provide for far-reaching reconstruction activities. Its conservative requirements sat uncomfortably with the transformative intentions of the Iraqi occupiers and, more generally, with the imperatives of state-building. As a result, the relevance and suitability of the conservationist principle in the rebuilding of Iraq became a wider test for the principle's relevance and suitability for occupations in the twenty-first century. The validity of the no-change rule was vigorously challenged by the occupiers and became the object of a lively debate amongst legal scholars. This debate has also seen scholars discussing the relevance and application of the right to self-determination in the context of occupation and is therefore of great interest to this review.

Self-determination is one of the key developments that have occurred in international law after the law of occupation has entered into force. As mentioned earlier, the Hague Regulations are more than a century old, and the Geneva Convention IV, which expands the Hague law, entered into force in 1949. Self-determination, instead, makes its first appearance as a legal principle in the UN Charter, but its development as a norm is strictly linked to the height of the decolonisation process, and so it has occurred during the second half of the twentieth century. A contemporary interpretation of occupation law, it is argued, must take into consideration other developments in general international law. How, then, should contemporary occupations take into account the law of self-determination? What role does the right play and what is the relationship between self-determination and the provisions of occupation law?

25 The Article reads: 'The authority of the legitimate power having in fact passed into the hands of the occupant, the latter shall take all the measures in his power to restore, and ensure, as far as possible, public order and safety, while respecting, unless absolutely prevented the laws in force in the country'. The Hague provisions were later expanded by the Fourth Geneva Convention (GCIV). Article 64 of GCIV unpacks the concept of necessity providing a specific set of circumstances in which passing legislative measures during occupation is possible. See Hague Convention Respecting the Laws and Customs of War on Land, Annex (18 October 1907) 36 Stat 277, Article 43 (Hague Regulations) and Geneva Convention IV relative to the Protection of Civilians Persons in Times of War (19 August 1949) 6 UST 3516 (GCIV).

Scholarly views on this issue can be summarised in three main positions:

(i) The two are mutually reinforcing. The conservationist principle of occupation law is a means of protecting self-determination and is a guarantee against any violation of this right.
(ii) The two are not mutually reinforcing and one should prevail over the other. The conservationist principle is anachronistic and occupation law must be adapted to the contemporary world in order to allow making the necessary changes to respect the obligations originating from the law of self-determination and human rights law.
(iii) The two must coexist and should be balanced. This position represents a middle-ground and adds complexity to the relationship between the two bodies of law. In this view, the two may overlap and carry partially conflicting obligations, so a balance must be struck between the authority afforded by the occupants under the conservationist provisions of occupation law and what the right to self-determination would require.

I shall proceed to analyse the three positions showing how the various authors can be located along a continuous spectrum of positions which start from those who firmly reject almost any form of revision of the conservationist Hague provisions to those who are decisively pro-change and welcome transformative occupations. In doing so, I aim to draw out similarities and contrasts in how self-determination is conceptualised by the different authors.

Jean Cohen is probably the most exemplificative supporter of the position which sees the conservationist principle as a protection shield for self-determination. She contends that the relevance of self-determination to occupation law is 'complex but compelling' because it poses serious limits to the action of occupiers.[26] Her view stems from a specific conception of self-determination that is based on two notions. First is the idea that self-determination is closely interconnected with popular sovereignty and that popular sovereignty is not antithetic to state sovereignty. On the contrary, she believes that the two are mutually reinforcing and that the latter can be viewed as the space within which former can be exercised.[27] Second is the idea that popular sovereignty regulates the relationship between a people and its government, and that this relationship cannot be confiscated or regulated by outsiders.[28]

26 Jean L Cohen, 'The Role of International Law in Post-Conflict Constitution-Making: Toward a *Jus Post Bellum* for "Interim Occupations"' (2007) 51 *New York Law School Law Review* 497, 524.

27 ibid 524–26.

28 ibid 525. See also Simone van den Driest, 'Pro-Democratic Intervention and The Right to Political Self-Determination: The Case of Operation Iraqi Freedom' (2010) LVII *Netherlands International Law Review* 29, who claims that in Iraq there has been a violation of the right to self-determination because the Iraqi Interim Government was not elected bottom-up but rather selected by the occupiers. The real conditions for an exercise of self-determination were created after the transition, with the instalment of an elected government (at 63–68).

As a consequence of these two points, Cohen argues that respect for the principles of popular sovereignty and self-determination entail as a general rule a prohibition on acting on behalf of the local population. This includes a virtually absolute prohibition on repealing offensive laws as well as a prohibition on imposing major reforms with irreversible effects on the occupied territory.[29] Similarly, Sassòli argues that the right to self-determination of a people under occupation cannot be implemented by an occupying power, thus 'the best way to respect it for an occupying power is not to legislate, but to withdraw'.[30] In his view, what forbids the occupying powers to pass sweeping legislation in an occupied territory is the principle that legislation must be based upon the will of the people, so the legislative activity must be kept to the absolute minimum necessary until it can be exercised by the local people.[31] On the same line, Wilde recognises that the essence of self-determination, as a legal concept, is radically to repudiate the legitimacy of foreign domination itself.[32] In his view, any alteration to existing law is acceptable only as far as it is made to ensure that the laws in force do not violate human rights. The acceptance of measures that go beyond this would legitimise the idea that trusteeship is back and that the self-determination paradigm has become qualified.[33] As Toone put it,

> The critical assumption underlying the US approach in Iraq and the theory that the conservationist principle is anachronistic is that the occupying power knows what is in the best interests of the occupied people and that it will act accordingly. Besides hearkening back to the colonialist shadows of yesteryear, this assumption is simply incorrect.[34]

29 ibid.

30 Also for Bhuta, who attributes a meaning of non-interference to self-determination, the departure of foreign troops is a precondition for the realisation of self-determination. See Nehal Bhuta, 'New Modes and Orders: The Difficulties of a *Jus Post Bellum* of Constitutional Transformation' (2010) 60 *University of Toronto Law Journal* 799 and Marco Sassòli, 'Legislation and Maintenance of Public Order and Civil Life by Occupying Powers' (2005) 16 *European Journal of International Law* 661, 677.

31 ibid. Sassòli identifies a case for necessity, however, when local legislation is clearly contrary or falls short of human rights standards and whereas the existing law makes the exercise of local self-determination impossible. On this point see also Gregory H Fox, 'The Occupation of Iraq' (2005) 36 *Georgetown Journal of International Law* 195, 276–77.

32 Ralph Wilde, 'From Trusteeship to Self-Determination and Back Again: The Role of the Hague Regulations in the Evolutions of International Trusteeship, and the Framework of Rights and Duties of Occupying Powers' (2010) 31 *Loyola of Los Angeles International and Comparative Law Review* 85, 131–32.

33 ibid.

34 Jordan E Toone, 'Occupation Law During and After Iraq: The Expedience of Conservationism Evidenced in the Minutes and Resolutions of the Iraqi Governing Council' (2012) 24 *Florida Journal of International Law* 469, 501.

A more nuanced position on this matter is proposed by Wheatley in his detailed commentary on the compliance of state-building in occupied Iraq with the law of self-determination.[35] Again, for Wheatley self-determination poses significant limit to the occupiers in the exercise of authority over an occupied territory as it forbids the endorsement of a specific form of government.[36] However, this prohibition is not absolute. Wheatley assumes that the right to self-determination, outside of colonialism, is one exceptional *jus cogens* norm that can be overridden by considerations of public interest in maintaining peace and security.[37] He allows, indeed, an exceptional condition under which a political order could be imposed over a people: when such a determination is made by the Security Council through a resolution 'properly adopted' to safeguard international peace and security.[38] In other words, for matters of peace and security a derogation to the right to self-determination could be permitted in virtue of an argument for the absolute deference to the judgment of Security Council, as far as the Resolution is adopted through proper procedures and in accordance with the Charter provisions.[39]

Moving along the spectrum of permissibility, we find ideas about a number of flexible limitations imposed by self-determination on the occupying power. By this I mean a set of factors and circumstances for which it is argued that the occupiers may carve out some space for introducing legal reforms. The first of these is the temporal factor: an occupation which is of 'limited', 'reasonable', or 'minimum possible' duration is not contrary to self-determination.[40] Secondly, occupation must be a temporary process and its outcome must be aimed at preparing the conditions for the realisation of self-determination. The case for action is particularly strong in situations where the ousted regime was not representative. The argument is important because it lays upon a complex, and at times contradictory, conceptualisation of self-determination. To put it simply,

35 Steven Wheatley, 'The Security Council, Democratic Legitimacy and Regime Change in Iraq' (2006) 17 *European Journal of International Law* 531.

36 ibid 540.

37 ibid 543.

38 ibid 542–44. The same argument is made also by Sean Butler, 'Separating Protection from Politics: The UN Security Council, the 2011 Ivorian Political Crisis and the Legality of Regime Change' (2015) 20 *Journal of Conflict and Security Law* 251.

39 In Iraq, however, Wheatley found that this limit was surpassed since Resolution 1546 endorsed a form of power-sharing government in absence of any free participation of the Iraqi people, of their freely elected representatives and without the advancement of a rationale for why change of political regime was necessary to maintain peace and security. Wheatley (n 35) 544–50.

40 This view is supported by a number of writers, see Bartram Brown, 'Intervention, Self-Determination, Democracy and The Residual Responsibilities of the Occupying Power in Iraq' (2004) 11 UC Davis Journal of International Law and Policy 23, 44; Alexander Orakhelashvili, 'The Post-War Settlement in Iraq: The UN Security Council Resolution 1483 (2003) and General International Law' (2003) 8 *Journal of Conflict and Security* Law 307; Jung Youngjin, 'In pursuit of Reconstructing Iraq: Does Self-Determination Matter?' (2005) 33 *Denver Journal of International Law and Policy* 391, 406.

for some self-determination requires, on the one hand, the occupants to refrain from introducing any significant changes to the legal systems of the occupied territory; on the other, it requires that the occupants prepare the ground on which the local population can choose their own government and with it exercise their right to self-determination. In so doing, the occupants are invited to 'resist the temptation to excessively nation-build' and a reasonable balance is auspicated between no involvement and too much involvement.[41] Going one step further, Benvenisti concedes that there may be solid reasons for occupiers to interfere in shaping the political choices of an occupied sovereign, in order 'to ensure that the process is practical, inclusive and fair'.[42]

Finally, there are a number of outright supporters of the pro-change view – according to which the conservationist principle is an actual impediment to the realisation of the right to self-determination. In this view self-determination is entirely conceived as an objective, the ultimate aim of the reconstruction process the attainment of which can be initiated through occupation (as in the case of Iraq) and facilitated by the actions of the occupying powers.[43] As David Scheffer put it, 'to pull Iraq out of its repressive past and return it to the community of civilised nations, the [Coalition Provisional] Authority will aggressively employ international human rights law, principles of democratisation (as the engine of self-determination), economic initiatives, and perhaps controversial use of force principles in the name of domestic security'.[44] Roberts also notes that: '[t]he prime stated purposes of the coalition forces include assisting the process of establishing a constitutional order, in the country and assisting the Iraqi people to exercise their right of self-determination'.[45] The authors supporting a mutually

41 Youngjin (n 40) 407–408.

42 Eyal Benvenisti and Guy Keinan, 'The Occupation of Iraq: A Reassessment' in Raul A Pedrozo (ed), *The War in Iraq: A Legal Analysis* (US Naval War College 2010) 273–76. See also Hanne Cuyckens, *Revisiting the Law of Occupation* (Brill Nijhoff 2018) 106–107.

43 Some do not argue this point as a general principle, but in relation to Iraq specifically they simply accept the fact that the occupation's aim was to realise the right to self-determination because the Security Resolutions which purposed to regulate the process explicitly stated so. See Andrea Carcano, 'End of the Occupation in 2004? The Status of the Multinational Force in Iraq after the Transfer of Sovereignty to the Interim Iraqi Government' (2006) 11 *Journal of Conflict and Security Law* 41, 54; Adam Roberts 'The End of Occupation: Iraq 2004' (2005) 54 *International and Comparative Law Quarterly* 27; Michael Ottolenghi, 'The Stars and Stripes in Al-Fardos Square: The Implications for International Law of Belligerent Occupation' (2007) 72 *Fordham Law Review* 2177; Nigel D White, 'The Will and Authority of the Security Council after Iraq' (2004) 17 *Leiden Journal of International Law* 645; Rudiger Wolfrum, 'Iraq – From Belligerent Occupation to Iraqi Exercise of Sovereignty: Foreign Power versus International Community Interference' (2005) 9 *Max Planck Yearbook of United Nations Law* 1. In his book, Carcano is critical of the actions of the Council in Resolution 1511 (2003). Andrea Carcano, *The Transformation of Occupied Territory in International Law* (Brill Nijhoff 2005) 302.

44 David Scheffer, 'Beyond Occupation Law' (2003) 97 *American Journal of International Law* 842, 844–45.

45 Roberts (n 43) 43.

exclusive view of the interpretation of the relationship between occupation law and self-determination indeed call for a revision of the former in order to allow a greater scope for transformative action in occupied territories. According to Roberts, changes to the system of government may not be imposed from the outside, except when transformative policies represent the best way to deliver certain goals such as democracy, human rights and self-determination.[46] It is difficult to imagine how self-determination, used in this sense, can pose any significant limitation to the agenda of transformative occupiers aiming to engage in state-building. In the words of Nehal Bhuta,

> Like a sovereign dictatorship, transformative occupation exceeds the legal order that authorizes its provisional assumption of control, in the name of 'a new and better order'. It derives its legitimacy, in other words, from the promise of the order to come, a horizon of expectation that is invoked to relativize the legal rules which bind it in the present.[47]

To sum up, a review of literature on occupation law shows that opinions on whether or not self-determination poses any limit to the action of occupying forces willing to transform the state structure of an occupied territory, hence whether the right to self-determination constitutes a challenge to the survival of the conservationist principle, depend essentially on what self-determination is taken to mean. Where self-determination is taken to mean popular sovereignty as a precondition for action, it poses strong limits to the actions of occupiers aiming to transform state structures and the laws in force. Where self-determination is taken to mean popular sovereignty as an objective then it does not impose restrictions against the transformation; rather, self-determination is seen to provide the impetus for transformation to wipe out unrepresentative structures.

2.2.1.1.3 THE LIGHT FOOTPRINT APPROACH

This last section is dedicated to reviewing the literature dealing with self-determination issues in the context of so-called 'light footprint' peace operations with a state-building mandate. As discussed in chapter 1, the light footprint approach, first used in Afghanistan, sees a reduced role for the international actors and a stronger participation of the local ones. Known also as the 'assistance model', this model sees the 'internationals' no longer assuming direct responsibility for managing transitions and implementing liberal-democratic transformations, as they are now more modestly mandated to 'assist', 'support', and work 'in coordination with' local authorities. Within the assistance model the

46 Adam Roberts, 'Transformative Military Occupation: Applying the Laws of War and Human Rights' (2006) 100 *American Journal of International Law* 580, 620–21.

47 Nehal Bhuta, 'The Antinomies of Transformative Occupation' (2005) 16 *European Journal of International Law* 721, 737.

primary responsibility for managing transitions therefore rests with the national authorities, which are to act in partnership with the international actors. The fact that the process is administered by a domestic government has at first made the assistance model appear unremarkable from the perspective of its compliance with the right to self-determination. In other words, the existence of an indigenous government has basically shielded this model of intervention from virtually any evaluative enquiry in relation to compliance with self-determination standards. For instance, de Brabandere writes: 'The case of Afghanistan of course cannot as such be seen as contravening the right to self-determination, as no foreign administration has been set up. Instead, the Bonn Agreement immediately envisaged National interim authorities to oversee its implementation'.[48] But is the assistance model truly unremarkable? One scholar, in particular, has questioned these assumptions.

Matthew Saul has written extensively on this topic.[49] He analysed the legal basis for the initiation of international involvement aimed at post-conflict reconstruction, and in so doing he paid unprecedented attention to the role and significance of self-determination in this context using case studies of international involvement in Afghanistan, Liberia, Iraq, Haiti and Somalia. In his work he understands self-determination as the right of the people of a state to political independence and popular sovereignty,[50] and set out to identify whether state-building reforms undertaken under the assistance model present any evidence of being undertaken by an authority that shows genuine attachment to the will of the people. Having done so, he critically discussed the legal basis on which the initiation of international involvement is authorised, finding that there are issues of compliance with political independence regarding both consent and Chapter VII authorisations.[51]

Saul notes that in the assistance model, only the security aspects are Chapter VII authorised, whilst political reconstruction is authorised by consent. Although both of these bases are legally valid, Saul argues that the model based on consent remains problematic in principle. The model allows governments in dysfunctional states to preserve their rights in virtue of the recognition they retain at

48 De Brabandere (n 19) 73.

49 See Matthew Saul, *Popular Governance of Post-Conflict Reconstruction: The Role of International Law* (CUP 2014); 'Creating Popular Governments in Post-Conflict Situations: The Role of International Law' in Carsten Stahn, Jennifer S Easterday and Jan Iverson (eds) *Jus Post Bellum* (OUP 2014); 'Local Ownership of Post-Conflict Reconstruction in International Law: The Initiation of International Involvement' (2011) 16 *Journal of Conflict and Security Law* 165; 'International Law and the Will of the People in Post-Conflict Rebuilding', conference paper delivered at *The Future of Statebuilding: Ethics, Power and Responsibility in International Relations*, University of Westminster, London (2010); 'From Haiti to Somalia: The Assistance Model and The Paradox of State Reconstruction in International Law' (2009) 11 *International Community Law Review* 119.

50 Saul, 'From Haiti to Somalia' (n 49) 126 and 'Local Ownership of Post-Conflict Reconstruction in International Law' (n 49) 16–17.

51 Saul, 'Local Ownership of Post-Conflict Reconstruction in International Law' (n 49).

the international level, even though they do not exercise effective control over their territory.[52] Effectively, in this way the model permits a government with no or little attachment to the will of the people to remain in control of the reconstruction process. The paradox, argues Saul, is that the continued existence of states with ineffective governments is itself explained and perpetuated in the name of self-determination and non-intervention, as the two fundamental principles of international law and basic principles of the UN Charter system which must regulate the relationship between states.[53] The paradoxical consequence of putting an ineffective government in control of the state in the name of self-determination is that it brings into doubt self-determination as political independence. This is so because such a model does not offer serious protection to ineffective states against 'the influence that the international actors can have over an ineffective government in respect of how the state is reconstructed'.[54] On the same point, Anne Orford writes: 'it seemed almost unremarkable to be told in November 2001, in the aftermath of a war on terror, that the government of Afghanistan was being *freely determined* by its people in Bonn, while the World Bank, the United Nations Development Programme and the Asian Development Bank co-hosted a meeting in Islamabad to decide how to transform Afghanistan into a market economy'.[55]

Once established that the assistance model allows an ineffective local government to consent to the initiation of international involvement in its internal affairs for state-building purposes, Saul argues that international law does not ensure any meaningful connection between reconstruction and will of the people.[56] This is, at least, concerning the initiation of international involvement. As a result, Saul remains sceptical about the significance of international law in imposing limits to the activities of state-builders.[57] As far as the law of self-determination is concerned, indeed, he sees no limits imposed on international actors willing to engage in state-building activities by means of

52 Saul, 'From Haiti to Somalia' (n 49) 136–37.
53 Saul, 'Local Ownership of Post-Conflict Reconstruction in International Law' (n 49).
54 Saul, 'From Haiti to Somalia' (n 49) 143 and 'International Law and the Will of the People in Post-Conflict Rebuilding' (n 49).
55 Orford (n 13) 128.
56 Saul, 'Local Ownership of Post-Conflict Reconstruction in International Law' (n 49) 23–26.
57 In his latest writings Saul argues that interveners, notwithstanding their lack of legal restraints, are generally not willing to outrightly neglect self-determination imperatives. For this reason, state-builders seem to exploit the connection existing between democracy and self-determination to favour the creation of democratic orders. However, the absence of a legal definition of democracy does not ensure that self-determination standards are applied by international law in any meaningful sense. The advantages of a substantive legal definition of democracy for regulating manifestations of state-building are advocated also by Charlesworth. See Hilary Charlesworth, 'Law After War' (2007) 8 *Melbourne Journal of International Law* 233; Matthew Saul, 'The Search for an International Legal Concept of Democracy: Lessons from the Post-Conflict Reconstruction of Sierra Leone' (2012) 13 *Melbourne Journal of International Law* 1 and 'Creating Popular Governments in Post-Conflict Situations (n 49).

providing ‘assistance’ to an ineffective domestic government. All in all, Saul argues that international law largely leaves the issue of who governs the state in the hands of international actors because ‘international actors can, paradoxically, provide the legal authority for a set of domestic actors to consent to the same international actors becoming involved in the affairs of the state with a view to providing the factual authority necessary for governance’.[58] In a similar fashion, Bhuta has also submitted that international law on self-determination does not provide any meaningful guidance or standards for how to proceed with the drafting of a new constitution in post-conflict states. The only requirements expressed by law in these circumstances are the mere need of a popular expression of will. However, there is no rule governing the production of the new order, just a procedural entitlement to say yes or no to the order produced.[59]

In conclusion, the existing literature on the light footprint approach reveals that the discourse on self-determination should be explored further, if we aim to understand its role in this context. Whilst the assistance model seemed unremarkable, it appears incapable of ensuring respect for self-determination as political independence and freedom from outside interference. Sceptical views on the content of this norm have argued also that guidance to action cannot be found for self-determination taken as a participatory right.

2.2.2 A critical appraisal of the evaluative approach

This review of literature has revealed the existence of a complex and multi-faceted understanding of self-determination in the context of state-building. Notwithstanding the wide variety of interpretations offered regarding its role, content and significance as a legal concept, the widespread use of an evaluative approach made it possible to draw out a series of recurring features with which the right is identified.

In the context of ITA, it was proposed that self-determination enforces a set of limits to the activity of international administrators. First, it mandates that foreign administrations must be temporary. Secondly, it prohibits international actors to impose a specific form of government. Thirdly, it mandates local participation in the administration of power. We have also seen that self-determination is not considered to be an absolute right, but one from which derogation is permitted. On this basis, it is argued that the limits above need to be balanced against imperatives of international security, including the fragility of the state and the adequacy of local institutions. In the context of occupation, we have seen that the way self-determination is conceived (i.e. popular sovereignty as a precondition for action *versus* popular sovereignty as an objective) determines its relationship with occupation law. Depending on the way it is understood,

58 Saul, *Popular Governance of Post-Conflict Reconstruction* (n 49) 227.
59 Bhuta, ‘New Modes and Orders’ (n 30).

self-determination becomes either the rationale for exercising wide administrative authority on behalf of international occupants or the reason to restrict it to the minimum necessary. Moreover, in this context we have seen that many argued, as well, that self-determination is not an absolute right but one which needs to be balanced with security imperatives. In the context of assistance missions, instead, literature is scant so that generalisations are not possible. The existing studies, however, submit that the significance of self-determination as a legal norm, in this context, is reduced in virtue of the fact that the reconstruction is undertaken, at least nominally, by a domestic government. However, it is argued that the model does not ensure respect for self-determination understood as political independence.

The most remarkable feature of the debate in question is not the variety of existing views, which generally characterises academic debates, neither the overall indeterminacy attached to self-determination, to which international lawyers are accustomed. The striking aspect of this debate is the superficiality with which it is acknowledged that self-determination is not an absolute right and that derogation from this right is permitted.

Although being a common submission, it is not clear on which basis one can argue that temporary foreign control does not contravene self-determination. The idea of temporariness as a mitigating factor for the exercise of foreign control is generally used to shield accuses of violating self-determination. Again, this is presented as a matter of fact, but where can this claim be substantiated in international law? In his work, Wilde has argued convincingly that the tolerance of domination in contemporary situations constitutes a legacy of trusteeship. Whilst recognising the impossibility of applying the legal framework of trusteeship to ITAs, many indeed accept the rules applied to the trusteeship regime to play a guiding role in conceptualising international administration and its relationship with the right to self-determination.[60] The question, in this case, is how this is possible from an international law perspective. In view of the incontrovertible fact that the trusteeship regime cannot be applied, on what legal basis do international lawyers justify temporary derogation from self-determination entitlements?

This view is presented as a statement, often by adding a footnote to secondary literature and commentaries on the powers of the Security Council. However, nowhere in the actual sources of law on self-determination it is mentioned whether they can be subjected to derogation. Also, authors do not engage in thorough analysis of the law and do not offer first-hand interpretations of its provisions in order to establish that derogation is permitted and to define the characteristics of the derogation regime. This aspect, so far, remains an unresolved feature of the debate on self-determination. The question brings us also

60 On this point see also Lindsay Cameron and Rebecca Everly, 'Conceptualizing the Administration of Territory by International Actors' (2010) 21 *European Journal of International Law* 221, 238.

to consider two problematic issues in relation to how scholarly literature has tackled self-determination: an issue of method and one of content.

2.2.2.1 The issue of method

I identified two problematic issues relation to the method used by authors in carrying out their analyses of self-determination. The first problem with the literature analysed, as mentioned above, is a lack of thorough, in-depth analysis of the law of self-determination.[61] Given the proverbial indeterminacy of the norm, it is expected that international lawyers would dedicate wide space to interpreting the sources of the law, paying detailed attention to their wording, context, object and purposes. In fact, authors pay scant attention to interpretative details, dedicating at maximum a couple of paragraphs to defining the scope and content of self-determination and a passing reference to treaties and jurisprudence of the International Court of Justice.

For their cursory analyses of the law, the authors use quotes from treaty law and General Assembly Resolutions (as an expression of custom), generally – and rightly – to acknowledge that self-determination implies a freedom from subjugation, a right not to have a government imposed and a general participative right to choose on behalf of the people. This definition is often taken to be comprehensive and little attention is dedicated to the fundamental task of explaining what the formula really means. Where this is done, indeterminacy of the law is the recurrent answer. For instance, what specific rights and obligations does the norm include and for whom? And do they change according to the context where it is applied? What kind of relationships does it establish/mandates between the local people and the external actors that engage in reconstruction? When, exactly, can a government be said to have been imposed? Thorough discussion of these issues is rarely offered and, when this is the case, answers

61 The law of self-determination is scattered throughout various sources of international law. See UN Charter, arts 1(2) and 55; International Covenant on Civil and Political Rights, 16 December 1966, 999 UNTS 171, art 1; International Covenant on Economic, Social and Cultural Rights, 16 December 1966, 993 UNTS 3, art 1; GA Res 1514 (XV), 14 December 1960; GA Res 1541 (XV), 15 December 1960, Declaration on Principles of International Law Concerning Friendly Relations and Cooperation among States in Accordance with the Charter of the United Nations, GA Res 2625 (XXV), 24 October 1970; The Final Act of the Conference on Security and Cooperation in Europe, 1 August 1975, 14 ILM 1292. The principle has also been a subject of discussion in a number of judgments delivered by the International Court of Justice: *Legal Consequences for States of the Continued Presence of South Africa in Namibia (South West Africa) Notwithstanding Security Council Resolution 276 (1970)* (Advisory Opinion) [1971] ICJ Rep 16; *Western Sahara* (Advisory Opinion) [1975] ICJ Rep 12; *East Timor (Portugal v Australia)* [1995] ICJ Rep 90; *Legal Consequences of the Construction of a Wall in the Occupied Palestinian Territory* (Advisory Opinion) [2004] ICJ Rep 136; *Accordance with International Law of the Unilateral Declaration of Independence in Respect of Kosovo* (Advisory Opinion) [2010] ICJ Rep 403.

are presented in the form of personal opinions on the matter, rather than as a set of arguments duly substantiated on the basis of careful legal analysis.

The second issue on which I would like to focus attention is the lack of detailed discussion concerning self-determination's status in the normative hierarchy of international law. Given its ascription amongst the very few norms of international law that enjoy *jus cogens* status,[62] claims about the non-absolute character of self-determination and annexed possibility to derogate from it require, at minimum, serious questioning on the right's normative status.[63] Once again, in the literature reviewed above such claims are often set out as unsubstantiated opinions. Most discussions quickly resolve the issue by claiming that self-determination may not be considered to enjoy *jus cogens* status outside of the decolonisation context, and that in its post-colonial form of 'internal self-determination' the right is too indeterminate to constitute *jus cogens*. Self-determination, especially outside the decolonisation context, is a multi-leveled and multi-dimensional norm, for which a determination on *jus cogens* status is remarkably complex. A serious discussion in this respect needs to identify what aspects may be *jus cogens*, in which circumstances, and if the right carries *erga omnes* obligations, what sort of obligations and for whom.

This kind of in-depth discussion is necessary if one aims to carry out a serious undertaking on whether certain aspects of the norm can be derogated or not. Even authors who claim a *jus cogens* character for this norm, avoid taking this complexity into consideration.[64] Wheatley, for instance, briefly considers the issue of normative status, then moves on to the next-level question of whether Security Council action can override self-determination concerns.[65] The question is explored into some detail by Fox, who points to a gap in knowledge: the few existing discussions on *jus cogens*' relation to the Council do not pursue the problem of self-determination.[66] The same view is shared also by Levitt, who calls for more research to be conducted in this area.[67] In his analysis of the situation in occupied Iraq, Carcano delves into the question of whether the Security Council is bound to take self-determination into account when

62 See Hector Gros Espiell, 'Self-determination as *jus cogens*' in Antonio Cassese (ed) *United Nations, Fundamental Rights: Two Topics in International Law* (Sijthoff and Noordhoff International 1979) and 'Article 40: Commentary, Report of the International Law Commission', 56 GAOR (2001) Supplement No. 10, (A/56/10) 284.

63 Saul's latest work tackles the issue of self-determination's normative status and argues that 'there is a haziness surrounding the normative status of the right to self-determination'. His article is a welcome contribution. Matthew Saul 'The Normative Status of Self-Determination in International Law: A Formula for Uncertainty in the Scope and Content of the Right?' (2011) 11 *Human Rights Law Review* 609.

64 See, for instance, Alexander Orakhelashvili, *Peremptory Norms in International Law* (OUP 2006).

65 Wheatley (n 35) 543.

66 Fox, *Humanitarian Occupation* (n 23) 214.

67 Jeremy I Levitt, 'Illegal Peace? An Inquiry into the Legality of Power-Sharing with Warlords and Rebels in Africa' (2006) 27 *Michigan Journal of International Law* 495, 526.

exercising its functions. He argues that the Security Council acting under the UN Charter shall remain bound by self-determination in the long term, but maintains that it can shape the content and modalities of the people's enjoyment of self-determination; thus effectively balancing this right with the right of UN member states to the maintenance of international peace and security.[68]

Aside from these few notable examples, the literature reviewed in this chapter makes no reference to the recent jurisprudence dealing with the relationship between peremptory norms and Security Council resolutions adopted in the public interest against threat to peace and security.[69] This has been the case even though the judgements in question precede much of the literature referenced in this review. The discussion on this matter, instead, to back up claims on the derogable nature of self-determination makes reference mainly to a piece written by Matheson on ITAs, where he stated:

> I believe that there can in fact be situations in which the Security Council would be justified in directing a permanent change in some aspect of the status, boundaries, political structure, or legal system of territory within a state, if the Council should determine that doing so is necessary to restore and maintain international peace and security.[70]

The statement is not only, at most, one author's interpretation of the law, and hence a subsidiary source of law, but it is such a general statement that it cannot be said to constitute a proper argument. Rather, it seems to suggest a view which needs testing and scrupulous analysis in order to be confirmed. Given the relative popularity of the derogation claim, as seen above, this lack of verification is surprising, to say the least.

To conclude, any claims on the nature of the right to self-determination who aim to demonstrate its derogable or absolute nature must be substantiated by proper analysis of its normative status. The non-absolute character of self-determination was put forward by a great number of commentators but does

68 Carcano, *The Transformation of Occupied Territory in International Law* (n 43) 189–203.

69 With two exceptions: Wilde and Wheatley did provide passing references to the *Kadi, Lockerbie, Behrami* and *Seramati* cases. See *Case concerning questions of interpretation and application of the 1971 Montreal Convention arising from the aerial incident at Lockerbie (Libya v United States)* [1992] ICJ Rep 114; *Case concerning questions of interpretation and application of the 1971 Montreal Convention arising from the aerial incident at Lockerbie* [1998] ICJ Rep 115; Case T 315/01 *Kadi v Council of the European Union and Commission of the European Communities*, judgment of the CFI, 21 September 2005; Case C-402/05 P and C-415/05 *Kadi and Al-Barakaat International Foundation v Council and Commission* [2008] ECR I-6351; App No 71412/01 *Agim Behrami and Bekir Behrami v France*, and App No 78166/01 *Ruzhdi Saramati v France, Germany and Norway*, Grand Chamber decision of 2 May 2007. See Wilde, 'From Trusteeship to Self-Determination and Back Again' (n 32) and Wheatley (n 35).

70 Michael J Matheson, 'United Nations Governance of Post-Conflict Societies' (2001) 95 *American Journal of International Law* 76, 85.

the claim find substantiation in practice? Where is the evidence that derogation from self-determination standards is actually and permissibly taking place and under what circumstances? In order to answer these questions, legal research first needs to draw a clear map of the content and scope of the right, as it applies to the context of state-building. Once a clear legal analysis is provided, research can move towards identifying what aspect(s) of the right may be absolute and what aspect(s), instead, may be derogable. This takes us to the next point.

2.2.2.2 *The issue of interpretation*

The second problematic issue identified in relation to how self-determination is studied in relation to state-building is related to interpretation. To understand self-determination, the first step is to identify which 'self' we are interested in. Self-determination is a right of peoples, whereas the definition of who constitutes a people was purposely left open.[71] Its consequent suitability for application to a multitude of selves (indigenous peoples, people under occupation or alien domination, colonies, the people of a state as a whole, and arguably also to selected sub-state groups and minorities) makes of self-determination an essentially multi-faceted right. Its specific aspects, substance and content change according to the self it applies to. It is, therefore, mandatory that any serious attempt at detailed analysis starts with the identification of a precise subject for analysis.

There is a standard way for narrowing down the 'self' in self-determination debates. The idea of self-determination embodied in international law is indeed informed on a territorial contextualisation of the 'self'.[72] On the one hand, the 'self' is the people of a defined territory, notwithstanding the characteristics of this people (homogenous, heterogeneous). The only attribute is that the people permanently live in a defined territory. On the other hand, the 'self' is a group contained within a larger territorial unit and so the two do not overlap. These groups, instead, claim an entitlement to self-determination in the name of identity-based characteristics. The two conceptions recall the two dimensions of self-determination: external and internal. Therefore, those who study self-determination from the perspective of territorially defined entities (former colonial territories, now independent states) focus on the so-called internal aspects of the concept. Others, in reverse, discuss the internal dimension of the concept but pay also due attention to the far-reaching implications of granting external self-determination rights to sub-territorial groups and minorities. This binary division is not questioned; the dismissal of either dimension of the right from the discussion is an automatism.[73]

71 See James Summers, *Peoples and International Law: How Nationalism and Self-determination Shape a Contemporary Law of Nations* (2nd edn, Brill 2014).

72 Jeremy Waldron, 'Two Conceptions of Self-Determination' in Samantha Besson and John Tasioulas (eds), *The Philosophy of International Law* (OUP 2010).

73 I will take issue with this method at length in Chapter 4.

In a way, the lack of detailed analysis of the theory is understandable. Attempts to establish the significance and application of self-determination run the risk of either being redundant or of being inconclusive.[74] In order to avoid these risks, contemporary studies on self-determination can either focus on under-analysed selves, or aim to monitor the developments of the law in a context where a set of significant practice in relation to that self can be observed and interpreted. In this respect, I believe that it is possible to point out two gaps in the literature reviewed here and I will address them in turn.

The first gap concerns a lack of substantial focus. State-building, which is a relatively recent phenomenon, constitutes a privileged setting to observe how self-determination is used in practice and what is its impact both in intra-state relations (people v. external actors) and at the domestic level of (state v. people). The right can therefore be studied with different focus as it applies to at least three possible selves: (a) sub-state groups with independence claims; (b) minorities; and (c) independent states. It is possible to distinguish three trends of scholarship according to the self under examination.

Trend (a) focuses on the rights of sub-state groups with independence aspirations. The lead example of this is the literature considering the debates on ITA, as we have seen above, and the most recent debate concerning the independence of Kosovo as a result of state-building efforts.[75] Trend (b) concerns the minorities within a state, and how their collective rights have been systematically accommodated in state-building processes. Its literature has paid great attention to peace-making, and to the dynamics that come into play during the elaboration and implementation of peace deals.[76] Christine Bell, a leading scholar in the field, dedicates a chapter of her book *On The Law of Peace* to self-determination.[77] Bell argues that the field of peace agreements and 'post-peace agreements reconstruction'[78] offers a valuable insight on the way self-determination has developed from indeterminacy and on how it was reconceptualised. Her main thesis is that self-determination developed through

74 There are already many lengthy studies on this, including a relatively recent comprehensive account of the subject: see Antonio Cassese, *Self-Determination of Peoples: A Legal Reappraisal* (CUP 1995).

75 James Summers (ed), *Kosovo: A Precedent? The Declaration of Independence, the Advisory Opinion and Implications for Statehood, Self-Determination and Minority Rights* (Brill 2011).

76 For recent examples see Levitt (n 67); Scott P Sheeran, 'International Law, Peace Agreements and Self-Determination: The Case of The Sudan' (2011) 60 *International and Comparative Law Review* 423; Cindy Daase, 'The Redistribution of Resources in Internationalized Intra-State Peace Processes by Comprehensive Peace Agreements and Security Council Resolutions' (2011) 3 *Goettingen International Law Journal* 23; Kelly Stathpoulou, 'Self-Determination, Peace-Making and Peace-Building: Recent Trends in African Intra-State Peace Agreements' in Duncan French (ed), Statehood and Self-Determination: Reconciling Tradition and Modernity in International Law (CUP 2013); Marc Weller, 'Settling Self-Determination Conflicts: Recent Developments' (2009) 20 *European Journal of International Law* 111.

77 Christine Bell, *On the Law of Peace* (OUP 2008).

78 ibid 108.

the practice of peace agreements that she calls 'hybrid self-determination',[79] is not, strictly, positive international law, but is a realm of practice that holds some legal effect. Bell's approach is innovative as it does not turn to practice in order to provide an evaluative assessment of whether peace agreements have respected the right to self-determination. On the contrary, she uses this specific set of practice, peace agreements, to understand what this concept currently means and what role it plays in the negotiations. In doing so, she provides the only notable exception to the dominant evaluative approach.

Finally, in relation to trend (c) above, scholarship has mostly overlooked the study of self-determination as the right of an independent people in the context of state-building. First, there has been a distinctive lack of focus on the self-determination entitlements of independent selves. By this, I mean that the right to self-determination as it applies to the people of a state as a whole has not been sufficiently studied. Whilst this lack of attention is to be attributed also to the wider body of literature on self-determination, the limited attention it received in the context of state-building is striking. As we have seen above, studies on ITA concern sub-state groups and thus deal with a different set of claims attached to a different layer of self-determination. The right of independent states, how it works and what it means, therefore, is to be studied in other contexts: we are left with occupation and the assistance mission. In relation to occupation, the right is to be interpreted in view of its relationship with occupation law, a special international law regime that applies at times of military occupations.[80] In general, therefore, it is in the planning and management of assistance model-led reconstructions that we are better able to observe the significance of self-determination and how it relates to other principles of international law. Analysis in this field, however, is scarce[81] and is affected by all the limits outlined above. This is a gap that legal research needs to address.

Concerning the second gap, I take issue with the role that has been attributed to practice in the evaluative studies I reviewed in section 2.2 of this chapter. A strong limit of this approach lays with two underpinning assumptions that were found in the literature. On the one hand, some see the law as being too obscure and undetermined to say anything meaningful for practice. On the other hand, state practice is used only to evaluate compliance with the law, rather than to interpret it as a means to add details to generic formulas. As stated above, the context of state-building, being a relatively recent phenomenon, constitutes by all means a privileged observatory to look at how self-determination is applied at intra-state and inter-state level, what is its significance and impact in the shaping of reconstruction programmes. Existing analyses aim to ascertain how self-determination shapes/limits state-building, without questioning whether the relationship could work the other way around. Is state-building providing

79 ibid 220.

80 See section 2.2.1.1 above.

81 The exceptions are works by Bhuta, 'New Modes and Orders' (n 30), van der Driest (n 28) and Saul (n 49).

the institutional space for the norm of self-determination to be developed or redeveloped? As long as studies of self-determination are carried out from an evaluative perspective, they will offer only a limited contribution to our understanding of the norm under contemporary international law, of its role and value in this context. A new interpretative framework is needed.

2.3 The need for a new interpretative framework to study self-determination

In this chapter I have shown that the way in which self-determination was studied in relation to state-building has contributed little to advance our legal understanding of this norm. I have submitted that existing scholarship has relied heavily on the adoption of an evaluative approach, which aimed to establish the limits, if any, that self-determination may pose to state-building, and in what circumstances such limits can be set aside. However, many scholars have argued in favour of a derogable nature of self-determination. I have also argued that the legal bases for this argument were not sufficiently explored, and that claims to the non-absolute nature of the right must be followed by a complex analysis of the normative status of the norm, rather than by unsubstantiated principled statements. In addition, a lack of analysis was also shown in relation to a specific layer of the right (the right of the people of a state).

At this stage, a significant challenge for new research on self-determination is to reinvent the way in which we look at self-determination. To add meaningful substance to what we know about self-determination, future legal research will need to overcome the methodological and interpretative issues that I have outlined in sections 2.2.2.1 and 2.2.2.2, and must think beyond the dominant evaluative approach. But what should the features of this new framework look like? For originality purposes, research should focus on self-determination as the right of the people of a state. In order to produce knowledge about the significance and impact of this specific aspect of self-determination, it should also have the following distinctive features. In the first place, it should start with a strong normative analysis. The research should look into the origins of the concept of self-determination; dig out the content of this norm by looking at sources of law; provide a first-hand interpretation of the scope and content of the right as it applies to the people of a state – an aspect of the right often overlooked by studies of international law. Existing studies have generally referred to it as a concept overlapping with state sovereignty, political independence and non-interference. The appropriateness of these analyses needs to be questioned.

On a methods level, future research must also be context-specific.[82] Contemporary practice can enlighten us on the post-colonial meaning of self-determination.

82 This point was stressed also by Drew, who points out the necessity of establishing the context in which her analysis of East Timor was carried out, not as a mere academic exercise, but because this has practical consequences: identifying colonialism as the proper basis for East-Timorese self-determination claims is important because in that context the right carries a specific content, which otherwise would be more indeterminate. Drew (n 22) 657–58.

Historically, the key normative development of self-determination took place in-context, and mainly during decolonisation. In this setting, it became a right of colonised people and developed much of its legal content. Can state-building constitute a similar historic opportunity to track the development of post-decolonisation self-determination as a legal right of the people of a state?

On the level of interpretation, the study should look at state practice, set in a specific context, in order to draw out the significance and impact of the norm in light of contemporary practice of international law. In so doing, new research should follow the avenue inaugurated by Bell's analysis of self-determination in the practice of peace agreements. State practice should be seen as the *locus* where the application of self-determination can be studied, and where developments in the law can be spotted. Future research should therefore monitor and aim to interpret any possible discrepancy found between what the law in theory requires and what the practice shows. Has the law of self-determination developed adding details to previously vague standards? Has the law transformed and/or collapsed into other norms or principles (i.e. has democratic governance become a substitute for internal self-determination)?

The benefits of having new research produced according to this innovative conceptual framework is to advance our knowledge of self-determination. The advantages of making some clarity on a notoriously obscure norm of international law would be useful to whoever is engaged in state-building, both at present and in the reconstructions to come.

2.4 Conclusion

This chapter has demonstrated that there is a dominant narrative which, so far, has dictated the way in which self-determination was looked at in scholarly work on post-conflict state-building. I suggested that this narrative does not, in fact, appreciate the way self-determination applies to state-building and is therefore unhelpful in exploring the relevance and significance of this principle in the post-decolonisation phase of its development. The analysis conducted here has unveiled the areas where our understanding of self-determination remains insufficient. In so doing, the chapter has carved out a vital space for more research to be conducted departing from this dominant narrative. The approach called for aims to better grasp the significance that self-determination plays in relation to state-building and would produce original knowledge in this field of scholarship.

After all, improving our understanding of the meaning of self-determination is not only an exercise of pure interest for those devote to the issue. It is also an important way to contribute to knowledge-making concerning the legality and legitimacy of external intervention, at a time in which outside intervention into failed states' internal affairs is all the more frequent.

3 The right to self-determination for the people of an independent state: an overview

3.1 Introduction

In the past fifty years, international law scholarship has devoted a great deal of attention to the study of self-determination. As a political principle, self-determination has a long-standing history, which dates back to the idea of popular sovereignty championed by the French Revolution of 1789.[1] It was not until the 1940s, however, that the principle entered into the realm of international law. As a legal concept, self-determination was included in the UN Charter in 1945, but it was in the following two decades, with the occurrence of decolonisation, that it gained real status as a norm of international law. As a consequence, academic interest in the topic was particularly intense between the 1950s and the mid-1970s. In these years historical events, which saw great changes happening in the international arena and a large number of new states coming into existence, took hostage the development of international law on self-determination. The decolonisation movement linked almost inextricably the notion of self-determination with the global movement for the liberation of colonised peoples, so that self-determination became one of the basic and most significant norms of international law of decolonisation.[2]

As a consequence, the meaning, scope and content of the legal principle of self-determination were spelled out in detail in relation to its application to peoples under colonial domination.[3] Norm-development took place in context and its content was therefore defined accordingly: self-determination came to mean first and foremost freedom from colonial domination and the right to attain independence. At a later stage, the definition of domination was expanded to

1 See section 3.2.1.2 below and works cited therein.

2 Malcolm N Shaw, 'The Western Sahara Case' (1978) 49 *British Yearbook of International Law* 119, 147.

3 Starting with the measures set out by General Assembly Resolution 1541 (XV) *Principles which should guide Members in determining whether or not an obligation exists to transmit the information called for under Article 73 of the Charter*, adopted on 15 December 1960, UN Doc A/Res/15/1541.

include also people under racial, alien or external domination.[4] At the same time, the meaning, content and legal significance of self-determination as it applies beyond the decolonisation context remained more obscure and underdeveloped in international law – so that most of its aspects are still largely disputed today. This even led some to question whether, with the end of decolonisation, self-determination, as such, might be 'dead'.[5]

Most writers today recognise that there is a role for self-determination outside the colonial context. More precisely, at present the discourse on self-determination outside decolonisation focuses around several streams. The main directions of work concern the following issues: the rights of indigenous peoples;[6] secession and the right to independence;[7] democratic governance and the right of autonomy for minority groups.[8] The latter branch of study is closely intertwined and often conflates into the discourse on human rights, minority rights and political participation.

The principal aim of this chapter is to take discussions over the meaning and significance of self-determination beyond the colonial context a step forward. I will do so by producing original knowledge about a specific sub-norm of self-determination that has received scant attention in existing literature. By 'sub-norm' I mean a small component of the wider, general principle of self-determination that exists in international law. A sub-norm, as understood here, attaches specifically to one of the 'selves' entitled to self-determination under

4 See art 1(4), Protocol Additional to the Geneva Conventions of 12 August 1949, and relating to the Protection of Victims of International Armed Conflicts (Protocol I), 8 June 1977.

5 Lung-Chu Chen, 'Self-Determination: An Important Dimension of the Demand for Freedom' (1981) 75 *Proceedings of the American Society of International Law* 88; Prakash Sinha, 'Is Self-Determination Passé?' (1973) 12 *Columbia Journal of Transnational Law* 260; Gerry J Simpson, 'The Diffusion of Sovereignty: Self-Determination in the Post-Colonial Age' (1996) 32 *Stanford Journal of International Law* 255, 255.

6 See eg Martin Scheining and Pekka Aikio (eds), *Operationalizing the Right of Indigenous Peoples to Self-Determination* (Abo Akademi University 2000) and Alexandra Xanthaki, *Indigenous Rights and United Nations Standards: Self-Determination, Culture and Land* (CUP 2007).

7 To cite but a few: Simone van den Driest, *Remedial Secession: A Right to External Self-Determination as a Remedy to Serious Injustices?* (Oxford 2013); Marcelo G Kohen (ed), *Secession: International Law Perspectives* (CUP 2006); Margaret Moore (ed), *National Self-Determination and Secession* (OUP 1998); Igor Primoratz, Aleksandar Pavković (eds), *Identity, Self-Determination and Secession* (Ashgate 2006); Milena Sterio, *The Right to Self-Determination under International Law: "Selfistans", Secession and the Rule of the Great Powers* (Routledge 2013); Christian Walter, Antije von Ungern-Sternberg and Kavus Abushov (eds), *Self-Determination and Secession in International Law* (OUP 2014).

8 For a few examples see Ulrike Barten, *Minorities, Minority Rights and Self-Determination* (Springer 2014); Hurst Hannum, *Autonomy, Sovereignty and Self-Determination: The Accommodation of Conflicting Rights, Revised Edition* (University of Pennsylvania Press, 1996); Thomas D Musgrave, *Self-Determination and National Minorities* (Clarendon Press 1997); Marc Weller and Stefan Wolff (eds), *Autonomy, Self-Governance and Conflict Resolution: Innovative Approaches to Institutional Design in Divided Societies* (Routledge 2005).

contemporary international law. Self-determination by definition applies to a 'self', and more specifically it applies to a number of selves. Here I will take into account only one, specific 'self', namely the people of an independent state, to study and shed light over the contours of the sub-norm that applies to it. In order to make sense of this complexity, I will use the metaphor of layers, according to which self-determination is composed of a number of layers, each attached to a specific self.[9] In this view, each 'layer' shall represent a sub-norm, or a specific, defined norm which composes the wider, macro-principle of self-determination in international law.

In Chapter 2, I found that there is a need to know more about self-determination as the right of the people of a state in order to assess its relevance and significance in-context. Such knowledge is lacking at present and leaves a gap in the literature, so that we do not know its role in governing transition from conflict to peace. The present chapter makes an original contribution to scholarship by offering a comprehensive insight into the features that distinguish this particular layer of self-determination, one that has generally been overlooked in previous studies.

The structure is articulated into three main sections. Sections 3.2 starts by introducing the sub-norm taken into account, and proceeds to outline the origins of self-determination as a legal principle, its meaning under the UN Charter and its association with decolonisation. Section 3.3 is devoted to an analysis of the meaning and content of the norm in treaty and customary international law. Overall, the chapter examines the origins, development and conceptualisation under international law of what remains an under-explored and under-acknowledged dimension of self-determination. An in-depth analysis of the content and scope is thus provided, in defiance of the proverbial indefiniteness which is usually said to characterise the principle of self-determination. This analysis is useful to prepare the ground for an interpretation of the character of this norm that will be set out in Chapter 4.

3.2 Subjects, selves and 'layers' of self-determination

As a preliminary step, I begin with a definition of what self-determination means and how it should be understood in this study. As I mentioned above, self-determination 'by definition' is attached to a certain 'self', where the self is a people: a collective entity.[10] Who qualifies as a people under international law and thus who can enjoy self-determination entitlements has always been

9 A similar understanding of self-determination as actuated on layered levels was put forward also by Maguire. See Amy Maguire, 'Law Protecting Rights: Restoring the Law of Self-determination in the Neo-colonial World' (2008) 12 *Law Text Culture* 12, 15.

10 The right to self-determination is listed among the rights of peoples. The International Court of Justice (ICJ) recognised it as such in its opinion on *Western Sahara* (Advisory Opinion) [1975] ICJ Rep 12, para 54. See also, more generally, James Crawford, 'The right to Self-determination in international law: Its development and future' in Philip Alston

a burning question and one that has deeply divided and continues to divide scholars, states and all those with a bearing on the interpretation of international law.[11] According to Helen Quane, there are at least three broad interpretations of the 'self' for self-determination. The term can either refer to: (i) the right of the population of a state; (ii) the right of the population of a colonial territory; (iii) the right of peoples, if they comprise the entire population of a state or colonial territory.[12]

The focus here is on the first of the three meanings that can be attributed to the 'self' to be determined. Therefore, I take 'people' to mean the population of an independent state and I look at self-determination to establish what it means for and how it applies to the people of an independent state. This interpretation of *whom* is entitled to self-determination is often considered as the least controversial amongst the three possibilities outlined above.[13] This particular interpretation is considered uncontroversial because it relies on a notion of people that identifies territorially defined selves and, in so doing, it speaks of self-determination without posing any challenge to the principle of territorial integrity of existing states. Indeed, with respect to self-determination it is believed that the real quagmire has to do with the claims of sub-state groups who cultivate secessionist ambitions.[14]

In fact, the approach to viewing territorially-defined selves as uncontroversial is far from being uncontroversial. The reality of post-colonial states, indeed, raises important questions concerning the appropriate delimitation of territorial

---

(ed), *People's Rights* (OUP 2001) and James Crawford, 'The rights of peoples: 'peoples' or 'governments'?' in James Crawford (ed), *The Rights of Peoples* (Clarendon 1988).

11 See James Summers, Peoples and International Law: How the Right of Self-Determination and Nationalism Shape a Contemporary Law of Nations (2nd edn, Brill Nijhoff 2014).

12 Hellen Quane, 'The United Nations and the evolving right to self-determination' (1998) 47 *International and Comparative Law Quarterly* 537, 537. For Doehring, there are three possible right-bearers: (i) an ethnic minority living inside a state; (ii) colonial peoples living beyond the boundaries of the colonial powers; (iii) the population of a foreign state, who can invoke the right in case of foreign domination. See Karl Doehring, 'Self-determination' in Bruno Simma and others (eds), *The Charter of the United Nations: A Commentary, Vol II* (2nd edn, OUP 2002) 55.

13 Crawford, referring to two possible meanings of self-determination as a right of states and as a right of the people in a specific territory to choose their own form of government, calls the first 'uncontroversial'. Raic also writes that, of all the different candidates for self-determination, the notion of people as the people of an independent state 'is without a doubt the least controversial'. See, respectively, J Crawford, *The Creation of States in International Law* (2nd edn, OUP 2006) 59 and David Raic, *Statehood and the Law on Self-Determination* (The Hague 2002) 244. On the same point see also Alexander Kiss, 'The people's right to self-determination' (1986) 7 *Human Rights Law Journal* 165.

14 This concept is condensed very well in the famous words written by Lansing in relation to the Wilsonian idea of self-determination: 'When the President talks of 'self-determination' what unit has he in mind? . . . Without a definite unit which is practical, application of this principle is dangerous to peace and stability. . . . The phrase is simply loaded with dynamite'. Robert Lansing, *The Peace Negotiations: A Personal Narrative* (Houghton Mifflin 1921) 97.

boundaries and the possible artificiality of state borders. In certain situations, indeed, the lines drafted by colonial powers can be seen to have divided and separated territories in an arbitrary manner, with the effect of arbitrarily dividing peoples with a homogeneous language, culture and traditions.[15] This issue renders the application of self-determination, within the borders of certain established states (particularly in former African colonial territories), notably controversial. International law has addressed the problem by elaborating the principle of *uti possidetis*.[16] This principle, which is said to be grounded on customary law, is primarily aimed at 'securing respect for the territorial boundaries now when independence is achieved'.[17] The way this principle was applied within certain, colonially-established, territorial boundaries has therefore led to constructing who is a people for the purposes of international law.

Here I will not question the relationship between *uti possidetis* and self-determination.[18] I recognise that a debate exists on this issue but, for the present purposes, I accept that existing state borders define a population and identify a people which constitutes a 'self' legitimately entitled to self-determination under international law. This approach is justified because I aim to study and discuss the character and significance of this precise layer of self-determination. I recognise, nonetheless, that in specific situations there may be solid arguments that would make such a perspective problematic, because various levels of self-determination claims may indeed overlap in this type of situation.[19]

Summing up, this enquiry will focus on the right to self-determination as it attaches to the people of an independent state. Throughout Chapters 3 and 4 I will show that this one, specific dimension of self-determination has a core legal meaning that contradicts the proverbial indeterminacy attached to the principle. I will show that his core content can be drawn from the sources of

15 See Edward McWhinney, *Self-determination of Peoples and Plural-ethnic States in Contemporary International Law: Failed States, Nation-building and the Alternative, Federal Option* (Brill 2007) 55.

16 See *Frontier Dispute (Burkina Faso v. Mali)* [1986] ICJ Rep 554 at 566–67; Conference on Yugoslavia, Arbitration Commission, Opinion No 2, 31 ILM (1992) 14979 at 1498 and Opinion No 3, ibid 1499–500.

17 *Frontier Dispute Case* (n 16) 566.

18 I acknowledge, nevertheless, that the legal validity and appropriateness of this principle have been strongly criticised and repeatedly called into question. See, for instance, Steven Ratner, 'Drawing a better line: *Uti possidetis* and the borders of new states' (1996) 90 *American Journal of International Law* 590; Gérard Kreijen, *State Failure, Sovereignty and Effectiveness* (Martinus Nijhoff 2004) 41–42; Musgrave (n 8) and Antonio Cassese, 'The International Court of Justice and the Right of Peoples to Self-determination' in Vaughan Lowe and Malgosia Fitzmaurice, *Fifty Years of the International Court of Justice: Essays in Honour of Sir Robert Jennings* (CUP 2008) 362. For a contrasting view incontrovertibly accepting *uti possidetis* as a binding norm of international law see Malcolm N Shaw, 'Peoples, territorialism and boundaries' (1997) 3 *European Journal of International Law* 478.

19 I will return to this point in Chapter 5, when I discuss, in context, the situation of state-building in Somalia.

international law and is also well-established in the literature. This task first requires putting together the information available, which is at present scattered in a number of sources. A comprehensive account does not exist for this layer of self-determination, so the following sections will proceed with identifying the scope and content of this specific dimension of self-determination, in order to offer a clear picture of what we know about this aspect of the norm.

3.2.1 Self-determination in international law

Self-determination emerged first as a political principle but it is widely accepted that it acquired a legal status in 1945, with the adoption of the Charter of the United Nations.[20] Before that, as one author put it, 'the nature of self-determination was that of a gift or a favor'.[21] To demonstrate the non-legal nature of self-determination before 1945, scholarly literature makes common reference to the case of the Aaland Islands.[22] The case concerned a dispute between Finland and Sweden in relation to the future of the Aaland Islands; an island territory populated mostly by persons of Swedish language, culture and traditions, that was ceded to Russia together with Finland in 1809. When Finland declared its independence in 1917, the Islands fell under Finnish jurisdiction.[23] It is then that a dispute arose on whether the Islands should have been part of the new Finnish state or reunited with Sweden. In deciding the case, both a Committee of Jurists and a Commission of Rapporteurs, appointed by the Council of the League of Nations, plainly excluded the possibility that the principle of self-determination could be considered an international legal norm – recognising however its value as an important political principle and its relevance in situations of transition and state formation.[24]

Only sporadic opinions exist to challenge the dominant view according to which self-determination had not effectively acquired a legal status in international law before 1945 and the drafting of the UN Charter.[25] Amongst these,

20 This view is accepted by most commentators. See eg Antonio Cassese, *Self-determination of Peoples: A Legal Reappraisal* (CUP 1995); Doehring (n 12); Rosalyn Higgins, *Problems and Process: International Law and How We Use It* (Clarendon Press 1994); Kiss (n 13), Michla Pomerance, *Self-determination in Law and Practice: The New Doctrine in the United Nations* (Martinus Nijhoff 1982).

21 Raic (n 13) 197.

22 *Aaland Islands Case* (1920) League of Nations Official Journal Spec Supp 3 (1920) 3.

23 For a background on the facts of the case see Philip M Brown, 'The Aaland Islands Question' (1921) 15 *American Journal of International Law* 268; N J Padeldorf and K G Andersson, 'The Aaland Islands Question' (1939) 22 *American Journal of International Law* 465.

24 *Aaland Islands Case* (n 22) and 'The Aaland Islands Question' (1921) 1 *League of Nations Official Journal* 691.

25 For instance, Lachs argues that the principle had already become part of the general principles of international law by the time the Charter was being drafted. Manfred Lachs, 'The Law in and of the United Nations (Some Reflections on the Principle of Self-Determination)' (1961) 1 *Indian Journal of International Law* 429, 432–33.

it is worth mentioning Brownlie, who has pointed out that the Atlantic Charter of 14 August 1941 was in fact the first instrument to collect a wide multilateral acceptance of some basic principles of self-determination – although the document does not mention the term itself.[26] In line with this view, Laing also argued it was in that moment, through the Atlantic Charter and the support it gained by US state practice during 1941-45, that a right to self-determination has in fact emerged under customary international law.[27] However, this view remains unconvincing for two main reasons: first, because – as we have already mentioned – the term self-determination fails to appear as such in the document; and, secondly, because the legal value of the Atlantic Charter and its capacity to create rights and obligations to signatory states is dubious, to say the least.[28]

Here, I support the generally accepted view according to which self-determination acquires a legal status in international law in 1945, with the inclusion of the actual word 'self-determination' in the UN Charter. On this basis, the next section will be devoted to ascertaining whether, in the UN Charter, the term self-determination can be said to have contained a reference to the 'self' to which this research is dedicated.

3.2.1.1 Self-determination in the UN Charter

In order to grasp what self-determination means in the Charter an interpretative exercise is required, because it is not sufficient to interpret the term through its ordinary meaning. The term is indeed controversial and its meaning also changes in-context, according to the self that it is attached to. In the attempt to attribute a meaning to self-determination in the UN Charter, I will therefore resort to supplementary means of interpretation such as the *travaux préparatoires*, with the aim to understand what meaning was originally infused to this term by the drafters.[29]

26 The Atlantic Charter was a statement through which subscribing states based their aspirations for future world order, not a treaty. It contained eight points, of which, two read: (ii) They [the participants] desire to see no territorial changes that do not accord with the freely expressed wishes of the peoples concerned; (iii) They respect the right of all people to choose the form of government restored to those who have been forcibly deprived of them'. The Atlantic Charter (1946–47) *Yearbook of United Nations Law* 3 http://www.nato.int/cps/en/natolive/official_texts_16912.htm (last accessed 15 April 2018). See Ian Brownlie, 'An Essay in the History of the Principle of Self-Determination' in Charles H Alexandrowicz (ed), *Grotian Society Papers 1968. Studies in the History of the Law of Nations* (Martinus Nijhoff 1970).

27 For a lengthy discussion of the value of the Atlantic Charter under customary international law see Edward A Laing, 'The Norm of Self-Determination, 1941-1991' (1991) 22 *California Western International Law Journal* 209.

28 For a discussion on this matter see Brownlie (n 26) and U O Omozurike, *Self-determination in International Law* (Archon 1972) 59–61, for a discussion of the debated applicability of the Atlantic Charter to colonial peoples.

29 For this approach to treaty interpretation see Vienna Convention on the Law of Treaties arts 31–32.

The Charter has two direct references to self-determination: the term appears in Articles 1 (2) and 55, but both provisions fail to provide a definition of the term.[30] A formula essentially identical to what was included as Article 1(2) was set out at San Francisco by the four inviting powers: China, US, UK and USSR.[31] The final version of Article 1(2) reads as:

> The purposes of the United Nations are:
>
> 1. . . .
> 2. To develop friendly relations among nations[32] based on respect for the principle of equal rights and self-determination of peoples, and to take other appropriate measures the strengthen universal peace.

Article 1 sets out the 'Purposes and Principles' of the organisation, which are 'designed to provide a guide for the conduct of the Organization and its organs'.[33] The Rapporteur to the First Commission on the drafting of the UN Charter stated that 'the Purposes constitute the raison d'être of the Organization . . ., the cause and object of the Charter to which member states collectively and severally subscribe.[34]

For many years, the binding character of the Purposes and Principles has been a matter of controversy and subjected to open debate. On the one hand, we have those who argue that whilst the legislative history of Article 1 points to the direction of attaching a legally binding status to it, the wording of this Article is more appropriate for political objectives than for legally binding principles.[35] The formula indeed is said to remain too vague and undefined to be said to impose any legal obligations or legal standards of conduct to Charter members.[36]

30 Charter of the United Nations art 1(2), outlining the Purposes of the United Nations, provides that one of these purposes is 'to develop friendly relations among nations based on respect for the principle of equal rights and self-determination of peoples, and to take other appropriate measures to strengthen universal peace'. Article 55 provides that the United Nations shall promote a number of goals 'with a view to the creation of conditions of stability and well-being which are necessary for peaceful and friendly relations among nations based on respect for the principle of equal rights and self-determination of peoples'.

31 Dumbarton Oak proposals, Committee I/1 3 Doc U.N. Conf. On Int'l Org. Vol III, 622, 5 May 1945.

32 The use of the word nations instead of states, is widely attributed to the fact that some of the founding members of the organisation were not yet states at the time when the Charter was drafted. The exceptions were: Byelorussia, India, Philippines and the Ukraine. For this interpretation see Higgins (n 20) 113 and Quane (n 12) 539.

33 Rudiger Wolfrum, 'Chapter 1: Purposes and Principles' in Simma and others (n 12) 40.

34 UNCIO Vol VI, 387.

35 Wolfrum (n 33) 40.

36 Daniel Thürer and Thomas Burri, 'Self-determination' (2010) *Max Planck Encyclopedia of Public International Law* http://opil.ouplaw.com/home/epil (last accessed 15 April 2018).

On the other hand, we have those who believe that the Purposes and Principles do have a binding force and thus that legal character was attached to self-determination in the Charter. Today, the majority of scholars support this view according to which self-determination acquired legal status under the Charter.[37] To mention but a few, Cassese argues that the Charter constitutes a real turning point in the life of self-determination, because it represents the moment in which the political postulate is turned into a legal standard of behaviour.[38] Doehring believes that self-determination in the Charter has a legal status because 'the legally binding nature of the Purposes is undoubtedly clear', given that Article 2(4) of the Charter requires all member states to abstain from all activities which could impair the Purposes of the Charter.[39] In recent years, even those who had remained sceptical about the legal value of the Purposes and Principles at the time of drafting of the UN Charter, accepted that in contemporary international law, thus in light of the developments of international law since 1945, it is widely appreciated that certain elements of Article 1(1) and (2) are considered binding under customary law, and that decisions taken by the UN under other Articles of the Charter can all be seen as examples of practice in implementing the Purposes and Principles set out in Article 1.[40]

Having established that self-determination in the UN Charter was (or has since been) given a legal character, we shall now move to the key task that this section set out to accomplish. More precisely, I will show that it is possible to draw out three key features that the drafters have attributed to this principle that are of interest to the present enquiry. First, it is clear that under the Charter self-determination does concern the people of independent states. Secondly, it appears that self-determination is intertwined with the principle of sovereign

37 The view according to which self-determination become a legal standard of conduct was first put forward by Wright in 1954. Wright was the first to argue that self-determination, to some extent, had become a legal right under the Charter. This view is shared by a number of scholars, amongst which we can list Cassese, Crawford, Doehring, Higgins, Umozurike and Quane. Amongst those who argue against this position, we have Blum, Kelsen, Pomerance and Sinha. For a clear summary of the early debate see Prakash Sinha, 'Has Self-determination Become a Principle of International Law Today?' (1974) 14 *Indian Journal of International Law* 332. More generally see Yehoda Blum, 'Reflections on the Changing Concept of Self-determination' (1975) 10 *Israel Law Review* 509, 511; Cassese, *Self-determination of Peoples* (n 20); Crawford, *The Creation of States in International Law* (n 13); Doehring (n 12); Hans Kelsen, *The Law of the United Nations: A Critical Analysis of its Fundamental Problems* (Praeger 1964) 53; Higgins (n 20); Umozurike (n 28); M Pomerance (n 20); Quane (n 12); Quincy Wright, 'Recognition and Self-determination' (1954) 48 *American Society of International Law Proceedings* 23.

38 Cassese, *Self-determination of Peoples* (n 20) 43.

39 Doehring (n 12) 49.

40 Wolfrum (n 33) 40. Cassese also recognised that, while at first the lack of a detailed definition meant that the principle was 'primarily intended to guide the Organization', over the years the development of the law at the treaty and customary level on behalf of UN member States 'turned that standard into a precept that was also directly binding on states'. See Cassese, *Self-determination of Peoples* (n 20) 43.

equality of states.[41] Thirdly, under the UN Charter the content of the layer of self-determination taken into exam here is essentially twofold.

In relation to the first point, the *travaux préparatoires* reveal that a lively debate surrounded the issue of 'who' was to be entitled to self-determination under Article 1. The issue was clearly put by the representative of Belgium, who warned that it would be dangerous to extend the right to self-determination as a basis of friendly relations between the nations.[42] The issue of whether national, sub-state groups should be entitled to self-determination was in fact taken up and repeatedly stressed by several state representatives. A study of the meetings minutes reveals that in several Committee sessions state representatives repeatedly stressed that that the right of secession was not included in the definition of self-determination, as this would not be in conformity with the purposes of the Charter.[43] In response to these concerns, the technical Committee summarised the position of participant members as follows: 'the principle [self-determination] conformed to the purposes of the Charter only insofar as it implied the right of self-government of peoples and not the right of secession'.[44]

On this point Quane provides a convincing elucidation by conducting a cross-referenced analysis of the way in which the word 'peoples' is used in other provisions of the Charter. In so doing, she draws attention to how the Preamble opens with the phrase 'We the Peoples of the United Nations' to then conclude with the statement that 'our respective Governments . . . have agreed to the present Charter'.[45] The reference to 'our respective Governments', in her view, suggests therefore that the term 'peoples' in the Preamble refers to peoples organised as states.[46] In addition, she reminds us of how the references to self-determination in Articles 1 and 55 would also make sense in an historical

41 On the inclusion of the term 'sovereign equality' as a new term in the UN Charter see Bardo Fassbender and Albert Bleckmann, 'Article 2(1)' in Bruno Simma and others (eds), *The Charter of the United Nations: A Commentary, Vol II* (2nd edn, OUP 2002) 83.

42 'Surely one could use the word "peoples" as an equivalent of the word state, but in the expression of the people's right to self-determination the word peoples means the national groups which do not identify themselves with the population of a state. As for the word "nations" used at the beginning of this article, it is not possible to determine whether it is used in the first or in the second meaning of the word "peoples". The second criticism on the text proposed by the amendment of the sponsoring governments is that it would be dangerous to put forth the peoples' right of self-determination as a basis for the friendly relations between the nations.' UNCIO, Vol VI, 300.

43 For instance, Colombia stated: 'if it [self-determination] means self-government, the right of a country to provide its own government, yes, we would certainly like it to be included; but if it were to be interpreted, on the other hand, as connoting a withdrawal, the right of withdrawal or secession, then we should regard that as tantamount to international anarchy, and we should not desire that it should be included in the text of the Charter'. Debates of the First Committee of the First Commission of the San Francisco Conference, 15 May 1945, 20 (unpublished). Reported in Cassese, *Self-determination of peoples* (n 20) 39–40. See also the Summary Report of Sixth Meeting of Committee I/1, UNCIO Vol VI, 296.

44 UNICIO, Vol VI (1945) 296.

45 Quane (n 12) 540.

46 ibid.

perspective to support this interpretation since 'the general view in 1945 was that only states had rights under international law'.[47]

The view is shared also by Rosalyn Higgins, who believes that the term as originally included in the Charter had a state-based meaning. In both Article 1(2) and Article 55, Higgins argues that self-determination is about 'the rights of the people of one state to be protected', because in 1945 it was the 'equal rights of states that was being provided for, not of individuals'.[48] James Summers, in his study of the meaning of peoples in the law of self-determination, also supports this point claiming that not surprisingly states welcomed a definition of peoples as the people of independent states.[49] In particular, he cites a statement by the Government of China which makes this point clear: "peoples' can be identified with states. China means the state of China and a logical meaning would be the people of the state of China'.[50]

Overall, it seems safe to argue that, in the Charter, self-determination was conceived to be attached to the people of independent states. This definition did not encounter resistance on behalf of states and of yet non-state nations who participated in the drafting of the Charter. This point is both easy to trace in the *travaux préparatoires* and well established in the academic literature. What is disputed, instead, is whether this could have been the one and only meaning associated to 'people', or whether the term has been conceived to apply also to other possible selves (colonial peoples and national minorities).[51]

A second aspect which emerges clearly from the debates surrounding the adoption of the Charter is the link existing between self-determination and the principle of equal rights of states. Article 1 of the Charter speaks of a singular 'principle of equal rights and self-determination'.[52] The *travaux préparatoires* show that it was clear in the intention of the drafters that the principles of equal rights of people and that of self-determination were to be 'two component elements or one norm'.[53] This connection is important because it defines a special

47 In fact, Quane does not only support the fact that self-determination acquired a legal status in the Charter; she brings the argument even further by stating that, to the extent that self-determination refers to sovereign equality of states, 'it is possible to speak of a legal right to self-determination in the Charter'. This interpretation is relatively audacious and does not seem to have been backed by other scholars. Quane (n 12) 539–44.

48 Higgins (n 20) 112.

49 To support this claim, he lists a number of states who shared this view during the discussions including Colombia (see n 43), Nicaragua and China. See Summers (n 11) 198. The point is also made by Milan Sahovic, *Principles of International Law Concerning Friendly Relations and Cooperation* (Belgrade Institute of International Politics and Economics 1972) 341.

50 See Summers (n 11) 198 and UNCIO Vol XVII, 280.

51 I have not engaged in making such a determination because it would have not been useful for the purposes of this research. However, Quane and Raic are good examples of discussions on this matter. See Quane (n 12) and Raic (n 13).

52 UNCIO Vol XVIII, 107.

53 UNCIO Vol VI, 703.

relationship between self-determination and its significance for the people of an independent state. As Rosalyn Higgins remarks, one cannot ignore the coupling of self-determination with equal rights under the Charter, and it was the equal rights of states that was provided for.[54] This relationship, in light of the point we established above concerning the meaning of 'peoples' in the Charter, attributes certain rights to states and, with it, to its people. In other words, the principle, as one, is there to assure the equality of peoples organised as states, and to ensure that no people can be denied the right to self-determination on the basis of any alleged inferiority.[55]

This brings us to the third aspect of the law on self-determination that we aim to address: the issue of content. There has been much criticism in relation to the content of self-determination in the Charter, accused of being left excessively vague, undefined, little explained and thus resulting all together of little substance. Cassese, for instance, seems to be disappointed about the fact that the concept of self-determination upheld in the Charter can only be negatively inferred for what it *did not* mean.[56] Conversely, here I show that if one considers self-determination from the perspective of the rights and entitlements that it gives to the people of independent states, its significance, meaning and conceptualisation in the UN Charter is far from being disappointing. The Charter sets out an important, core meaning attached to this specific layer of self-determination. Moreover, through this chapter we will see that this precise meaning will hold on to the law of self-determination through the development of the principle in the following decades.

A careful analysis of the drafting history of the Charter demonstrates that there is agreement on at least two aspects of the norm's content. Firstly, it is accepted that self-determination provides peoples with an entitlement to establish a regime of their choice, and that this regime must be a genuine expression of the will of the people. Secondly, self-determination requires that other states do not interfere into a state's internal affairs. I will elaborate on these two aspects in turn.

In relation to the first, there are two separate passages of the drafting subcommittee's reports, in which the Rapporteur's text is very clear in relation to the meaning of the norm.[57] One passage reads: 'It was understood . . . that a core, essential element of the principle in question [self-determination] is a free and genuine expression of the will of the people'.[58] The second passage then adds to this, stating that 'the principle conformed to the purposes of the Charter only insofar as it implied the right of self-government of peoples and not the right of secession'.[59] On a further request from the Commission, the

54 Higgins (n 20) 112.
55 Wolfrum (n 33) 44.
56 Cassese, *Self-determination of Peoples* (n 20) 42.
57 These reports represent and authoritative guide to the reading of how self-determination should be understood in the Charter. See Omozurike (n 28) 46.
58 UNCIO Vol VI, 455 and Vol VI, 704.
59 UNICIO Vol VI, 296.

Ukrainian chairman of the subcommittee, Mr Manuilsky, was called upon to explain further the meaning of the principle and he explained as follows: 'the right of self-determination meant that a people may establish any regime which they may favour'.[60] The Rapporteur also stressed that cases of alleged fictitious expression of the will of the people, such as those of Nazi Germany and Italy, were to be excluded.[61] These remarks were made in order to stress that the attachment to the will of the people, as Cassese has rightly observed, must be 'real and substantial and not formalistic and legalitarian'.[62]

These statements show that self-determination in the Charter gave to the people of an independent state a right to govern themselves through a regime that is not imposed on them but that is a result of the people's genuine choice. This generic 'right to self-government', however, was not a means to grant individual rights and it did not mean democratic government; nor did it advance a specific definition of self-government. This right is to be understood simply as a collective entitlement on behalf of the people of a state, as a whole, to govern themselves.

The second core legal meaning that can be safely attributed to self-determination under the Charter is to be drawn from two facts: i) that self-determination is to be read in function of other aspects of the Charter;[63] ii) that self-determination is inherently linked to the principle of equality of states, because the two principles are, in fact, one. As we have established above, the close interconnectedness between sovereign equality and self-determination is there to ensure the equality of peoples organised as states, so that no people can be denied the right to self-determination on the basis of any alleged inferiority. For this to happen, the choice of each people to self-government must be genuine and free from external intervention, in accordance with the provisions of Article 2(7). Essentially, by coupling self-determination with the equal rights of states the Charter guarantees for the people of an independent state a right to self-government without interference from other states.[64] In this respect, Crawford recognises that 'both references [to self-determination] in the Charter seem to mean . . . the sovereign equality of states, and in particular the right of the people of a state to choose its own form of government without external intervention'.[65] This point was set out also by Higgins, who argued that in the context of 1945, when the Charter was drafted, self-determination

60 UNCIO Vol XVII, 163.

61 UNCIO Vol VI, 704.

62 Antonio Cassese, 'Political Self-determination: Old Concepts and New Developments' in Antonio Cassese (ed), *UN Law and Fundamental Rights: Two Topics in International Law* (Sijthoff & Noordhoff 1979) 139.

63 UNCIO Rapporteur, Committee I/1, 1 June at 17. 'The principle in question [self-determination], as a provision of the Charter, should not be considered alone but in connection with other provisions'. Quoted in Summers (n 11) 198.

64 UNCIO Vol VI, 703–704.

65 James Crawford, *The Creation of States in International Law* (n 13) 114.

was clearly taken to mean that the peoples of one state were to be protected from interference by other states or governments.[66]

To sum up, a close analysis of the UN Charter and its *travaux préparatoires* has shown that it is possible to claim with confidence that self-determination, in all its proverbial vagueness, was thereby attributed a twofold meaning. Indeed, we now know that self-determination, as a legal principle, can apply to the people of independent states and, for them, it contains two aspects: (i) a strong anti-interventionist connotation; (ii) a strong participatory requirement. These are important features that have defined and characterised the principle since its crystallisation into a principle of international law. In the next section, I will show that the existence of these two components can be traced out in the origins of the concept, and that they followed its transformation from a political postulate into a legal norm.

3.2.1.2 Legacies of the law

This section will provide a concise summary of the origins of self-determination. A variety of in-depth discussions on this matter have already been offered, so it is not the aim of this section to contribute to an already rich debate.[67] Instead, the purpose of this brief discussion is to provide a synthetic account of the origins of self-determination that is functionally designed to explain the existence of two distinguished meanings attributed to it in the UN Charter – as we saw in the above paragraph. Where do these meanings come from? How did they make it into the Charter and, with it, into the realm of legal norms? Also, why were the drafters able to provide two relatively detailed meanings to self-determination when the 'self' is the people of an independent state?

The answer to these questions is to be found in the history of self-determination. The term 'self-determination', as such, appeared in the early 20th century, but, as Theodore Woolsey put it in 1919: '[t]his is no new thing, though the phrase is new'.[68] If one looks for the origins of the concept, there are indeed two main trails to follow: the Western and the socialist path. In the Western tradition, the roots of the idea of self-determination can be traced back to the principle of the consent of the governed set out in the American and French Revolutions.[69] This principle conveyed the idea that the people are the source of all legitimate governmental power and that decisions about the future status

66 Rosalyn Higgins, 'Postmodern Tribalism and the Right to Secession, Comments' in C Brölmann and others (eds), *Peoples and Minorities in International Law* (Springer 1993).

67 For an overview of the main texts see Cassese, *Self-determination of Peoples* (n 20); Raic (n 13); A Rigo-Sureda, *The Evolution of the Right to Self-determination: A Study of United Nations Practice* (Sijthoff 1973); Summers (n 11); Omozurike (n 28).

68 Theodore S Woolsey, 'Self-Determination' (1919) 13 *American Journal of International Law* 302.

69 On this point see Brownlie (n 26) 90–99. For two synthetic accounts see also Omozurike (n 28) 3–11 and Raic (n 13) 172–75.

of a people must be taken from the people themselves. This basic idea was later elaborated upon and came to form the basis of the so-called 'Wilsonian idea' of self-determination. This wider concept, which encompassed Wilson's own idea and definition of self-determination, included the right of peoples to decide about their destiny and to govern themselves;[70] certain guarantees for minorities[71] and, according to several commentators, even a full 'right to democracy' as well.[72]

On the other hand, in the socialist conception self-determination carried a different meaning. The term's first ever appearance, dating back to 1896, was made in a resolution of the London International Socialist Congress.[73] In the socialist tradition self-determination means that all nations have a right to determine their own destiny free from external intervention, to include also a

70 'We believe these fundamental things: First, that every people has a right to choose the sovereignty under which they shall live' and also 'there is a deeper thing involved than even equality of right among organised nations. No peace can last, or ought to last, which does not recognise and accept the principle that governments derive all their just powers from the consent of the governed, and that no right anywhere exists to hand peoples about from sovereignty to sovereignty as if they were property'. See, respectively, Woodrow Wilson, 'Address delivered at the First Annual Assemblage of the League to Enforce Peace: American Principles' (27 May 1916) http://www.presidency.ucsb.edu/ws/?pid=65391 (last accessed 15 April 2018); and his 'Address to the United States Senate, 22 January 1917' in Arthur S Link (ed), *The Papers of Woodrow Wilson, Vol 40* (Princeton University Press, 1982) 536–37.

71 In this respect the principle was conceived in an intrinsically selective fashion. It only applied to the former Ottoman, Austro-Hungarian and Russian empires but was not deemed to be applicable to colonies. Many scholars have been critical of such a selective stance, to the point of calling it the 'Wilsonian patchwork'. The expression was used by Harold Nicholson, and is reported in Michla Pomerance, 'The United States and Self-Determination: Perspectives on the Wilsonian Conception' (1976) 70 *American Journal of International Law* 1. Others instead, have emphasised how such a treatment reflected a general understanding, existing in public opinion at that time, according to which the principle was meant to be applied only to those nations or populations which had been seriously affected and disturbed by the war. See Gilbert Murray, 'Self-Determination of Nationalities' (1922) 1 *Journal of the British Institute of International Affairs* 6, 9. For other critical voices see Hannum (n 8) 28–29; Rigo Sureda (n 67) 22 and Anthony Whelan, 'Wilsonian Self-Determination and the Versailles Settlement' (1994) 43 *International and Comparative Law Quarterly* 99.

72 Alfred Cobban, *National Self-determination* (OUP 1947) 20; Hannum (n 8) 30; Pomerance, 'The United States and Self-Determination' (n 70) 26; Whelan (n 71) 100.

73 The resolution reads: 'This Congress declares that it stands for the full right of all nations to self-determination [Selbstbestimmungsrecht] and expresses its sympathy for the workers of ever country now suffering under the yoke of military, national or other absolutism. This Congress calls upon the workers of all these countries to join the ranks of the class-conscious [Klassenbewusste – those who understand their class interests] workers of the whole world in order jointly to fight for the defeat of international capitalism and for the achievement of the aims of international Social-Democracy'. The Resolution is included in Lenin's 1914 essay on *The Right of Nations to Self-Determination*. VI Lenin, *The Right of Nations to Self-Determination* in V I Lenin, *Collected Works, Vol 20* (Progress Publishers 1967) 599, 632.

right to secession.[74] The concept, however, was conceived first and foremost as an instrument for class struggle against capitalism. Indeed, the application and realisation of the right was not meant to uphold the expression of any singular collective identity, but was simply a means to advance the cause of socialism. In other words, in Soviet thinking self-determination could only take place through socialism, with the integration of all nations in a universal socialist community – as opposed to all nationalisms.[75] As Raic puts it, for Lenin 'oppression as a result of bourgeois nationalism was the principal constitutive factor for the right to self-determination' and secession was seen as a remedy to which every people was entitled – including colonial peoples.[76]

Another important aspect of the Soviet idea of self-determination is that a people has a right to sovereign self-rule. This however does not mean that the people have a democratic entitlement to choose their government. In the view that socialism is the ultimate form of self-determination, a people need not, according to Soviet thinkers, choose to retain control over their own future, but they must at least have 'the opportunity to decide the issue on its own', without external interference.[77] This means that the Soviets sponsored a right to self-determination, as self-government, that must be understood differently from that promoted by the Western tradition. The Soviets understood self-determination as strongly attached to sovereign independence and to include also a strong non-intervention connotation. In Cassese's words, for socialist states self-determination is actually tantamount to non-intervention: it 'means the right that foreign States shall not interfere in the life of the community against the will of the government. It does not include the right that a foreign State shall not interfere in the life of the community against the interests of

74 In relation to self-determination, Stalin wrote: 'The right to self-determination means that only the nation itself has the right to determine its destiny, that no one has the right forcibly to intervene in the life of the nation .... The right of self-determination means that a nation can arrange its life according to its own will. It can arrange its life on the basis of autonomy. It has the right to complete secession. Nations are sovereign and all nations are equal'. The passage is taken from Stalin's 1913 essay on *Marxism and the National Question* and is quoted in Cassese, *Self-determination of Peoples* (n 20) 14. Also in his essay on the topic Lenin writes that 'it would be wrong to interpret the right to self-determination as meaning anything but the right to existence as a separate state'. See Lenin (n 73) 603.

75 'We Social-Democrats are opposed to all nationalism and advocate democratic centralism. We are opposed to particularism, and are convinced that, all other things being equal, big states can solve the problems of economic progress and of the struggle between the proletariat and the bourgeoisie far more effectively than small states can. VI Lenin, *The Question of National Policy* (1914) in VI Lenin (n 73). On this point see also Cassese, *Self-determination of Peoples* (n 20) 18; Cobban (n 72) 107; Raic (n 13) 184–88; Thürer and Burri (n 36).

76 Raic (n 13) 185.

77 George Ginsburgs, '"Wars of National Liberation" and the Modern Law of Nations – The Soviet Thesis' in Hans W Baade (ed), *The Soviet Impact on International* Law (Oceana 1965) 79.

the population, but at the request or at any rate with the tacit approval of the government'.[78]

To sum up, in the Western tradition self-determination was rooted in the ideals of equality and popular sovereignty. For 19th century European nationalists it meant a nation's right to constitute a state and was used in the Paris Peace Conference to settle minority claims. For Wilson, moreover, it was a synonym for a right to democratic government. On the other hand, for the Soviets it was a means to achieve socialism and meant the right of a nation to decide its own destiny, to free itself from oppression and to determine its sovereign status – if necessary through secession – free from external intervention. In this sense, it also meant that all nations are equal and equally entitled to this right.

Overall, there are two important differences between the Western and socialist conceptions of self-determination. First, in the Western tradition self-determination is conceived to apply selectively and not to colonial peoples – unlike for the Socialists', for which the right applies universally to all oppressed peoples. Secondly, a key distinction has to do with the individual versus the collective character of the right. The Western tradition attributes a focus on the individual as the constituent of the people, whereas the will of the people is to be expressed through a vote, either in the form of a plebiscite or possibly through democratic government. Conversely, the socialist tradition conceived self-determination as a collective right, attributed to the people of a state, as a whole, to be independent. Moreover, this right needs not be exercised directly by the people, it can also be legitimately exercised by their governments.

This section has showed that in the history of the development of self-determination, as a political concept, there are two separate meanings: one strictly linked to the principle of non-interference attached to state sovereignty, and one participatory principle linked to the idea of popular sovereignty. These two interpretations can be traced respectively in the socialist and Western origins of the concept of self-determination. Now, if one goes back to the interpretation that we offered through a close study of the term's meaning in the UN Charter, it is easier to explain where this meaning came from and why self-determination in the UN Charter was taken to mean two different things at the same time.

Before moving on to the new section, I wish to stress the importance of the socialist contribution to the creation of international law on self-determination. It is generally acknowledged that the inclusion of self-determination provisions in the Charter is indeed to be credited to the strenuous work of the socialist delegation at the San Francisco Conference.[79] Thereby the delegation is said to

78 Cassese, 'Political Self-determination' (n 62) 140.

79 Cassese, *Self-determination of Peoples* (n 20) 19; Bill Bowring, 'Positivism *versus* Self-determination: The Contradictions of Soviet International Law' in Susan Marks (ed), *International Law on the Left: Re-examining Marxist Legacies* (CUP 2008) 158; and Ginsburgs (n 77) 79.

have 'done everything to ensure that the right became one of the fundamental principles of contemporary international law',[80] as a result of which Article 2(1) of the Charter was drafted. The socialist contribution to the development of the law continued also in the years following the adoption of the Charter. Primarily, socialist states and scholars pushed for the right to be applied to non-self-governing territories seeking independence from their colonial rulers. Secondly, they continued to stress the link between self-determination, sovereign equality of states and non-interference in domestic affairs.[81] As Cassese reminds us, in the Eastern Bloc conception, once independence was achieved, the principles of sovereign equality and non-intervention were paramount, because only then adequate protection for the free expression of the will of the people could be guaranteed.[82]

To conclude, so far we have established that in the UN Charter self-determination acquired a legal status and a precise, twofold meaning as a legal concept. This brief excursus on the origins of self-determination was important in order to elucidate what are the sources of these two trails of meaning. It was also meant to explain that the two can, to some extent, be traced back to the history of the idea since the early days of life of self-determination as a political principle. As we will see, this twofold arrangement will have important consequences for the future developments of the norm and for this reason, it was an aspect that the analysis was keen on setting out clearly.

3.2.1.3 Self-determination and its application in decolonisation

The years following the adoption of the UN Charter have been of vital importance for the development of self-determination under international law. Starting in 1960, with the adoption by the UN General Assembly of a resolution called *Declaration Granting Independence to Colonial Countries and Peoples*,[83] the right to self-determination was essentially interpreted as the right of colonial, foreign and alien-dominated peoples to claim independence.

The socialists had championed since the early days a concept of self-determination as the right of oppressed people to decide over their future, hence it is not surprising that the draft Resolution 1514 was submitted to the Assembly by the USSR.[84] At that stage, the Western countries were indeed reluctant to extend the right to all colonies, because, as Cassese noted, they had not yet realised that 'between 1945 and 1965 the concept of self-determination had necessarily to identify itself with that of anti-colonialism since, in that period of history, the principal aim in the struggle for the freedom of peoples was

80 Bowring (n 79) 158.
81 See para 3.1 below.
82 See Cassese, *Self-determination of Peoples* (n 20) 45.
83 General Assembly Resolution 1514 (XV), 14 December 1960.
84 Bowring (n 79) 161.

to disrupt colonial domination'.[85] In spite of the strong reaction and protests that the resolution raised between member states in the General Assembly, the Declaration was adopted with a large majority[86] and constituted a historical moment in the development of international law on self-determination and of international law more generally.

From that moment, the association between self-determination and decolonisation, which was not spelled out in the Charter (and according to some, was not included at all)[87] became an established fact. The resolution indeed proclaimed the existence of a 'right' of self-determination for all peoples. Paragraph 2 of the document reads:

> 2. All peoples have the right to self-determination; by virtue of that right they freely determine their political status and freely pursue their economic, social and cultural development.

Whilst the resolution has a non-binding character, hence being not a law-making instrument in itself, its effects on the development of international law today are undisputed.[88] The Declaration has indeed influenced a highly significant number of subsequent assembly resolutions, declarations and conventions, creating a set of consistent practice and, with it, of *opinio juris*, around the issue of decolonisation. In brief, today it is possible to say that it was with the Declaration, in 1960, that self-determination became a right vested in the colonial peoples residing in non-self-governing territories.[89] Thus, it can be said that, at that moment in time, a new layer of self-determination was created, and that the principle acquired a new, additional meaning in international law.

Here I will not analyse in detail the contribution of the Declaration to the development of international law on self-determination. This point has already been dealt with at length in other occasions and is well-established in the

85 Cassese, 'Political Self-determination' (n 62) 141.

86 The Resolution was passed on 14 December 1960 by a vote of 89 to 0, with 9 abstentions (Australia, Belgium, Dominican Republic, France, Portugal, Spain, Union of South Africa, United Kingdom, United States).

87 See Higgins (n 20).

88 Even though the legal value of GA Resolutions can be disputed, given their non-binding character, it is established that it is the cumulative effect of the resolutions that indicate the emergence of general customary international law around a certain issue. See Rosalyn Higgins, 'The United Nations and Lawmaking: The Political Organs' (1970) 64 *American Journal of International Law* 43. See also ICJ cases: *Legal Consequences for States of the Continued Presence of South Africa in Namibia (South West Africa) Notwithstanding Security Council Resolution 276 (1970)* (Advisory Opinion) [1971] ICJ Rep 16 paras 52–53 and *Western Sahara case* (n 10) para 55, where the Court considers the development of international law on non-self-governing territories as resulting in large part from the application of Charter norms by the political organs of the United Nations, and in particular the General Assembly. On this point see also James Crawford, 'The General Assembly, the ICJ, and self-determination' in Vaughan Lowe and Malgosia Fitzmaurice, *Fifty Years of the International Court of Justice: Essays in Honour of Sir Robert Jennings* (CUP 2008) 591.

89 Doehring (n 12) 52.

literature.[90] For the purposes of this study, it shall be sufficient to accomplish a much less ambitious task. Simply, in this section I wish to explain that the Declaration brings an important conceptual development in the life of self-determination as a principle of international law. Moreover, I wish to highlight how this development represents a departure from the meaning originally attributed to self-determination which was set out in the UN Charter, and that the existence of these two branches of the principle is not mutually exclusive. In so doing, I take side with those who argue that the concretisation of self-determination into the right of non-self-governing territories to decide their international status is but one single aspect of the multi-faceted principle of self-determination.

The view is indeed not novel and can be found elsewhere in the literature. For instance, Thurer argues plainly that 'it is undisputed that decolonization is a special concretization of the right to self-determination'.[91] Raic notes that the 'right to decolonization', championed by the United Nations between the 1950s and 1970s and acknowledged also by the International Court of Justice in its Advisory Opinions on Western Sahara and Namibia 'is *not* a specific *meaning* of self-determination, rather it is a form of implementation of' the core meaning of self-determination (the idea that a people should have a say about its political status and future).[92] Doehring also believes that 'decolonization is only one of several occurrences which contributed to the establishment of the principle of self-determination', but he admits that it was precisely through UN practice in implementing the decolonisation process that self-determination 'achieved the stature of an applicable legal right'.[93] On the same line, some referred to the application of self-determination in the colonial context as an arbitrary limit,[94] in the nature of a *lex specialis*,[95] or even viewed the association of the two as a 'historical aberration'.[96] According to this logic, it is argued that the identification of self-determination with decolonisation as the result of a sort of misinterpretation of the principle, that has in fact restricted its meaning and excluded other aspects of it (democracy, autonomy, right of secession, etc),

90 See references cited in nn 11, 20, 28 and 67.
91 Thürer and Burri (n 36) 366.
92 See Raic (n 13) 221–22.
93 Doehring (n 12) 52–53.
94 Martti Koskenniemi, 'National Self-Determination Today: Problems of Legal Theory and Practice' (1994) 43 *International and Comparative Human Rights Quarterly* 241, 242.
95 Robin A White, 'Self-Determination: Time for a Re-Assessment' (1981) XXVIII *Netherlands International Law Review* 147, 148. Also Doehring writes: 'If one considers the right to self-determination, taking into account all its variations, i.e. its "defensive" variety, as a defence by the people of a state against foreign domination, and "offensive" self-determination as the right of a minority to maintain its special status, decolonization appears to have an exceptional position. . . . It is therefore surprising to note that for some time many writers have considered decolonization to be the only legally recognized exercise of self-determination'. Doehring (n 12) 60.
96 Simpson (n 5) 260.

diminishing its overall revolutionary potential. In so doing, the development of the norm, which became strictly intertwined with the struggle for the liberation of colonial peoples, has threatened self-determination with obsolescence after the momentum of global liberation came to a close.[97]

Overall, it is clear that decolonisation has contributed to the development of international law on self-determination, to the point that it became its most widely known application and most popular setting. Here, in order to take this notion a step further, I will discuss whether the way self-determination has developed in relation to a specific self (colonial peoples) has implications also for its development in relation to the self that is object of this study (the people of independent states). In other words, I aim to explore whether the contextual developments of the norm specific to one of its selves carry wider resonance also for other layers of the principle that have been shadowed by the mainstream decolonisation discourse on self-determination.

In this study, I focus only on a single dimension of the principle, and thus it is important for the analysis to maintain the perspectives separate in order to produce knowledge that is layer-specific. In order to maintain this analytical angle, one must depart from univocal interpretations of 'the' right or principle of self-determination and aim to offer a more nuanced interpretation of its content and components. My focus, therefore, is on the need to discern the various dimensions of the norm (using the metaphor of layers), to see whether and how they overlap in relation to meaning and content. Hence, what was the contribution of decolonisation-related developments in the area of self-determination law for the principle as it applies to the people of independent states?

A first important point is made by Doehring. He argues that decolonisation caused

> [t]he third potential holder of the right of self-determination, namely the population of a sovereign state, to become increasingly relevant. The population of an established and reorganized State may also be qualified as a 'people' under Art 1(2) of the UN Charter. If a nation . . . has organized a State, it is then entitled to maintain and defend that status. . . . Former colonies or minorities which have organised their own States do not in this way lose their right of self-determination, but retain possession of that right.[98]

Lachs adds to this by pointing out that the 1960 Declaration

> [l]ays down a series of directions, which constitute the very essence of [self-determination]'s substance. It also penetrates that sphere of the principles of self-determination which is of concern to those peoples who have

97 ibid 265–74. See also Sinha for a discussion regarding the possible obsolescence of the principle: Sinha, 'Is Self-determination *Passé*?' (n 5) 260.
98 Doehring (n 12) 56.

already attained independence. In this respect it recalls the duty of states to observe the principles of 'equality', 'non-interference in the internal affairs of all states' and 'the respect of the sovereign right of all peoples and their territorial integrity'.[99]

On this basis one can see how the two dimensions of self-determination that we have seen, the one attached to the people of a state and the one attached to a colonial people, are not made to overlap. Instead, the two are distinct, they co-exist and actually complement each other. Indeed, when the self-determination rights of a colonial people are exhausted self-determination continues to apply because the self, having become independent, is transformed into a new self with certain, specific, self-determination entitlements that are well-rooted in international law. The relationship between these two layers of self-determination is therefore regulated by three key principles:

(i) coexistence of the layers – the two exist at the same time, only they apply to different selves;
(ii) consequentiality – after a colonial people becomes independent through an act of self-determination it becomes an independent people with other, different, self-determination rights;
(iii) reinforcement – the realisation of self-determination for a colonial people does not reduce the right into obsolescence but instead it reinforces its meaning and applicability to the people of independent states.

In the next section we will expand the discourse on the basic idea that self-determination is a right that continues even after its realisation through independence. For the time being, I will conclude with a summary of what was shown in present section.

So far, I have demonstrated that the legal developments undergone by the principle of self-determination through decolonisation brought a number of significant contributions for the study of the norm. First, we saw that in the decolonisation setting a new layer of self-determination was created. This new layer is attached to a self (the people of colonial territories) that had not been entitled to self-determination before and this was an important development in international law. Secondly, we saw that with these developments the concept of self-determination became multi-dimensional, and so univocal views and interpretations are unsuited to describe its meaning and content. Thirdly, we understand that a multi-faceted interpretation must pay attention to what each layer of the norm means and what content is attached to it. Fourth, we found that the developments of the right in relation to one of its self-specific dimensions had also repercussions on other self-specific dimensions of the norm. More specifically, we noted how the creation of new independent states through the

99 Lachs (n 25) 438.

process of colonial self-determination has contributed to ascertaining and defining an increasing relevance for self-determination entitlements that are attached to the people of an independent state.

3.3 Self-determination in human rights treaties and customary international law: the articulation of the norm's content and scope

In this section I will discuss the contribution of treaty and customary international law to the development of self-determination law as it applies to the people of an independent state. Before starting our analysis, it needs to be highlighted that these developments mostly took place at the same time as the process of decolonisation. The importance of the timing factor is relevant because it will show that self-determination as the right of the people of an independent state, other than being a legal concept that precedes the idea that self-determination as a right vested in the colonial people, is also not merely a transformation of the right to colonial independence which seeks to ensure its survival in the post-colonial world. Instead, the existence of the two dimensions of the right is separated and their development can be tracked to show that it took place simultaneously. In other words, the conceptualisation of self-determination as the right of the people of an independent state exists separate from and in addition to the elaboration of the law on decolonisation.

The adoption of GA resolutions on decolonisation indeed precedes the adoption of treaty law, but not their development and the discussions that preceded its adoption. It is important to present a narrative of the development of the law that does not contradict reality, because doing so would pose the risk to undermine also the conception of a multi-layered idea of self-determination that is so important in this study. An overview of the development of treaty and customary international law on self-determination that remains mindful of this complexity will therefore help us to delineate the multi-dimensionality of the concept and to trace out clearly its separate layers in every phase of its legal development.

3.3.1 Self-determination in the international covenants on human rights

An important milestone in the legal history of self-determination is the adoption of the International Covenant on Economic, Social and Cultural Rights (ICESCR) and the International Covenant on Civil and Political Rights (ICCPR) (the Covenants), opened for signature in 1966.[100] The two Covenants contain

100 International Covenant on Economic, Social and Cultural Rights, adopted 16 December 1966, 993 UNTS 3 and International Covenant on Civil and Political Rights, adopted 16 December 1966, UST, 999 UNTS 171.

an identical Article 1, which provides a definition of self-determination drafted and adopted by independent states. The Article, of which the first draft was discussed as early as 1950, provides to date the most comprehensive definition of self-determination enshrined in a primary source of international law.[101] In draft, Common Article 1 had already adopted a formula that would later constitute the basis of GA Resolution 1514 of 1960, reading as follows:

> 1. All peoples have the right of self-determination. By virtue of that right they freely determine their political status and freely pursue their economic, social and cultural development.
> 2. All peoples may, for their own ends, freely dispose of their natural wealth and resources without prejudice to any obligations arising out of international economic co-operation, based upon the principle of mutual benefit, and international law. In no case may a people be deprived of its own means of subsistence.
> 3. The States Parties to the present Covenant, including those having responsibility for the administration of Non-Self-Governing and Trust Territories, shall promote the realization of the right of self-determination, and shall respect that right, in conformity with the provisions of the Charter of the United Nations.

The text of this Article is absolutely fundamental for detailing the content and scope of self-determination in many respects. First and foremost, because the Covenants are, in Cassese's words, 'the only international agreements in force which explicitly make it a duty of States to respect this right and so to grant self-determination to all peoples'.[102] The idea of having an article on self-determination included in the human rights treaties was advocated by the Soviets, who viewed self-determination as a precondition for the respect of individual rights.[103] The first proposal was made in 1950, 10 years before the passing of GA Resolution 1514, in a formulation of the right which included both colonial territories and national minorities.[104] Later, the inclusion of the right in the two International Covenants on Human Rights was decided by the

101 A first draft was submitted to the Third Committee of the General Assembly in 1950, but the proposal was rejected (UN Doc A/1559 at 28).

102 Cassese, 'Political Self-determination' (n 62) 142.

103 See Cassese, *Self-determination of Peoples* (n 20) 47 and Manfred Nowak, *UN Covenant on Civil and Political Rights: CCPR Commentary* (2nd rev edn, Engel Verlag 2005) 10.

104 Cassese, *Self-determination of Peoples* (n 20) 48. The first draft submitted to the Third Committee of the General Assembly stated: 'Every people and every nation shall have the right to national self-determination. States which have responsibilities for the administration of Non-Self-Governing territories shall promote the fulfillment of this right, guided by the aims and principles of the United Nations in relation to the peoples of such Territories. The State shall ensure to national minorities the right to use their native tongue and to possess their national school, museums and other cultural and educational institutions'. See UN Doc A/C.3/L.96 at 17.

Commission on Human Rights in 1952 and by the Third Committee of the UN General Assembly in 1955.[105] The Article is thus said to remain the most important expression of self-determination in the 1950s.[106]

Over the years, the debates which led to the adoption of the Article led to a watering down of its provisions in the final written formula. Nonetheless, the debates still contributed to expanding the meaning of the concept and show that self-determination was thereby attributed a number of meanings concerning who is entitled to what. Here I will focus specifically on the contribution that Article 1 has brought to the articulation of self-determination as the right of the people of an independent state, bearing in mind that the its contribution to the development of the law of self-determination is in fact wider.

3.3.1.1 The wording 'all peoples'

As we have seen, in the UN Charter it was not clear who was entitled to self-determination, but we ascertained that one of the selves surely entitled to it (and possibly the only one) was the people of an independent state.[107] The first important development of self-determination under the Covenants is thus the enlargement of this entitlement to 'all peoples', as worded in paragraphs 1 and 2 of Article 1. Here I will not dwell with the issue of who, exactly, the Article includes and excludes, but it shall suffice to say that the discussion was more concerned with whether minority groups could constitute peoples rather than whether other categories, such as colonial peoples and the people of independent states, shall be included in the definition.

The bulk of the discussion among experts in Commission on Human Rights indeed concerned the issue of how expansive the definition of people should be. It was ultimately decided that the term 'should be understood in its most general sense and that no definition was necessary', but that 'the right of minorities was a separate problem of great complexity'.[108] States' representatives also stated that '[t]he right would be proclaimed in the covenants as a universal right and for all time', but that 'the article was not concerned with minorities or the right of secession, and the terms 'peoples' and 'nations' were not intended to cover such questions.[109] It was instead stressed by several states that the term people

105 General Assembly Resolution 545 (VI) (1952) adopted on 5 February 1952. See also Hector Gros Espiell, *The Right to Self-determination: Implementation of United Nations Resolutions*, UN Doc E/CN.4/Sub.2/405/Rev.1 para 52 (and footnotes) and R Baxter, 'Official Documents: United Nations Draft International Covenants on Human Rights' (1964) 58 *American Journal of International Law* 857.

106 Summers (n 11) 287.

107 See para 3.2.1.1 above.

108 See the comments cited in Marc J Bossuyt, *Guide to the 'Travaux Préparatoires' of the International Covenant on Civil and Political Rights* (Martinus Nijhoff 1987) 32 and 45.

109 ibid 27.

would instead cover the people of independent states.[110] On this issue, Summers notes that it shall not be surprising that states' representatives were inclined to accord self-determination to the people of independent states. In doing so, independent states – and specifically Western states – aimed at strengthening the independence of those people.[111] By the time the Article on self-determination was finally adopted in 1955 only a few states still maintained that it should be limited to colonial situations.[112]

Years later, at the time of ratification of the Covenant, the Indian Government entered a reservation where it declared that 'the words 'the right of self-determination' . . . apply only to the peoples under foreign domination and that these words do not apply to sovereign independent States or to a section of a people or nation – which is the essence of national integrity'.[113] The statement raised objections on behalf of three countries: the Netherlands, Germany and the Federal Republic of Germany, that stressed how the application of the right to self-determination should instead be universal.[114] As Cassese notes, the fact that India decided to enter such a reservation, as well as the reactions to it, reveal that general consensus was leaning in the other direction.[115]

Today, this view is widely accepted and it is therefore undisputed that Article 1 speaks for several selves entitled to self-determination, including at least the people of a state and colonial peoples.[116] A key implication of such a diversification

110 Clyde Eagleton, 'Self-Determination in the United Nations' (1953) 47 *American Journal of International Law* 88, 92.

111 Summers (n 11) 305.

112 These were: Greece, Saudi Arabia, Liberia, Syria, Lebanon and Pakistan. See Cassese, *Self-determination of Peoples* (n 20) 51. For a complete list of minutes with references to statements on self-determination issues submitted by states' representatives to the Third Committee at its Fifth Session see UN Doc E/CN.4/514 at 59–62.

113 The text of the reservation is available on the United Nations Treaty Collection web site https://treaties.un.org/pages/ViewDetails.aspx?src=TREATY&mtdsg_no=IV-3&chapter=4&lang=en (last accessed 15 April 2018).

114 Cassese, *Self-determination of Peoples* (n 20) 51; Crawford, The right to Self-determination in international law' (n 10) 28; Higgins (n 20) 116.

115 Cassese, *Self-determination of Peoples* (n 20) 60.

116 For instance, Crawford notes that: 'Just as a matter of ordinary treaty interpretation, one cannot interpret Article 1 as limited to the colonial case. Article 1, paragraph 1 does not say that some peoples have the right of self-determination. Nor can the term 'peoples' be limited to colonial peoples. Paragraph 3 deals expressly, and non-exclusively, with colonial territories. When a text says that 'all peoples' have a right – the term 'peoples' having a general connotation – and then in another paragraph of the same article, it says that the term 'peoples' includes the peoples of colonial territories, it is perfectly clear that the term is being issued in its general sense. Any remaining doubt is settled by paragraph 2 . . . No one has ever suggested that the principle of permanent sovereignty over natural resources is limited to colonial territories. So far as the interpretation of Article 1 goes, that surely settles the point'. Crawford, 'The Right of Self-Determination in International Law' (n 10) 27. On the same token see also Doehring (n 12) 60; Robert McCorquodale, 'Self-Determination: A Human Rights Approach' (1994) 43 *International and Comparative Law Quarterly* 860; Quane (n 12); Raic (n 13) 245; Summers (n 11) 303–24; Christian

is that in this way the survival and relevance of self-determination in the post-colonial world are ensured. Anne Bayefsky indeed pointed out that 'the direct and universal language of the first paragraph [of Article 1] makes clear that the principle of self-determination has survived the era of decolonization in international law'.[117] On this point, Nowak also stresses that the use of a declaratory present tense in 'all people have' instead of 'shall have' demonstrates the character of self-determination in Article 1 as a continuing right.[118] The question of whether the right to self-determination has been exhausted with decolonisation can thus be answered simply by pointing at the multi-dimensionality of this principle.

3.3.1.2 The content of the right

Having established that the people of an independent state is one of the selves that are entitled to self-determination under common Article 1 of the Covenants, we now needed to ascertain what the right means and what it entails for the self in question. For the people of a dependent territory, indeed, self-determination means first and foremost the possibility of choosing their international status and to achieve independence.[119] But what does the right mean for a people that is already organised into an independent state? There are two provisions included in the Article that need to be interpreted in order to answer this question: (i) *in virtue of that right they freely determine their political status and freely pursue their economic, social and cultural development*; (ii) *all peoples may, for their own ends, freely dispose of their natural wealth and resources.*[120]

There is no easy way to draw out the meaning of self-determination in the Covenants. State representatives in the Third Committee of the General Assembly dedicated twenty-six meetings to consideration of Article 1 of the draft Covenants.[121] Ultimately, states decided not to adopt any of the suggestions put forward that would define the substance of the right. It was preferred instead a more abstract form, because any numeration of the components of the right

---

Tomuschat, 'Self-Determination in a Post-Colonial World' in Christian Tomuschat (ed), *Modern Law of Self-Determination* (Martinus Nijhoff 1993) 2–3.

117 Anne F Bayefsky, *Self-determination in International Law: Quebec and Lessons Learned, Legal Opinions/Selected and introduced by Anne F. Bayefsky* (Kluwer 2000) 2.

118 Nowak (n 103) 15–16.

119 As convened in GA Resolution 1514 (XV).

120 See arts 1(1) and 1(2) respectively.

121 641th to 655th and 667th to 677th meetings during the Tenth Session of the Third Committee. The debates are contained in the records UN Doc A/C.3/SR.641-55, 667–77 and a summary of discussion held can be found in Report of the Third Committee UN Doc A/3077 of December 1955. For a good summary of debates see Hurst Hannum, 'Rethinking Self-Determination' (1993) 34 *Virginia Journal of International Law* 1, 19–25.

was seen as likely to be incomplete.[122] The starting points of our analysis are therefore twofold.

First, I will refer to the interpretation of self-determination provided by the two UN Special Rapporteurs of the Sub-Commission on Prevention of Discrimination and Protection of Minorities, Mr Gros Espiel and Mr Critescu, who were mandated by the Commission on Human Rights to prepare a study on the development of self-determination in UN law and practice.[123] The two, separate opinions are of great interest in many respects, but for the present purposes they are particularly relevant since Gros Espiel writes that the Special Rapporteurs were invited to pay particular attention 'to the question of self-determination after the attainment of political independence'.[124] Aureliu Critescu in his report dwells on the discussion held among states in the Third Committee of the General Assembly concerning Article 1 of the Covenants and states that 'with regard to the nature of the right, it was held to be a true right possessing political, economic and legal elements. The right of peoples to self-determination had two aspects: from the domestic point of view it signified the people's right to self-government and from the external point of view their independence'.[125]

Secondly, the Article will be read in its context, namely as a provision included in a human rights treaty.[126] A key focus will therefore be on the work of the Committee on Human Rights, as the body mandated to interpret the ICCPR[127] and to review individual applications under its Optional Protocol.[128] In 1984 the Committee issued a General Comment focused specifically on the right to self-determination, in which it provided an elucidation of the content of

122 Discussion held at the Commission on Human Rights, reported in UN Doc E/CN.4/SR.257, cited in Bossuyt (n 108) 35.

123 The studies were commissioned to the Rapporteurs in 1974, hence after the adoption of the two Covenants and only a couple of years before their entry into force in 1976.

124 Gros Espiel (n 105) 2.

125 Aureliu Critescu, *The Right to Self-Determination: Historical and Current Development on the Basis of United Nations Instruments* UN Doc E/CN.4/Sub.2/404/Rev.1 (United Nations 1981) para 32.

126 According to art 31 of the Vienna Convention on the Law of Treaties. For a similar approach see also Allan Rosas, 'Internal Self-Determination' in Christian Tomuschat (ed), *Modern Law of Self-Determination* (Martinus Nijhoff 1993) 225, 243.

127 ICCPR, Pt IV.

128 The Committee has systematically refused to examine complaints based solely on claims brought under art 1 of the ICCPR, arguing that the complaint procedure set up under the Optional Protocol is reserved to individuals, and thus that it can only be invoked for cases related to arts 6 to 27 of the Covenant. See Anna Batalla, 'The Right to Self-Determination: ICCPR and the Jurisprudence of the Human Rights Committee', paper prepared for the Symposium on The Right to Self-Determination in International Law, 29 September–1 October 2006, The Hague, Netherlands http://unpo.org/downloads/AnnaBatalla.pdf (last accessed 15 April 2018) and decisions cited therein; Optional Protocol to the International Covenant on Civil and Political Rights, adopted and opened for signature and accession by General Assembly Resolution 2200 (XXI) of 16 December 1966.

the right and of the obligations that arise under Article 1, which put forward three important points.[129] First, it sets out that Article 1 is interrelated with other provisions of the Covenant – without further specification but general consensus leads to the inclusion of, at least, Article 25 (political participation) and 47 (natural wealth and resources), and possibly Article 27 (rights of persons belonging to minorities) as well.[130] Secondly, it establishes that paragraph 3 of the Article imposes corresponding obligations on state parties concerning the implementation of self-determination. These obligations are not only in relation to their own peoples but towards all peoples who have not been able to exercise or have been deprived of the possibility to exercise their right to self-determination.[131] Thirdly, the Comment specifies that states have reporting obligations towards the Committee in relation to Article 1 and, as part of this obligation, states are requested to report on each paragraph of the right.[132] In regard to paragraph 1, which sets forward the political content of the right, states are requested to describe the constitutional and political processes which in practice allow the exercise of the right of peoples to 'freely determine their political status and freely pursue their economic, social and cultural development'.[133] In relation to paragraph 2, states are required to indicate any factors or difficulties which prevent a people from 'freely dispose of their natural wealth and resources'.

In more general terms, the practice of the Committee on Human Rights has contributed to the interpretation of self-determination by putting in evidence that the right to self-determination has both political and economic content, and that the two should be treated separately.[134] It has also made an inescapable connection between a state's constitutional structure and the realisation of political self-determination. As Cassese put it, Article 1 'established a permanent link between self-determination and civil and political rights', so that 'the issue of whether a state has respected its people's right to self-determination cannot be resolved without an inquiry into the state's decision making process'.[135] The point was raised also by Raic, who argued that 'the inclusion of self-determination

129 Human Rights Committee, General Comment No 12, CCPR/C/21/Add.3 of 5 October 1984 (GC12). Others have taken more critical views on the contributions of GC12 to the clarification of self-determination. For instance, Hannum is very unenthusiastic of the Comment, arguing that 'it does nothing to clarify the meaning of self-determination or the scope of state obligations under Article 1'. See Hannum, *Autonomy, Sovereignty and Self-determination* (n 8) 27.

130 GC12, para 1.

131 ibid paras 2 and 6. This issue will be further discussed in ch 5.

132 ibid paras 3–5.

133 ibid para 4.

134 The inclusion of an identical art 1 in the International Covenant on Economic, Social and Cultural Rights also reinforces this view. More generally see Nowak (n 103) 24 and Matthew Craven, *The International Covenant on Economic, Social, and Cultural Rights: A Perspective on its Development* (Clarendon 1998).

135 Cassese, *Self-determination of Peoples* (n 20) 54.

in a *human rights* treaty makes it difficult to exclude the application of self-determination in the relationship between the state and its population'.[136]

This aspect of self-determination, the one which Critescu called 'the right to self-government' from the domestic point of view, is essentially a right for the population of a state to have a say in the choice of their rulers, and to choose its form of government.[137] The extent to which this right can be conceived as a right to democratic governance is highly disputed, but for the time being it should be sufficient to see Article 1 as the basis for the realisation of other Covenants' rights, including Article 25 concerning political participation. The key elements of this Article, namely the right to take part in the conduct of public affairs and the right to vote and to be elected, have indeed a clear connection with a people's right freely to determine their status and to choose the form of their constitution or government.[138] However, the two remain distinct, as Article 1 is a right of peoples to determine their status freely, whilst Article 25 is a right of individuals to take part in the conduct of public affairs and to participate in electoral processes.[139]

3.3.1.3 The word 'freely'

As we have seen above, in Article 1 self-determination has both a political and an economic content and this content applies to all selves entitled to self-determination. It gives rights to peoples and imposes obligations to state parties to the Covenants, including obligations that touch upon states' decision-making arrangements at the constitutional level. Here we will see how these provisions can be interpreted in favour of the people of independent states, or, in other words, how the rights and obligations can be defined for this specific self. We already know that, for a colonial people, the right to choose their status means the right to become independent, or to join another state, etc. We also know, however, that the meaning of the term 'status' more generally is not clear, and no clarification in this sense is provided in the *travaux* either.[140] What comes to help in this interpretative exercise, therefore, is our knowledge of what self-determination meant in the UN Charter. In paragraph 2 of this chapter I established that, under the Charter, self-determination included for the people

136 Raic (n 13) 235.

137 See statement from the USA, UN Doc E/CN.4/SR.257 6–7, cited in Bossuyt (n 108) 34.

138 This connection was made also by the Human Rights Committee in its General Comment No 25, CCPR/C/21/Rev.1/Add.7 of 27 August 1996 and in the *Gillot v. France* decision. See *Gillot et al v France*, Communication no 932/2000 of 26 July 2002, UN Doc CCPR/C/75/D/932/2000.

139 In *Gillot et al v France* (n 138) the Human Rights Committee has elaborated on the relationship between the two rights, arguing that restrictions on art 25 could be justified in view of the provisions of art 1.

140 'The definition was not self-explanatory or self-sufficient, and the meaning of the word 'status' was far from being clear'. Bossuyt (n 108) 33.

of an independent state the right to establish a regime of their choice, and that this regime shall be an expression of the will of the people. Moreover, there is also a requirement that other states do not interfere into a state's internal affairs.[141]

In view of the above, we should focus our attention on a key element of the Covenants' definition: the word *freely.* The Article indeed provides a right for the people to '*freely* determine' their status, '*freely* pursue' their development and *freely* dispose' of their wealth. United Nations Rapporteur Gros Espiel explains the meaning of this wording very clearly, stating that:

> The Special Rapporteur feels obliged to stress the point, in order that all the necessary conclusions may be drawn from it, that the right to self-determination, which is *sine qua non* for the existence of human rights and freedoms, basically implies that peoples must be able to exercise their will freely and independently, without any kind of external interference and under a legal system which guarantees them freedom of expression. Although every people possesses the right to choose its own political, economic, social and cultural status, this right must be recognized in such a way that it can be exercised in conditions of complete freedom.[142]

It is indeed in the word *freely* that we can trace out the two components of the right attributed to the people of an independent state that were already included in the UN Charter. To put it differently, the word 'freely' effectively both mediates and condenses the two strands of meaning attributed to self-determination by Soviet and Western states. The word includes the right to choose their legislators 'free from manipulation or undue influence from the domestic authorities'[143] as well as the right to do so free from the outside interference of other states. Concerning the first aspect, Cassese valuably demonstrated that the drafting history of the Article shows that the view according to which the concept of self-determination should include freedom from an authoritarian regime was forcefully propounded by Western states when they realised that they could no longer oppose the introduction of a provision on self-determination.[144] In relation to the issue of outside influence, Doehring recognises that under Article 1 self-determination means that 'a people, having organized into a state, is free to decide on a form of government and may prohibit any intervention in this respect'.[145] This Article hence reinforces the prohibition on state parties to

141 See para 2.1.a above.
142 Gros Espiel (n 105) 65, para 279.
143 Cassese, *Self-determination of Peoples* (n 20) 53.
144 The states in question were the USA, UK, Greece, New Zealand and Denmark. The initiative was also supported by a number of developing countries, among which were India, Syria, Pakistan, Lebanon and Egypt. See Cassese, *Self-determination of Peoples* (n 20) 60 and references to meeting minutes of GA debates cited therein.
145 Doehring (n 12) 56.

interfere in the affairs of other state parties in a manner that seriously infringes upon the right of a people to self-determination.

All in all, the formula adopted in Article 1 of the Human Rights Covenants seems to have gone where the UN Charter did not go. In the drafting process the scope of self-determination was indeed widened to include both strands of meaning that were already set out at San Francisco but which made it only partially in the Charter provisions.[146] The formula used in the Covenants indeed managed to find a definition of self-determination that was able to include also the people of non-self-governing territories (by referring to *all* peoples), a cause championed by Third World and socialist countries; yet the same formula managed also to move beyond the socialist conception of self-determination as equal to non-interference once independence has been achieved, adding a domestic dimension to it. The formula drafted for Article 1 thus managed to incorporate the colonial self into a definition of self-determination which went beyond the mere maintenance of the independent status for already independent people, adding a substantial self-governance content which regulates the relationship between a state, its people and the decision-making processes enacted at state-level. In this sense, the right to self-determination enshrined in the human rights Covenants can be said to be a complex and multi-faceted legal concept that develops in greater detail the embryonic ideas that had been already set out a decade earlier in the UN Charter.

3.3.1.4 Other characteristics

It is established that in Article 1 of the human rights Covenants self-determination has both retraced and widened the meaning attributed to it in the UN Charter. The development of self-determination as the right of the people of an independent state has therefore benefitted from its inclusion in the two human rights treaties. A number of points can be made to advocate further the claim that the meaning and content of the right was expanded by treaty law.

First, one should note that in the human rights treaties the right was attributed an economic content, a feature which it did not have in the Charter.[147] The economic aspects of self-determination are the freedom to determine the

146 See para 3.2.1.2 above.

147 In 1952, at the request of the General Assembly, the Commission on Human Rights recommended the establishment of a commission to conduct a full survey on the right of peoples and nations to permanent sovereignty over their natural wealth and resources, having noted that this right formed a 'basic constituent of the right to self-determination'. Following this recommendation, the General Assembly established the United Nations Commission on Permanent Sovereignty over Natural Resources on 12 December 1958 under GA Resolution 1314 (XIII). In 1961, this Commission adopted a draft resolution outlining principles concerning permanent sovereignty over natural resources. Following consideration of this draft resolution by the Economic and Social Council and the Second Committee of the General Assembly, the General Assembly adopted resolution 1803 (XVII). See Abelard's Kilangi, 'Introductory Note to Permanent Sovereignty Over

economic system or regime under which a people should to live. The UN Rapporteur describes this concept as a condition

> [w]here the people has formed a free and sovereign state or has established some other political formula through the exercise of the right to self-determination, the people of that state naturally retains its right freely to determine the economic regime which is to exist in that state. This right will be of lasting efficacy and will continue to take effect in the future, which is of particular significance, in view of all the neo-colonialist and neo-imperialistic schemes, whatever form they make take, to dominate the new states which have come into being as a result of the exercise of the right to political self-determination.[148]

Again, in relation to the content aspects of the right, UN Rapporteur Critescu reports that the Commission on Human Rights considered the question of the right to self-determination at its eighth session in 1952, and 'as regards the definition of the right to self-determination, some members maintained, *inter alia*, . . . that the right to self-determination should be regarded not only from the political, but also from the economic viewpoint, since political independence was based on economic independence, and that the right of peoples freely to dispose of their natural resources should be recognized'.[149]

Secondly, the right was explicitly made to apply to *all peoples* knowing that various forms of selves were to be included. In so doing, the right implicitly acquired a context-specific character: according to whether the self inhabits an independent or a dependent territory, the way self-determination applies to it will change. This feature is important because it also means that self-determination has never fully collapsed into a right to decolonisation, even at the height of the decolonisation movement. The dominant narrative which presents the development of self-determination from a right of colonial peoples that strives to find its own content and application in the post-colonial world is therefore deviant.[150] Instead, we have seen that the development of the right as a right of people of non-colonial territories (the people of a state) did not take place in a way

---

Natural Resources, General Assembly Resolution 1803 (XVII) of 14 December 1962' http://legal.un.org/avl/ha/ga_1803/ga_1803.html (last accessed 15 April 2018).

148 Gros Espiell (n 105) 26. See also Critescu (n 125) para 44: 'Any state should acquire complete control on its national resources and should place it in a position to apply its national laws to any private industry, even if those laws authorized expropriation or nationalization'.

149 Critescu (n 125) para 44.

150 See eg Quane (n 12). For a contrary view, more in line with what is argued here see Tomuschat, who argues that 'self-determination could never be considered an exclusive right of colonial people. Even GA Res 1514 (XV), in spite of its specific object of bringing about speedy decolonization, provides that self-determination is a right of all peoples. The two International Covenants on Human Rights use identical language'. Tomuschat (n 116) 2.

that was one-dimensional, subsequent to decolonisation and linear in time. Its existence indeed precedes the existence of a legal right of self-determination of colonial selves and was *de facto* articulated and expanded at the same time when the right of colonial selves was being ascertained and developed. The two are therefore not subsequent but co-existent, they are not mutually exclusive but they run in parallel, they do not contradict each other but complement each other.

Thirdly, self-determination, as a contextually-related right, does not die when the context changes, it rather transforms the way it is implemented and applied, whilst it continues to apply. More specifically, it continues to apply as long as the self on which is attaches to is a self entitled to self-determination in some form. As Emerson put it: 'once the major original exercise of self-determination has been undertaken, the small prints takes over and becomes the big print which establishes the new and far more restrictive guidelines'.[151]

Fourthly, the various aspects of the right are mutually related and mutually reinforcing. This point can be made both in relation to the relationship between human rights and self-determination, and with respect to the content aspects of self-determination. In relation to the first, Thurer and Burri argue that by being included in Articles 1 ICCPR and ICESCR, the concept of self-determination as a whole was given the characteristics of a 'source or essential prerequisite for the existence of individual human rights, since these rights could not genuinely be exercised without the realization of the collective right of self-determination'.[152] The same point was made also by the Commission on Human Rights in its General Comment on self-determination, where it stated that 'its realization is an essential condition for the effective guarantee and observance of individual human rights and for the promotion and strengthening of those rights'.[153]

To conclude, the inclusion of a right to self-determination in the international human rights treaties has significantly developed the meaning of self-determination in treaty law. The right has thereby acquired a contextual and diversified application, which appeals to a number of selves, and a multi-faceted content which includes several aspects related to the conditions under which a people can be given rights against the state and other states alike. In the next sections we will now consider whether and how the scope and content of self-determination in customary international law can be said to have further expanded the meaning attributed to it under treaty law in the decades following the entry into force of the Covenants.

151 Rupert Emerson, 'Self-determination' (1971) 65 *American Journal of International Law* 459, 459.

152 See Thürer and Burri (n 36) para 10. Cassese also supports this view by saying that 'the right of self-determination, though not in itself sufficient, is nonetheless an essential pre-condition for the effective recognition of the rights and freedoms of individuals'. Cassese, 'Political Self-determination' (n 62) 142.

153 GC12, para 1.

3.3.2 *The Declaration on Friendly Relations and Co-operation among States*

In 1970 the General Assembly adopted Resolution 2625 (XXV), which contains the annexed Declaration on Principles of International Law Concerning Friendly Relations and Co-operation among States in Accordance with the Charter of the United Nations (the Declaration).[154] The resolution was adopted without a vote on 24 October 1970, after several years of debates,[155] hence showing the level of general consensus reached in the final version of the document. Per se, General Assembly Resolutions are not legally binding documents. Many states however submitted that they understood the principles set out in this particular resolution to be part of general international law or of customary international law.[156] On the issue of custom, the International Court of Justice stated that:

> The effect of consent to such resolutions [and particularly Resolution 2625 (XXV)] cannot be understood as merely that of a "reiteration or elucidation" of the treaty commitment undertaken in the Charter. On the contrary, it may be understood as an acceptance of the validity of the rule or set of rules declared by the Resolution by themselves. . . . It would therefore seem apparent that the attitude referred to expresses an *opinio juris* respecting such rule (or set of rules), to be thenceforth treated separately from the provisions, especially those of an institutional kind, to which it is subject on the treaty-law plane of the Charter.[157]

And again later, the Court reiterated that:

> As already observed, the adoption by States of this text [GA Res 2625] affords an indication of their *opinio juris* as to customary international law on the question.[158]

A more nuanced view, offered by Cassese, advances the argument that not the whole Declaration can be regarded to be customary law, but that 'only those

154 GA Res 2625 (XVV) of 24 October 1970, UN Doc A/RES/25/2625.

155 A summary of the points raised by state representatives are contained in the two main reports of the Special Committee mandated to oversee the drafting of what became Resolution 2625 (XXV) see *Report of the Special Committee on Principles of International Law Concerning Friendly Relations and Co-operation Among States*, 24 UN G.A.O.R. Supp. 19, UN Doc A/7619 (1969) and *Report of the Special Committee on Principles of International Law Concerning Friendly Relations and Co-operation Among States*, 25 UN GAOR Supp 18, UN Doc A/8018 (1970).

156 Among the states in favour of considering the Declaration an expression of customary international law we Iraq, Hungary and the USA. Those against Italy and Australia. See UN Doc A/C.6/SR.1178 (23 September 1970) 1181–82.

157 *Military and Paramilitary Activities in and against Nicaragua (Nicaragua v. United States of America)*, Merits, Judgment [1986] ICJ Rep 14 para 188.

158 ibid para 191.

provisions on which a broad measure of substantial and unreserved agreement was possible have become a major element of international rules'.[159] More generally, the Declaration is said to constitute an authoritative and arguably the most important single statement in which state members of the United Nations agree on the interpretation of the law of the Charter in relation to seven fundamental principles of international law – among which there is the principle of equal rights and self-determination of peoples.[160]

Starting from the view established above, according to which self-determination under the UN Charter applies to the people of independent states,[161] and knowing that the Declaration is an interpretation of UN Charter provisions, it can be inferred that the same is valid also for the Declaration, and it is therefore of great interest to see how the principle was clarified in this document.[162] For this purpose, it is worth citing at length two key passages of the Declaration dealing with self-determination, which read as follows:

> By virtue of the principle of equal rights and self-determination of peoples enshrined in the Charter of the United Nations, all peoples have the right freely to determine, without external interference, their political status

159 It is submitted that these rules are the following: (a) peoples under colonial or alien domination have a right to 'external' self-determination; . . . (b) peoples under racist regime have the right to 'internal' and 'external' self-determination; . . . (c) States controlling peoples who find themselves in one of the aforementioned situations have a duty to respect and implement this right and in particular to refrain from using force to deprive those peoples of their right to self-determination; (d) third States are on the one hand duty-bound to refrain from interfering with the exercise of that right and, on the other hand, authorised to grant peoples struggling for their self-determination any form of support (short of the dispatch of troops). Cassese, 'Political Self-determination' (n 62) 146.

160 C D Johnson, 'Toward Self-Determination: A Reappraisal as Reflected in the Declaration on Friendly Relations' (1973) 3 *Georgia Journal of International and Comparative Law Quarterly* 145, 154–59 and Robert Rosenstock, 'The Declaration of Principles of International Law Concerning Friendly Relations: A Survey' (1971) 65 *American Journal of International Law* 713, 714.

161 See section 3.2.1 above.

162 The same view is shared also by UN Special Rapporteur Critescu in his study of the principle. See Critescu (n 125) para 58. Cassese, on the other hand, leans towards a restrictive interpretation which would make the principle set out in the Declaration only applying to colonial peoples. Cassese reaches this conclusion through a close reading of the debates in the GA, which were not conclusive and presented both universalistic and restrictive interpretations. It is not clear, however, how the Declaration could exclude the people of independent states from the meaning of peoples, given that the purpose of the Declaration was to clarify and better define – not to modify – certain political principles enshrined within the legal framework of the UN Charter. The inclusion of a territorially uncontroversial definition of peoples is given for granted also by McWhinney in 1966, at the start of the work of the Committee. See Cassese, *Self-determination of Peoples* (n 62) 109–11 (in particular footnotes 14 and 15) and Edward McWhinney, 'Friendly Relations and Cooperation among States: Debate at the Twentieth General Assembly, United Nations' (1966) 60 *American Journal of International Law* 356.

> and to pursue their economic, social and cultural development, and every State has the duty to respect this right in accordance with the provisions of the Charter.
>
> . . . Nothing in the foregoing paragraphs shall be construed as authorizing or encouraging any action which would dismember or impair, totally or in part, the territorial integrity or political unity of sovereign and independent States conducting themselves in compliance with the principle of equal rights and self-determination of peoples as described above and thus possessed of a government representing the whole people belonging to the territory without distinction as to race, creed or colour.[163]

In the light of what we have seen above concerning the interpretation of the word 'freely' enclosed in Article 1 of the Human Rights Covenants, we understand that the Declaration has gone a step further in making its dual meaning explicit. In paragraph 1, there is indeed a clear reference to the fact that the determination to which the self is entitled must be done 'without external interference'.[164] This wording substitutes the word 'freely' and precedes the formula used to define self-determination, which is essentially identical to the one used in Article 1 of the Covenants. In paragraph 7, instead, there is an elaboration of the domestic standards that a state is required to respect in order to fulfil its self-determination obligations and allow the self to exercise its self-determination rights free from internal oppression. It is precisely in relation to this aspect that most commentators command the Declaration for having expanded and refined the meaning of self-determination. By adding a representativeness requirement, international law was indeed being infused with more detailed self-determination standards that states are called to respect at the domestic level.

For this reason, it can be argued that in the Declaration there is a clear intention to develop the principle in its domestic aspects. It is far from clear, however, the extent to which the document has actually refined domestic self-determination standards. Under international law, who is entitled to be represented at the state-level on self-determination grounds? Amongst legal scholars there is a great deal of debate around the meaning that should be attributed to the representativeness clause set out in paragraph VII quoted above. Some argue that a wide, liberal interpretation can be advanced (one that would, for example, encompass political opinions, minorities and secessionist groups);[165]

163 Respectively, paras I and VII of the section on the Principle of Equal Rights and Self-Determination of the Declaration. On the Declaration more generally see P H Houben, 'Principles of International Law Concerning Friendly Relations and Co-Operation among States' (1967) 61 *American Journal of International Law* 703 and R M Witten, 'The Declaration on Friendly Relations' (1971) 12 *Harvard International Law Journal* 509.

164 Some argued that this provision means nothing more than a right to non-intervention in domestic affairs. See Cassese, 'Political Self-determination' (n 62) 144; Pomerance, *Self-determination in Law and Practice* (n 20) 46.

165 Raic (n 13) 253–55; Rosenstock (n 160) 732; Summers (n 11) ch 7.

others instead take side for a more restrictive interpretation that would cover only racial groups.[166] According to Cassese, this formulation was a strategic compromise advanced by the Italian delegation, which replaced the words 'governments representative of the whole people', included in the original draft.[167] The substitution of such a general formula with a more specific one which enumerates race, creed or colour as standards for representation would therefore introduce a qualification – and with it a limitation – of the notion of 'representative government'.[168]

Here I will not dwell into this issue in detail because, with time, the interpretation seems to have expanded. For instance, in both the Vienna Declaration and Programme of Action, and the formula already contained in the Declaration 'without distinction as to race, creed or color' was substituted with the wording 'without distinction of any kind'.[169] The Vienna Declaration is also a non-legally binding instrument, adopted in 1993 and endorsed by General Assembly Resolution 48/121 of 20 December 1993, adopted without a vote and referred to in all subsequent GA Resolutions on self-determination.[170]

A second, important way in which the Declaration decisively expands the provisions of the Charter is by ascertaining the existence of an obligation for every state to respect this right. In fact, the formulation goes even a step further and defines this obligation as a duty, imposed on every state, to promote the realisation of the principle of equal rights and self-determination, and to 'render assistance to the United Nations in carrying out the responsibilities entrusted to it by the Charter concerning the implementation of this principle'.[171]

Summing up, we have seen that, by 1970, the principle of self-determination originally introduced in the Charter had significantly developed from its cryptic formulation adopted 25 years earlier. Its content had expanded to include some sort of domestic standard of representativeness to which the people of independent states were entitled to, as well as an obligation for all states to contribute to the realisation of the right. We have also seen that the two trends of meaning, one attached to the socialist interpretation, more connected to non-intervention aspects, and one attached to the Western conception of self-determination as

166 Cassese, 'Political Self-determination' (n 62); Cassese, *Self-determination of Peoples* (n 20) 113–14; Johnson (n 160) 152; Pomerance, *Self-determination in Law and Practice* (n 20) 39.

167 UN Doc A/8018, 44–49 (referring to the original proposals submitted in UN Doc A/AC.125/L.86 and A/AC-125/L.80) and Cassese, *Self-determination of Peoples* (n 20) 118.

168 ibid.

169 United Nations World Conference on Human Rights, Vienna Declaration and Programme of Action, 25 June 1993, 32 *ILM* (1993) 1661. The same formula is also used in the Declaration on the Occasion of the Fiftieth Anniversary of the United Nations, General Assembly Resolution 50/6, adopted on 24 October 1995, para 1.

170 UN Doc A/Res/48/121 of 20 December 1993.

171 Paragraphs 1 and 2 of the section on the Principle of Equal Rights and Self-Determination of the Declaration. See also Sahovic (n 49) 370.

popular participation, were consistently traceable in the way the principle has developed, in its formulation as well as in its content.

3.3.3 Regional instruments in Europe, Africa and the Arab world

In the previous sections we analysed self-determination provisions contained in various sources of international law. Here, we shall consider three regional instruments dealing with self-determination. Whilst bearing in mind that their significance is limited under international law, the aim is to see how self-determination was conceptualised in regional instruments.

3.3.3.1 The Helsinki Declaration

The Final Act of the Conference on Security and Co-operation in Europe closed at Helsinki on 1 August 1975 with the adoption of a Declaration (the Helsinki Declaration)[172] in which 35 countries were involved.[173] The Declaration is not legally binding, but rather a document reflecting a moral and political commitment to act in accordance with the stated principles advanced by states parties to the Conference. It thus does not have a universal significance but more of a regional relevance confined to Europe and Northern America. However, participating states recognised that the Declaration is based directly and expressly on Charter law; and many states also recalled the Principles of International Law Concerning Friendly Relations and Co-operation among States, adopted as GA Resolution 2625.[174] It can be said, therefore, that the document is 'consistent with international law, and, given the level at which it was concluded, many observers think it may become in fact one of the most widely quoted sources of customary international law'.[175] Indeed, the Final Act was also cited, in relation to the principle of non-intervention, by the International Court of Justice as evidence of *opinio juris* of the participating states.[176]

Principle VIII of the Declaration specifically calls into question the 'equal rights and self-determination of peoples'. The key passage in this respect reads:

> By virtue of the principle of equal rights and self-determination of peoples, all peoples *always* have the right, *in full freedom*, to determine, *when and as they wish*, their *internal and external* political status, without external

172 14 *ILM* 1293 (1975).

173 All European countries, except for Albania, plus the USA and Canada.

174 Gros Espiell (n 105) para 240.

175 Harold S Russell, 'The Helsinki Declaration: Brobdingnag or Lilliput?' 70 *American Journal of International Law* (1976) 242, at 246–48.

176 *Case Concerning Military and Paramilitary Activities in and against Nicaragua* (n 157) para 189. The Act was cited also by the Canadian Supreme Court within the merits of the case Supreme Court of Canada, *Re Secession of Quebec*, 161 *Dominion Law Reports* [1998] 4th Series 436, para 121 and 4389, para 129.

> interference, and to pursue as they wish their political, economic, social and cultural development.[177]

The text is of particular interest to this study since it was clearly drafted having in mind the peoples of independent states. For instance, Raic has noted that, at the time of adoption of the Helsinki Declaration, there was no situation of colonialism in Europe or North America, hence the document proves the relevance of self-determination outside of the colonial context.[178] According to Cassese, 'it appears incontrovertible that the Helsinki Declaration, when it discusses the principle of self-determination, only extends the right to the entire populations living in and identifying with sovereign states (for example, Italian or French citizens).[179] All in all, the subject of contention is whether the word peoples could include also other selves other than the people of independent states, not whether the people of independent states are included. For the present purposes, here it shall suffice to know that the inclusion of this specific self is undisputed.

Going into the substance of the provisions, the text appears to reinforce and clarify the content that was already set out in the Declaration on Friendly Relations five years earlier by stressing some of its aspects that were not spelled out too explicitly in previous documents. First, the addition of 'always' and 'as they wish' as a means to 'convey the idea that the right of self-determination is a continuing right, a right that keeps its validity even after a people has chosen a certain form of government or a certain international status'.[180] For the people of independent states, self-determination is not a one-off right to choose, but an ongoing, continuous right to decide on their status and to pursue their political, social and cultural development.

Secondly, the Helsinki Declaration introduces in the language of self-determination a division between 'internal' and 'external' political status, hence distinguishing between an entitlement to decide over a people's international status versus its right to decide upon the form of government under which it is to live. This passage can be seen as a means to develop the domestic standards requirements that were set out in the Declaration on Friendly Relations, as no saving clause was included at Helsinki. This view can be further supported by the inclusion of two formulas: 'in full freedom' and 'without external interference'. If the two were synonymous, this would be a repetition. It can thus be argued that the first is to be taken as to mean freedom from internal oppression. This interpretation is set out also by Cassese, who argues that:

> [t]he phrase 'in full freedom' reflects the Western view whereby the right of self-determination cannot be implemented if basic human rights and

177 Principle VIII (Equal rights and self-determination of peoples), Helsinki Declaration [emphasis added].

178 Raic (n 13) 231, noting also that the argument that reference to self-determination outside of colonialism was unnecessary was expressly rejected during the conference.

179 Cassese, *Self-determination of Peoples* (n 20) 289.

180 Cassese, 'Political Self-determination' (n 62) 150.

> fundamental freedoms ... are not ensured to all members of the peoples concerned. ... It therefore sanctions the right of peoples to exercise self-determination free *from internal interference* (i.e. from oppression from an authoritarian government). The expression "without external interference" denotes freedom *from possible encroachment by third states.*[181]

The provisions laid down at Helsinki, therefore, at least on the level of political commitment, move beyond the meaning attributed to self-determination in international law 'as we know it'. Their agreed text indeed came to reflect more closely the Western conception of self-determination, which carries a strong focus on anti-authoritarianism. Moreover, the formula adopted at Helsinki markedly reaffirms the co-existence within the idea of self-determination of two trends: one stressing upon freedom from internal oppression and one stressing on freedom from external interference. Once again, the two are interrelated, interconnected and complementary; they are co-existent and only combined and fused together they give full meaning to the right of self-determination.

3.3.3.2 *The African Charter of Human and People's Rights*

A second regional instrument that shall be mentioned is the African Charter on Human and People's Rights [hereinafter the African Charter], adopted by the Assembly of Heads of States and Governments of the Organization of African Unity in 1981.[182] With 53 state parties that have signed and ratified it, the African Charter is the largest regional human rights instrument in place today.[183] Drafted by independent states, the document recognises that some rights, as collective rights, are vested in peoples. Among them, there is the right to self-determination. Article 20 of the African Charter reads:

> 1. All peoples shall have the right to existence. They shall have the unquestionable and inalienable right to self-determination. They shall freely determine their political status and shall pursue their economic and social development according to the policy they have freely chosen.
> 2. Colonized or oppressed peoples shall have the right to free themselves from the bonds of colonization by resorting to any means recognized by the international community.

181 ibid 152.

182 African [Banjul] Charter on Human and People's Rights, adopted on 27 June 1981, OAU Doc CAB/LEG/67/3Rev.5 (1981), 520 UNTS 217, 21 *ILM* 58 (1982).

183 The only African state which has signed but not yet ratified the African Charter at the time of writing is South Sudan. Ratification status available at http://www.achpr.org/instruments/achpr/ratification/ (last accessed 15 April 2018). The European Convention for the Protection of Fundamental Rights and Freedom as of 15 April 2018 counts 47 ratifications. Ratification status available at https://www.coe.int/en/web/conventions/full-list/-/conventions/treaty/005/signatures (last accessed 15 April 2018).

3. All peoples shall have the right to the assistance of the State parties to the present Charter in their liberation struggle against foreign domination, be it political, economic or cultural.

The first thing to highlight in relation to this document, and to the article more specifically, is that in the African Charter the meaning of 'peoples' was purposely left undefined by the drafters. The committee of experts who drafted the document indeed deliberately refused to 'indulge in the definition of such notions as "peoples" so as not to end up in difficult discussions'.[184]

Most amongst those who have written on the interpretation of 'peoples' in this document agree on the fact that at least the people of independent states were included in the mind of the drafters.[185] Arguments in favour of this interpretation in existing literature are made mainly by indirect reasoning. Some scholars reached this conclusion by offering a combined reading of paragraphs 1 and 2 of Article 20. Paragraph 1 states that *all peoples* have the right to self-determination, and paragraph 2 applies specifically to *those people* that are oppressed or colonised. Thus, the argument goes, if paragraph 2 deals with a specific category of peoples, it seems reasonable to adduce that the word *peoples* in the first paragraph is given a more general, wider meaning.[186] Others, instead, view the applicability of self-determination on the people of a state as a necessary implication of a very restrictive view according to which self-determination in African states would apply only to ex-colonial peoples. In this sense, self-determination would apply only to the peoples of independent states that had formerly been colonised by European states, such as the Nigerians, without a distinction between the groups of peoples within Nigeria.[187]

An additional, decisive case can be made in favour of this interpretation of the term 'people' in light of a recent judgment of the African Commission on

184 *Report of O.A.U. Secretary-General on Draft African Charter on Human and People's Rights*, OAU Doc C.M./1149, para 13 cited in Michael K Addo, 'Political Self-Determination within the Context of the African Charter on Human and People's Rights' (1988) 32 *Journal of African Law* 182, 184.

185 For commentators what is left highly uncertain instead, is whether minorities, sub-state groups such as ethnic or religious groups can be considered 'peoples' under art 20, especially in view of their potential secessionist claims. See S Kwaw Nyameke Blay, 'Changing African Perspectives on the Right of Self-Determination in the Wake of the Banjul Charter on Human and People's Rights' (1985) 29 *Journal of African Law* 147; Mtendeweka Mhango, 'Governance, Peace and Human Rights Violations in Africa: Addressing the Application of the Right to Self-Determination in Post-Independence Africa' (2012) 5 *African Journal of Legal Studies* 199. For a sceptical view instead see Kiwanuka, who argues that, regretfully, in the African Charter the meaning of 'peoples' can be equated with 'states' but possibly not (or not strongly so) with the meaning of 'all persons within a state'. Richard N Kiwanuka, 'The Meaning of "People" in the African Charter on Human and People's Rights' (1988) 82 *American Journal of International Law* 80.

186 Blay (n 185) 158.

187 Mhango (n 185) 208.

Human and People's Rights – the body mandated to interpret the Charter.[188] In a case brought by a former Head of State against The Gambia the Commission wrote:

> 73. It is true that the military regime came to power by force, albeit, peacefully. This was not through the will of the people who, since independence have known only the ballot box, as a means of choosing their political leaders. The military coup d'état was therefore a grave violation *of the right of Gambian people to freely choose their government as entrenched in article 20(1) of the Charter.* Article 20(1) provides: 'All peoples shall . . . freely determine their political status . . . according to the policy they have freely chosen. (See also the Commission's Resolution on the Military of 1994).[189]

In this passage the Commission clearly ascertains that the provisions of Article 20(1) do apply to the people of the Gambia as a whole, and that the right of a people freely to choose their government is included in the right to self-determination, as enshrined in Article 20(1). It can thus be said that, under the African Charter, the right of the people of a state 'freely to determine their political status' and to 'pursue their economic and social development according to the policy they have freely chosen' includes, at the very least, an entitlement to choose their government.[190] This point is set out also by Summers, who argues that there is evidence in African states reporting practice that self-determination under the African Charter draws from a right to self-government that can be attached to the whole population of a state.[191] Moreover, another significant feature of Article 20 is in its paragraph 3, which gives to people a 'right to the assistance of State Parties . . . in their liberation struggle against foreign domination, be it political, economic or cultural', hence reinforcing the basic concept that self-determination is a right which generates obligations for other state parties.

A second important element of the African Charter is that the economic aspects of self-determination are included in two separate Articles, namely Article 21 (right to free disposal of wealth and natural resources) and 22 (right to economic, social and cultural development).[192] In this respect, Summers observes that states

188 Protocol to the African Charter on Human and People's Rights on the Establishment of an African Court on Human and People's Rights, adopted June 9, 1998, OAU Doc OAU/LEG/EXP/AFCHPR/PROT (III).

189 *Jawara v The Gambia* (2000) AHRLR 107 (ACHPR 2000) (emphasis added).

190 In addition to this collective, people's right, under art 13(1) the African Charter gives to every citizen also the individual, human right to participate in government. It reads as follows: 'Every citizen shall have the right to participate freely in the government of his country, either directly or through freely chosen representatives in accordance with the provisions of the law'.

191 Summers (n 11) 380 (especially see references cited in footnotes).

192 See Kiwanuka (n 185) 95. For a detailed analysis of economic self-determination see Alice Farmer, 'Towards a Meaningful Rebirth of Economic Self-determination: Human

in their periodic reports reveal a similar understanding of Article 21 to that of Article 1(2) of the Covenants.[193]

Concluding, the right to self-determination enshrined in the African Charter of Human Rights does attach to the people of independent African states. We have seen that, for this self, the right can be interpreted in a way that essentially resembles the scope and content that is attributed to it under international law more generally. The document does, however, provide some significant scope for substantial developments to take place on the economic contents of the right.

3.3.3.3 The Arab Charter of Human Rights

In contrast with the expansive approach taken by the African Charter, we shall now look at another, more recent, regional human rights instrument where self-determination was used in a rather restrictive sense. The Arab Charter on Human Rights [hereinafter the Arab Charter] indeed remains, to date, possibly the most cryptic amongst regional instruments dealing with the right to self-determination. Its Article 2 provides that:

> 1. All peoples have the right of self-determination and to control over their natural wealth and resources, and the right to freely choose their political system and to freely pursue their economic, social and cultural development.
> 2. All peoples have the right to national sovereignty and territorial integrity.[194]

The formula used in paragraph 1 clearly retraces the definition provided in the Human Rights Covenants without adding any further element of substance. A significant element to bring to attention, instead, is the wording used in paragraph 2. By saying that *all peoples* have the right to national sovereignty and territorial integrity, the Arab Charter noticeably sets forward a notion of 'people' that is state-centered. The people of a state are therefore clearly included as a self entitled to self-determination under Article 2 of this document.[195] There is an apparent conflict, however, between the provisions of Article 2(1) and the absolute forms of government which characterise some of the states in the Arab region. For this reason, in the future it will be necessary to monitor the activities

---

Rights Realization in Resource-Rich Countries' (2006) 39 *New York University Journal of International Law and Policy* 417.

193 Summers (n 11) 383.

194 League of Arab States, Arab Charter on Human Rights, adopted 22 May 2004, reprinted in 12 *International Human Rights Reports* 893 (2005), entered into force 15 March 2008. The Arab Charter builds on an earlier text drafted in 1994 that failed to gain enough support to enter into force.

195 Excluding the Palestinians, that seem to have been clearly in the mind of the drafters, the people of independent states in fact seem to be the only possible selves entitled to self-determination under the Arab Charter. See also Summers (n 11) 392.

of the Arab Human Rights Committee, the body mandated to review reports submitted every three years by ratifying states, in order to understand whether and how Arab states will report on the implementation of self-determination measures.[196]

To conclude, in the last three sections we have seen that the right to self-determination is present not only in purely international treaties and sources of customary international law, but also in a number of other instruments – with a wide degree of legal significance – that have a more limited, regional application. We have also seen that, in all of these instruments, the right to self-determination unequivocally applies to the people of independent states. In Europe, the definition of self-determination incorporated in the Helsinki Declaration moves forward from self-determination as we know it under international treaty and customary law. More specifically, it entails a strong non-interference component, both understood as freedom from external interference and freedom from authoritarian rule. In Africa, the scope and content of the right seem to reflect the interpretation that is offered under international law more generally, with a possible further elaboration of economic standards – which are treated separately from political aspects. Finally, in the Arab region the meaning seemingly attributed to self-determination is more restricted than in other regional instruments. Also, the recent nature of the review mechanism put in place by the Arab Charter does not yet provide, at present, sufficient material to discuss the way in which ratifying states are implementing their obligations under Article 2.

3.3.4 General Assembly resolutions: competing efforts

This chapter showed that between 1940s and the late 1970s the right to self-determination has developed along two main interpretative lines. The first, promoted by Western countries, draws from the concept of popular sovereignty and sees self-determination as a means to ensure that a government holds attachment to the will of the people and that it has a participative character. The second, promoted by the socialist bloc, was instead more focused on presenting self-determination as a freedom right: the right of a people to choose their form of government free from any kind of external interference. We have also seen that states which have participated in the drafting of all international law sources on self-determination have constantly and strenuously had to mediate between these two interpretations, until they could be reconciled and a proper, inclusive wording could be found to incorporate and fuse them together into a unitary formula. In this section we shall now see that attempts were also made, starting in the late 1980s, to try and separate the two trends of meaning.

196 Several reports have been submitted by ratifying States but none of these is available online and/or in a language other than Arabic. See http://www.lasportal.org/en/Pages/default.aspx (last accessed 15 April 2018).

In 1988, the United States sponsored a draft resolution in the General Assembly, under an agenda item dealing with self-determination and human rights, called E*nhancing the Effectiveness of the Principle of Periodic and Genuine Elections*'.[197] This was only the first of a set of resolutions that, from there, every year for several years the Assembly came to adopt on the same issue.[198] The resolutions were intended to put forward a model of democratic governance based on the enforceability of participatory rights. In the operative paragraphs of these resolutions the Assembly clearly set out a requirement that governments shall be attached to the will of the people and spelled out that determining the will of the people requires genuine and periodic elections.[199]

In contrast to this trend, a second set of concurring resolutions was introduced in 1989, sponsored by Cuba and titled *Respect for the principles of national sovereignty and non-interference in the internal affairs of States in their electoral processes*.[200] This second set of resolutions was adopted in parallel to the ones

197 Before being adopted the draft resolution (UN Doc A/C.3/43/L.80) was changed to include a clear reference to the condemnation of Apartheid. The Resolution was adopted without a vote but several states raised issues concerning the respect for the principle of non-intervention and self-determination of peoples (Mexico, Panama, Pakistan) and the possibility of states to hold elections in accordance with their own traditions and culture (Ghana, Zambia). See UN Doc A/C.3/43/SR.57, 7–8.

198 These resolutions are: UN Doc A/Res/43/157 of 8 December 1988; UN Doc A/Res/44/146 of 15 December 1989; UN Doc A/Res/45/150 of 18 December 1990; UN Doc A/Res/46/137 of 17 December 1991; UN Doc A/Res/47/138 of 18 December 1992; UN Doc A/Res/48/131 of 20 December 1993. From 1994 onwards, the subject and title of the Resolutions changed slightly and began to focus more on the role of the United Nations in enhancing elections and promoting democracy. For a full list of subsequent resolutions and their voting records see Annex 1.

199 Operative paragraphs 1–3 of Resolution 45/150 (1990) read as follows: 'The General Assembly . . .

1. *Underscores* the significance of the Universal Declaration of Human Rights and the International Covenant on Civil and Political Rights, which establish that the authority to govern shall be based on the will of the people, as expressed in periodic and genuine elections;
2. *Stresses*, its conviction that periodic and genuine elections are a necessary and indispensable element of sustained efforts to protect the rights and interests of the governed and that, as a matter of practical experience, the right of everyone to take part in the government of his or her country is a crucial factor in the effective enjoyment by all of a wide range of other human rights and fundamental freedoms, embracing political, economic, social and cultural rights;
3. *Declares* that determining the will of the people requires an electoral process that provides an equal opportunity for all citizens to become candidates and put forward their political views individually and in co-operation with others, as provided in national constitutions and laws'.

200 A total of twelve resolutions with an almost identical name were adopted by the General Assembly between 1989 and 2005. These resolutions are: UN Doc /A/Res/44/147 of 15 December 1989; UN Doc A/Res/45/151 of 18 December 1990; UN Doc A/Res/46/130 of 17 December 1991; UN Doc A/Res/47/130 of 18 December 1992; UN Doc A/Res/48/124 of 20 December 1993; UN Doc A/Res/49/180 of 23 December

on genuine elections and intended to promote a different model of governance, one that values non-interference and aims to defend the preservation of the diversity of national systems.[201] The sponsoring states indeed saw the involvement of the international community in promoting democracy and the holding of elections as an undue incursion into a state's internal affairs, namely the prerogative of each state to choose and develop its government system without external interference.[202]

It is of interest to note that, in the operative text of this resolution, explicit reference is made to self-determination as the Assembly:

> 1. *Reiterates* that, by virtue of the principle of equal rights and self-determination of peoples enshrined in the Charter of the United Nations, all peoples have the right, freely and without external interference, to determine their political status and to pursue their economic, social and cultural development, and that every State has the duty to respect that right in accordance with the provisions of the Charter;
> 2. *Affirms* that it is the concern solely of peoples to determine methods and to establish institutions regarding the electoral process, as well as to determine the ways for its implementation according to their constitution and national legislation; . . .
> 4. *Urges* all States to respect the principle of non-interference in the internal affairs of states and the sovereign rights of peoples to determine their political, economic and social system.[203]

It seems clear that, with such wording, the resolution stresses the link between the principle of non-interference and the right of people to self-determination, understood as the right of the people of a state to choose its political status and, in so doing, to determine methods and establish institutions which regulate the electoral process. In response to this submission, in 1991 the competing resolution on genuine elections saw the introduction of an extended preamble paragraph, which reads:

> *Recognizes* that there is no single political system or electoral method that is equally suited to all nations and their people and that the efforts of the

1994; UN Doc A/Res/50/172 of 22 December 1995; UN Doc A/Res/52/119 of 12 December 1997; UN Doc A/Res/54/168 of 25 February 2000; UN Doc A/Res/56/154 of 19 December 2001; UN Doc A/Res/58/189 of 22 December 2003; UN Doc A/Res/60/164 of 16 December 2005. For a list of voting records of these resolutions see Annex 1.

201 On this point see also Gregory H Fox, 'The Right to Political Participation in International Law' (1992) 17 *Yale Journal of International Law*' 539, 590–91.

202 See Ignacio de Moral, 'An approach to the democratic debate in international law' [in Spanish] (2010) 10 *Anuario Mexicano de Derecho Internacional* 97, 114.

203 GA Resolution 44/147.

> international community to enhance the effectiveness of the principle of periodic and genuine elections should not call into question each State's sovereign right, in accordance with the will of its people, freely to choose and develop its political, social, economic and cultural systems, whether or not they conform to the preferences of other States.[204]

Other commentators argued that the two strands in the two resolution series appear to contradict each other.[205] In fact, to some extent the two could be seen as reinforcing each other. Both resolutions indeed reaffirm the right of each state and of its people to choose and develop freely its national institutions, according to the will of the people and to the electoral processes locally developed. The two, however, seem to differ substantially in relation to what are the conditions which should be given priority in order to ensure that a free determination is made. Namely, the first set of resolutions stresses more the need to have an electoral process that guarantees periodic and genuine elections, which provide equal opportunities for all citizens and highlight the role of the UN in providing electoral assistance.[206] The second set focuses instead on the link between diversity of democratic systems and national sovereignty, stressing that states themselves should ensure all the necessary mechanisms for peoples to develop freely its national electoral processes – which shall include periodic and genuine elections.[207]

In any case, these resolutions can hardly be said to have a legal value under international law. Only very general inferences can be made by looking at the voting records.[208] For instance, concerning the first set Jure Vidmar writes: 'The proclamations of these nearly unanimously adopted GA resolutions may be regarded as expression of *opinio juris* in regard to obligations imposed on states by the right to political participation'.[209] The resolutions had indeed very wide acceptance, and were adopted every year with an increasing number of favourable votes until they started being adopted without a vote in 2009.[210] In relation to the second set, instead, consensus is weaker: voting records remain far from unanimous or near-unanimous adoption which may be capable of expressing an adherence to customary law. Moreover, the last

204 GA Res 46/137.

205 See Rosas (n 126) 240 and, to a lesser extent, Niels Peters, 'The Principle of Democratic Teleology in International Law' (2008) 34 *Brooklyn Journal of International Law* 33, 59.

206 The role of the UN was central starting from Resolution 46/137 (1991) onwards.

207 See in particular Resolution 60/164, where all references to non-intervention are eliminated.

208 In general terms, the first set of resolutions was promoted by the US and supported by Western states; the second was introduced by Cuba and supported by Third World countries. The vast majority of states, however, have supported both series of resolutions. See Annex 1.

209 Jure Vidmar, 'The Right of Self-Determination and Multiparty Democracy: Two Sides of the Same Coin?' (2010) 10 *Human Rights Law Review* 239, 262.

210 For voting records of all resolutions see Annex 1.

resolution was passed in 2006, and after that no more were passed on the same agenda item. As a result, the debate on whether there is a right to democratic governance in international law is therefore still open; whether at present there is a nascent requirement to have multi-party elections or only a general right to political participation which does not impose a particular political system for states remains indeed a topic for fierce discussion among international law academics.[211]

Despite these due warnings as to their precise legal relevance, this group of General Assembly resolutions is an important set of documents in at least three ways. First, their parallel existence reinforces the idea advanced in this chapter which sees self-determination attached to two different meanings, championed from two fronts. On the one side, the focus is on the concept of popular sovereignty and on the participatory element of a people's right to choose its status; on the other, the focus is on the non-interventionist aspects of the people's freedom right to choose its status free from external interference. Secondly, the resolutions were important in that they showed that it is extremely difficult to divide and separate the two meanings neatly, as they are closely entangled and referred to at the same time in both sets of resolutions. What can more readily be discernible in the two approaches, however, is the focus on what aspects shall be prioritised in order to ensure that a 'free' determination can be made. Thirdly, the resolutions were important because, even if their legal value is far from ascertained – and possibly very limited – it seems clear that no unanimous *opinio juris* has yet crystallised on a specific model or system of democracy that states are required to adopt under international law.

3.3.5 Self-determination in the sources of international law: a tale of two meanings and one content

Sections 3.2 and 3.3 above were devoted to a detailed discussion of the meaning and content that can be attributed to self-determination, as a right attached to the people of independent states, in current international law. Now, before moving to a discussion of the character of this sub-norm that will be offered in the next chapter, we will recall briefly the key points established so far.

In the first place, the analysis has demonstrated that if one focuses on a specific self, namely the people of independent states, the content of the right

211 For reference to the main voices in this debate see: Jean D'Aspremont, '1989-2010: The Rise and Fall of Democratic Governance in International Law' in James Crawford and Sarah Nouwen (eds), Select Proceedings of the European Society of International Law, *Vol 3* (Hart Publishing 2011); Russell Buchan, *International Law and the Construction of the Liberal Peace* (Hart Publishing 2013); Thomas M Franck, 'The Emerging Right to Democratic Governance' (1992) 86 *American Journal of International Law* 46; Jure Vidmar, *Democratic Statehood in International Law: the Emergence of New States in Post-Cold War Practice* (Hart Publishing 2013); Steven Wheatley, *The Democracy, Minorities and International Law* (CUP 2005).

to self-determination is neither so indeterminate nor as controversial as it is generally deemed to be. Indeed, we have shown that there is both evidence in the sources of international law and general agreement between academics that a core, definite and substantial content for this sub-norm exists and that its contours can be identified. More specifically, we have seen that the core content to be attributed to this specific layer of self-determination consists in a right for people freely to choose and shape their own political status and freely to pursue their economic, social and cultural development. UN Rapporteur Critescu interpreted this content to include the right of a people:

> [t]o equip themselves with the political, economic and social institutions of their choice; the right to decide their own future, to choose their own form of government, to set their political objectives, to construct their systems and to draw up their philosophical programmes without any pressure, whether direct or indirect, internal or external.[212]

We have also seen that self-determination, as a legal right, was first introduced in the UN Charter and from there its content and meaning has developed through treaty and custom in the following decades. Little space was dedicated, on the contrary, to ICJ rulings on this matter. This is due to the marginal relevance that ICJ rulings can have for the analysis developed here. ICJ judgments indeed dealt with a number of cases concerning self-determination but all of them were cases of self-determination happening within the colonial context.[213] As Cassese rightly put it,

> [t]he historical and political circumstances led the Court to deal with only the most 'classical' and 'traditional' dimension of self-determination: anti-colonialism. ... By the same token, states avoided taking up another dimension of self-determination at the judicial level, that is internal self-determination *qua* the right of the whole population of a sovereign state to free and unhindered access to government without any discrimination based on race.[214]

212 Critescu (n 125) para 319.

213 *Legal Consequences for States of the Continued Presence of South Africa in Namibia* (n 88); *Western Sahara, Advisory Opinion* (n 10); *East Timor (Portugal v. Australia) Judgment* [1985] ICJ Rep 90; *Legal Consequences of the Construction of a Wall in the Occupied Palestinian Territory* (Advisory Opinion) [2004] ICJ Rep 136; *Accordance with International Law of the Unilateral Declaration of Independence in Respect of Kosovo* (Advisory Opinion) [2010] ICJ Rep 403. Some aspects of self-determination were also involved in the cases of *Burkina Faso/Mali Frontier Dispute* (n 16) and *Burkina Faso/Niger Frontier Dispute (Burkina Faso v. Niger)* [2013] ICJ Rep 44. For a general overview of the ICJ jurisprudence on this matter see Andrew K Coleman, *Resolving Claims to Self-Determination: Is there a Role for the International Court of Justice?* (Routledge 2014).

214 See Cassese, 'The International Court of Justice and the Right of Peoples to Self-determination' (n 18) 352.

In delivering its Advisory Opinion on Kosovo in 2010, the ICJ could have taken a chance to expand its jurisprudence on self-determination outside the colonial context.[215] Instead, the Court did not dwell into the substance of self-determination and decided the case on other bases.[216] In their separate opinions, Judges Simma and Yusuf both regret that the Court did not reflect on the substance of self-determination arguments, as a means to respond and settle considerations that were made by states in their pleadings before the Court.[217] In particular, Judge Yusuf argued that:

> [a]n assessment by the Court of the existence of an entitlement could have brought clarity to the scope and legal content of the right of self-determination, in its post-colonial conception, and its applicability to the specific case of Kosovo. The Court has in the past contributed to a better understanding of the field of application of the right of self-determination with respect to situations of decolonization or alien subjugation and foreign occupation. It could have likewise used this opportunity to define the scope and normative content of the post-colonial right of self-determination.[218]

Overall, ICJ jurisprudence has not been particularly helpful in shedding light on the contours of the layer of self-determination that is studied here. The one reference that is surely worth recalling from ICJ rulings, however, is the one made by the Court in the *Western Sahara Case*. Here, the ICJ provided its own general definition of self-determination as 'the need to pay regard to the freely expressed will of the people'.[219] To date, this statement constitutes an important, authoritative interpretation of what is at the core of the right. However, what it means that self-determination is essentially about the right for people to making a free choice is a concept open to interpretation.

The only case in which the ICJ dealt with self-determination outside the context of decolonisation is in its advisory opinion on the *Construction of a Wall in the Occupied Palestinian Territory* (the *Wall* advisory opinion).[220] Here, the Court found that self-determination applied to the situation in question by virtue of the fact that the right to self-determination is generally recognised in the UN Charter and reaffirmed in General Assembly 2625 (XXV), and because the existence of the Palestinian people was deemed to be 'no longer an issue'.[221] This judgment is of great interest because it represents a first attempt to articulate

215 *Kosovo Advisory Opinion* (n 213).

216 ibid paras 79 and 82.

217 *Kosovo case,* Separate Opinions of Judge Simma, paras 6–7 and of Judge Yusuf, para 6.

218 *Kosovo Case*, Separate opinion of Judge Yusuf, para 5.

219 *Western Sahara* Advisory Opinion (n 10) para 59.

220 Judge Higgins made this point in her separate opinion, paras 29–30. *Wall* Advisory Opinion (n 213).

221 Respectively, paras 88 and 118 of the *Wall* Advisory Opinion (n 213).

the right to self-determination outside the realm of decolonisation and does, therefore, reveal some important features of what this right may look like.

For instance, the opinion highlights a very strong connection between self-determination and territory.[222] This doing, the Court conveys the idea that 'self-determination is essentially a territorially based right and that there is an organic, definitional link between a people and the territorial base upon which they claim to exercise their right to self-determination'.[223] Moreover, the opinion stresses the *erga omnes* character of the obligations that arise from self-determination, recalling its previous judgment on the *East Timor case* and the text of GA Resolution 2625 (XXV) where it is stated that every state has the duty to promote the realisation of the principle.[224] Although the *Wall* opinion does not deal with the right as it applies to the people of an independent state, the findings highlighted above are nonetheless significant and should be borne in mind. The way the Court dealt with self-determination allows us to think that some of the essential characters of this right remain valid and relevant, even if we do not consider the right in its anti-colonial form, and rather wish to examine a different layer of the principle.

Throughout the present chapter we have also seen that the core content of the right of self-determination for the people of an independent state was interpreted as being attached a twofold meaning: (i) the right of a people to choose its form of government and to pursue their economic, social and cultural development free from external interference; (ii) the right of a people to choose its form of government and to pursue their economic, social and cultural development free from internal oppression and authoritarian rule. Of these two meanings, the first focuses on the non-intervention requirements that render a people's choice free; whilst the second focuses on the participatory requirements at state-level that ensure a choice is made freely. It was shown how these two meanings have always been present since the early days of self-determination as a political principle, and that they can also be traced into every step of the history of its development as a legal norm. Furthermore, it was argued that over the decades the two meanings were amalgamated to the point that they seem to have condensed into a unitary, compact legal concept that indicates what self-determination means for the people of independent states. As a result, the

222 ibid para 122.

223 Jean-Francois Gareau, 'Shouting at the Wall: Self-determination and the Legal Consequences of the Construction of a Wall in the Occupied Palestinian Territory' (2005) 18 *Leiden Journal of International Law* 489, 520.

224 *Wall* advisory opinion (n 213) para 155–56. See also Gareau (n 223) 518–19 and Gentian Zyberi, 'Self-determination through the lens of the International Court of Justice' (2009) 56 *Netherlands International Law Review* 429, 441–42. According to some, the statement in the *Wall* case on the *erga omnes* character of the obligations imposed by self-determination is an example of a judicial statement that has the benefit to add more weight to comments made by commentators such as the Special Rapporteur Gros Espiell, who had also argued that self-determination as an *erga omnes* character. See Coleman (n 213) 236.

two components now seem almost impossible to dissect without substantially altering the meaning of the right.

Finally, the continuous character of the right was also spelled out. In the colonial context, it has been questioned whether self-determination had any meaning after the act of 'determination' was made (i.e. notably the choice for independence).[225] On the other hand, for already-independent states we have seen that the right assumes an ongoing character, as it provides a continuous entitlement to 'freely determine' their status and 'freely pursue' their development. If it seems reasonable that a 'determination' can be made through a single one-off act; the idea of pursuing one's development, instead, hints to a gradual process, one with an ongoing character because it is attached to an entitlement that is continuous in time. This is explained well by Rapporteur Gros Espiell, who states that:

> The implementation of the right of peoples to self-determination involves not only the completion of the process of achieving independence or other appropriate legal status by the peoples under colonial and alien domination, but also the recognition of their right to maintain, assure and perfect their full legal, political, economic, social and cultural sovereignty. The right of peoples to self-determination has lasting force, does not lapse upon first having been exercised to secure political self-determination and extends to all fields, including of course economic, social and cultural affairs.[226]

Hence, self-determination is not exhausted once a determination is made about a people's political status at the international level. Independent peoples are indeed one of the selves legitimately entitled to self-determination and, for them, it is a permanent right to maintain and defend their independent status.[227] What was found here is not an isolated view, but rather a common understanding amongst scholars. Others indeed notice how 'self-determination is not a single choice to be made in a single day. It is the right of a group to adapt their political position in a complicated world to reflect changing capabilities and changing opportunities'.[228] The same position was maintained by ICJ Judge Yusuf in his separate opinion on the *Kosovo case*, where he wrote that self-determination, in its post-colonial conception, 'is a right which is exercisable continuously, particularly within the framework of a relationship between peoples and their own state'.[229] Finally, Professor Cassese is also clearly supportive of this interpretation. In his

225 See, for instance, Crawford, 'The General Assembly, the ICJ, and self-determination' (n 88) 598–99; Pomerance, *Self-determination in Law and Practice* (n 20) 74–75; Sinha, 'Is Self-determination *Passé*?' (n 5).

226 Gros Espiell (n 105) 8.

227 ibid paras 114–15.

228 Roger Fischer, 'The Participation of Microstates in International Affairs' (1968) 1968 *Proceedings of the American Society of International Law* 164, at 166.

229 *Kosovo Case* (n 213) separate opinion, of Judge Yusuf, para 8.

detailed analysis of the *travaux préparatoires* of the Human Rights Covenants, he finds that:

> The right to self-determination provided for in the Covenant is a continuing right. The language of Article 1 and the attendant preparatory work compel such a conclusion. Although the draft of Article 1 proclaimed 'all peoples *shall have* the right to self-determination', the final text reads 'all people *have* the right to self-determination'. This change was intended to 'emphasize the fact that the right referred to is a permanent one'.[230]

To conclude, so far I have outlined the contours and content of a norm that is known for its proverbial indeterminacy. Contrary to what one might have expected, it was found that if one focuses on a specific layer of this norm its indeterminacy is not so pervasive and an interpretation of the right's content can be advanced in a fairly confident manner. Now that the core meaning and content of the right have been set out, in order to offer a more complete picture further analysis will be directed to study the character of this norm.

3.4 Conclusions

This chapter has provided a detailed analysis of the meaning and content of one specific layer of self-determination: namely the right as it applies to the people of independent states. It has studied its origins as a legal concept and its use in the UN Charter and more widely in treaty and customary international law. Through a detailed analysis of the development of international law on self-determination, an interpretation of the scope and content of this layer was provided. It was found that for self-determination as it applies to the people of a state a core legal meaning can be traced out and that is neither so indeterminate nor as controversial as other aspects of the norm are generally understood to be. Further, it was shown that this norm has an essentially twofold content which gives the people a right to choose its form of government and to determine its economic, social and cultural development and to do so free from external interference. The next chapter is dedicated to study the character of this norm and sets out to provide an original interpretation that revisits existing conceptualisations of self-determination set out in the literature.

230 Comment made by the Chairman of the Working Party of the Third Committee when presenting the draft of the Third Committee (UN Doc A/C.3/SR.668, para 3), cited in Cassese, *Self-determination of Peoples* (n 20) 54.

4 The right to self-determination for the people of an independent state: an interpretation

4.1 Introduction

Chapter 3 provided an in-depth, first-hand analysis of the meaning and content of one specific dimension of self-determination, namely the right as it attaches to the people of independent states. In so doing, it outlined a core legal meaning attributed to self-determination that can be traced in the law and literature alike. The present chapter builds on these findings and sets out an interpretation of the character of self-determination that is to be conceptualised into a complex and multi-faceted norm of international law. Taken together, the two chapters provide the first systemic account of this specific dimension of self-determination.

This chapter is divided in three parts. Section 4.2, which includes the core of the analysis, submits that the layer of self-determination under examination possesses specific traits which make it unique and unfit to being understood on the basis of other, more classical, interpretations of self-determination, namely, the division into external and internal self-determination is revisited and an alternative way of thinking about the sub-norm in question is proposed. Section 4.3 suggests a context and direction for future research on self-determination to shed light on the way this norm works in practice. The chapter thus concludes by pointing to state-building as a specific context to which we should turn if we aim to observe how this specific layer of self-determination is used in state practice and to establish its significance in contemporary international law.

4.2 The character of the norm

This section will examine the character of self-determination as a legal norm. More specifically, we will start by looking at whether self-determination, for the self in question, holds the character of a principle or of a right. We will then move on to assess the validity of the interpretation commonly offered of self-determination, according to which the right can be divided into internal and external counterparts and will discuss the appropriateness of this division to study the self in question. Finally, we will focus on the power of self-determination to impose obligations and we will establish what obligations it imposes and on whom. We shall now discuss these three issues in turn.

4.2.1 Self-determination as a principle and a right

Amongst international law scholars there has long been a debate on the character of self-determination, with differing views on whether it shall be considered a principle or a right under international law.[1] Principles differ from rules in that they are more general and constitute overarching standards that must be interpreted and used for guidance when decisions are made. Rules, instead, are more precise and give rise to claims for their exercise. A rule also has clearer features than a principle because it defines subjects, matters to which it applies as well as means and methods of implementation. This is explained clearly by Dworkin, who argues that:

> the difference between legal principles and legal rules is a logical distinction. Both sets of standards point to particular decisions about legal obligation in particular circumstances, but they differ in the character of the direction they give. Rules are applicable in an all-or-nothing fashion. If the facts a rule stipulates are given, then either the rule is valid, in which case the answer it supplies must be accepted, or it is not, in which case it contributes nothing to the decision. . . . All that is meant, when we say that a particular principle is a principle of our law, is that the principle is one which officials must take into account, if it is relevant, as a consideration inclining in one direction or another.[2]

In relation to self-determination, deciding whether it should be considered as a principle of international law or as a set of one or more specific rules is therefore important. In the first case, self-determination would be seen as a normative standard, one holding great potential for normative development and from which several specific rules can be deduced – to be extracted according to the context and situation in which self-determination is called to apply. The positive aspects of this perspective are that, as a principle, self-determination would enjoy significant flexibility and would be highly adaptable in the way it is applied. Among the negative aspects, instead, one can list the fact that its application may lead to contrasting and even contradictory interpretations.[3] Conversely, if one sees self-determination as constituted by a set of rules of international law, this approach would leave less space to indeterminacy as it would identify certain selves that, under certain circumstances, can benefit from certain rights; it would also be possible to identify certain subjects on which certain obligations are imposed if the above rights are to be given effect.[4] To put it in Knop's words,

1 For a discussion of this matter see Karen Knop, *Diversity and Self-Determination in International Law* (CUP 2002) 29–49.
2 Ronald Dworkin, *Taking Rights Seriously* (Bloomsbury 2013) 40–42.
3 Antonio Cassese, *Self-determination of Peoples: A Legal Reappraisal* (CUP 1995) 128–29.
4 Examining Crawford's work, Knop also finds that a key difference between the principle and the right to self-determination is not in relation to content, it is about the determinacy of the subject – namely the definition of the people. Knop (n 1) 34.

'logically, rules may elaborate, but not replace, principles; just as principles may summarize, but not replace, a body of rules'.[5]

Debate on this matter is ongoing and whilst it is difficult to find voices who argue that self-determination outside of the colonial context is a right, we can distinguish at least two main positions. On one side, we have those more inclined to see self-determination, in its post-colonial formulation, as a principle rather than a right.[6] For instance, UN Rapporteur Critescu thinks that 'as a general rule of international law the principle of equal rights and self-determination plays an important part in international law as a whole; it generates the specific rules and institutions necessary for its application'.[7] The flexibility of the principle is valued positively as self-determination would thus be more capable of adapting to the international order and develop its full potential.[8] On the other side, we have those who argue that self-determination can be both a principle and a right, and that the two can exist in parallel or at the same time. An example of this position is contained in the writing of the other UN Rapporteur, Gros Espiell, who states that 'in international law self-determination other than being a principle is also a right of peoples under colonial and alien domination'.[9] The same view is shared also by Crawford, who compliments Cassese for taking the same stance;[10] and by Raic, who sees self-determination as composed of a complex *set* of legal norms and rules, rather than one specific and all-embracing legal norm or rule.[11]

5 ibid 45.

6 'The concept of self-determination is related to freedoms "a people" can have; it is about giving peoples the freedom to determine their lives and destinies. In this way, it incorporates political, economic, cultural and social claims of all kinds. Yet, this generic understanding is better left to the *principle* rather than the *right*.' See Alexandra Xanthaki, *Indigenous Rights and United Nations Standards: Self-Determination, Culture and Land* (CUP 2007) 30. Also, in a study of ICJ jurisprudence, Klabbers argues that the Court has turned self-determination from a substantive and enforceable right into a more open-ended principle. See Jan Klabbers, 'The Right to be Taken Seriously: Self-Determination in International Law' (2006) 28 *Human Rights Quarterly* 186.

7 Aureliu Critescu, *The Right to Self-Determination: Historical and Current Development on the Basis of United Nations Instruments* UN Doc E/CN.4/Sub.2/404/Rev.1 (1981) para 136.

8 Daniel Thürer and Thomas Burri, 'Self-determination' (2010) *Max Planck Encyclopedia of Public International Law* para 26 http://opil.ouplaw.com/home/epil (last accessed 15 April 2018).

9 Hector Gros Espiell, *The Right to Self-determination: Implementation of United Nations Resolutions*, UN Doc E/CN.4/Sub.2/405/Rev.1 para 52.

10 In reviewing Cassese's monograph on self-determination, Crawford writes: 'One of the difficulties with the literature on self-determination is its tendency to search for a single, self-sufficient norm and to lament when, inevitably, it cannot be found. It is as if one were to assume that the law relating to the use of force in international relations could be expressed in terms of a single norm. Cassese does not make this mistake. He sees self-determination as consisting both of general principle and of particular rules'. James Crawford, 'Book Review of Antonio Cassese, *Self-determination of Peoples*: A Legal Reappraisal' (1996) 90 *American Journal of International Law* 331, 332.

11 David Raic, *Statehood and the Law on Self-Determination* (The Hague 2002) 224.

Drawing from this second view, I argue that self-determination, for the people of a state, can be understood to be both a principle and a right. It can be taken to be a right in terms of the strength and detailed nature of its provisions in relation to the self analyzed. We have indeed seen above that the norm gives this self specific entitlements to a people in the form of both freedoms and participative rights. It is also relatively specific in what the substance of the right includes (to choose a form of government; to choose its economic system and pursue its economic policies) and in relation to the obligations that it imposes on third party states (not to interfere in these choices; to assist a people in realising these choices).[12]

However, it is also a principle because it can be used as a normative and interpretative tool to adapt to new situations where self-determination is called upon to apply and further to define the way it should apply. For instance, the essence of the principle can be used to regulate the relationship between the various actors involved in the implementation of the right to self-determination, and could be used to interpret the way conflicting obligations can and should be balanced. In this sense, one could refer to both a principle of self-determination as well as a right of self-determination, because the norm includes a number of rights and obligations attached to a variety of selves: states, peoples, third party states or institutions that can adapt to different contexts. As Summers put it, to argue that self-determination was transformed from a principle into a right is to ignore a more fluid reality.[13] The normative character of the layer of self-determination examined here can thus be defined as to have a hybrid nature, that alone can encompass the complexities of a norm possessing both the distinctive traits generally attributed to a right and the traits proper of a principle.

4.2.2 Self-determination revisited: an indivisible norm

As discussed in Chapter 3, the development of self-determination in international law has been strongly influenced by its association with decolonisation, to the point that this connection has almost hijacked the future of the norm outside that specific context. As a means to uproot the principle from its anti-colonial past, and as a way to mitigate both the risk for the right to fall into desuetude and the potentially disruptive effects of applying a right to self-determination beyond the colonial context, legal scholarship has supported the establishment of a distinction between 'external' and 'internal' aspects of self-determination.[14] According to this distinction, external self-determination broadly refers to the right of a people to choose its international status (including the right to claim

12 This will be explored further below in section 4.2.4.

13 James Summers, *Peoples and International Law: How the Right of Self-Determination and Nationalism Shape a Contemporary Law of Nations* (2nd edn, Brill Nijhoff 2014) 75.

14 A similar point was made also by Jean-Francois Gareau, 'Shouting at the Wall: Self-determination and the Legal Consequences of the Construction of a Wall in the Occupied Palestinian Territory' (2005) 18 *Leiden Journal of International Law* 489, 492–93.

independence); whilst internal self-determination refers to the right of a people to decide its form of government at the state-level.[15] To put it differently, external self-determination is understood to regulate the relationship between the people of a state and other actors at the international level; whilst internal self-determination regulates the relationship between the people and the state itself.[16] The same remarks were made also by the Committee on the Elimination of Racial Discrimination, in its General Comment 21, where it stated that:

> In respect of the self-determination of peoples two aspects have to be distinguished. The right to self-determination of peoples has an internal aspect, that is to say, the rights of all peoples to pursue freely their economic, social and cultural development without outside interference. . . .The external aspect of self-determination implies that all peoples have the right to determine freely their political status and their place in the international community based upon the principle of equal rights and exemplified by the liberation of peoples from colonialism and by the prohibition to subject peoples to alien subjugation, domination and exploitation.[17]

Today, virtually all studies on self-determination purport to deal with either the internal or the external dimension of the right of self-determination. In fact, this binary conceptualisation is so pervasive that it constitutes the first methodological stance that one comes across in any study on self-determination that one may approach. The aim of this section is to show that this distinction can be inappropriate to talk about the self-determination entitlements of the people of independent states. To do this, I will challenge the usefulness of this dual interpretation by explaining why it is not suitable to being applied to the right in relation to this specific self.

To begin with, it is worth noting that despite its undeniable popularity in the literature, the internal/external division is nowhere to be found in the actual sources of the law of self-determination.[18] The distinction seems to have been suggested for the first time by the Netherlands – later joined by Denmark and Australia – in the General Assembly in 1952, during the discussion which led

15 See Michla Pomerance, *Self-determination in Law and Practice: The New Doctrine in the United Nations* (Martinus Nijhoff 1982) 37.

16 This description was suggested also by Thornberry. Spijkers also phrases the distinction as self-determination as applied to the relationship between peoples and their 'own' rulers (internal self-determination) and the relationship between peoples and oppressive forces 'from outside' (external self-determination). See Otto Spijkers, *The United Nations, the Evolution of Global Values and International Law* (Intersentia 2011) 389 and Patrick Thornberry, 'The Democratic or Internal Aspect of Self-determination with Some Remarks on Federalism' in Christian Tomuschat (ed), *Modern Law of Self-Determination* (Martinus Nijhoff 1993) 101.

17 General Recommendation XXI (48) UN Doc CERD/C/365/Rev.1 (2000) 16, para 4.

18 The exception is the wording used in the Helsinki Final Act, which is however a non-binding instrument. See ch 3.3.3.1.

to the adoption of the draft Human Rights Covenants.[19] At the time it did not, however, make it into the text of Article 1 because it was seen by the proponents of self-determination as a means to water down its provisions and essentially viewed as an attempt at 'hair splitting'.[20] In the literature, the division appears to have been first proposed by Wengler in 1957,[21] but it is more commonly known for having been introduced in English literature by Cassese in 1979.[22] Since then, the dual structure has become the dominant paradigm for interpreting self-determination, to the point that it has literally informed the whole academic discussion on the matter.[23]

The cornerstone around which the distinction was created is the principle of territorial integrity. This is because international law generally employs a territorial definition of self-determination, so that any time that territorial integrity is at stake in self-determination claims, we speak of 'external self-determination'; whilst any time in which the territorial integrity of a certain unit is not at stake, we speak of 'internal self-determination'.[24] This interpretation was bred in the

19 The representative of the Netherlands argued that: 'The idea of self-determination was a complex of ideas rather than a single concept. Thus the principle of internal self-determination, or self-determination on the national level, should be distinguished from that of external self-determination, or self-determination on the international level. The former was the right of a nation, already constituted as a state, to choose its form of government and to determine the policy it meant to pursue. The latter was the right of a group which considered itself a nation to form a state of its own'. UN Doc A/C.3/SR.447 (1952) para 4. See also statements by representatives of Australia and Denmark in, respectively, UN Doc A/C.3/SR.669 (1955) para 22 and A/C.3/SR.644 (1955) para 6.

20 'The Greek delegation would therefore not take part in arguments on technicalities which had aptly been described as "hair splitting". For his part, he could not accept subtle distinctions drawn by some representatives between individual and collective human rights and between "internal" and "external" self-determination.' UN Doc A/C.3/SR.454 (1952) para 25. On this point see Summers (n 13) 342.

21 The attribution is made by Cassese, who cites W Wengler, 'Le droit à la libre disposition des peuples comme principe de droit international' (1957) 10 *Revue hellenique de droit international* 27. See Cassese (n 2) 70.

22 Antonio Cassese, 'Political Self-determination: Old Concepts and New Developments' in Antonio Cassese (ed), *UN Law and Fundamental Rights: Two Topics in International Law* (Sijthoff & Noordhoff 1979) 139.

23 The division between external and internal self-determination has inspired also the Supreme Court of Canada in its judgment *Re Secession of Quebec (1997)*, DLR 161 (1998) 4th Series para 126. The ideas of external and internal self-determination have also been cited by several states in their written statements to the ICJ in the *Accordance with International Law of the Unilateral Declaration of Independence in Respect of Kosovo* (Advisory Opinion) [2010] ICJ Rep 403. On this point see James Summers, 'The Concept of Internal and External Self-Determination Reconsidered' in Duncan French (ed), *Statehood and Self-Determination: Reconciling Tradition and Modernity in International Law* (CUP 2013) 231. A rare sceptical concern was raised by Maguire, who claims that this dichotomy is a colonial artificiality. See Amy Maguire, 'Law Protecting Rights: Restoring the Law of Self-determination in the Neo-colonial World' (2008) 12 *Law Text Culture* 12, 27.

24 For a similar definition see written statement of the Netherlands, 17 April 2009, *Kosovo Advisory Opinion* (n 23) para 3.5. For a conceptualisation of 'territorial self-determination'

colonial context – where self-determination meant first and foremost a right to secede from the parent state and to constitute an independent territorial unit – and it is precisely the view that the representative of the Netherlands had in mind when it suggested that the right could be split into two counterparts.[25]

According to this territorial logic, therefore, looking at the 'self' as the people of already independent states means looking at internal self-determination only.[26] This is because the exercise of this right does not involve any re-definition of international boundaries and no disputes over territory are at stake. However, this right does concern international boundaries: only it deals with them in relation to their maintenance, safeguard and defense. The argument advanced here is that this classification is unsuited to make sense of the layer of self-determination under examination. Indeed, the right to self-determination, as defined in this study encompasses not only internal but both internal and external aspects of self-determination as it is generally understood.

In essence, the argument submitted here is that the appropriateness of the mainstream understanding of the internal/external divide can be challenged if one is to view the distinction not from the standpoint of territorial integrity, but from the perspective of the 'self' considered. In other words, if our point of reference is not the principle of territorial integrity but the self in question, the internal/external divide becomes a more nuanced and articulated concept, whose function is to regulate the relationships between the various actors involved in the realisation of self-determination rights. In this respect, Summers proposes a convincing analysis of the internal/external dichotomy and argues that this

---

see Jeremy Waldron, 'Two Conceptions of Self-determination' in Samantha Besson and John Tasioulas (eds), *The Philosophy of International Law* (OUP 2010).

25 In 1955 the representative of the Netherlands speaking to the GA Third Committee stated: 'The concept of self-determination was a complicated one, consisting as it did of several different ideas and being capable of different forms of application. Moreover, it comprises the two aspects of self-determination, the external and the internal, the latter being the right of a nation already constituted as a state to choose its own form of government and freely determine its own policies. That aspect was ignored by the most fervent adherents of self-determination'. UN Doc A/C.3/SR.642 (1955) para 25.

26 Only some attempt to make sense of how to reconcile the fact that internal self-determination shall include also the prohibition of external interference component of self-determination. For instance, Doehring argues that the right to internal self-determination, i.e. the right to decide freely on a form of government, includes also that 'any outside pressure designed to enforce the installation of a particular form of government or to enforce the maintenance of an existing form of government must be defined as an internationally prohibited intervention'. In more general terms, Rosas has elaborated a list of elements that are generally deemed to be contained in the legal concept of self-determination and attempted to divide which of these pertain to external and which to internal self-determination. He noticed, however, that there is no consensus on what is exactly to be regarded as pertaining to the internal and external dimensions, and that this confusion is not accidental, as the two cannot be sharply distinguished. See Karl Doehring, 'Self-determination' in Bruno Simma and others (eds), *The Charter of the United Nations: A Commentary*, *Vol II* (2nd edn, OUP 2002) 56 and Allan Rosas, 'Internal Self-Determination' in Christian Tomuschat (ed), *Modern Law of Self-Determination* (Martinus Nijhoff 1993) 225, 231.

division does not make sense in absolute terms, but rather it relates to emphasis and perspective.[27] For Summers, what constitutes an external and internal aspect of self-determination cannot be pre-determined but depends on the perspective of the particular unit, or self, that is entitled to this right. Moreover, these perspectives can also apply simultaneously across various elements of a self-determination process, so that there cannot be a single understanding of internal and external self-determination.[28] In particular, he submits that, with regard to the people of an independent state, the internal and external dimensions of self-determination retrace the internal and external aspects of state sovereignty.[29]

Seeing division in these terms, it appears that the internal/external division is about defining what kind of relationships are defined by self-determination. The proposition that the people of a state hold only a right to 'internal' self-determination seems therefore inappropriate and, to some extent, deviant for the purposes of clarifying our understanding of this layer of the right. The people of an independent state do indeed hold a right to self-determination, which includes a number of entitlements pertaining to both dimensions of self-determination. Articulating the concept along the internal/external divide is helpful because it provides a detailed interpretation of the rights and obligations contained in this norm. Moreover, the division can also be helpful to explain how the principle, as it applies to the people of independent states, should be conceptualised. Nonetheless, I submit that it is methodologically inappropriate to first divide the right into two counterparts and then assign one to the self in question.

Up until now, scholars have first divided the right and then claimed that only one-half of it, namely internal self-determination, applied to the people of independent states. This method has had the effect of playing down some aspects of self-determination which do not fully fit within this division. For instance, by accepting that independent people have a right to 'internal' self-determination, one is already conceptualising self-determination as a principle that regulates the relationship between a state and its people, rather than an instrument to protect the people against the interference of third party states. Overall, by arbitrarily dividing the right and claiming that only one dimension of it applies to the people of independent states, the result is that the self-determination claim of the people of independent states may be weakened.[30]

27 Summers, 'The Concept of Internal and External Self-Determination Reconsidered' (n 23).
28 ibid 247.
29 ibid 234. He also notices how the idea of state and people being made to coincide 'was particularly strong in the drafting of the Helsinki Final Act, where there was a focus on the independence of Easter European countries from the Soviet Union.
30 This approach is expressed very clearly by Dam-de Jong who writes that 'once a people has organised itself within an autonomous State, whether through secession, integration or association, it may be argued that the right to external self-determination including economic self-determination, is mainly assimilated into the principle of state sovereignty and the related principles of territorial integrity and non-intervention, which must be respected by other States. What remains is a right of peoples within the State to internal self-determination'. Daniella Dam-de Jong, *International Law and Governance of Natural Resources in Conflict and Post-Conflict Situations* (CUP 2015) 82.

For the people of independent states, the core content of the norm of self-determination, as we have seen throughout this chapter, is a combination of internal and external aspects of self-determination (as commonly defined in the literature, thus based on the principle of territorial integrity). In considering this right, neither the internal nor the external dimension can be downplayed without the content of the right being put at risk of being fundamentally modified. Once more, the content of this layer of self-determination has both internal and external aspects and it is unsuited to being identified with either solely the internal or the external dimension of self-determination as for its general understanding.

4.2.2.1 Articulating the indivisible: external and internal aspects of unitary self-determination

The unsuitability for binary division of the layer of self-determination suggested here can be explained by looking at the way in which the different aspects of the norm are connected and intrinsically intertwined. In this section, we will look at how the content of the norm is articulated along the internal/external divide, in order to understand what aspects of the right are set out to regulate the relationship between the people of a state and external actors (other states, peoples or actors at the international level) and what aspects regulate the relationship between the people of a state and the state itself. These are, respectively, the external and internal aspects of self-determination.

In the first place, it is important to notice that the division between internal and external self-determination, as it is generally understood in the literature, goes back to the two-fold interpretation of the content of the norm which we have traced above as pertaining to the Socialist and Western traditions.[31] The legacy of the development of self-determination, as a norm of international law, is such binary division of the norm as we know it today. However, this division has never been openly mentioned in the sources of the law, because at all stages in the making of international law on self-determination, international law makers have strived to unify the two tendencies.

As a result of a constant mediation exercise, under international law the right of self-determination gives the people of a state the right to choose their government, determine their status and pursue their development, free from external interference. The formula includes both internal and external self-determination entitlements, but it does not simply add together internal and external aspects: it has in fact strictly intertwined and intrinsically linked the two components. In other words, the external aspects of the right are not merely a substantial component to be added to a core 'internal' meaning of self-determination (or vice versa), but they are both necessary elements for the realisation of the core components of the right.

31 See ch 3 2.1.2.

My key argument is that the layer of self-determination studied here is particularly suited to study the internal/external interplay, what each dimension means and what it might include. At the same time, this layer of the norm is also utterly inappropriate for the division to be applied to it. Since this layer of self-determination includes both internal and external aspects, it is not possible to indicate one dimension (either external or internal) which fully explains the right. Making any choice in this sense would indeed arbitrarily diminish the right's content, or at least sideline the importance of some of its aspects. For this reason, the view generally accepted, according to which the right of self-determination, as it applies to the people of independent states, concerns only the internal dimension of self-determination is fundamentally problematic.[32] The right does in fact include also external aspects, which are irreducible as they underwrite, define and complete the meaning of the right itself.

This argument is exemplified by Figure 4.1 below, which attempts to explain this complex idea in a visual manner. According to the scheme provided, the right of self-determination for the people of an independent state can be separated into its external and internal components. Each component, in its turn, has a specific content which includes a number of substantial, procedural and immunity rights. The figure was filled in relation to the right of the people of a state to choose their political status (one of the aspects of the wider right of self-determination of the people of a state) but it can be valid also for the economic, social and cultural development components of self-determination. The scheme provides a conceptualisation of the binary division between external and internal self-determination and shows two things. First, that the right in question includes both external and internal components, which give rise to separate rights entitlements. Secondly, it shows that the two components can be sub-divided into more detailed right components, none of which can be collapsed into another, either because they mean different things, or because each component regulates the relationship between different actors.

As we can see, the self-determination component i.a regulates the relationship between the people of a state and various external actors – other states and international actors more generally, such as international organisations, coalitions of states, regional organisations, etc. This component is essentially an immunity right which attaches to the people of a state a right to non-interference in their choices concerning their political status. Component ii.a and ii.b, instead, regulate the relationship between a people and its government at the state level. Component ii.a sets out a procedural right to participate,[33] so that any time that a determination of the will of the people is made, the people has a right to participate.[34]

32 See amongst others, Doehring (n 26); Rosas (n 26); Tomuschat (n 16); Raic (n 11).

33 For an interpretation of self-determination as a procedural right to take part in decision-making see Klabbers (n 6).

34 This component has its origin in the claim that a right to democracy is included in the concept of self-determination, because participation is to be guaranteed as an individual right; in particular, the link is made between arts 1 and 25 of the ICCPR, recognising that every citizen has the right to take part in the conduct of public affairs.

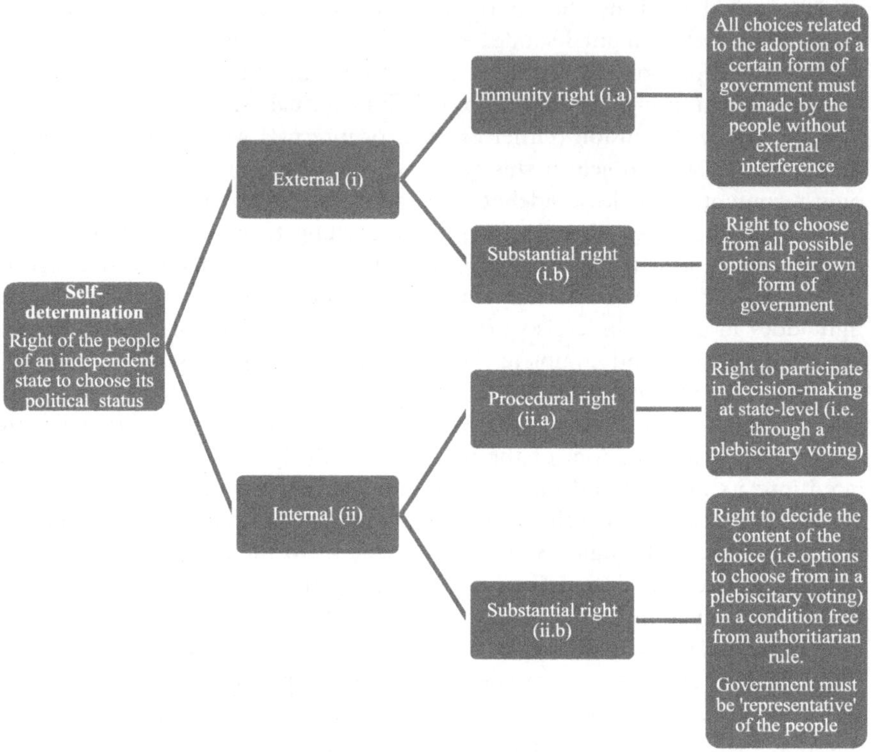

Figure 4.1 The binary division of self-determination

Component ii.b regulates the way in which the substantive determination of the will of the people is to be made. It includes, for instance, a right to choose the substance in a plebiscitary voting, which must be decided by the people freely from authoritarian rule;[35] and a right for the whole people to be represented at the state level (i.e. through certain constitutional arrangements), without distinction of any kind. Finally, component i.b is a right, which gives to the people of a state the right to choose its political status, both understood as maintaining their independence and as the right to decide about the system of government that the state shall assume.

35 This point was made also by Gareau, who argues that self-determination '[e]ntails that, by definition, 'peoples' possess the right to select the outcome of their choice, but it also means that they have the right to be provided a process through which the choice will be expressed'. ... On the other hand, control over the process employed to ascertain the will of the people can be, and often has been left in the hands of a third party and/or of the parent state'. Gareau (n 14) 495–96.

The scheme can also be used as a tool to understand what it means that independent states have a right to external self-determination. Independence, an entitlement so crucial and controversial in self-determination cases that are in conflict with territorial integrity, holds a less controversial meaning in the case of already-independent selves. It was already established above that self-determination does not cease with the achievement of independent statehood, but that in such circumstances it is transformed to be applied to a new, independent self. Retracing the figures reported in the table, we can see that for the people of an already independent state the entitlement to independence simply translates into a right of the people to remain politically independent (i.b) and to defend their independence from threats of external intervention (i.a). All in all, this amounts to the right of a people to maintain and defend the independence achieved.

4.2.3 Self-determination as a right: for whom to exercise?

Section 4.2.2 has shown that self-determination is a complex norm to which a number of rights are attached. The present section elaborates on the specificity of these rights, showing that although their content can sometimes overlap with other rights which already exist in international law, self-determination entitlements are unique because they are irreducible. In order to show this, let us start by an analysis of the significance and *raison d'être* for the right of self-determination in a state-based context.

As discussed above, there is a significant conceptual overlap between self-determination and other principles of international law. Several scholars have indeed highlighted how, for independent peoples, the right to self-determination is closely related to the principles of non-intervention, the equality of states, state sovereignty and sovereign equality.[36] Yet the nature of this link, and hence the exact nature of the relationship between self-determination and other principles, is debated. For instance, Crawford submits that self-determination is *represented* by non-intervention;[37] Raic believes that self-determination could *equate* in scope to non-intervention and sovereign equality;[38] Spijkers argues that non-intervention is a *continuation* of self-determination;[39] Summers thinks that self-determination is a *corollary* of non-intervention;[40] whilst Critescu sees sovereign equality to be a *corollary* of self-determination.[41] Here I take the view that the relationship between self-determination and other principles of

36 Cassese, *Self-determination of Peoples* (n 3) 45; Crawford, *The Creation of States in International Law* (2nd edn, OUP 2006) 128; Raic (n 11) 146 and 233; Rosas (n 26) 250; Summers, Peoples and International Law (n 13) 305 and 448–55.

37 Crawford, *The Creation of States in International Law* (n 36) 128.

38 Raic (n 11). 233.

39 Spijkers (n 16) 415.

40 Summers, Peoples and International Law (n 13) 305.

41 Crtitescu (n 7) para 163.

international law is not of simple overlap and that it can be defined in relation to two main issues. First, self-determination fundamentally differs from other principles of international law because it is a right of peoples. Secondly, it differs from other principles in view of both its scope and of its multi-faceted nature. Let us now explore these two points in turn.

The first key difference between self-determination and other principles of international law is in relation to the subject to which the right is attached. The beneficiaries (or right holders) of a people's right are peoples, not states. Many scholars have already stressed this point, starting with UN Rapporteur Critescu, who by examining the UN Charter provisions, states that 'the authors of the Charter conceived the principle of equal rights and self-determination of peoples as a single norm applicable to states, nations and peoples, for states in the international meaning of the word are obviously peoples'.[42] Raic distinguishes self-determination from all other principles and rights because the latter apply to states and this, he argues, is an important difference because 'it cannot be denied that the relevant instruments [of international law on self-determination] clearly refer to peoples as the holders of the right of self-determination and refer to states as the main addressees of this right'.[43]

In his thorough analysis of the Covenants, Cassese also acknowledges that:

> Article 1 common to the Covenants addresses itself directly to peoples, whatever the 'dimension' (internal or external) of the legal entitlement it provides for. Peoples are thus holders of international rights to which correspond obligations incumbent upon contracting states *vis-à-vis* both peoples and other contracting states.[44]

Even Higgins, who was initially more cautious arguing that in the UN Charter it was states – rather than people – who were subject to rights, recognises that, with decolonisation, the right of self-determination has then developed from a right of states to a right of peoples.[45] Spelling out this difference is significant because conceptualising self-determination as a people's right and not a state's right has important implications. If self-determination belonged to states, and could be exercised by their governments, it could become a pretence for governments to dispose of the peoples.[46] Cassese reminds us that

42 ibid para 260–66. See also James Crawford, 'The Rights of peoples: 'peoples' or 'governments'?' in James Crawford (ed), *The Rights of Peoples* (Clarendon Press 1988) 55–67 and Alexander Kiss, 'The people's right to self-determination' (1986) 7 *Human Rights Law Journal* 165, 170–71.

43 Raic (n 11) 233.

44 Cassese, *Self-determination of Peoples* (n 3) 144.

45 Rosalyn Higgins, *Problems and Process: International Law and How We Use It* (Clarendon Press 1994) 114.

46 Alexandra Xanthaki, 'The Right to Self-Determination: Meaning and Scope' in Nazila Ghanea and Alexandra Xanthaki (eds), *Minorities, Peoples and Self-determination* (Martinus Nijhoff 2004) 23.

this was indeed the view historically advanced by the Eastern bloc countries, that would view self-determination as a right held by the government of a state, and not by its people.[47]

As a people's right, self-determination is therefore different from other principles of international law that give rights to states. Self-determination indeed confers rights on peoples to exercise both against other states as well as through their own state and against their governments.[48] Interestingly, Crawford argues that self-determination, as a right attached to a people, to the extent that it applies 'it qualifies the right of governments to dispose of the peoples in question in ways that conflict with their rights of self-determination'.[49] Summers further elaborates on this point by providing a sharp insight on the dynamic relationship between the people and the state under self-determination provisions. He argues that for independent peoples there is an important role that the state and its institutions can play in the exercise of self-determination:

> [e]ither as medium for the right (through elections, participation in the legislature, government, etc.) or as a goal for the right (statehood). . . . If self-determination is understood as determining political status and social, economic and cultural development, state institutions provide an extensive framework for its exercise. This can be achieved through elections, participation in the legislature and government, as well as other institutions such as the civil service, legal system, army and police, as well as health and education.[50]

This way of explaining the relationship between the people and their state through the lenses of self-determination provides an important tool through which we can enhance our understanding of self-determination as a right. Indeed, it appears clear that this right, as a right attached to a people and which may be exercised through governmental functions and structures by the people themselves – it works differently from a right that is attached to a state and exercised by the state through its government.

The second key difference between self-determination and other principles of international law is in relation to the scope of their provisions. Surely it is easy to spot a striking similarity between self-determination and two principles in particular: non-intervention and sovereign equality. The ICJ, in the *Case Concerning Military and Paramilitary Activities in and against Nicaragua*,[51]

47 Cassese, *Self-determination of Peoples* (n 2) 103–104.
48 Crawford, 'The Rights of 'Peoples' (n 42) 56.
49 ibid 59.
50 Summers, 'The Concept of Internal and External Self-Determination Reconsidered' (n 23) 247–48.
51 *Military and Paramilitary Activities in and against Nicaragua (Nicaragua v. United States of America)*, Merits, Judgment [1986] ICJ Reports 101.

presented non-intervention as a corollary of the principle of the sovereign equality of States and defined a prohibited intervention as:

> [o]ne bearing on matters in which each state is permitted to decide freely. One of these is the choice of a political economic, social and cultural system and the formulation of foreign policy. Intervention is wrongful when it uses methods of coercion in regard to such choices, which must remain free ones.[52]

The same provision was used also in the Declaration on Principles of International Law Concerning Friendly Relations and Co-operation among States, which also adds that 'armed intervention and all other forms of interference or attempted threats against the personality of the State or against its political, economic or cultural elements, are in violation of international law'.[53] The Declaration seems to distinguish between outright intervention and lesser forms of interference, thus suggesting a wider prohibition that extends to non-military means of coercion.[54] In brief, these provisions confer to states the freedom to make independent choices about their political system and constitutional arrangements, which closely retraces the entitlement conferred on their people by self-determination. As noticed by Emerson, the principle thus makes clear that any effort on behalf of states or organisations to become involved in the affairs of other sovereign states in order to promote one or another decision would seem to be an evident violation of the prohibition of intervention.[55] On this point, Saul argues that adding the right to self-determination provides an ethical buttressing to the case for non-intervention, as it places the emphasis on the protection of the interests of the people rather than the state.[56]

The second striking similarity in relation to the scope of international law principles is between self-determination and sovereign equality. The latter, as a right of states, is known simply to mean independence, but under a different name.[57] At the time of its insertion in Article 2 of the UN Charter, the principle

52 ibid para 205. The freedom of states to choose their political, economic and cultural system was affirmed also by the *Declaration on the Inadmissibility of Intervention in the Domestic Affairs of States and the Protection of their Independence and Sovereignty*, GA Res 2131 (XX) of 21 December 1965, UN Doc A/RES/2131(XX). See Declaration on Principles of International Law Concerning Friendly Relations and Co-operation among States in Accordance with the Charter of the United Nations [the 1970 Declaration], GA Res 2625 (XVV) of 24 October 1970, UN Doc A/RES/25/2625.

53 1970 Declaration (n 52).

54 See also Maziar Jamnejad and Michael Wood, 'The Principle of Non-intervention' (2009) 22 *Leiden Journal of International Law* 345, 346 n 7.

55 Rupert Emerson, 'Self-determination' (1971) 65 *American Journal of International Law* 459, 466.

56 Matthew Saul, *Popular Governance of Post-Conflict Reconstruction: The Role of International Law* (CUP 2014) 70–71.

57 Juliane Kokott, 'States, Sovereign Equality' *Max Planck Encyclopedia of Public International Law* (August 2007) para 20 http://opil.ouplaw.com/home/epil (last accessed 15 April

was discussed by Sub-committee I/1/A and kept in the text on the assumption and understanding that it conveys the following:

(1) That states are juridically equal;
(2) That they enjoy the rights inherent in their full sovereignty;
(3) That the personality of the state is respected, as well as its territorial integrity and political independence.[58]

The principle was also listed amongst the seven fundamental principles of international law in the 1970 Declaration, where to the three points above was also added:

(4) The territorial integrity and political independence of the state are inviolable;
(5) Each state has the right to choose and develop its political, social, economic and cultural systems.[59]

Again, the overlap between the scope of self-determination rights and rights attached to the principle of sovereign equality is self-evident in each of these points, but particularly in point (5), concerning the freedom to choose a political system.

Hence, it is undisputable that self-determination overlaps, in terms of scope, with other fundamental principles of international law. However, the argument here is that this overlap is only partial and does not cover all aspects of self-determination. As we have seen above, the scope and content of self-determination as the right of the people of a state is more articulated than a right to non-interference or a right to choose and develop its political system. Self-determination includes both of these provisions at the same times, as well as a right to participation and representation on behalf of the people as a whole. All in all, it is the amalgam, the entirety of these entitlements that constitutes self-determination, and it is in this respect that the uniqueness of the right comes to play. Viewing self-determination in its complexity and as a whole, is essential to understand its uniqueness in international law.

Above we have seen that the way in which the content of self-determination at state-level can be articulated in relation to internal and external aspects – as was described above and exemplified by Figure 4.2 – can be of help to understand its significance and application. In addition, we can also look at the type of right(s) which constitute self-determination to better understand the way in which its uniqueness plays out its difference from state rights. In other

2018); B Fassbender and A Bleckmann, 'Article 2(1)' in Bruno Simma and others (eds), *The Charter of the United Nations: A Commentary, Vol II* (2nd edn, OUP 2002) 82.

58 Fassbender and Bleckmann (n 57) 77.

59 1970 Declaration (n 52).

words, as it applies to the people of a state, self-determination functions first of all as a collective, immunity right that the people can exercise externally against other states and actors at the international level. In so doing, the people's right of self-determination works similarly to a state's right to non-interference. At the same time, however, self-determination also functions as: (a) a collective, immunity right that the people of a state can exercise internally, against interference from an authoritative government; (b) a collective right to being represented in government at the state-level; (c) a collective right to take part in decision-making processes at the state-level;[60] (d) possibly, also an individual right to participation in decision-making processes.[61] It is apparent how in this second (internal) manifestation the people's right to self-determination works differently, and often against, state-centred rights. In relation to its content, some wondered whether internal self-determination means anything more than political participation or whether it has developed into something more definite than an expression of a state's constitutional provisions and human rights obligations.[62]

Concluding, the key difference between self-determination and other, related principles of international law is not as much in relation to the content of the right but more concerning the functioning and operation of the right. Essentially, the *raison d'être* for self-determination is that it differs from other existing provisions of international law because it complements them and adds something very specific: it gives to the people the right to exercise certain claims against their government, to participate in and, to some extent, also to shape state structures.

4.2.4 *Self-determination as a source of obligations*

So far we have discussed self-determination in relation to its character and for the power it has to attach rights to a certain self that is entitled to it. This section is dedicated to discuss self-determination in relation to the duties that it attracts. It was pointed out earlier that certain international law instruments dealing with self-determination contain obligations aimed at ensuring the realisation of the right.[63] What are these obligations and on whom are they imposed?

60 Klabbers (n 6) refers to this as 'a right to be taken seriously' and 'a right to be heard'.

61 Rapporteur Gros Espiell writes: 'To assert that self-determination constitutes a collective right of peoples does not mean that an individual right, to which all human beings are entitled, cannot exist at the same time. A right can be simultaneously and individual right and a collective right. The presumed incompatibility between the two types of rights is inadmissible. This conclusion, already recognised, for instance, with respect to the right to development, the right to form trade unions and the right to freedom of information, is perfectly applicable to the case of the right to self-determination'. Gros Espiell (n 9) para 57.

62 See, respectively, Rosas (n 26) 246 and Summers, 'The Concept of Internal and External Self-Determination Reconsidered' (n 23) 237–38.

63 See ch 3. 3.1 and 3.3.2.

A major role in defining the scope of self-determination and the duties that it attracts was played by the Human Rights Committee [the Committee]. The Committee has elaborated on this matter in its General Comment 12.[64] In this document the Committee first acknowledges that Article 1 of the Human Rights Covenants imposes obligations on all state parties concerning its implementation, and that these obligations 'are interrelated with other provisions of the Covenant and rules of international law'.[65] In relation to the substance of obligations, the Committee reminds states of their reporting obligations concerning Article 1, which must cover all aspects of the right and detailed description on how they meet their obligations in relation to every paragraph of the Article.[66] The Comment further states that this reporting obligation is particularly important, because:

> it imposes specific obligations on States parties, not only in relation to their own peoples but *vis-à-vis* all peoples which have not been able to exercise or have been deprived of the possibility of exercising their right to self-determination. ... The obligations exist irrespective of whether a people entitled to self-determination depends on a State party to the Covenant or not. It follows that all States parties to the Covenant should take positive action to facilitate realization of and respect for the right of peoples to self-determination. Such positive action must be consistent with the States' obligations under the Charter of the United Nations and under international law: in particular, States must refrain from interfering in the internal affairs of other States and thereby adversely affecting the exercise of the right to self-determination. The reports should contain information on the performance of these obligations and the measures taken to that end.[67]

In fact, the content of this paragraph is relevant in many respects. First, because it highlights the universal character of the obligations imposed by self-determination.[68] It was specified that the obligation to assist in the realisation of the right is imposed on states towards all people, and not only towards people under colonial situations.[69] The same point was raised also by Cassese, who

64 See Human Rights Committee, General Comment No 12, CCPR/C/21/Add.3 of 5 October 1984.

65 ibid para 2.

66 ibid para 3.

67 ibid para 6.

68 The same view is held also by Sahovic, who studied obligations which rise from the 1970 Friendly Declaration and writes: 'The efforts by some states to have a special listing of the duties of states responsible for administering non-self-governing and trust territories to assist peoples in these territories to exercise their right to self-determination did not succeed, because the majority wished to stress the universal character of this principle'. Milan Sahovic, *Principles of International Law Concerning Friendly Relations and Cooperation* (Belgrade Institute of International Politics and Economics 1972) 371.

69 This was set out by the Committee when it considered Azerbaijan's report See UN Doc CCPR/C/79/Add.38 of 3 August 1994, para 6. This approach may lead one to think that reporting obligations are not only intended for actions aimed at the realisation of

acknowledges that the obligations that rise from self-determination, particularly so under the Human Rights Covenants, are not bilateral but have an *erga omnes* character.[70] Secondly, the Committee's passage is important because it elaborates on the type of duties that come from self-determination entitlements. Namely, the right gives rise to both negative and positive obligations. It imposes negative obligations in that it calls states and other international actors not to interfere in a people's choices in relation to its political status, and economic, social and cultural development. As one author put it, when it comes to sovereign peoples 'no positive step is required, nor is any particular kind of government or social, economic, or cultural system called for or favored; all that is needed is that there not be external interference which impairs the ability of the state freely to make its own choices'.[71] However, self-determination imposes also a set of positive obligations, or steps that must be taken in order to respect, promote and assist in the realisation of the right. Rapporteur Gros Espiell allows that 'these duties must of course be interpreted, and their limits determined, in the light of the purposes and principles of the United Nations Charter and on the basis of systematic co-ordination of all the relevant instruments of the Organization'.[72] In so doing, he recognises that not only states but also international organisations, and the UN have an active role in the realisation of the right.

Indeed, self-determination can also act as a constitutional limitation for international organisations. For instance, according to the provisions of Article 1(2) of the UN Charter, the United Nations shall act in respect of self-determination in developing friendly relations amongst nations.[73] The same applies also to the African Union, whereby under Article 3(h) of its Constitutive Act it declares an objective of the organisation to promote people's rights in accordance with the African Charter of Human Rights, which includes amongst others the right to self-determination.[74]

---

self-determination of peoples within the jurisdiction of the state but widely, in relation to any effort that a state may exercise aimed at promoting the realisation of self-determination of people more generally.

70 Cassese, *Self-determination of Peoples* (n 3) 134. The *erga omnes* character of obligations imposed by self-determination was highlighted also by the ICJ in its East Timor judgment (para 29) and in the Advisory Opinion on the Construction of the Wall (para 156). Yet, in none of these cases the Court was referring to the right of the people of independent states, that is instead clearly included in the Covenants and thus undoubtedly contemplated by Cassese. See *East Timor (Portugal v. Australia) Judgment* [1995] ICJ Rep 90; *Legal Consequences of the Construction of a Wall in the Occupied Palestinian Territory* (Advisory Opinion) [2004] ICJ Rep 136.

71 He further states that the only exception, one single higher principle which may override the ban on intervention is the elimination of racial discrimination. See Emerson (n 55) 465–67.

72 Gros Espiell (n 9) para 91. In relation to positive obligations see also Robin A White, 'Self-Determination: Time for a Re-Assessment' (1981) 28 *Netherlands International Law Review* 147, 168.

73 On this point see discussion in ch 1.2.

74 See ch 3 3.3.2. Constitutive Act of the African Union, Doc CAB/LEG/23.15, adopted 11 July 2000.

In sum, it is clear that self-determination is a right which gives rise to a number of obligations in international law. These obligations are imposed not only on the state under whose jurisdiction lives the people who aims to exercise its right to self-determination. Under Article 1 of the Human Rights Covenants and under the provisions of the 1970 Declaration it is advanced that these obligations are universal and can even be said to have an *erga omnes* character.

In relation to the people of an independent state, self-determination surely imposes a negative obligation on all states not to interfere with the exercise of this right – meaning non-interference with the choices that a people is entitled to made in relation to choosing its political status and the development of its economic, social and cultural systems. At the same time states have a positive obligation to respect, promote and assist peoples in the realisation of this right. In relation to decolonisation, the framework for the realisation of the right in Trust Territories and consequent obligations of administering states were spelled in some detail.[75] In relation to the people of independent states, instead, there is no clear picture of what are these positive obligations, of how they work, in what circumstances they may apply and, most importantly, of what is their relationship with the negative obligations brought in by the external aspects of self-determination.

4.2.5 Self-determination as a hybrid indivisible norm

The interpretation of self-determination provided here has set forward the contours of a right that, applied to the people of an independent state, has a number of peculiar features. First, self-determination was defined as a norm which contains some specific rules for its application (more typical of a right) together with the normative and interpretative strength of a principle, always capable to adapt to new situations and contexts. Secondly, self-determination applied to sovereign selves was described as a compact, indivisible right that is unsuited to be classified as pertaining to either the internal or external dimension of a territorially-defined concept of self-determination. Instead, the right as considered here can be seen as a hybrid norm, because it contains elements of both dimensions of self-determination (as classically divided). However, these elements are so intertwined in the meaning and scope of this particular layer of the right that their separation would be impossible without the scope and content of the right being compromised. Thirdly, it was spelled out that self-determination is a right of peoples and not of states, and in so being it gives rights to peoples and imposes obligations on governments and not vice versa. It also regulates the relationship between peoples and their states, as well as

75 See GA Resolution 1541 (XV) of 15 December 1960, UN Doc A/RES/1541(XV); Articles 73 and 74 (Chapter XI) of the UN Charter and *Legal Consequences for States of the Continued Presence of South Africa in Namibia (South West Africa) notwithstanding Security Council Resolution 276 (1970)*, (Advisory Opinion) [1971] ICJ Rep 16.

peoples and other states and international actors. Finally, it was shown how self-determination imposes both negative and positive obligations on states and international organisations to assist in the realisation of the right.

Figure 4.2 visually outlines the complexity inherent to the right to self-determination as it was studied here. It shows that the right consists not of a straightforward, univocal provision but, rather, that it is constituted of a bundle of rights and obligations that attach to a number of players. The figure can be also used to show the way in which the various components of self-determination (rights,

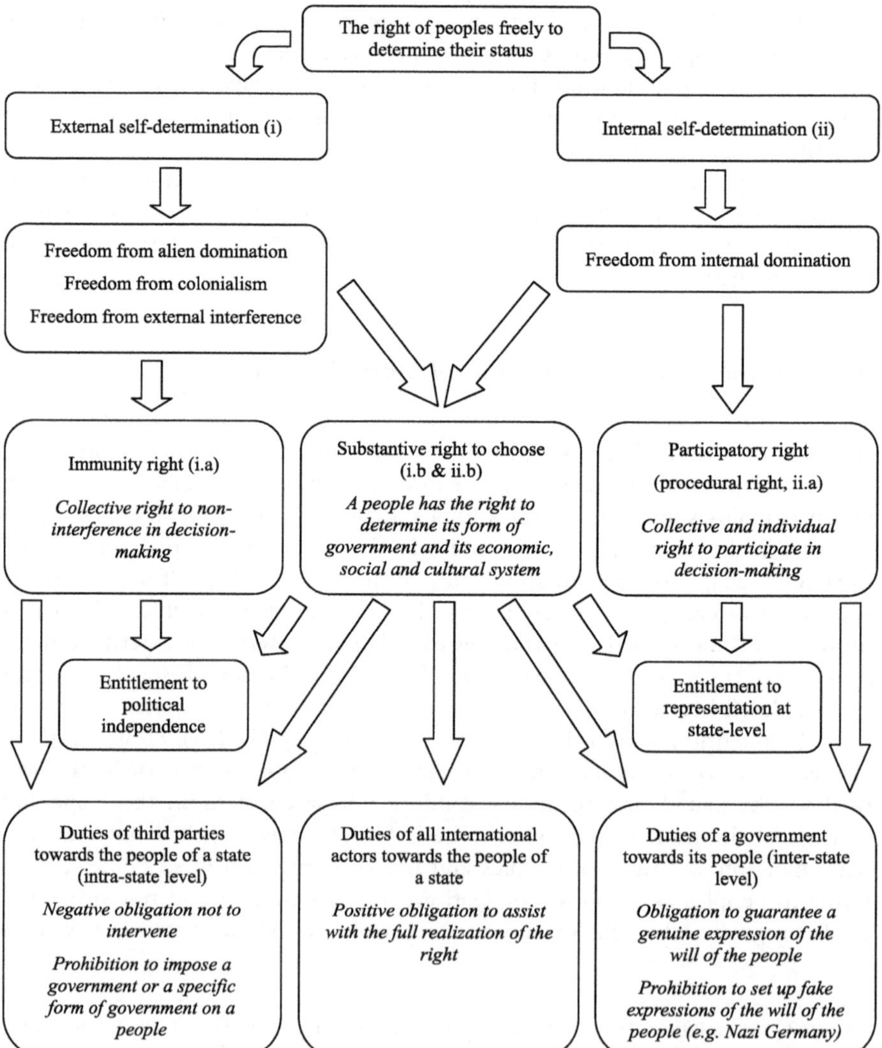

Figure 4.2 The multi-dimensional complexity of the right of self-determination

entitlements, obligations) can be disposed, or allocated, in relation to the division into internal and external aspects. This is meant to show that the right, as it applies to sovereign selves, is unsuited for being classified as pertaining to either internal or external self-determination (as classically divided in function of the implications for territorial integrity linked to the exercise of the right).

Conversely, the figure shows that the allocation of the right's component is disposed in a fluid manner across the internal/external divide and so that this division should be seen as more fluid, or as a spectrum, along which the various component of the right can be placed. The figure is also meant to show that each sub-principle/right included in this layer of self-determination is specific and irreducible. By this I mean that each of its components is unique and cannot be collapsed into another. It is the sum of these components that characterises a 'full' expression of the right and, all in all, it is only the full mosaic of these components that may guarantee complete respect for the right of self-determination applied to sovereign selves.

4.3 Self-determination in use: a study of state-building practice

This chapter has questioned what it means that self-determination gives a people the right freely to decide about their political status and to determine their economic, social and cultural development. In so doing, the chapter has provided an in-depth overview of the law concerning a precisely defined layer of self-determination. The picture provided here is about the law 'as we know it' from a study of treaties, customary international law, opinions of international courts and scholarly interpretations. One issue concerning self-determination, however, is that the development of this norm happens in context, because it is attached to a number of different selves. The next step, therefore, will be to identify a context where this layer of self-determination is applied, in order to see whether contemporary practice reflects this interpretation of the law.

In order to answer this question, the remaining part of this book will look at how the principle of self-determination, attached to the people of independent states, applies in the context of state-building. As we have seen in Chapters 1 and 2, state-building, and the consequent dynamics through which political reconstruction is directed in collapsed, failed and disintegrated states constitute an ideal setting for international lawyers to observe how the principle is used and what is its significance in the post-colonial world. They provide an important chance for international law scholars to ascertain the importance of this fundamental principle and to observe its functioning as it applies to the people of an independent state.

The nature of state-building brings in self-determination concerns for two main reasons. First, because state-building implies an exercise of power-allocation at the national level in states that are being rebuilt. These exercises often include a radical re-structuring of the state, of its political, constitutional and economic structures. In the aftermath of conflict, states undergo a phase of deep political restructuring and change which seriously affects the ways in which power is administered at the national level. In this context, the significance and role of self-determination – both as an organising principle for international relations[76] and as a source of rights and obligations – is clearly called into question in situations when the future of a people is at stake.[77] Secondly, the process of state re-structuring can see an involvement of external actors. What further characterises state-building against ordinary political transitions is indeed the close (and sometimes heavy) involvement of external actors in the process of reorganisation of power.[78] State-building processes are often orchestrated at the international level and offer a variety of roles and levels of engagement to external actors (international organisations; NGOs; coalitions of states; contact groups; single states) involved with the engineering and re-modelling of states in transition.

It seems imperative, therefore, to investigate what role the legal principle of self-determination plays in regulating state-building processes. In normal circumstances, the people of an independent state would be entitled to a right to non-interference in their choices concerning the state structures in accordance with the provisions of Article 2(7) of the UN Charter. This entitlement, which retraces the external aspect of their right to self-determination, is normally exercised by governments rather than by its people. This is explained very well by Doehring, who argues that in relation to already independent people:

> [t]he right to decide freely in a form of government, does not present any particular problems. Any outside pressure designed to enforce the installation of a particular form of government or to enforce the maintenance of an existing form of government must be defined as an internationally prohibited intervention. Only if international obligations to install or to preserve a particular form of government have been established, perhaps through a treaty, could such intervention be lawful.[79]

This is not the case for state-building. Here, the distinction between self-determination and non-interference is vital and the distinction made above between the right-bearer of the two rights gains an unprecedented importance.

76 For Koskenniemi self-determination is a legal-constitutional principle which 'aims to offer a principal (if not the only) basis on which political entities can be constituted, and among which international relations can again be conducted normally'. Martti Koskenniemi, 'National Self-Determination Today: Problems of Legal Theory and Practice' (1994) 43 *International and Comparative Human Rights Quarterly* 241, 246.

77 *Aaland Islands Case* (1920) League of Nations Official Journal Spec Supp 3 (1920) 3; 'The Aaland Islands Question' (1921) 1 *League of Nations Official Journal* 691 and Nathaniel Berman, 'Sovereignty in Abeyance: Self-determination and International Law' (1988) 7 *Wisconsin International Law Journal* 51.

78 On this issue see generally Simon Chesterman, *You The People: The United Nations, Transitional Administration and State-Building* (OUP 2002); David Chandler, *Empire in Denial: The Politics of State-building* (Pluto 2006).

79 Doehring (n 26) 56.

Weak, failed, collapsed states undergoing reconstruction with a heavy degree of international assistance in most cases are deemed to constitute a threat to international peace and security under Article 39 of the UN Charter. As such, their rights under international law, as provided by the UN Charter, can be reduced.[80] External interference in their international affairs may indeed be justified in order to maintain peace and security and, as shown in Chapter 1, various forms of intervention are not only allowed under international law but sometimes also welcomed and encouraged by the international community.

In these circumstances, what happens to the rights held by the people of these states? Does the principle of self-determination provide their people with a shield from external interference in matters related to the decisions to be made on the reconstruction of state structures? And if so, to what extent and in what circumstances? The character and normative status of self-determination as the right of a people of independent states has not yet been sufficiently explored in the literature for an answer to be given. This is because the right was always made to coincide with non-intervention and, for this reason, in standard circumstances it would not have been possible to observe how it can function independently from the state-right with which it overlaps. For instance, some had even argued that the guarantees contained in Article 1 of the Covenants, in so far as they refer to independent states, are superfluous, because any restriction on freedoms to determine by third states must be seen as an unlawful intervention, so that 'the invocation of the right of self-determination in this context is meaningless'.[81]

Today, after 25 years of state-building practice at UN level, time has come to discuss the role, significance and normative status of this layer of self-determination by looking at the practice of international law and not only at the theory. For these purposes, state-building should be viewed as a laboratory of practice where the right plays out, and as a privileged observation point to see how the principle is being interpreted, or whether it is being ignored, violated, or (re)defined. It is not unusual for legal concepts over time to alter their meaning or emphasis as new circumstances arise. Whether this has happened to the principle of self-determination in the post-colonial era is something that might be revealed by a close study of state-building practice.

4.4 Conclusions

This chapter has provided an interpretation of the scope and content of self-determination as it applies to the people of independent states, along with an interpretation of the norm's character. It was established that the norm is not merely a principle or a right, but it is a complex norm constituted by a bundle of rights and obligations. Whilst the rights are attached to the people, and to the people only; the obligations imposed by self-determination are distributed

80 According to art 2(7) and Chapter VII of the UN Charter.
81 Doehring (n 26) 54.

to several actors – i.e. the territorial state, other states and peoples, international actors. Moreover, the chapter has also argued that the 'classic' distinction between internal and external self-determination, based on the potential conflict between self-determination and territorial integrity, sits uneasy with the layer of self-determination studied here. In fact, this distinction is helpful because it helps to articulate the meaning and content of this layer of self-determination, but it is unsuitable to divide the right along the internal/external line.

For independent peoples, self-determination is a hybrid, indivisible norm which encompasses both internal and external aspects (as generally understood) in the framework of a single norm that recalls the contours of a state's right to sovereign equality and the principle of non-intervention. Nonetheless, it was also shown that with self-determination the attachment to a people, and not to governments, makes this norm unique, irreducible and profoundly different from all other rights and principles of international law.

The next chapter studies the way in which self-determination is used in practice in order to test the applicability of this normative framework. It looks at whether state practice reflects the interpretation of self-determination provided here and, in so doing, it aims to assess whether practice expands, further details or maybe contradicts the interpretation of international law on self-determination that was offered here.

5 State-building in Somalia 2000–2012: what role for self-determination?

5.1 Introduction

In the previous chapters we looked at the meaning, nature and scope of self-determination as a principle of international law. It was established that, for the people of independent states, self-determination has a complex, multi-faceted content which includes a right for the people to choose its form of government and to pursue its economic, social and cultural development free from external interference. Furthermore, it was demonstrated that the importance of self-determination, in international law, is to be attached to right being a right of peoples – meaning that it gives rights to the people of a state and imposes obligations on their governments, on other states and on international actors alike.[1]

In the present chapter I set out to study the application of this model of self-determination through a study of practice. To do this, I will engage in an in-depth analysis of state-building efforts conducted in Somalia from 2000 until 2012. I analyse and interpret Security Council resolutions, peace agreements, regional organisations' communiqué(s) and states' official records where self-determination issues are directly or indirectly addressed. The aim of this enquiry is to determine what role, if any, self-determination standards have played in situations where the right of the Somali people freely to determine their political status was at stake. Chapter 2 set out the argument that a new approach is needed to the study of self-determination to move beyond the well-established evaluative approach which dominates the literature. For this purpose, the analysis here is not aimed simply at assessing whether practice in Somalia complies with or violates the law. Conversely, the analysis aims to understand what the Somalia state-building process can tell us about the role and impact of self-determination law and standards in shaping and influencing state-building programmes. Such an exercise is intended to illustrate how self-determination provisions are interpreted and translated into practical rules and policies in rebuilding governance institutions in a situation of power vacuum. In so doing, this study contributes to assessing whether practice reflects, expands, further details or maybe contradicts the model of self-determination set out in this study.

1 See the scheme provided in Figure 4.2 at ch 4. 2.5.

The chapter proceeds in five steps. Section 5.2 explains why Somalia was selected as an illustrative example to study the application of self-determination and to understand its significance. Section 5.3 provides a summary of events which make up the story of the peace process which managed to re-establish a national government in Somalia after almost 20 years of anarchy caused by the collapse of state institutions. Section 5.4 is dedicated to accomplishing a key task: to advance an analysis of the self-determination issues at stake in the political reconstruction of Somalia. It analyses in detail the steps and phases of the Somali state-building project in order to identify the moments in which the political future of the Somali people was at stake and, in these moments, it will discuss whether and how 'external' and 'internal' self-determination standards have played out. Three phases of the Somali state-building project will be analysed: (i) the creation of a new government; (ii) the adoption of a new constitution; and (iii) the adoption of a federal system of government. Section 5.5 then offers a critical perspective on how self-determination aspects and standards have been applied to the Somali context – throughout the state-building process and over the years in question. It will be shown that there is a contradiction between the normative model set out in Chapters 3 and 4, and state practice in relation to the application of self-determination standards to the reconstruction of Somalia. A tentative interpretation will be advanced to explain how we can make sense of this apparent contradiction. Is Somalia a peculiar case of non-compliance or is this case study telling us something more general in relation to the way states understand self-determination to apply in state-building settings?

Finally, section 5.6 offers conclusive remarks and highlights the need for further comparative analysis to be conducted on this matter in order to make sense of states' behaviour in relation to self-determination issues in a more comprehensive sense. It is further stressed how future research shall focus on less extreme situations, namely when the condition of power vacuum is due to a momentum in which state structures are ineffective rather than to a long-standing condition of state-disintegration.

5.2 Somalia: the choice of a case-study

The present chapter studies the significance of self-determination in the context of state-building efforts conducted as part of the Somali National Reconciliation process. The right to self-determination, as explained in Chapter 3, is understood here as the right of the people of the state of Somalia as a whole.[2] The period

2 It is important to specify this because in Somalia self-determination claims have several layers that co-exist. First, there is the right of the people of the state of Somalia as a whole – and this is the layer under examination here. Secondly, the Northern territory of Somaliland claims independence from Southern Somalia. Third, Somali-populated areas of Ethiopia (Ogaden region) also have their self-determination claims to reunite with the rest of the Somali people in the project of a Greater Somalia. On the latter point, see Abdirahman Y Duale, 'Less and more than the sum of its parts: The failed merger of Somaliland and Somalia and the tragic quest for 'Greater Somalia'' in Redie Bereketeab, *Self-Determination and Secession in Africa: The Post-colonial State* (Routledge 2015) 104–18.

taken into consideration goes from April 2000, when a Somalia National Peace Conference was organised at Arta, in neighbouring Djibouti,[3] to September 2012, when the first non-transitional Somali Government – the Somali Federal Government (SFG) – was established[4] and a new President elected.[5] In greater detail, I will look at the events which took place between April 2000 and early 2007 because, as we will see from the analysis below, it was during this time that self-determination issues have been more central to state-building initiatives.

Amongst many examples of post-conflict reconstruction and state-building, Somalia was chosen as a suitable context for research for three key reasons. In the first place, for almost two decades Somalia has been the most cited example of a completely failed (collapsed) state as it was left without a government since 1991, when the state structure collapsed.[6] This unique situation of a state in a condition of power vacuum (at times it was also referred to as a 'situation of anarchy' in spite of the existence of local, unofficial forms of authority)[7] makes Somalia the ideal context where one can study the application of self-determination standards in situations where state-building initiatives are conducted in a country that has witnessed the prolonged lack of a central authority. This is an undoubtedly valuable analytical perspective because, as we have seen in Chapter 4, state institutions play an important role in facilitating its people to exercise the right to self-determination.[8] The state can indeed be either the medium for the realisation of the right (i.e. through the participation in elections or referenda held by the state) or it can itself be the goal of the self-determination exercise

3 'Somalia National Peace Conference' *SN News* (6 April 2000) http://www.banadir.com/whatisthere.htm (last accessed 15 April 2018).

4 Natasya Tay and David Smith, 'Somalia's first Parliament since 1991 inaugurated in Mogadishu' *The Guardian* (London, 20 August 2012) http://www.theguardian.com/world/2012/aug/20/somalia-first-parliament-inaugurated (last accessed 15 April 2018).

5 Mohammed Ibrahim, 'Somalia Selects Activist as Leader' *New York Times* (New York, 10 September 2012) http://www.nytimes.com/2012/09/11/world/africa/parliament-selects-mohamud-as-somalias-president.html (last accessed 15 April 2018).

6 The country had no formal justice system, no government, no formal education system, no police, no tax authorities, no custom regulation and no formal border control systems. See generally Rikka Koskenmaki, 'Legal Implications Resulting from State Failure in Light of the Case of Somalia' (2004) 73 *Nordic Journal of International Law* 1; Yemi Osinbajo, 'Legality in a Collapsed State: The Somali Experience'(1996) 45 *International and Comparative Law Quarterly* 910 and Alexandros Yannis, 'State Collapse and Prospects for Political Reconstruction and Democratic Governance in Somalia'(1997) 5 *African Yearbook of International Law* 23; Abdulqawi A Yusuf, 'Government Collapse and State Continuity: The Case of Somalia' (2003) 13 *Italian Yearbook of International Law* 11.

7 In the absence of a central governmental authority, Somalis instituted a diversified array of forms of government and revitalised economies, with different degrees of regional success. Such forms of authority include military administrations, long-distance trading enterprises, civic structures, religious authorities and state-like structures – especially in the northern part of the Somali territory. On this point see Mark Bradbury, *Becoming Somaliland* (Progressio 2008) 3 and Ken Menkhaus, 'If Mayors Ruled Somalia: Beyond the State-building Impasse' (2014) The Nordic Africa Institute, *Policy Note 2* http://www.nai.uu.se/news/articles/2014/04/29/154351/index.xml (last accessed 15 April 2018).

8 See ch 4.2.3, n 50.

(realised through the choice of statehood and/or through decision-making of the people about the shape that the political structure of their state should take). In addition, in Chapter 4 we have also seen that the state is also a holder of certain obligations in relation to self-determination, such as the obligation that the government must be representative of the whole of the people and that in decision-making exercises a genuine expression of the will of the people must be guaranteed.[9]

For these reasons, it is important first of all to study the situation in Somalia in order to understand how, without an existing state framework, self-determination entitlements play out in the absence of their privileged medium for realisation. Moreover, this study should also enable us to appreciate who, in a situation where no government, state structure or institution is in place, is left to take charge for the observance of self-determination standards.

In the second place, over the many years in which Somalia was without a government, the choice to focus only on the period 2000–2012 also needs to be explained. The Somali National Reconciliation Process, which spans across this period of time, indeed constitutes the only successful attempt at rebuilding a stable state structure in Somalia since the country's breakdown in 1991. Moreover, since its inception the Process has engaged steadily with state-building objectives. It provided for the creation of a new governmental authority and of new state institutions, including a new Constitution and a new judicial system, with a view to engineering a system of governance that could ensure long-term stability in the country. Such sweeping changes operated on the political and constitutional order of the state, provide a fertile ground for observing how self-determination rights and standards are mainstreamed into the process and to see how they actually play out in practice. Moreover, the peculiar situation of collapsed Somalia provides an additional opportunity to observe how self-determination concerns and standards were integrated into a process of outright creation of state structures – as opposed to modification or replacement of existing ones that one would see in most other state-building contexts.

In the third place, it is of further importance to study the situation in Somalia because it provides a chance to examine the role of external actors in promoting self-determination standards in a context of power vacuum. Since its inception, the Somali National Reconciliation Process has been essentially externally driven – and this is not surprising, given the extended lack of a central authority. The process of reconstruction of Somalia's state structures has indeed seen external actors being actively involved in all phases of the planning, organisation and implementation of the transition to peace. In Chapter 4, we have seen that the right to self-determination imposes a number of duties and obligations on third party states towards the people of independent states.[10] These are, in specific,

9 See ch 4.2.4 and Figure 4.2.
10 See ch 4.2.4.

a negative obligation not to interfere with a people's free choices (such as the prohibition to impose a government or a specific form of government on a people) and a positive obligation to assist with the full realisation of the right.[11] It is significant to study what happened in Somalia because this case offers the chance to see how the international community, and in particular those involved in the reconstruction efforts, have interpreted their obligations towards the Somali people. In this sense, it will also be critical to look at how external players have understood and balanced their duty to assist with their obligation not to intervene in the absence of a legitimate local government representative of the Somali people.

In sum, there are a number of important reasons why the process of political reconstruction of Somalia should be of interest for legal research on self-determination. In the following section I will thus provide a brief summary of the reconstruction process, with a view to highlighting the state-building components of the process, in preparation for the legal analysis of the relevance of self-determination that will be offered in sections 4 and 5 below.

5.3 Emerging from anarchy: the political reconstruction of Somalia (2000–2012)

Somalia becomes independent in 1960. Only days after gaining independence, the two states of Northern and Southern Somalia (respectively former British and Italian colonies) united under one single state.[12] Initially set out as a democratic state, a military coup in 1969 turned Somalia into a single-party Socialist state, led by Siyad Barre. Barre installed a regime which was extremely corrupted, violent and authoritarian. Its overthrow, in 1991, signed the beginning of a state of ravaging chaos. The opposition which overthrew the Barre regime indeed failed to construct a central authority and Somalia remained without an internationally recognised government until the Somali Federal Government was installed in August 2012.[13]

In 2000, almost ten years after authority collapse and over a dozen failed peace conferences, Somalia's Northern neighbour state, Djibouti, organised the Somalia National Peace Conference in Arta, to be held between 20 April and 5 May 2000.[14] The conference was backed by the United Nations and the Arab League, and saw extensive participation of Somali actors including clan leaders and civil society organisations. Participation was wider than any previous attempt, yet the process was boycotted by several powerful faction leaders as

11 See ch 4, Figure 4.2.

12 Ayfare A Elmi, *Understanding the Somalia Conflagration: Identity, Political Islam and Peacebuilding* (Pluto Press 2010) 17.

13 For a regularly updated summary of events see 'Somalia Profile: Timeline' *BBC News* http://www.bbc.com/news/world-africa-14094632 (last accessed 15 April 2018).

14 See note 3.

well as by the autonomous regional authorities of Somaliland and Puntland.[15] As a result of the negotiations, the Arta conference established a Transitional National Government (TNG), a National Transitional Charter was drafted and a provisional parliament was 'democratically selected' by official delegates.[16] In the following two years, however, the TNG was not successful in establishing control over Somali territory and remained unable to function effectively.

In March 2001, Ethiopia convened a meeting in Awasa for the warlords opposed to the TNG, where the various factions grouped under an umbrella structure called the Somalia Reconciliation and Reconstruction Council (SRRC).[17] The declared purpose on behalf of Ethiopia to convene this meeting was to agree on a common platform to facilitate dialogue with the TNG. In fact, the real purpose was to undermine the TNG and ultimately push for the holding of a new reconciliation conference to elect a new transitional government.[18] As the competition between these two groups intensified, the need for a new peace conference was indeed called for at the January 2002 summit of the Intergovernmental Authority on Development (IGAD).[19]

In October 2002 a new peace conference was thus convened under the auspices of IGAD, with the stated purpose of reconciling the TNG with the SRRC. Responsibility for managing the process was given by IGAD to a Technical Committee composed of the three 'frontline states': Djibouti, Ethiopia and Kenya. Due to regional rivalries and to the ongoing conflict between Ethiopia and Eritrea, Kenya was seen to be more neutral and hence designated to act as Chair.[20] The conference was held in the Kenyan town of Eldoret and constitutes an important turning point in the process of reconciliation. The conference indeed seemed to offer 'the best opportunity in many years to restore peace and government to Somalia' – with all key political actors involved except only the Somaliland administration.[21] It also was to develop in three phases, the first of which resulted in the signing of the Eldoret Declaration in October 2002

15 Kidist Mulugeta, *The Role of Regional and International Organizations in Resolving the Somali Conflict: The Case of IGAD* (Friederich Ebert-Stiftung 2009) 27, http://library.fes.de/pdf-files/bueros/aethiopien/07937-book.pdf (last accessed 15 April 2018). Whilst the leaders of Puntland and Somaliland boycotted the conference, all clans in these territories were represented in the Conference, according to the Report of the UN Secretary General on the situation in Somalia, UN Doc S/2000/1211.

16 See Ahmed I Samatar and Abdi I Samatar, 'Somali Reconciliation: Editorial Note'(2008) 3 *Bildhaan: An International Journal of Somali Studies* 1, 4.

17 See Elmi (n 12) 94 and International Crisis Group (ICG) 'Salvaging Somalia's Chance for Peace' (2002) Africa Brief n° 11, 2.

18 See Report of the Secretary-General, UN Doc S/2001/963, paras 11–13.

19 IGAD is a sub-regional organisation created in 1996 with a mandate of resolving conflicts in the region, including the Somali conflict. The organisation comprises six member countries in the Horn of Africa: Djibouti, Ethiopia, Kenya, Somalia, Sudan and Uganda. For more information, see the organisation's website www.igad.int (last accessed 15 April 2018).

20 See ICG (n 17) 3 and Mulugeta (n 15) 28.

21 ICG, 'Negotiating a Blueprint for Peace in Somalia' (2003) Africa Report N°59.

(Declaration).[22] The Declaration provided for a cessation of hostilities (although infringed several times) and set out the basic Principles of the Somalia National Reconciliation Process, to which all parties were mandated to adhere.

This Declaration signposts a turning point on the history of conflict resolution and state-building in Somalia because a decision was thereby made that Somalia would become a federal state. Under Article 1 of the Declaration, Somali representatives accepted a commitment to creating a decentralised, federal state.[23] This commitment was novel because it reversed the unitary structure developed at Arta, which was more incline to leave an open choice to the Transitional mechanism to choose between a system or regional autonomies and a federal structure.[24] This passage is therefore important because it was at Eldoret that a commitment was made for the form and system of the Somali state to be changed accordingly. Here parties to the peace process made a commitment to substitute the unitary model adopted throughout the history the Somali state (1961-1991) with a federal one and accepted the commitment to create a decentralised, federal system as the blueprint for any future state-building development in the country.[25]

The steps which followed as part of the National Reconciliation process for Somalia were indeed informed by the federalist approach and by the various efforts to implement such a design. At the reconciliation conference, the TNG and SRRC governmental movements fused together to create a unitary movement from which originated the Transitional Federal Government (TFG). The following year, a conference was organised in Nairobi where the structure of the TFG was further developed, a Transitional Federal Charter was adopted,[26] a national Parliament was inaugurated, a president elected and the TFG itself

22 Declaration on Cessation of Hostilities, Structures and Principles of the Somalia National Reconciliation Process, adopted at Eldoret, Kenya on 27 October 2002.

23 Article 1 'Federalism' reads as follows: '(1) To create federal governance structures for Somalia, embodied in a Charter or Constitution, which are inclusive, representative, and acceptable to all the parties; (2) To endorse the principle of decentralisation as an integral part of Somalia's governance structure'. http://theirwords.org/media/transfer/doc/1_so_2002_27-1cc947333efb6592d19dbf3273e848d8.pdf (last accessed 15 April 2018).

24 'Draft Agenda of the Conference: (3) The establishment of transitional, national, representative government (national assembly, cabinet and judiciary), and the creation of a decentralized system based on regional autonomy for the transition period. The form of government shall be a parliamentary democracy, with a bicameral national assembly . . . The Transitional mechanisms shall be based on a ***decentralized*** system of governance (***regional autonomy or federal structure)*** during the transitional period' (emphasis added). See Somalia National Peace Conference (n 3).

25 The formalisation of federalism took place only in July 2003, after intense negotiation, and on agreement that the federal process would develop gradually in the first years of the transition. See United Nations Report of the Secretary-General on the situation in Somalia, UN Doc S/2003/987, para 6.

26 *Somali Transitional Charter. Transitional Federal Charter for the Somali Republic* [Somalia], February 2004 http://www.unhcr.org/refworld/docid/4795c2d22.html (last accessed 15 April 2018).

established.[27] Although enjoying formal international recognition, the TFG could not enter Somalia and sat in Nairobi at the time of its formation, in October 2004, because the capital city Mogadishu was still controlled by warlords.[28] In June 2005, the president and the prime minister moved inside Somalia, to Jowhaar, but the parliament was unable to meet in Jowhaar because the speaker of the Transitional Federal Parliament was in Mogadishu and refused to go to Jowhaar. In January 2006, the president and the speaker agreed to hold the first meeting of the parliament on Somali soil in February 2006 in Baidoa.[29] The Parliament was therefore able to first convene inside of Somalia only after more than one year since its formation and was able to relocate to the capital Mogadishu in December 2006, thanks to the military assistance of the Ethiopian army.[30]

Established in exile, the TFG suffered from a severe lack of legitimacy within Somalia, which reflected in part its inability to exercise effective control over Somali territory.[31] The TFG's ineffectiveness was indeed due to many factors, including rampant corruption, its inherent weakness and lack of legitimacy amongst the Somali population; but it was also confronted by armed opposition at home. In the early days of its establishment a new force emerged inside the country, promoting an alternative form of governance to the internationally backed government and named the Union of Islamic Courts (UIC). The UIC was an umbrella organisation comprising 'a variety of Islamist organizations, centred on a long-standing network of local Islamic or *sharia* courts in Mogadishu'.[32] In fact, the courts were not a union of Islamic judges or scholars adhering to a specific form of Islam. Rather, they were mainly seen as yet another manifestation of clan power, which varied significantly in religiosity.[33] The courts were

27 See Statement by the President of the United Nations Security Council, 19 November 2004, S/PRST/2004/43.

28 Gerard Prunier and Barabara Wilson, 'A World of Conflict Since 9/11: The CIA coup in Somalia' (2006) 33 *Review of African Political Economy* 749. See also Apuuli P Kasaija, 'The UN-led Djibouti peace process for Somalia 2008–2009: Results and Problems' (2010) 28 *Journal of Contemporary African Studies* 261, 265.

29 The first meeting of the Transitional Federal Parliament inside Somalia was held on 26 February 2006. See United Nations Security Council, Statement by the President, S/PRST/2006/11, 15 March 2006 and 'Somalia: Parliament will meet in Baidoa, confirms President' *Irin News* (14 February 2006) http://www.irinnews.org/printreport.aspx?reportid=58133 (last accessed 15 April 2018).

30 United Nations Report of the Monitoring Group on Somalia, submitted in accordance with Resolution 1724 (2006), UN Doc S/2007/436 of 18 July 2007, at 11.

31 Tim Murithi, 'Inter-Governmental Authority on Development on the Ground: Comparing Interventions in Sudan and Somalia' in Frederic Soderbaum and Rodrigo Tavares, *Regional Organizations in African Security* (Routledge 2011) 79.

32 Cedric Barnes and Haran Hassan, 'The Rise and Fall of Mogadishu's Islamic Courts' (2007) 1 *Journal of Eastern African Studies* 151.

33 ibid 152 and Kirsti Samuels, 'Constitution-building during the war on terror: the challenge of Somalia' (2008) 40 *New York University Journal of International Law and Politics* 597, 604.

an endogenous mechanism originally created to deal with lawlessness in the country, and their judgements were enforced by militias who served specific clan interests in providing 'security' in the capital city.

Starting from Mogadishu, by July 2006 the UIC gradually managed to take over power and extend their control to the Southern and central parts of Somalia.[34] Ethiopia, seeing the threat of hostile Islamists gaining power in neighbouring Somalia, in July started sending troops into the country to fight the UIC.[35] In response to the Ethiopian presence in Somalia, the UIC declared a holy war against Ethiopia, which they saw as an occupying power in Somalia.[36] This threat provided Ethiopia with the leeway to justify a full-scale military intervention in Somalia on the basis of self-defence.[37] In fact, the justification used by Ethiopia to defend outright military intervention was two-fold, and included also an invitation to intervene launched by the TFG, who had been trying with little success to fight the UIC for over six months.[38] Since the early days of its establishment, the TFG had requested IGAD, the African Union (AU) and the international community to support its efforts to assert its authority and re-establish peace and security in the country with the deployment of an international peace support operation (IGASOM).[39] Despite its approval by IGAD members in early 2005 and its endorsement from the AU, the force was authorised only in December 2006 by the UN Security Council under Resolution 1725 (2006) and

34 Report of the Monitoring Group on Somalia pursuant to Security Council resolution 1676 (2006), S/2006/913, 22 November 2006. See also Abdi I Samatar, 'The Miracle of Mogadishu' (2006) 33 *Review of African Political Economy* 581.

35 Ezra W Yihdego, 'Ethiopia's military action against the Union of Islamic Courts and others in Somalia: Some legal implications' (2007) 56 *International and Comparative Law Quarterly* 666, 667. The presence of Ethiopian troops in Somalia during the second half of 2006 was recorded also in the report of the Report of the Monitoring Group on Somalia pursuant to Security Council resolution 1676 (2006), S/2006/913, 22 November 2006. Ethiopia, however, in a letter annexed to the report, denied the presence of its troops in Somalia. Ethiopia only acknowledged its presence in Somalia in late December 2006, claiming it was acting in self-defence. See United Nations Security Council meeting records, S/PV.5614, 26 December 2006.

36 'Somalis vow a holy war against Ethiopia' *BBC News* (London, 9 October 2006) http://news.bbc.co.uk/1/hi/world/africa/6032907.stm (last accessed 15 April 2018). See also Bjorn Moller, 'The Somali Conflict: The Role of External Actors' (2009) Danish Institute for International Studies Report No 3, 17–18.

37 Jeffrey Gentleman, 'Ethiopia Hits Somali Targets, Declaring War' *New York Times* (New York, 25 December 2005) http://www.nytimes.com/2006/12/25/world/africa/25somalia.html (last accessed 15 April 2018).

38 On this point see the excellent piece by Ahmed A M Khayre, 'Self-Defence, Intervention by Invitation, or Proxy War? The Legality of the 2006 Ethiopian Invasion of Somalia' (2014) 22 *International and Comparative Law Quarterly* 208.

39 Matt Bryden, 'Storm Clouds over Somalia as Rivals Prepare for Battle' *The Nation* (Nairobi, 8 December 2006) http://old.crisisgroup.org/ar/Regions%20Countries/Africa/Horn%20of%20Africa/Somalia/op-eds/storm-clouds-over-somalia-as-rivals-prepare-for-battle.html (last accessed 29 May 2018).

never de facto implemented due to a lack of technical capacity on behalf of IGAD to deploy the mission.[40] In this situation, Ethiopia's military action in Somalia was highly problematic and its legality dubious to say the least, given that the intervention was carried out in presence of a long-standing arms embargo imposed on Somalia by UNSC Resolution 733 (1992) and on invitation by a local government which, at the time, had virtually no effective control over Somali territory and enjoyed limited recognition at the international level.[41]

In a matter of weeks, the UIC were heavily defeated in confrontation with the Ethiopian army, and by January 2007 Ethiopian troops managed to escort the TFG into Mogadishu.[42] In the months which followed the return of the TFG in the capital Mogadishu, the Security Council authorised the African Union to establish a peacekeeping mission (AMISOM) with the mandate to protect the TFG and support national reconciliation dialogue,[43] whilst the TFG and Ethiopian forces continued to battle against the local insurgents. At that time, the insurgency consisted of three main groups: the Al-Shabaab, a well-trained splinter group of the UIC which represented its most radical fringe; a large group of Hawiye clan militia who loathed the presence of the Ethiopian military in Mogadishu; and a group of nationalist fighters who opposed Ethiopian involvement in Somali affairs.[44]

This situation of widespread violence and insecurity which followed the defeat of the UIC led to considerable pressure being made both at the national and international level to the TFG to seek reconciliation with all national stakeholders. TFG President, Abdullahi Yusuf Ahmed, proposed to organise a National Reconciliation Congress to which former UIC heads agreed to participate as a political entity.[45] However, the TFG insisted that only clan representatives could participate since the TFG did not recognise the political party of the former UIC leaders and the reconciliation was between clans and not political parties. For these reasons, no one from the UIC attended the conference. The Congress took place in July–August 2007 and thereby the participants agreed to a

40 United Nations Security Council Resolution 1725 (2006) of 7 December 2006. See also Paul D Williams, 'Into the Mogadishu Maelstrom: The African Union Mission in Somalia' (2009) 16 *International Peacekeeping* 514 and Mulugeta (n 15).

41 United Nations Security Council Resolution 733 (1992) of 23 January 1992; Khayre (n 38) and Yihdego (n 35).

42 Menkhaus reports that 'the coat-tails of the Ethiopian forces rode the TFG, which assumed control over key government buildings under heavy Ethiopian protection'. Ken Menkhaus, 'The Crisis in Somalia, Tragedy in Five Acts' (2007) 106 *African Affairs* 357.

43 United Nations Security Council Resolution 1744 (2006) of 20 February 2007.

44 Human Rights Watch, 'Shell-Shocked: Civilians under Attack in Mogadishu' (2007) vol 19, No 12(A) www.hrw.org/sites/default/files/reports/somalia0807webwcover.pdf (last accessed 15 April 2018).

45 Report of the Secretary General on the situation in Somalia, UN Doc S/2007/381 of 25 June 2007, 1–2.

number of outcomes, including the holding of free and fair elections in 2009.[46] Meanwhile, in September 2007 groups opposed to the TFG (including some former UIC leaders, clan elders, civil society representatives, some parliamentarians and the Somali Diaspora) held a parallel congress in Eritrea, where they founded the Alliance for the Liberation and Reconstitution of Somalia (ARS), and claimed to be ready to engage in talks with the TFG only after the withdrawal of Ethiopian forces.[47] On 9 June 2008 the TFG and ARS at a meeting in Djibouti reached a political agreement (hereinafter the Djibouti Agreement), which – amongst other things – provided for the cessation of hostilities and requested the UN to deploy an international stabilisation force, which would exclude neighbouring states, to fill the security gap that would be left by the departure of Ethiopian troops.[48]

The Djibouti Agreement was rejected by Al-Shabaab, the hard-liners in the defunct UIC, and possibly seen with suspicion by the hard-line elements from within the TFG – namely President Yusuf and his supporters – who were suspicious of the opposition as well as of the TFG Prime Minister and his supporters.[49] By the end of 2008 Al-Shabaab, who started as a movement of 500 to 700 fighters,[50] had been gaining strength and managed to retake most of Southern Somalia, with its leadership concentrated in the port city of Kismayo.[51]

In late 2008, growing disagreements internal to the TFG prompted IGAD to call the parties to order. In November the organisation, in an effort to avoid the derail of the peace process, imposed targeted sanctions to all those inside and outside Somalia who had become obstacles to the achievement of peace, a position endorsed immediately after by the AU and the UN in Security Council Resolution 1844 (2008).[52] In late December, sanctions were imposed on President Yusuf and its close associates, ultimately causing the resignation of the president and the establishment of a new government.[53] In parallel to the

46 Report of the Secretary General on the situation in Somalia, UN Doc S/2007/658 of 7 November 2007, 1–2.

47 UN Doc S/2007/658, 2 and 'New Somali Alliance Threatens War' *BBC News* (London, 12 September 2007) http://news.bbc.co.uk/2/hi/africa/6990928.stm (last accessed 15 April 2018).

48 Agreement between the Transition Federal Government of Somalia (TFG) and the Alliance for the Re-liberation of Somalia (ARS), done in Djibouti on 9 June 2008.

49 Ken Menkhaus, 'Somalia: A Country in Peril, a Policy Nightmare' (2008) ENOUGH Strategy paper, 6 http://www.enoughproject.org/publications/somalia-country-peril-policy-nightmare (last accessed 15 April 2018).

50 Human Rights Watch (n 44).

51 'The Rise of the Shabaab' *The Economist* (London, 18 December 2008) http://www.economist.com/node/12815670 (last accessed 15 April 2018).

52 Respectively, Communiqué of the 30th Extraordinary Session of the IGAD Council of Ministers on the Prevailing Political and Security Situation in Somalia, Addis Ababa, Ethiopia, 18 November 2008, para 11; African Union, *Communiqué of the 163th Meeting of the Peace and Security Council*, PSC/MIN/Comm.4 (CLXIII), 22 December 2008, para 10 and UN Security Council Resolution 1844 (2007) of 20 November 2008.

53 For a detailed summary of events see Kasajia (n 28).

withdrawal of Ethiopian troops, in January 2009 the new government, guided by the Chairman of ARS, Sheikh Sharif, extended the transitional period of two years, hence moving forward the date for holding democratic elections to August 2011.[54] Levels of conflict and insecurity remained high throughout 2009 and 2010, due to the continued opposition of armed groups such as Al-Shabaab, Hizbul Islam and Ahlu Sunna Wal Jma'a (ASWJ). At this stage, the conflict involved a religious connotation, strong links to clan politics and raged alongside an international force deployed in support of the TFG with the mission to establish a functional government.[55]

Then, in 2011 history seemed to repeat itself in Somalia: in June an accord was signed in Kampala to bring together the President of the TFG and the Speaker of Parliament, in order to overcome a political impasse internal to the TFG. In the accord it was agreed to postpone elections of another 12 months, thus extending the transitional period to August 2012.[56] A new Roadmap for ending the transition was then adopted with the facilitation of the UN Special Representative Augustine Mahiga, for the purposes of setting out the key tasks and priorities for the Transitional Federal Institutions (TFI) in order to comply with the August 2012 deadline.[57] Moreover, two external military interventions led by neighbouring countries, Kenya and Ethiopia, took place to fight Al-Shabaab's armed opposition to the TFG in Southern Somalia. In October 2011, Kenya decided to intervene in Somalia after a series of cross-border kidnappings targeting Western tourists on the Kenyan border and aid workers in the Dadaab refugee camp, which Kenya attributed to Al-Shabaab.[58] One month after Kenya, also Ethiopia sent troops into the country,[59] so that by 2012 the TFG battle against Al-Shabaab was fought on several levels and by a multiplicity of players: security forces, AMISOM and forces sent in from neighbouring countries.

54 See Report of the Secretary General on the situation in Somalia, UN Doc A/2009/132 at 2.

55 Ricardo Real Pedrosa de Sousa, 'External Interventions and Civil War Intensity in South-Central Somalia (1991–2010)' (2014) 29 *Cuadernos de Estudios Africanos* 57, 80.

56 Agreement between the President of the Transitional Federal Government of Somalia and the Speaker of the Transitional Federal Parliament of Somalia (The Kampala Accord), Kampala, Uganda, 9 June 2011 https://reliefweb.int/report/somalia/agreement-between-president-transitional-federal-government-somalia-and-speaker (last accessed 15 April 2018).

57 The need to comply with the Roadmap as a condition for continued support to the TFI was set out in UN Security Council Resolution 2010 (2011) of 30 September 2011, under operative paragraph 2 and acting under Chapter VII of the Charter. UN Doc S/Res/2010/2011.

58 See International Crisis Group, 'The Kenyan Military Intervention in Somalia' (2012) *Africa Report n. 184* and UN Security Council Report on the situation in Somalia, UN Doc S/2011/759 at 1–4.

59 Daniel Howden, 'UN-backed invasion of Somalia spirals into chaos' *The Independent* (London, 15 December 2011) http://www.independent.co.uk/news/world/africa/unbacked-invasion-of-somalia-spirals-into-chaos-6276959.html (last accessed 15 April 2018).

This situation was partially addressed with the UN Security Council endorsing AMISOM strategic concept of 5 January[60] through Resolution 2036 (2012) of 22 February 2012, which requested AMISOM to increase force strength and accepted part of the rehatted Kenyan forces assigned to the southern border regions of Somalia in support of Somali TFG forces.[61] The resolution further authorised AMISOM to take: '*all necessary measures* as appropriate in those sectors in coordination with the Somali security forces *to reduce the threat* posed by Al-Shabaab and other armed opposition groups in order to *establish conditions* for effective and legitimate governance across Somalia'.[62] In so doing, the resolution essentially entrusted AMISOM with a wide peace-enforcement mandate to fight Al-Shabaab as the armed opposition to the TFG, and implicitly acknowledged also the government's lack of legitimacy across the country.

During 2012, despite both the intricate security situation and serious political conflicts within the Parliament, the Roadmap for transition continued to advance under the aegis of the international community. By the end of February 2012, the leaders of the TFI, together with the leaders of the regional administrations of Puntland and Galmudug, and representatives from ASWJ had met twice in Garowe to agree on a detailed approach to end the transition. The Garowe principles included the formation of a provisional Constitutional Assembly and the creation of a bicameral legislature, established that elections of the Parliament and President would be held by August 2012 and national elections in 2016.[63]

By 20 September 2012, with the adoption of a Provisional Constitution; the selection of a new Parliament – operated by a group of Elders and by the members of a Technical Selection Committee; the appointment of a new, non-transitional Somali Federal Government (SFG); and the election of a new President, the transitional phase was declared over. After more than 10 years of transition, Somalia had its first non-transitional government since 1991, a President and a Provisional Constitution which delineates the contours of the new structure of the Somali state. Many aspects concerning the shape that the state of Somalia should take, including how federalism should be worked out, still need to be defined, yet the basic foundations for effective governance have been laid out for the country.

60 Communiqué of the 306th Peace and Security Council Meeting on the Situation in Somalia, Addis Ababa, Ethiopia, 5 January 2012 http://amisom-au.org/2012/01/commuique-of-the-306th-psc-meeting-on-the-situation-in-somalia/ (last accessed 15 April 2018).

61 See UN Security Council Resolution 2036 (2012) of 22 February 2012 and UN Security Council Report on the Situation in Somalia, UN Doc SC/2012/74 at 1–8.

62 UN Security Council Resolution 2036 (2012), operative paragraph 1.

63 The Garowe Principles on the Finalization and Adoption of the Constitution and the End of the Transition, adopted at the Somalia National Consultative Constitutional Conference, held on 21–23 December in Garowe, Puntland, Somalia. http://piracyreport.com/index.php/subcategory/1/Home_LAND/Government/122011///1 (last accessed 15 April 2018).

At this stage, from the perspective of international security, there are still giant steps forward that Somalia is expected to take before the country can be stabilised and may constitute a safe environment. Indeed, the government is still under attack in its own compound and threats from the Somali armed opposition, in particular from Al-Shabaab, are still worrying neighbour states.[64] From the perspective of international law, considerations can be made concerning what role is played by the law in guiding the transition. For this purpose, the efforts at constructing peace and stability in Somalia will be analysed with a view to assess the role that self-determination concerns have played alongside security and state-building imperatives in driving the process onwards. The next sections will therefore examine whether and how state practice in relation to the Somalia National Peace and Reconciliation Process included self-determination concerns into the efforts deployed by states and the international community in order to bring about peace and stability to war-torn Somalia.

5.4 Power vacuum, state-building and national reconciliation efforts: a space for self-determination?

An analysis of state practice which is meant to flesh out how the right to self-determination of the people of a state has been protected and promoted in a process of state-building must address two key tasks. First, it must identify situations and conditions where self-determination rights and entitlements apply to the context in question. Secondly, it must study state practice with a view to detect and assess whether, how and to what extent self-determination concerns have informed and shaped state practice in these situations. In approaching these two tasks, I start off from the interpretation of self-determination as the right of the people of independent states that was provided in Chapters 3 and 4. According to the scheme provided, self-determination can be articulated (but not divided) into internal and external components.

External self-determination gives a people the right to determine their political future, including their form of government, as well as to pursue their economic, social and cultural development free from external interference. In essence, the principle sets the requirement that any sweeping changes in the form and structure of the state must be a genuine expression of the will of the people. In the case of Somalia, the state-building project created state institutions

64 Abdi Sheikh and Feisal Omar, 'Al-Shabaab militants attack Government building, at least 10 dead' *Reuters* (New York, 14 April 2015) http://www.reuters.com/article/2015/04/14/us-somalia-blast-attacks-idUSKBN0N50T520150414 (last accessed 15 April 2018); 'Kenya attack: 147 dead in Garissa University assault' *BBC News* (London, 3 April 2015) http://www.bbc.com/news/world-africa-32169080 (last accessed 15 April 2018). See also Vanda Felbab-Brown, 'Why are Efforts to Counter Al-Shabaab Falling so Flat?' *Brookings* (Washington, 5 April 2016) http://www.brookings.edu/blogs/order-from-chaos/posts/2016/04/05-counterterrorism-state-building-somalia-felbabbrown (last accessed 15 April 2018).

virtually from scratch, attributing the state a certain shape and form first with the adoption of a Transitional Constitution, then with its transformation into a Provisional Constitution. In this passage, Somalia passed from being a country with collapsed state structures that were based on a unitary, centralised form of state, to purporting to become a democratic, federal Republic committed to the principle of decentralisation. This passage was carried out in the midst of an ongoing civil war which saw the TFG falling short of internal legitimacy and the capacity to control territory, and being constantly engaged in reaching agreements with the various armed factions controlling significant areas of state territory. Moreover, the process has been strongly guided by external actors, to the extent that the Somali conflict can be considered one of the conflicts most heavily subjected to the threat of external interference.[65]

From the standpoint of external self-determination, therefore, one needs to assess whether the changes in the form and system of government of Somalia, put in place through the state-building process, were made as part of a process which guaranteed a genuine attachment to the will of the people and by means of a determination made free from external interference. Analysis therefore needs to be conducted to appreciate whether this was the case and, if so, to point out how this attachment to the will of the people was ensured in practice. Such an analysis will be useful to understand how the various actors involved in state-building in Somalia overall conceptualised and translated into practice the right of the Somali people to determine their future, as well as their own obligations to promote and protect internal and external aspects of self-determination.

Specific rights and obligations are also attached to the internal aspects of self-determination. These latter mandate that in decision-making exercises governments avoid fake expressions of the will of the people and that, this doing, they ensure that the people as a whole are represented. In the case of Somalia, the issue of representativeness was crucial to any of the conferences and meetings organised to mediate between the parties in question. Thus, how was this concept interpreted and with what results? Also, how has the government (or who for it) ensured that the genuine expression of the will of the people was manifested in moments when important decisions on the political future of the people were being made?

65 The Fund for Peace's *Guide to the Indicators for Conflict Assessment* suggests a number of factors that are taken into account in order to assess the level of intervention of other states or external political actors in any given country (indicator n 12). According to the scheme provided, Somalia during the years in exam would rank very high in any of the given measures, ticking all the boxes contained in the indicator: presence of covert operations; economic intervention or aid; dependency on aid; external support for factions; military attacks across borders; presence of foreign troops; military assistance or training exercises supported by other states; presence of a peacekeeping operation on the ground; external support for police training. See (2011) *The Fund for Peace Country Analysis Indicators and Their Measures*, The Fund for Peace Publication CR-10-97-CA (11-05C) 20 https://issuu.com/fundforpeace/docs/cr-10-97-ca-conflictassessmentindicators-1105c (last accessed 15 April 2018).

This set of questions will help us in identifying the role and significance that self-determination standards have had in the process of political reconstruction of Somalia. The questions must therefore be posed specifically in relation to situations where the right attaches. More precisely I have identified three situations that can be singled out within the state-building process as being of particular relevance to self-determination issues. First, the establishment of a new government in the midst of chaos; second the adoption of a new Constitution; third the adoption of a federal system of government. We will examine these situations in turn.

5.4.1 *First situation: the creation of a new government in the midst of chaos*

During the process of state-building in Somalia (2000-2012) the country has witnessed the establishment of three different set of institutions and attached governments. First, the TNG, created at Arta in 2000; second the TFG created in Nairobi in 2004 and last the SFG, created within Somalia in 2012. As Saul remarks, post-conflict governments have an important role in reconstruction because they are required to determine the priorities for the reconstruction period, including the interpretation of any peace agreement, and to develop strategies for the implementation of reconstruction priorities.[66] In the present section we will consider what are the key issues at stake with the creation of new governments, through the lens of international law on self-determination, starting from a situation of protracted lack of a central authority – often referred to as political vacuum or anarchy.

5.4.1.1 *Representativeness criteria*

As we have seen in Chapter 3, the right to self-determination in its internal connotation sets out the requirement for governments to be representative of the whole people belonging to the territory of a state without distinction as to race, creed or colour.[67] Somali transitional governments have not been elected through an exercise of popular will and have not been put in place within the framework of a national electoral law. They were established as a result of international conferences organised for the purposes of leading Somalia out of chaos. For this reason, in order to make an assessment concerning self-determination and representation issues, two things need to be considered.

66 Matthew Saul, *Popular Governance of Post-Conflict Reconstruction: The Role of International Law* (CUP 2014) 23.

67 Declaration on Principles of International law on Friendly Relations and Co-operation among States in Accordance with the Charter of the United Nations, GA/RES/2625 (XXV) of 24 October 1970, UN Doc A/RES/25/265, paragraph VII of the section on the Principle of Equal Rights and Self-Determination. See discussion in ch 3.3.

First, we need to look at how conference delegates were selected. Both the Arta and Eldoret conferences (as well as their sub-conference components) were held outside of Somalia. Somali delegates were invited by the organising powers and sponsoring organisations to attend the meetings. Who drafted the list of attendees, who figured on these lists and who did not are thus the first steps to be considered in establishing whether any formation or institution emerging from this process can be said to be representative and inclusive. Secondly, we will look at the procedures which enabled the selection of said institutions, the appointment of leaders and of transitional governments. In order to make an assessment, one would indeed need to know who elected and/or appointed representatives and on the basis of what criteria.

5.4.1.2 Selection of peace conference participants

The Arta Conference has been described as a real attempt to bring together a cross-sectional selection of delegates to debate the future of Somalia and, in this sense, it was intended to have a broader basis and broader legitimacy than any previous initiatives.[68] Nearly 5,000 delegates were involved in the Conference including Somali elders from all regions, former politicians, intellectuals, representatives of clans and civil society and, for the first time, also Somali women.[69] Representatives gathered to discuss how to bring peace and reconciliation to the war-torn state and several outreach missions were also conducted inside the country by conference representatives. Faction leaders and warlords were invited to participate but not as veto holders and many refused to attend.[70] As explained by the representative of Djibouti, the organising country:

> In initiating this National dialogue, Djibouti was unambiguous. The process would be comprehensive in addressing all facets of Somalia's ills; it would be transparent, inclusive and independent of undue influences. The participation of leaders of factions and administrative regions was sought and aggressively pursued directly and indirectly throughout the Conference and since the formation of the new Government. The criteria for their participation were never spelled out in advance. The door has always been open, and it will continue to be open. But it was implicit that they had to affirm the unity and territorial integrity of the country, that they had to agree to peace, reconciliation and the primacy of law, and that they had to commit

68 United Nations Secretary General, Report on the Situation in Somalia, UN Doc S/2000/1211, 19 December 2000, p. 10. See also Ioan Lewis, *Understanding Somalia and Somaliland* (Hurst & Company, 2008) 81.

69 In the initial phases of the conference, also representatives from Somaliland and Puntland participated. The two regions however pulled out of the process by mid-2000 and labelled the process as unrepresentative and externally imposed. See UN Doc S/2000/1211 and Mulugeta (n 15) 27.

70 S/2000/1211 and Samatar and Samatar (n 16) 3.

> to complete and verifiable disarmament. Not only did they [warlords] opt to stay away, but they also embarked on obstructing and undermining the Conference in order to maintain the status quo. Despite their absence, genuine representatives from every district, region, clan, sub-clan and minorities converged at Arta, Djibouti.[71]

Despite the efforts and the good intentions, the Arta process produced a dysfunctional government and the peace process derailed after less than two years due to the TNG's incapacity to function effectively.[72] Such failure, coupled with the parallel formation of the warlord alliance SRRC (with Ethiopian support) called for a new 'all-inclusive National Reconciliation conference' aim at forming a new government.[73] Attended by fewer delegates, the IGAD-sponsored Eldoret conference saw a rather different selection of attendees invited as representatives of the Somali people. The delegates included TNG representatives, civil society and also all the main warlords. Admittedly, these latter were invited in the hope of creating a more effective government yet paying little attention to the past record of these individuals.[74]

The Eldoret conference was to be organised into three phases. First, a representative delegation of 300 participants would be gathered in October 2002 to agree on the fundamental terms of the discussion. Secondly, a selection of roughly 75 delegates would discuss the core, substantial issues concerning reconciliation organised into 'Reconciliation Committees'.[75] These were to include, for instance, discussing the adoption of a constitution and the resolution of land and property conflicts. Thirdly, the proposals of the Committees were to be submitted to the plenary for deliberation and approval.

To begin with, the selection of delegates to participate was a major source of controversy since the conference started off at Eldoret. The International Crisis Group reported that, instead of 300, over 1,000 Somalis turned up at the conference due to a failure of the organisers to set out clearly established participation criteria.[76] This resulted in heavy negotiation to be undertaken in relation to whom should be selected to participate and several commentators denounced both mismanagement on behalf of the IGAD Technical Committee and the lack of neutrality in selecting participants.[77] According to Crisis Group,

71 Djibouti representative, Security Council Meeting Records, 10 October 19 October 2001, S/PV.4392.

72 See section 3 above.

73 United Nations Secretary General, Report on the situation in Somalia, UN Doc S/2001/963. 11 October 2001.

74 Lewis (n 68) 83.

75 Report of the Secretary General October 2002, S/2002/1201, at 6.

76 ICG, 'Salvaging Somalia's Chance for Peace' (n 17) 4.

77 See Mohamed A Eno, 'Inclusive but unequal: the enigma of the 14th SRNC and the four-point-five (4.5) factor' in Abdulahi A Osman and Issaka K Souaré (eds), *Somalia at the Crossroads: Challenges and Perspectives on Reconstructing a Failed State* (Adonis & Abbey 2007).

'disputes between Ethiopia and Djibouti over allocations for their respective Somali clients led to roughly a dozen revisions of the list during the first week of November alone'.[78] In the end, it is reported that selection criteria were so bias that the view of many Somalis is that Ethiopia, rather than Somalis themselves, had dominated the conference.[79]

In the end, neither of the two conferences managed meaningfully to address the problem of representativeness of delegates invited to attend. A general issue is that many delegates – including faction leaders, so-called 'scholars' and civil society representatives – were simply self-appointed and had a limited capacity to sell the peace process to constituencies in Somalia.[80] In fact, how this could have been done in a situation of chaos remains an open question. To outsiders, it is almost impossible to understand who speaks for whom in Somalia. The country's societal tissue is organised through lineage and has a clan-based structure.[81] However, the clan is not a fixed, stable entity: it is a dynamic, fluid, infinitely adaptable one which is constantly being remoulded according to the political situation.[82] All in all, dynamic clan-based affiliations, political fragmentation and long years of anarchy have essentially dismantled most forms of known order structures in great part of the country, leaving a void that is mainly filled by power struggles.

5.4.1.3 *Representativeness, (s)election and appointment of government representatives*

A second means to test the validity of representativeness criteria is by looking at the procedures elaborated to appoint leaders, transitional parliaments and institutions. Indeed, a key problem in both conferences was whether and how to allocate seats by faction or by clan.[83] Several models were elaborated and, finally, a clan-based formula for fixed proportionality was adopted. This controversial model, known as the '4.5 formula', distributes parliament seats equally

78 ICG, 'Salvaging Somalia's Chance for Peace' (n 17) 4.

79 This issue was highlighted in many of the interviews included in the International Crisis Group reports on the conference. See ICG, 'Salvaging Somalia's Chance for Peace' (n 17) and 'Negotiating a Blueprint for Peace in Somalia' (n 21). The same issue was stressed by Samatar and Samatar (n 16) at 7, according to whom by early 2003 'representatives of the international community and other observers confirmed that Ethiopia single-handedly controlled two-thirds of the list of conference participants'.

80 On this point see Lewis (n 68) 81–82; ICG, 'Negotiating a Blueprint for Peace in Somalia' (n 21).

81 According to anthropologist Lewis, a leading expert on Somali culture, the Somali nation consists of six main divisions: four major (Dir, Isaq, Hawiye, Darod) and two minor clans (Digil and Rahanweyn), which are to some extent geographically distinct. Lewis (n 68) 4 – see also diagram at page 109.

82 Mary Harper, *Getting Somalia Wrong? Faith, War and Hope in a Shattered State* (Zed Books 2012) 11 and 35–40.

83 ICG, 'Salvaging Somalia's Chance for Peace' (n 17).

among the four dominant clans with the remaining clans collectively assigned half as many seats as a dominant one.[84] The formula was first elaborated at a conference in Sodere, Ethiopia, in 1996–97.[85]

Different views have been advanced on the appropriateness of the 4.5 model as a formula for ensuring representation. Anthropologist Lewis welcomes the adoption of the 4.5 formula at Arta, which sees an arrangement based on clan quotas for being able for the first time to create an assembly which was openly to reflect 'political realities'.[86] According to the International Crisis Group, the formula was considered to be better able to favour authentic leaders at the Eldoret Conference and to reduce the power of the Technical Committee to steer the process.[87] Somali scholars, however, seem more reluctant to embrace the advantages of the 4.5 arrangement because they see it more as a crude and simplistic power-sharing exercise than anything which has to do with representation of the people. This is due both to practical downsides – the formula results in often very large parliaments and cabinets[88] – as well as to reasons of principle. Eno, describing the adoption of this formula at Arta, writes: '[the Committees] were without the morality to consider the controversy within their respective documents, as the infamous 4.5 clan power sharing formula contrarily purported injustice, inequality and the rightlessness of a section of the society'.[89]

The weight of clan identity in defining the conflict in Somalia and, as a result, what its relevance should be against state-building is indeed not a settled matter. What is for Lewis a 'political reality', indeed, is to other Somali scholars a legacy of the colonial strategy of 'divide and rule'.[90] Two main schools of thought indeed explain the link between Somali politics, culture and the civil war. According to Samatar,

> The dominant theory introduced by Somalist discussions [Lewis' theory] asserts that indifference to the centrality of clan identity in public affairs has been a major factor in Somali political crises. Advocates argue that the current predicament can be resolved by recognising 'traditional' clan identity as the foundation stone for the reconstruction of legitimate political and

84 ibid. See also Report of the Secretary General on the Situation in Somalia, UN Doc S/2003/231, 26 February 2003.

85 Abdullahi M Hersi, 'Application of power-sharing models in managing intractable clan conflict in Somalia' (2015) 2 *International Journal of Political Science* 1, 7.

86 Lewis (n 68) 82.

87 ICG, 'Salvaging Somalia's Chance for Peace' (n 17).

88 Katabaro Miti, 'Somalia: The Endless Search for Peace' (2010) AISA Briefing No 25 http://www.ai.org.za/wp-content/uploads/downloads/2011/11/No-25.-Somalia-The-Endless-search-for-Peace.pdf (last accessed 15 April 2018). See also Report of the Secretary General on the situation in Somalia, UN Doc S/2004/469, 9 June 2004.

89 Eno (n 77) 68. For a brief overview of the place of Somali lineage structure in relation to state collapse see Abou Jeng, *Peacebuilding in the African Union* (CUP 2012) 234–43.

90 Abdi I Samatar, 'Debating Somali Identity in a British Tribunal: The Case of the BBC Somali Service' (2010) 10 *Bildhaan: An International Journal of Somali Studies* 36.

> professional life. Opponents posit that Somalia's calamity is a product of the politicisation of genealogical difference and that the remedy to this crisis is to remove genealogy from state-driven politics. They note that recent experiences indicate that a clan-based strategy will only deepen divisions among Somalis rather that healing the discords.[91]

Since its adoption in 2000, the controversial 4.5 formula has become the major system for appointment and distribution of power at all levels in Somalia. At Eldoret, once the formula was embraced, the contentious issue became how to allocate parliament seats within each clan according to the formula – with faction leaders remaining to decide who shall occupy most of them.[92] As a result, the election of the TFG became, in the words of the International Crisis Group 'an unimaginative "cake-cutting" exercise of power-sharing between an un-elected and only partially representative political elite'.[93]

Most recently, the formula was also used in the formation of the SFG, Somalia's putative first non-transitional government, and of other institutions such as the National Constituent Assembly – created with the mandate to review and adopt a draft constitution. Nonetheless, discontent with the formula is all the more evident in the agreement that was reached at Garowe a few months before the establishment of the SFG. In the Garowe Principles, where Somali leaders set out to delineate how to proceed with the implementation of the Roadmap, was inserted a significant clause concerning the 4.5 formula. The Principles adopted state that, since the security situation did not permit elections, the lower house of the new Federal Parliament would be selected using the 4.5 formula of representation 'for this selection process only and shall prevail only for the term of parliament proposed under this agreement'.[94] The provision continues stating that:

> (ii) The 4.5 formula shall never become the basis for power sharing in any future political dispensation after the above-mentioned term concludes.
>
> (iii) The new Federal Constitution shall not include any provisions using the 4.5 formula and shall not be amended to abrogate this stipulation in any manner.
>
> (iv) The new federal parliament that comes into being in June 2012 shall not amend or enact any law or implement any policy that takes into account or attempts to reinstate the 4.5 power sharing formula.[95]

91 ibid 38. The point is also shared by Eno, who argues that '[t]he 4.5 mechanism is framed in the context of an erroneous but general myth of clan division, in which all the people are categorically put into significant and insignificant tribal groups'. Eno (n 77) 72.

92 See generally ICG, 'Salvaging Somalia's Chance for Peace' (n 17) and 'A Blueprint for Peace in Somalia' (n 21) 15.

93 ICG, 'A blueprint for peace in Somalia' (n 21) 1.

94 Garowe Principles (n 63) Principle 2 (c)(i).

95 Garowe Principle n. 2 (c)(ii)–(iv).

In essence, the Garowe Principles exceptionally allow the next Somali Parliament to be created according to the 4.5 formula, yet also agreeing that after the first mandate of the new non-transitional government expires, this very formula of representation will be unequivocally abandoned. The clause is surely significant. The 4.5 formula was indeed elaborated as a subsidiary means to ensure a certain degree of representativeness of selected bodies, given that no direct input was coming from the Somali people at large in the selection process. Its provisional, experimental and contextually related character was unequivocally enshrined into the ban for its future use in any post-transition, power-sharing arrangements. In spite of this ban, the formula resurfaced in January 2016 during political talks held to decide on the electoral model for forthcoming national elections. After intense disagreement and a first conference ended in stalemate, on 27 January 2016 the National Leaders Forum, comprising the federal government and regional state leaders, issued a Communiqué in which it was announced that the best scenario for the 2016 elections sees seats in the Lower House of Parliament allocated according to the 4.5 formula.[96]

Despite the widespread criticism attracted by the 4.5 formula – in particular amongst Somali civil society – international law seems not to have much to say about its legality. As far as the law is concerned, understanding representativeness based on clan affiliation and enacting the concept through a provisional *modus operandi* is a viable path. As we have seen in Chapter 3, the concept of representativeness under international law on self-determination is indeed still so vague[97] that without further specification and articulation no serious evaluation can be made concerning its accordance with experiments made in practice. This is true in particular of ethnically and religiously homogeneous people such as the Somalis. In sum, whether this method can be said to have ensured representation of all the people of Somalia, or not, is an issue open to interpretation.

On the contrary, a positive note can be made with regards to the idea of gender representation. At Arta, for the first time, delegates agreed that women were to be represented in the Transitional National Parliament (TNP) and that 25 posts, or about 11% of the number of seats, would be reserved to women.[98] Article 29 of the Transitional Federal Charter provided that women constitute at least 12% of the Transitional Federal Parliament, and effectively roughly

96 Communiqué on the Electoral Model for 2016 http://www.somalilandpress.com/somaliacommunique-on-the-electoral-model-for-2016/ (last accessed 15 April 2018), and the subsequent Agreement between the Federal Government of Somalia and the Government of Puntland State of Somalia of 4 April 2016 https://horseedmedia.net/2016/04/04/agreement-between-the-federal-government-of-somalia-and-the-government-of-puntland-state-of-somalia/ (last accessed 15 April 2018).

97 See ch 3.3.2.

98 United Nations Secretary General, Report on the situation in Somalia, UN Doc S/2000/1211 of 19 December 2000. In fact, however, the total of women elected was only 5%.

12% of women obtained a Parliament seat.[99] Once again, at the second Constitutional Conference held in Garowe in January 2012 the delegates decided that the new parliament would include a 20% of women members and that the National Constituent Assembly would have included 30% of women delegates.[100] In fact, the percentage of women who made it to Parliament was close to 14%,[101] and the Constituent Assembly convened with a 24% of women.[102] Even though the final results did not entirely fulfil the percentages required, it nonetheless appears that in Somali politics and society the concept of representativeness has developed to include at least certain level of female representation.

5.4.1.4 *Representativeness, (s)election of government representatives and the will of the people*

As we have seen so far, the transitional governments set up by the Arta and Eldoret conferences (the TNG and TFG respectively) were constituted by selected – rather than elected – individuals, who were often part of self-appointed, corrupted and violent elites. Their existence was constantly plagued by a lack of representativeness and of perceived legitimacy, by a lack of capacity to control territory, as well as by a significant lack of approval and support amongst the Somali people. It is therefore not surprising to know that these governments, even if they had *de jure* authority over the territory of Somalia, were questioned in terms of their ability to represent the Somali people. Doubts about the lack of a meaningful attachment to the will of the people were indeed raised by a number of states discussing the standstill of the TNG at the Security Council in late 2001 and early 2002. Neither the European Union nor the United States ever recognised the TNG, the second arguing that inside Somalia, no political group had reached a sufficient level of legitimacy to represent the Somali people.[103] Conversely, the OAU recognised

99 See United Nations Development Programme (UNDP), Country Office for Somalia (2012) *Gender in Somalia Brief*, 3 http://www.undp.org/content/dam/rbas/doc/Women's%20Empowerment/Gender_Somalia.pdf (last accessed 15 April 2018).

100 Garowe Principles (n 63), principle 1(d) and 1(b). See also M H Mukhtar, 'Somali Reconciliation Conferences: The Unbeaten Track' in Abdulahi A Osman and Issaka K Souaré (eds), *Somalia at the Crossroads: Challenges and Perspectives on Reconstructing a Failed State* (Adonis & Abbey 2007) 128.

101 UNDP (n 99).

102 United Nations Security Council, 'Report of the Secretary General on Somalia' UN Doc S/2012/643, para 8.

103 The representative of the US, in October 2001 stated: 'We believe that the people of Somalia control their own political destiny. A future expansion of the United Nations presence in Somalia, however important, cannot substitute for the will of the Somali people to reclaim their country from chaos. The search for political legitimacy must proceed inside Somalia, and it must go Somali by Somali. In our view, no single group has yet succeeded in achieving that legitimacy. It is not for the United States Government, the Security Council or any other outside power to determine who is the legitimate representative of the Somali people. … Our responsibility as the Security Council and as individual member States is to figure out how we can support the coming together of that critical mass'. Security Council meeting records, S/PV.4392, 19 October 2001.

the TNG in December 2000 and the UN followed suit in November 2001.[104] Similarly, a few other states recognised the TNG as an expression of the will of the people. Among them the obvious Djibouti[105] – the prime architect of the project which brought the government into being – together with other Arab states, namely Tunisia and Libya.[106]

On behalf of these states, however, no real motivation is brought for why the TNG, despite its fragility and shortcomings, is to be rightfully considered to be an embodiment of the will of the people. The only possible exception being Djibouti, who argued that the open-ended character of invitations sent out for the Arta conference made it a people-driven process. It would have been useful if these states provided an explanation on which concrete elements led them to decide that the TNG represented the will of the people as this sort of information on states' interpretation of self-determination standards at present is missing.

A couple of years later, things went much better for the TFG. Despite not being elected by popular vote and being also affected by significant legitimacy issues, the TFG was however recognised by the UN, the AU and IGAD and openly supported by the international community[107]. Lewis notices that, whilst the government had no public electoral mandate and no real local support, at least it was internationally backed; both financially and by being proclaimed as the legitimate, transitional government of Somalia.[108] Most significantly, in late 2006, after the rise of the UIC (who controlled great part of Southern and Central Somalia but excluded from the Transitional Federal Institutions (TFI)) the international community backed the TFG, recognising it as the principal

104 See Moller (n 36) 14.

105 'Indeed this was a people-oriented, people-led and people-driven process, embracing all segments of Somali society. . . . Let us not forget that the TNG represents the will of the people of Somalia, irrespective of its fragility, its lack of resources and the lack of meaningful and credible support from the international community despite being the only recognized Somali national framework in existence today'. Statement of the Representative of Djibouti, Security Council meeting records, SP/V.4392, 19 October 2001.

106 The representative of Tunisia stated: 'the TNG continues to make efforts to involve the recalcitrant parties in the peace process, which, I stress, has been endorsed by the entire people of Somalia'. Security Council, Meeting records, S/PV.4392, 10 October 2001. The representative of Libya stated: 'The international community must stand shoulder to shoulder with the Transitional National Government, truly chosen by the majority of the people of Somalia. There is no alternative. . . . . The shortest route to regaining stability in Somalia is to support the Transitional National Government and enable it to exert and extend its authority throughout Somalia. Ultimately, it is indeed transitional: it is not a permanent Government. When the transitional period ends, the people of Somalia will be able to elect their representatives and their legitimate Government at the ballot box'. Security Council meeting records, S/PV.4487 (Resumption 1), 11 March 2002.

107 See International Crisis Group, 'Somaliland: Time for African Union Leadership' (2006) Africa Report n° 110, 3.

108 Lewis (n 68) 85.

political player in Somalia and authorising an international protection mission to support the TFG's mandate.[109]

The question of why the international community was willing to recognise the TFG despite its lack of legitimacy is a difficult one to answer. One possibility is that, at least from 2007-2008 onwards, a major driving factor was that the TFG could provide some level of legitimacy for the international effort to suppress Somali piracy. At that time, indeed, the increase of piracy-related attacks had turned the Gulf of Aden and the waters off the Somali coast into one of the most dangerous lanes in the world. This forced the international community to consider the situation in Somalia and led to a necessity to engage with the TFG, in order to protect international economic shipping interests. In this view, international recognition of the TFG in exchange for authorisation of anti-piracy activity could provide a certain level of legitimacy to what would otherwise be a set of forceful measures of uncertain lawfulness.

In December 2007, the International Maritime Organization (IMO) had indeed requested the TFG to take urgent action regarding piracy, including the conclusion of agreements with other states concerned to enable warships and military aircrafts to escort ships employed to carry humanitarian goods into Somali ports.[110] The TFG gave consent to such measures on 27 February 2008.[111] Starting from June of the same year, a set of Security Council resolutions further decided that 'cooperating states', namely states operating with the consent of the TFG as notified in advance to the UN Secretary General, could engage on counter-piracy actions on Somali soil with all necessary means.[112] The resolutions were adopted under Chapter VII of the UN Charter, so that their call into question of TFG consensus may seem at first glance superfluous. However, this can be explained by the fact that a number of states engaged internationally in counter-piracy activities either did not recognise the TFG or did not trust its ability to give authorisation in a timely fashion.[113] The Council's actions on counter-piracy can thus be seen as a general encouragement to promote the role of the TFG as the internationally recognised authority of Somalia amongst other states.

Overall, neither the TNG nor the TFG were elected by the Somali people or by truly legitimate representatives of the people. If the Arta process included representatives' visits inside Somalia, the Eldoret conference provided for no mechanism to reach out to and actively engage with the Somali population. The governments had been established abroad by means of a peace conference

109 See para 4.1.5 below.
110 IMO Resolution A.1002 (25), 29 November 2007, para 6.
111 Douglas Guilfoyle, 'Counter-piracy Law Enforcement and Human Rights' (2010) 59 *International and Comparative Law Quarterly* 141, 146.
112 See Resolutions 1816, 1838, 1846, 1851 of 2003.
113 Douglas Guilfoyle, 'Piracy Off Somalia: A Sketch of the Legal Argument' *EJIL: Talk!* (20 April 2009) http://www.ejiltalk.org/piracy-off-somalia-a-sketch-of-the-legal-framework/ (last accessed 15 April 2018).

organised by foreign states, had only a nominal presence in the country and often excluded important local players who controlled instead significant parts of the territory of Somalia.[114] None of the means and procedures for appointment of Parliament members and government officials presented an even slight resemblance to a guarantee that the result of the selection could ensure a genuine attachment to the will of the Somali people. As a result, many Somali grassroots groups, civil society organisations and independent media organisations were unhappy with the international backing of the TFG, which they saw as a coalition of warlords created in exile and installed on Somalia through a peace agreement.[115]

In international law, plebiscites, referenda and free and fair periodic elections are generally accepted to constitute evidence of an expression of popular will, although this list of means is not exhaustive.[116] Despite this indeterminacy in the law, any sort of compliance with self-determination standards on this matter seems difficult to be located in state practice in relation to the establishment of governments in Somalia. This is so, mainly owing to the fact that the Somali population was essentially not involved by any means in the decisions made concerning the establishment of a government. It should therefore not be surprising that, notwithstanding the international community's backing of the TFG, during the transition and until the establishment of the SFG in September 2012, in Somalia there was a widespread view that no government had achieved an acceptable level of internal legitimacy since the fall of Siyad Barre.[117]

The SFG, the first non-transitional Somali Government, was also the result of a selective process but, differently from its predecessors, the selection and appointment of both Parliament and government took place inside Somalia. The process initiated with the adoption of a Roadmap in September 2011, as part of a three-day Somalia National Reconciliation Conference held in Mogadishu and aimed at defining the terms on which to end the transition after yet

114 With control being exercised both in a coerced (warlords and various armed groups) and non-coerced manner (i.e. Somaliland).

115 On this point see Elmi (n 12) 26.

116 In his separate opinion on the *Western Sahara Advisory Opinion*, Judge Ammoun argues that the legitimate struggle for liberation from foreign domination qualifies as an expression of popular will in absence of a lack of consultation of the people of a given territory. Roth notices how, in the practice of decolonisation, the plebiscites are an instrumentality, not the essence, of self-determination. Saul also argues that reference to art 21 of the Universal Declaration of Human Rights 'which provides for periodic and genuine elections 'can lend support to claims of elected governments to enjoy governmental status, but it does not provide a clear legal basis for such an assertion'. *Western Sahara* (Advisory Opinion) [1975] ICJ Rep 12, para 59; Brad R Roth, *Governmental Illegitimacy in International Law* (OUP 2000) 226 and Saul (n 66) 75.

117 Several scholars share this view, see, for instance, Apuuli P Kasaija, 'Somalia after the United Nations-led Djibouti peace process' (2011) 20 *African Security Review* 45.

another unilateral extension of the transitional period declared by the TFG.[118] The Roadmap was supported by representatives of the international community, facilitated by the representative of the UN Secretary General, Augustine Mahiga, and its purpose was to enshrine the commitment of the key Somali leaders and stakeholders to end transition by 20 August 2012.[119] By that date it was agreed that a number of objectives would be achieved, including the creation of a new elected or selected government.[120]

Soon after the process started once again electoral ambitions were betrayed. Objectives were soon remodelled and expectations lowered. At a meeting held in Gaalkacyo in March 2012, it was agreed that the new Federal Parliament would have not been elected but selected by 135 traditional clan Elders – themselves appointed by clan families according to the 4.5 formula[121] – who would in their turn nominate the 225 members of the new Parliament. It was also established that elders' nominations would be reviewed by a Technical Selection Committee, mandated to ensure that nominations meet the agreed standards.[122] By the set deadline the Elders completed their work – amidst strong accusations of corruption[123] – and as a result Somalia witnessed the election of a new Parliament, of a new President and the creation of the SFG, Somalia's first non-transitional government, by November 2012.

This move was met with renewed trust by the international community. The United States recognised the SFG in January 2013[124] and normalised its relationship with the country; a British embassy opened in Somalia, and also Italy, Turkey, Sweden, the Netherlands, Kenya and Ethiopia have officially or de facto recognised Somalia and established relations with the SFG.[125] Optimism shines also through the words of the UN Special Representative for Somalia: 'it is

118 'Somali leaders launch reconciliation bid' *Al-Jazeera* (Doha, 4 September 2011) http://www.aljazeera.com/news/africa/2011/09/201194153630941320.html (last accessed 15 April 2018).

119 Roadmap on Ending the Transition, adopted in Mogadishu, 6 September 2011 https://unpos.unmissions.org/roadmap-ending-transition (last accessed 15 April 2018).

120 ibid Benchmark 2, page 9.

121 'Somalia Swears in Historic New Parliament' *Al-Jazeera* (Doha, 23 August 2012) http://www.aljazeera.com/news/africa/2012/08/2012818183718864689.html (last accessed 15 April 2018).

122 Report of the Secretary-General on Somalia, UN Doc S/2012/283, para 9 and Andrew Atta-Asamoah, 'Long way to restoration: Lessons from Somalia's transition process' (2013) *ISS Situation Report* 7 https://www.issafrica.org/uploads/SitRep2013_9July-Asamoah.pdf (last accessed 15 April 2018).

123 Abdi I Samatar, 'Somalia's fleeting opportunity for hopeful change?' *Al-Jazeera* (Doha, 18 September 2012) http://www.aljazeera.com/indepth/opinion/2012/09/20129161225583 2176.html> 15 April 2018.

124 See *U.S. Relations With Somalia*, US Department of State Bureau of African Affairs (16 August 2013) http://www.state.gov/r/pa/ei/bgn/2863.htm (last accessed 15 April 2018).

125 See Chiara Giorgetti, 'Using International Law in Somalia's Post-Conflict Reconstruction' (2014) 53 *Columbia Journal of Transnational Law* 48, 52–53.

going to be collectively a different parliament than anything you have witnessed before and certainly the beginning of legitimate, representative and accountable institutions which has never happened in 21 years of Somali crisis.[126] Yet, taking a closer look, this optimism seems at least partially unjustified. The widespread accusations of corruption, attached to virtually all phases of implementation of the Roadmap, including the work of the Elders and also their appointment of nominees to the new Parliament, posed indeed serious questions about the perceived legitimacy and representativeness of the SFG. In the words of the International Crisis Group:

> In the rush to monopolise the roadmap's implementation they [the TFG] ignored the Transitional Federal Charter, bypassed the parliament, sidelined the cabinet, and otherwise manipulated the process in an effort to predetermine who would lead the next Somali government. . . . Some elders foisted on the council were phony and, after two months of incessant delays and brazen politicking, the outcome was anything but dignified. Some elders allegedly nominated uneducated and objectionable individuals, some sold seats to highest bidders, and others even nominated their own family members.[127]

All in all, being yet another non-elected entity, appointed under the 4.5 formula and by means of disputable (and disputed) procedures, and by methods which once again did not witness any kind of popular consultation at large, the SFG also lacked legitimacy, and was viewed by many Somalis de facto as yet another provisional government. In the words of Matt Bryden, former coordinator of the UN Monitoring Group on Somalia and Eritrea and Director of the Horn of Africa Section at the International Crisis Group,

> The new government is neither permanent, representative, broadly based, nor even inherently democratic. It is an interim government, established on the basis of a provisional constitution for a period of four years. It enjoys de jure sovereignty over all of Somalia, but exercises de facto authority over Mogadishu and parts of the South, largely thanks to a presence of foreign troops. . . . The SFG's principal virtue was simply that Hassan Sheikh had been elected President. Had sheikh Sharif been re-elected instead, few observers would have felt compelled to describe the new government as "credible", "legitimate", "democratic" or "representative" – and an even

126 Mohammed Yusuf, 'More than 200 approved for new Somali Parliament' *Voice of America* (19 August 2012) http://www.voanews.com/content/more-than-200-approved-for-new-somali-parliament/1491225.html (last accessed 15 April 2018).

127 See International Crisis Group, 'Somalia: from troubled transition to a tarnished transition?'(2012) *Media Release* https://www.crisisgroup.org/africa/horn-africa/somalia/somalia-troubled-transition-tarnished-transition (last accessed 15 April 2018).

smaller number of foreign governments would have been moved to recognize it.[128]

The President of the SFG, Hassan Sheikh was indeed a respected figure, as a former civil society activist and researcher, and his election was a reason of optimism for many in Somalia.[129] Nonetheless, it seems impossible to establish a link between the creation of the SFG and the will of the Somali people. The procedure through which the new government was set up, namely by appointment on behalf of a group of 135 elders, cannot be said to constitute a popular consultation *strictu sensu*. It is submitted here that it would be against the essence of the principle to consider valid as an expression of the will of a *people*, the expression of the will of a few representatives themselves appointed by a handful of clan leaders. In other words, the extent to which a people at large is involved in an alleged exercise of the will of the people is an aspect which I think should be considered relevant when making an assessment in relation to compliance with self-determination standards.

In creating unelected transitional authorities, the criteria for deciding who sits at the negotiation tables, who can be elected and/or appointed, on which basis and through what kind of procedures, are critical issues. More specifically, these points are critical to both ensuring the perceived legitimacy of transitional authorities in the eyes of the local people,[130] as well as to interpret whether concerns on self-determination standards concerning the attachment of the will of the people have been taken seriously. In the Somali National Reconciliation Process, the choice of criteria was operated entirely by conference organisers – Djibouti at Arta, and IGAD 'Frontline States' at Eldoret. As a result, the two processes not only have produced transitional governments created abroad which lacked any sort of legitimacy inside Somalia itself; it also created a system of government that did not provide for a single, serious guarantee that the governmental entities in place would be attached to an expression of the will of the people. Differently, the SFG was created inside Somalia, and notwithstanding the large degree of international support, the mechanisms which brought it into being also made it suffer from significant legitimacy issues in the eyes of the people it is supposed to represent. The selection of Traditional Elders, and also the Elders' selections of people in their turn, along with widespread accuses

128 Matt Bryden, 'Somalia Redux: Assessing the New Somali Federal Government'(2013) *Report of the Center for Strategic and International Studies* 4–6 http://csis.org/publication/somalia-redux (last accessed 15 April 2018).

129 See Giorgetti (n 125) 51 and Samatar, 'Somalia's fleeting opportunity for hopeful change?' (n 123).

130 According to Saul, 'the input of domestic elites that owe their status to some form of prior popular vote has a claim to represent better-quality popular involvement than input from domestic elites that are prominent in the society only because of the ability to wield force'. See Saul (n 66) 39.

of corruption, are all issues that pose serious questions about the possible link between the SFG and the will of the Somali people.

In the language of political analysis, Somali governments suffer from a problem of lack of effectiveness. This means that selection criteria, being inappropriate, led to peace processes being difficult to implement – and the Somali National Reconciliation was an example of that. As explained by the International Crisis Group (writing in 2003):

> Ultimately, what matters most is not who "deserves" to sit at the table, but rather who possesses authority and legitimacy in sufficient measure to implement an agreement and deliver a lasting peace. Unless this is resolved, there is a real risk that the current negotiation will produce another "government in exile", unable to provide a working administration inside the country that represents the general will.[131]

From the perspective of international law, self-determination standards bring in two further concerns in relation to government formation in addition to effectiveness. In the first place, these governments are problematic because, having failed to control the territory which they were trying to govern, they also failed to show any meaningful connection to the will of the people of this territory. An attachment to the will of the people, however demonstrated (for instance through conducting a popular consultation, general elections or a referendum), is a requirement to establish the compliance with self-determination of an ineffective government with no control on territory. It is known that there is no norm of international law requiring a people to exercise its right to self-determination by any particular method, although in general practice a referendum has always been considered satisfactory evidence in UN practice on decolonisation.[132] In making an assessment of what may constitute an exercise of the will of the people, however conceived, I argued that the extent to which the population at large is involved should be a determinant factor.[133] The methods used in Somalia cannot be said to have involved a large portion of the Somali people and for this reason it is submitted that they failed to show a meaningful connection to the will of the people.

131 ICG, 'Negotiating a Blueprint for Peace in Somalia' (n 21) 16.

132 Stefan Talmon, 'Who is a legitimate government in exile? Towards normative criteria for governmental legitimacy in international law' in Guy Goodwin-Gill and Stefan Talmon (eds), *The Reality of International Law. Essays in Honour of Ian Brownlie* (OUP 1999) 405. See also the Separate Opinion of Judge Dillard on the *Western Sahara Advisory Opinion* (n 116), p. 123; Peter Radan, 'Secessionist Referendum in International and Domestic Law' (2012) 18 *Nationalism and Ethinic Politics* 8 and James Summers, *Peoples and International Law* (2nd edn, Martinus Nijhoff, 2014) 47 and 338–39.

133 On a similar stance, Saul argues that 'a consultative exercise that covers the whole of a country has the potential to provide better-quality popular involvement than one that focuses only on a particular area'. Saul (n 66) 39.

In the case of transitional authorities, security concerns and feasibility issues related to the chances of conducting successful peace negotiations make generally accepted standards, such as the holding of a national referendum, often inapplicable. Under such conditions, state-building leads us to consider two alternatives. We are either called upon to redefine what can legitimately be considered to be evidence of an expression of the will of the people, in a way that possibly lowers the scale of popular involvement at large in order to adapt to hostile security situations. Or, in the alternative, we can consider a suspension in time of the exercise, to include at a minimum a decisive commitment to hold a general consultation as soon as the situation allows it. This is an issue that international law scholarship should discuss further, particularly if we aim to maintain that the principle of self-determination has a role in guiding transitions.

In the second place, moreover, issues can be raised also in relation to an additional concern specific to the Somali situation. The governments in question can be questioned about how much they can be considered representative of the entirety of the people of Somalia. It should indeed be noticed that, in both cases, the Somaliland region (comprising about 1/5 of the entire territory and over 1/3 of the entire population) did not took part in the deals. At Arta, however, whilst the elites did not participate, representatives from clans from all over Somalia joined the conference.[134]

A key question concerning the definition and interpretation of self-determination standards is about ascertaining who has the authority to do so. In relation to state-building, one peculiar feature of external actors that have a role in the process is that their involvement constitutes a chance to make sense of how states attribute meaning to self-determination standards. For this reason, the statements of Arab states, which recognised the TNG as an expression of the will of the people without further clarification, together with the backing of the TFG and SFG at international level despite its dubious representativeness and legitimacy seem to demonstrate that, in Somalia, the threshold of proof for attachment to the will of the people, in the context of a power vacuum, was either subordinated to concerns of a different nature, or interpreted to be set extremely low.

In normal circumstances, one could classify these shortcomings as issues of 'internal self-determination': a matter of rights and entitlements held by Somalis against their partially representative government. However, the peculiar situation in which Somalia had been lingering for almost a decade before the Arta process took off, does complicate the picture. As it was already pointed out above, the issue of who is invited to the conferences and what model of representativeness is more appropriate are decided not only by Somali faction (or non-faction) leaders who are generally self-appointed, but also by the external actors who

134 See section 5.3 above. On the size of the majority in relation to turnout in referenda see Summers (n 132) 50–51.

drive the entire process forward. The involvement of external actors thus makes this situation also a matter of concern to external self-determination.

5.4.1.5 External interference issues

In this section we will examine the issues surrounding the creation of a new government in a situation of power vacuum from the perspective of external self-determination. This means questioning whether decisions concerning the process of creation of transitional governments in Somalia were made freely by Somali elites – arguably representative of the whole people; or whether any external actor interfered in the process so as to impose transitional institutions on the Somali people.

In Chapter 3 we saw that that the prohibition of non-intervention attached to the right to self-determination confers on the people of a state the freedom to make independent choices about issues on which a people has a right to decide freely, including the choice of a political status, of a political system and related constitutional arrangements. Moreover, we also established that the prohibition of interference under the law of self-determination includes a wider prohibition than mere military intervention, to include non-military methods of coercion.[135] Overall, it can be said that all acts that amount to severe political pressure exercised by external actors (states and international organisations) aimed at stage-managing the process of state-building can be said to be contrary to external self-determination standards and to international law.

It was mentioned above that a heavy degree of external involvement in Somalia's internal affairs reportedly took place on behalf of various states and international actors. This happened constantly throughout the whole phase of conflict, instability and protracted transition, involving both military and non-military means of interference. In the period of time under consideration, interference in Somalia was so insidious that was indeed a matter of concern to the Security Council. In a Presidential statement issued in 2001, the Council '*called* on all States and other actors to comply scrupulously with the arms embargo established by Resolution 733 (1992) of 23 January 1992'; and insisted 'that all States, in particular those of the region, should not interfere in the internal affairs of Somalia. Such interference could jeopardize the sovereignty, territorial integrity, political independence and unity of Somalia'.[136] In this section we will consider several examples of how external actors attempted to interfere into Somalia's internal affairs and to promote certain strategic choices in the process of state-building, including first and foremost the creation of a new government.

Concerns over external interference in Somalia come indeed from many angles. In the *Nicaragua* case, the ICJ had established that training, arming,

135 See ch 4.2.2.1 and 4.2.3.

136 United Nations, Statement by the President of the Security Council, UN Doc S/PRST/2001/30, 31 October 2001.

equipping, financing and supplying the anti-government forces or otherwise encouraging, supporting and aiding military and paramilitary activities in and against the government of a country, is a breach of customary international law obligations on non-interference.[137] The Security Council, in relation to Somalia, has been primarily concerned with such acts which were in violation of the arms embargo imposed by Resolution 733 (1992).[138] The violation amounts to alleged provision of assistance and supply of arms, on behalf of certain governments, to groups inside Somalia in order to advance a set of political and strategic objectives. These acts, mostly operated by Somalia's neighbouring states, have been denounced in several of the reports submitted by the UN Monitoring Group on Somalia and constitute a clear violation of the principle of non-interference.[139]

Intervention in the form of training and assistance to anti-government factions is well documented both in relation to Ethiopian support of selected warlords, of anti-TNG factions and of the TFG; and also in relation to Arab states (Djibouti, Egypt, Libya, Iran, Syria and Hizbollah from Lebanon) as well as Eritrea supporting first the TNG, the ICU and then its splinter group, Al-Shabaab.[140] In fact, the mere existence and ruling of any faction and government over another in Somalia during the years in object can be seen entirely as an effect of greater or lesser degrees of external interference. To begin with, the TNG was created abroad, as a result of a conference convened at Arta under the auspices of Djibouti and with the support of a number of other Arab states. The government however had no control over territory because it was not supported locally by the warlords who were holding de facto power in Somalia and who had not been invited to the conference.

Yet the TNG itself, half way through the implementation of the Arta process, is reported to have raised issues on several occasions against the threat of external interference by expressing concern over Ethiopia's alleged intervention in Somalia's internal affairs. TNG officials claimed that Ethiopia was 'disregarding

137 *Military and Paramilitary Activities in and against Nicaragua (Nicaragua v. United States of America)*, Merits, Judgment [1986] ICJ Rep 14 at 146.

138 See note 41.

139 A first, general, accusation in this respect was moved by the 2002 Report of the Monitoring Group on Somalia. The following year the Monitoring Group affirmed that such assistance had been provided regularly since the imposition of the arms embargo, and notwithstanding the participation of those same actors in the IGAD peace process. The 2003 report also presented in greater detail assistance activities to Somali faction groups provided by the Ethiopia, Eritrea, Yemen, Djibouti. By 2003, hence mid-way through the Eldoret process which had started with the signing of the Eldoret Declaration on the Cessation of Hostilities, it was clear to the monitoring Group that neighbouring states were still playing a significant role in militarily assisting various factions in Somalia. See, respectively, UN Doc S/2002/722, 3 July 2002, para. 30; UN Doc S/2003/223, 25 March 2003.

140 See UN Report of the Monitoring Group on Somalia pursuant to Security Council Resolution 1676 (2006), UN Doc S/2006/913 para 6-145.

the sovereignty, territorial integrity and independence of Somalia by supplying arms and ammunition to Somali groups opposing the Transitional National Government'.[141] Indeed, after the establishment of the TNG, Ethiopia has first helped to establish the SRRC, and then provided its members with military training and arms supplies in order to make of this umbrella organisation a credible counterpart.[142] Surely this form of interference severely hindered the peace process set out at Arta, also given that Ethiopia successfully lobbied at the OAU and other international organisations to unseat the TNG and to convene a new, IGAD-sponsored, process.[143]

As a consequence of both the internal failures of the TNG – despite the support that it received from Eritrea and other Arab states – and of Ethiopian assistance in making the SRRC a credible counterpart, the Arta process derailed and a new peace conference had to be organised under the auspices of IGAD.[144] Hence, the origins of the Eldoret peace process, which later created the TFG, lie within a significant degree of external interference exercised by Somalia's neighbouring states – and by Ethiopia in particular. This was both in the form of discretion exercised drafting invitees' lists and appointing personnel, as was seen above, as well as in the form of military support to the TFG against the ICU, so that it could remain in power as the internationally recognised government of Somalia. Also, the fact that the TFG was able to return to Mogadishu only as a result of Ethiopian military intervention did not make it popular within Somalia. It is indeed reported that the TFG was known within Somalia with the derogatory nickname *daba dhilif*, meaning 'government set up for a foreign purpose'.[145]

It was external actors – and Ethiopia most blatantly amongst all regional powers – that conditioned the Kenyan-hosted IGAD peace talks. They did so by determining the conditions for the talks to be conducted and by means of providing selective military assistance to warring factions. On top of that, also the talks themselves, in the way they were conducted and administered, were heavily manipulated by external players – primarily IGAD member states themselves.[146] This type of interference is not only self-serving and, when forceful, also illegal; but it is deeply detrimental for peace and stability because it perpetuates conflict. In the case of Somalia, Ethiopian military interference undermined the peace processes set out at Arta, which had reached unprecedented levels of

141 United Nations Security Council, Report of the Secretary-General on the situation in Somalia, UN Doc S/2009/709 of 27 June 2002, at 4.

142 See Report of the Monitoring Group on Somalia, UN Doc S/2003/223, 25 March 2003.

143 See Samatar and Samatar (n 16) 5.

144 See section 5.3 above.

145 Harper (n 82) 177.

146 This view is supported by most writers and will be discussed at length in section 5.4.3 below. See eg Elmi (n 12) 94–95; ICG reports (nn 17 and 21); Mulugeta (n 15) 29.

representativeness, and ultimately led to the imposition of a new government and of a number of state-building measures on the Somali people.[147]

In 2006 foreign intervention in Somalia reached unprecedented levels. The TGF, established in exile under pressure from Ethiopia and with little connection to the territory, was initially unable to relocate from Kenya to Somalia and had been asking for international protection to do so. In January 2005 the AU Peace and Security Council accepted, in principle, the deployment of a Peace Support Mission.[148] At that time the TFG was particularly keen on receiving the military support of an international presence because it was facing the fast-growing threat of the UIC at home. At that time, the UIC was indeed controlling a large part of the territory of Southern and Central Somalia. In so doing, it was a major player in the political scene and was also enjoying a moderate level of popular support which made it represent a de facto viable alternative to the ruling of the TFG.

It was at this point, hence in the midst of a civil war between the UIC and the TFG, that the UN Security Council, acting under Chapter VII, adopted Resolution 1725 to authorise an IGAD protection and training mission in Somalia.[149] With this resolution the international community took a stance in Somalia, effectively taking sides and imposing the TFIs as the only viable and legitimate route to achieve peace and stability in Somalia.[150] In the preamble, the resolution recalls a few times the importance of an inclusive political process and the need to restore dialogue between the UIC and the TFG, but in operative paragraph 1 the Council:

1. *Reiterates* that the Transitional Federal Charter and Institutions offer the only route to achieving peace and stability in Somalia, *emphasizes* the need for continued credible dialogue between the Transitional Federal Institutions and the Union of Islamic Courts.

Within the terms of this resolution, the UIC could not have aspired to become the new government of Somalia, but it could, at maximum, have aspired to

147 On this point see Elmi (n 12) 96.

148 African Union Peace and Security Council, 29th Meeting, 12 May 2005, Addis Ababa, Doc PSC/PR/2(XXIX).

149 United Nations Security Council Resolution 1725 (2006) of 7 December 2006.

150 The same position was taken also a few months earlier by the Council of the European Union at the conclusion of a Council meeting a number of conclusions on Somalia were adopted, including: '3. The Council expresses its deep concern about the continuing tensions in Somalia between the UIC and the TFIs. The Council reconfirms its support to the TFIs as the only legitimate political representation in Somalia as defined in the Transitional Federal Charter'. See Council of Europe, 2748th General Affairs Council Meeting, 15 September 2015, ref. CL06-182EN http://europa.eu/rapid/press-release_PRES-06-241_en.doc (last accessed 15 April 2018). The same view on the partisan character of the support provided to the TFG by international actors is shared by Tobias Hagmann, *Stabilization, Extraversion and Political Settlements in Somalia*, Rift Valley Institute & Political Settlements Research Programme (2016) 40.

gain a role in the TFG and related institutions that were already in place.[151] It is important to recall that at the time the UIC enjoyed a certain (although limited) degree of local support and a wide level of effective control on Somali territory, two characteristics which the TFG lacked almost entirely. According to Jeng, 'by proclaiming that the TFG offered the only solution to Somali crisis, the resolution placed unrealistic faith in a fragile institution lacking attributes of empirical statehood or support from its social constituencies'.[152] In the preamble the resolution indeed seemingly acknowledges that there are effectiveness and legitimacy issues with the TGF by

> *underlining* the importance for stability in Somalia of broad-based and representative institutions and of an inclusive political process, *commending* the crucial efforts of the League of Arab States and the Intergovernmental Authority on Development (IGAD) to promote and encourage political dialogue between the Transitional Federal Institutions and the Union of Islamic Courts.

By adopting operative paragraph 1 above under Chapter VII, the Security Council accepted that the political future of Somalia would be linked to the TFG. In so doing, it agreed to protect and preserve what was a sort of 'façade' government against the threat of disintegration posed by the ICU.

There are many reasons why this is problematic. First, because international support was granted in favour of a government which was established abroad under the directives of foreign actors; that had not been elected, which presented no concrete guarantee that it could embody the will of the people and

151 In an interview with Mario Raffaelli, former Special Envoy of the Italian Government to Somalia from 2003 to 2008, it was highlighted that this paragraph of the resolution contained a form of political recognition for the UIC. In the interview, Raffaelli also stated that the final version of the resolution presented in fact a watered-down version of the original draft presented by the United States. With the help of British mediation in the Security Council, the mandate of the resolution was tied to the Khartoum Agreement and to its follow ups, hence linking the resolution to an ongoing process to which the UIC was part. In addition, the resolution prevented Somalia's neighbouring states to deploy troops to Somalia (operative paragraph 4). Together with the Representative of the European Union, Raffaelli travelled to Mogadishu on 12 December 2006 to meet with the Executive Council of the UIC and to explain the terms of the resolution to them. The delegation attempted to convince the UIC to accept the terms of the resolution, showing that accepting the resolution would have led to the basis for Ethiopian presence in the country to become inconsistent. Nonetheless, the UIC never accepted the resolution, being opposed to any foreign presence in the country. Interview with Mario Raffaelli, Special Envoy of the Italian Government to Somalia from 2003 to 2008 (Trento, Italy, 4 May 2015). See also Mohamed O Hassan, 'EU Delegation Pushes Somalia Peace Talks' *The Washington Post* (Washington, 13 December 2006) http://www.washingtonpost.com/wp-dyn/content/article/2006/12/13/AR2006121300956.html (last accessed 15 April 2018).

152 Jeng (n 89) 259.

as a consequence had suffered enormously from a legitimacy deficit. Support was also given at a time when that government was simply being kept in place by the presence of foreign troops – whereby said troops were present in the country in violation of a UN arms embargo and perceived as occupiers by the Somali population.[153] In this picture, the UN Security Council's backing of the TFG and of the TFIs as the *only route* to achieving peace and stability in Somalia transpires a certain degree of escalation in the level of foreign intervention allowed at the international level into Somalia's internal affairs. Essentially, in late 2006 some claim that the TFG had become just another party in the country's ravaging civil war but the one which was getting international support.[154]

In light of the above, it is surprising, to say the least, to see how no state raised any meaningful concern about any of the points mentioned above on the debates preceding the adoption of the resolution. The only significant reaction was provided by the state of Qatar, which explained its vote as follows:

> Our support for the resolution stems from our understanding that it aims to encourage all Somali parties to reach a peaceful political settlement through a comprehensive dialogue among all groups. This would accomplish the hoped-for stability. It is important that this resolution not have a negative impact; it must not be construed as being directed at one party at the expense of another. This must be kept in mind when the resolution is implemented.[155]

Ethiopia had started sending troops in Somalia to fight the UIC several months before the adoption of Resolution 1725, but it was not until late December that the operation escalated into a full-blown intervention, conducted with the support of the TFG. The controversies surrounding an alleged 'intervention by invitation'[156] in a similar context are almost self-evident. The intervention was sent out by a government established in exile and with only a nominal presence inside Somalia, not constitutionally elected and affected by serious legitimacy problems. In addition, the intervention was to be conducted against an arms embargo established under Chapter VII by resolution 733 (1992). Not only the legitimacy, but also the legality of such an intervention is disputable, to say the least.[157]

153 See Menkhaus, 'Somalia: A Country in Peril' (n 49) 11.; Abdi I Samatar, 'Ethiopian Invasion of Somalia: US Warlordism and AU Shame' (2007) 34 *African Review of Political Economy* 111, 153-54; Williams (n 40) 517.

154 See Williams (n 40) and Menkhaus, 'Somalia: A Country in Peril' (n 49) 11. After 2008, with the inclusion of Al-Shabaab into the US list of foreign terrorist organisations, the international backing of the TFG gained a greater level of legitimacy internationally, and also a greater level of intensity after the passing of Resolution 2036 (2012).

155 United Nations Security Council, Meeting records, 5579th meeting of 6 December 2006, UN Doc S/PV.5579 at 3–4.

156 On this point see Khayre (n 38), arguing that there is no actual evidence that the Somali Government has invited the Ethiopian army to intervene.

157 On the legality of the intervention see Kayre (n 38) and Yihdego (n 35).

An attempt on behalf of Qatar to circulate a presidential statement 'calling for an immediate cease-fire and the immediate withdrawal of all international forces, specifying Ethiopian troops' was blocked as other Council members 'opposed to singling out Ethiopia and calling for withdrawal'.[158] The lack of negative reactions at the international level can thus be interpreted as a more or less tacit approval of the intervention.[159] The intervention was indeed never condemned by the Security Council and was in fact praised by IGAD members.[160] There is also leaked evidence that a few months before the Ethiopians had sought and received US support for an intervention if things with the ICU would have escalated.[161] The 2006 US National Security Strategy document identified Africa as high priority, and this proved useful for the Ethiopians, who managed to take advantages of the US concerns about the expansion of the ICU in Somalia.[162] Overall, whilst the international community seemed not to have a problem with Ethiopian intervention in Somalia, inside Somalia the intervention was perceived as an occupation and a biased attempt forcefully to install an illegitimate regime.[163]

The Ethiopian military intervention led to a quick defeat of the ICU and to its disintegration as a political group. In the months following their defeat,

158 Statements reported in Yihdego (n 35) 671.

159 ibid. Saul argues that, whilst Ethiopia was arguably free to intervene under international law, the situation run contrary to the political principle of self-determination. Matthew Saul, 'Local Ownership of Post-Conflict Reconstruction in International Law: The Initiation of International Involvement' (2011) 16 *Journal of Conflict and Security Law* 165.

160 Mulugeta (n 15) 32.

161 Human Rights Watch obtained a leaked UN cable where it is reported that, in a conversation with UN officials, US Assistant Secretary of State for African Affairs, Jendayi Frazer, worried on the 'uncertain' situation in Somalia outlines a worst-case scenario where the expansion of the ICU throughout Somalia causes the disintegration of the TFG. Ms. Frazer is also reported to have said that this scenario would have a major negative impact in the Horn and that the US and IGAD would not allow it. She allegedly expressed the view that while the US feared an Ethiopian intervention could rally 'foreign elements', the US would rally with Ethiopia if the Jihadists took over. In a leaked US Government cable of 31 October 2006, it is also reported that the position of Ethiopia on a potential military success of the ICU over the TFG: 'The bottom line for the Government of Ethiopia (GOE), however, is that it cannot allow the TFG to fall to the Council of the Courts (ICU). If Baidoa is attacked, the GOE will defend it. The GOE's hope is that the international community will rally more forcefully behind the TFG before so that Ethiopia can legitimately defend it from being ousted by the Islamic Courts. . . . If the UN lifts the embargo, the TFG can seek to protect itself and strengthen the anti-ICU coalition, including the international community, rather than leaving Ethiopia as the sole "enemy" (in the ICU's rhetoric)'. Cable ID: 06ADDISABABA2901_a of 31 October 2006; original classification: SECRET https://search.wikileaks.org/plusd/cables/06ADDISABABA2901_a.html (last accessed 15 April 2018). See also Human Rights Watch (n 44) 22.

162 On this point see Harper (n 82) 169–70.

163 Williams (n 40) 517.

some of the group's former leaders started negotiating an agreement with the TFG, whilst Al-Shabaab, the hardliners in the former ICU, vowed for armed opposition to the TFG and started to regain territorial control in most of Southern Somalia.[164] Things got sharper in March 2008, when Al-Shabaab entered the US list of foreign terrorist organisations under suspicion that their leaders were responsible for the 1998 US embassy attacks in Nairobi.[165] With the inclusion of Al-Shabaab into this list the Council reinforced its position on Somalia's ongoing conflict and also decided to expand the role of the international force mandated to protect the TFG.[166] In Security Council resolution 2036 of 22 February 2012, operative paragraph 1, the Council, acting under Chapter VII:

1. *Decides* that . . . AMISOM shall be authorised to take all necessary measures as appropriate in those sectors in coordination with the Somali security forces to reduce the threat posed by Al Shabaab and other armed opposition groups in order to establish conditions for effective and legitimate governance across Somalia, *further decides* that AMISOM shall act in compliance with applicable international humanitarian and human rights law, in performance of this mandate and in full respect of the sovereignty, territorial integrity, political independence and unity of Somalia.[167]

The paragraph is of particular significance, for three main reasons. First, by authorising AMISOM to 'take all necessary means' the Council gives AMISOM a clear peace enforcement mandate against a specific group – something that has rarely been seen in security resolutions since the 1990s. According to Michael Pugh, in fact it was the first time for the Security Council to designate 'a specific enemy in mandating the AU peacekeeping mission in Somalia'.[168] Secondly, the Council admits that the peace enforcement mandate is necessary in order to *establish* the conditions for effective and legitimate governance across the country, hence implying that the supported government was significantly short

164 See section 5.3 above.

165 United States Government, Department of State, 'Designation of Al-Shabaab' 18 March 2008 https://web.archive.org/web/20080319184009/http://www.state.gov/r/pa/prs/ps/2008/mar/102338.htm (last accessed 15 April 2018).

166 The establishment of the IGAD mission (IGASOM), authorised by Resolution 1725 (2006) proved to be short-sighted. Operative paragraph 4 provided that, according to the plan presented by IGAD, no neighbouring country could send troops into Somalia and, as a consequence, the resolution was never implemented. The mission was later replaced with an AU mission (AMISOM), authorised by Security Council resolution 1744 (2007) of 21 February 2007.

167 United Nations Security Council Resolution 2036 (2012), UN Doc S/RES/2036, 22 February 2012.

168 Michael Pugh, 'Reflections on aggressive peace' (2014) 19 *International Peacekeeping* 410, 414.

of legitimacy and capacity to govern effectively.[169] Thirdly, the resolution suggests that, by carrying out its enforcement mandate on the side of an ineffective government with strong legitimacy issues, AMISOM not only shall but also can act in full respect of the political independence of Somalia.[170]

The only two significant statements of vote on adoption of this resolution came from the representatives of the United Kingdom and Germany. The UK representative explained that his government had voted in favour of the resolution because an expanded AMISOM would 'help increase areas of stability in Somalia. It will help the political process in Somalia by enabling Somalis outside the capital to take part in the political and constitutional process, making that process more representative and legitimate'.[171] In this view, a stronger mandate of the international presence is encouraged by a third-party external actor because it is conceived as an instrument to improve popular engagement in the process of drafting a new constitution. Likewise, for Germany, an expansion of AMISOM's mandate is functional to state-building and to assist the legitimacy of the constitutional process. In the words of the German representative:

> The ultimate goal of all efforts remains a united and functioning Somali State. AMISOM cannot continue indefinitely. The current situation calls for the establishment of security and of a responsible and representative Somali Government that promotes the political process and the delivery of basic services to Somali citizens. All of this requires a solid framework. The adoption of a new, legitimate constitution would be a very important step in this direction. Only such steps, implemented by responsible Somali actors, can lay the basis for a State in which AMISOM would be able to leave after having successfully fulfilled its tasks.[172]

In these words, it is clear that both the UK and the German governments believe that assigning AMISOM a peace enforcement mandate is a necessary means to establish the conditions in Somalia for promoting the political process and, with it, the adoption a legitimate constitution. In Chapter 4, we have seen that under international law states have a positive obligation to assist with the full

169 Legitimacy here is to be understood in the sense of 'governmental legitimacy', as explained by Talmon for the case of governments in exile: 'the attribute "legitimate" is used in diplomatic and legal language to distinguish a "government" in the sense of international law, either in exile or in situ, from a non-government, i.e. from an authority in exile not meeting the criteria for governmental status'. Talmon (n 132) 537.

170 In their vote statements Security Council members unanimously supported the TFG and called for steady progress to be made in implementing the Roadmap to End Transition. Were Al-Shabaab not included in the US terror list, it would have been less likely that the international community could have backed a dysfunctional government with legitimacy issues in such a straightforward manner.

171 United Nations Security Council, Meeting records, 6718th meeting of 22 February 2012, UN Doc S/PV.6718.

172 ibid.

realisation of the right to self-determination. The adoption of a new, legitimate constitution through a process which genuinely engaged the people of the state surely qualifies as an important milestone for the realisation of the right. The voting clarifications provided by Germany and the UK, therefore, seem to suggest that the two states may have voted in favour of this resolution keeping in mind that their action is in line with the obligation to assist a people with the full realisation of their right to self-determination. More state practice in this respect would be needed in order to tell whether this interpretation is correct; hence whether the two states acted in the belief that they had an obligation to assist the Somali people in ensuring that a legitimate constitutional process would take place, or whether their vote was motivated by necessity, self-interest or other strategic considerations.

To sum up, the role played by Somalia's neighbours in the process of rebuilding order and security in the country seems to have crossed the fine line that separates assistance from interference. From the perspective of international law, this cross-over is problematic for at least two main reasons. First, because such interference has violated the arms embargo imposed under Chapter VII by resolution 733 (1992) because it included the provision of military assistance, training and intervention. Secondly, because it appears to clash with the self-determination entitlements of the Somali people, who enjoy the right freely to decide, without external interference, about their political system and to pursue their economic, social and cultural development. This entitlement includes a right not to have a government imposed on the people and a right to develop its political system free from coercion.

Overall, the conditions under which the TNG, TFG and the SFG were created show that the progressive success of the transition rests on a set of foundations which seem to contradict basic international law standards attached to the principle of self-determination. External actors involved in Somalia, throughout the years 2002–2012, actively supported governments that had no demonstrable attachment to the will of the people, no control over Somali territory and which essentially could not function independently without foreign military assistance that they were enjoying in violation of the international arms embargo. Through various coercive means (including the provision of training, assistance and military aid), as well as through a Chapter VII recognition of the TFG as an exclusive, irreducible and legitimate political actor at a key moment in the history of peace-making in Somalia, this government became entitled to enjoy international military protection and support in the form of a peacekeeping operation, as well as to bring the state-building process ever closer.

The adoption of Resolution 1725 had consequences related to the impact and significance of external self-determination standards in the Somali context. By reducing the weight of non-intervention concerns in virtue of security interests, the international community has essentially lowered self-determination standards applicable to Somalia. Against what the law mandates, the Council has in this way ***determined for*** the Somali people that the TFG, a dysfunctional, unelected and unrepresentative government, was the only viable institutional route to achieve peace. In so doing, one can argue that the international community in Somalia has not only disregarded the absence of any tangible guarantee concerning the attachment of the reconstruction process to the will of the people; it has also disregarded very basic standards of non-interference attached to self-determination, depriving the Somali people of its international legal protection against external interference.

5.4.2 *Second situation: the adoption of a new constitution*

The second situation in which state-building practice can be of concern to self-determination is when a new constitution is adopted. The making of a new constitution is indeed a moment in which the future shape of the state is at stake, because decisions are made about the form and system of government that shall be adopted by a certain state.[173] In this section, therefore we aim to assess whether the government and the external actors involved in state-building exercises in Somalia, have done anything to ensure that the process of adoption of a new constitution reflected a genuine expression of the will of the Somali people.

5.4.2.1 *We, the delegates*

Somalia's first Constitution was adopted in 1960[174] and ratified by a national referendum in 1961.[175] This Constitution remained valid until the coup which brought to power Siyad Barre in 1969, which led to the suspension of the Constitution and later to its amendment, by means of another popular referendum through which Somalia was turned into a single-party Presidential Republic.[176] Following more than 10 years of total breakdown of government structures, the first attempt to re-establish order through a constitution took place at the Arta peace Conference, and led to the adoption of a three-year Transitional National Charter (TNC) which provided for elections in 2003. With the collapse of the TNG, also the TNC expired in 2003.[177]

The next attempt at drafting a Constitution was made in 2004, as part of the IGAD-led peace process. The Transitional Federal Charter (TFC), Somalia's

173 See generally Kirsti Samuels, 'Post-Conflict Peace-Building and Constitution-Making' (2006) 6 *Chicago Journal of International Law* 663.

174 The Constitution of the Somali Republic (1961) http://www.ilo.org/dyn/travail/docs/2176/Constitution1960.pdf (last accessed 15 April 2018).

175 For the results of the voting see 'Elections in Somalia' African Elections Database http://africanelections.tripod.com/so.html#1961_Constitutional_Referendum (last accessed 15 April 2018).

176 ibid. See 1979 referendum.

177 United Nations, UNDP/UNPOS Joint Constitution Unit (2012) *Guidebook on the Provisional Constitution of Somalia* http://docplayer.net/29951376-Guidebook-on-the-provisional-constitution-of-somalia.html (last accessed 15 April 2018).

proto-constitution for the transitional phase, was adopted in August 2004 in Nairobi.[178] As a transitional document to regulate the transitional phase to stability, it was adopted by the delegates invited to a peace conference and not approved by popular vote. Noteworthy, the overture of the TFC's preamble recites:

> We, the delegates representing the people of the Somali Republic have solemnly resolved to enact a Transitional Federal Charter for the Somali Republic.

With a view to ending the transition, the TFC itself envisages the creation of a proper constitution. The task to design a new constitution that can accommodate the request of creating a federal system of governance is specifically attributed to a purpose-built body, an independent Federal Constitution Committee (FCC).[179] More precisely, the task given to the FCC was to design a constitution suitable for a federal state to be submitted for official adoption. In June 2010, the draft document was presented to the public but, due to the security situation, the FCC reportedly regretted that it did not manage to consult the people before the draft was produced.[180] As a consequence, the draft presented was again provisional, pending revision and the formulation of a proper final draft, one elaborated following a process of consultation with the people. The final draft would then be ready for adoption by means of a referendum or, if the situation on the ground would dictate that a referendum would not be possible, an alternative consultative mechanism was to be decided by December 2011.[181] The Roadmap for transition, adopted on September 2011, established that a New Constitution was to be drafted by 1 July 2012 and adopted by referendum (or other consultative procedure provided by new constitution).[182] In December 2011, following delays with the implementation of the Roadmap and the renewed postponing of national elections, referendum aspirations were once again lowered and reformulated. At the Garowe I Constitutional Conference, held in December 2011, Somali leaders developed the idea proposed by the FCC of creating a National Constitutional Assembly (NCA) mandated to approve the new constitution.[183] In February 2012, at the second conference held in Garowe, the leaders convened on the terms of operation of the NCA and later a protocol was added to the Roadmap which established the means of work of

178 See note 26.
179 TFC, Art. 11(5).
180 The Main Report of the Federal Constitution Commission (FCC) on Consultation Draft Constitution, 30th July 2010, at 3 http://www.tandemproject.com/pdf/final_main.pdf (last accessed 15 April 2018).
181 Progress Report of the Independent Federal Constitution Commission on the Consultation Draft Constitution, July 2011 at 21–22 http://www.dastuur.org (last accessed 2 July 2012).
182 Roadmap, 'Benchmark 2: Constitution – (b) the Draft Constitution adopted' (n 119) 7.
183 FCC (n 181) 22.

the NCA. According to it, the Assembly mandated to vote on the new Constitution was to comprise 825 delegates (of which 30% were women), selected and appointed on the basis of the 4.5 formula by the Traditional Elders – the same Elders who selected the members of the new Somali Federal Parliament.[184]

In the words of the former Somali Prime Minister Abdiweli Mohamed Ali, the 825-member body was 'inclusive and representative' of Somali society.[185] From the perspective of international law on self-determination, however, its representativeness can be questioned in relation to two key aspects. First, because the body mandated to scrutinise the constitutions was indeed adopted with the same, flawed mechanisms used to select a government that was affected by important legitimacy issues. Secondly, the scope of action that was afforded by the NCA further complicates the issue. The Protocol annexed to the Roadmap included several provisions which greatly limited the possibilities of the NCA to shape the Constitution in view of the people's perspective which they allegedly represented. In particular, Article 7 of the Protocol provided the following:

> Article 7(2)(1) At the conclusion of the NCA's deliberations, the delegates shall vote on the following question: "Should this draft provisional constitution be provisionally adopted to provide for a better Somalia, help reconstruct our country and set us on the right path to justice and lasting peace, pending final adoption at the referendum?"
>
> Article 7(2)(5) In the event of a NO vote, this draft provisional constitution will nevertheless take effect until a new constitution is adopted.
>
> Art 7(3)(3) If the provisional constitution is ratified in the referendum, the provisional constitution as reviewed and amended takes full effect as the new constitution; and
>
> Article 7(3)(4) If it is rejected in the referendum, it will nevertheless continue as the provisional constitution until a further constitutional draft has been prepared, presented and ratified by referendum.[186]

The provisions set out in the various provisions of Article 7 reported above severely limit the space of action of the NCA. This body could indeed only have a yes or no vote over the constitution; and, should the outcome of the vote be negative, the same constitution would nonetheless have entered into effect as a provisional constitution.

In July 2012, the NCA adopted the new Provisional Constitution of the Federal Republic of Somalia with an overwhelming majority. Of the 645 members

184 Articles 3(1), 4(1) and 4(2), Somali Roadmap Signatories, *Protocol Establishing the Somali National Constituent Assembly* (2012), Nairobi, 22 June 2012 http://unpos.unmissions.org/Default.aspx?ctl=Details&tabid=9737&mid=12701&ItemID=19234 (last accessed 15 April 2018).

185 Abdiweli M Ali, Prime Minister of Somalia, 'Keynote address' (Chatham House, London, UK, 20 February 2012).

186 *Protocol Establishing the Somali National Constituent Assembly* (n 184).

of the constituent assembly that were present during the vote, 621 backed the document and only 13 voted against, while 11 abstained.[187] Nonetheless, the limited engagement of civil society and lack of popular engagement in the drafting process led to the legitimacy of this document within Somalia and for Somalia's civil society being disputed.[188] Without doubt, the holding of a popular consultation throughout Somalia and approval by referendum would have improved the situation, but as Menkhaus reminds us, 'Security and access are so poor in much of south-central Somalia that principles of inclusivity and local ownership are beyond the reach of a government that is under siege in its own compound'.[189] At all stages of the long-standing transition in Somalia, no government has ever been in a position realistically to aspire to holding a referendum or other type of truly universal consultative mechanism.

All in all, the latest Provisional Constitution of Somalia was adopted by a Committee composed by a few hundred people who claimed to be representative of the whole of the Somali people. Little debate has taken place within Somalia concerning the shape that the new State should assume and also the contribution brought by civil society representatives has been minimal. The process was essentially UN-driven and involved only the local elites and external actors. As Hay recounts, the involvement of other parties in creating the *pouvoir constituent* is a distinctive character of internationalised constitutions:

> Internationalized constitutions force us to reformulate the traditional understanding of legitimacy as a purely internal matter, because the international community effectively becomes part of the constituency being expressed and consenting to the constitution. Because they are made by an 'internationalized *pouvoir constituant*', legitimacy is measured by the additional imperatives and concerns of those actors. ... These objectives may be in tension with the norm of self-determination which is the primary concern of the local *pouvoir constituant*. The legitimacy of internationalized constitutions, therefore, depends on a level of acceptability for all parties concerned. For the local population, ownership is necessary to consider the constitution an exercise of self-determination. A sense of ownership is difficult to

187 See 'Somali Leaders Back New Constitution' *BBC News Africa* (Nairobi, 1 August 2012) http://www.bbc.com/news/world-africa-19075685 (last accessed 15 April 2018).

188 Mary Harper, 'Somalia: Whose Country is it, Anyway?' (2013) 37 *Fletcher Forum of World Affairs* 161, 166; Antonios Kouroutakis, 'The Provisional Constitution of the Federal Republic of Somalia: Process, Architecture, and Perspectives' (2014) 3 *Cambridge Journal of International and Comparative Law* 1. See also Gabe Joselow, 'Drafting Somalia's constitution opens debate on religion, law' *Voice of America* (Washington, 29 March 2012) http://www.voanews.com/english/news/Drafting-Somalias-Constitution-Opens-Debate-on-Religion-Law-144862645.html (last accessed 15 April 2018).

189 Menkhaus, 'If Mayors Ruled Somalia' (n 7) and Jason Burke, 'Mogadishu truck bomb: 500 casualties in Somalia's worst terrorist attack' *The Guardian* (London, 16 October 2017) https://www.theguardian.com/world/2017/oct/15/truck-bomb-mogadishu-kills-people-somalia (last accessed 15 April 2018).

orchestrate, although it is often attempted through a programme of formal public participation in the process.[190]

The lack of participation and popular endorsement by referendum led to the perception amongst the Somali people that the new Provisional Constitution is an elite-driven, externally imposed document.[191] The common perception is that during the whole of the transitional phase important constitutional decisions were made behind closed doors and without much concern for their broader acceptance by the Somali society.[192] On these bases, it is difficult to argue that that the formulation of the Provisional Constitution was a process which embodied the will of the Somali people, or one in which the Somali people had any significant input.

5.4.3 Third situation: the adoption of a federal system of government

The peace process in Somalia, between Arta in 2000 and Eldoret in 2002 has seen an important twist regarding the political organisation of the Somali state. Whilst the Arta process stood on a unitary model, on the basis of the 1961 Constitution, at Eldoret the representatives made a commitment to having a federal system of state.[193] This doing, the power-structures on which the Somali state should be organised were significantly altered by the IGAD peace process and Somalia was given a new imprinting for political organisation. With federalism being enshrined as a provision of the Transitional Federal Charter (Article 11), the former became a condition for the development of all subsequent arrangements and power-sharing negotiations that were to be conducted for the implementation of the federal constitutional model.

In scholarly literature, as well as in several opinion pieces written by Somali authors, it is clear that the adoption of federalism does not find unanimous

190 Emily Hay, 'International(ized) Constitutions and Peacebuilding' (2014) 27 *Leiden Journal of International Law* 141, 155.

191 Heritage Institute for Policy Studies, 'Federal Somalia: Not If but How' (2015) Policy Brief http://www.heritageinstitute.org/federal-somalia-not/ (last accessed 15 April 2018). A recent survey by the Heritage Institute for Policy Studies has however revealed that citizens have developed a more positive perception of the Provisional Constitution. See Heritage Institute for Policy Studies, 'Survey of Public Opinion on Somalia's Provisional Constitution' (2017) Policy Brief http://www.heritageinstitute.org/survey-public-opinion-somalias-provisional-constitution/ (last accessed 15 April 2018).

192 Abdihakim Ainte, 'Somalia: Legitimacy of the Provisional Constitution' (2014) 25 *Conciliation Resources, ACCORD* 60, 64 http://www.c-r.org/accord/legitimacy-and-peace-processes/somalia-legitimacy-provisional-constitution (last accessed 15 April 2018).

193 Ahmed I Samatar, 'The Porcupine Dilemma: Governance and Transition in Somalia' (2007) 7 *Bildhaan: An International Journal of Somali Studies* 39, 75. For a comparison on the various Somali constitutions concerning the system of government and decentralisation see Tom Ginsburg, José Cheibub and Justin Frosini, *Analytic Report on the Consultation Draft Constitution of the Somali Republic* (2012) International Development Law Organization (on file with author).

support amongst Somalis. Here I attempt to make sense of the process which brought about a constitutional 'model shift' in the organisation of the Somali state against external self-determination standards and requirements. I do so by considering two fundamental and closely inter-related questions: (i) what guarantees, if any, have been put in place to ensure that the commitment to turning Somalia into a federal state is (and has been since 2002) supported by the will of the Somali people? (ii) Was federalism a free choice of the Somali people?

5.4.3.1 The shift to a federal Somalia and the will of the people

The tension between centralism and federalism in Somalia has been a recurrent feature of Somali politics for many decades, but renewed interest on decentralisation awakened after the state collapse in 1990s.[194] In the history of the Somali Peace and Reconciliation Process, federalism makes its first appearance at Eldoret. Article 1 of the Eldoret Declaration provides that the parties undertake a commitment to:

1. Create federal governance structures for Somalia, embodied in a Charter or Constitution, which are inclusive, representative, and acceptable to all the parties;
2. Endorse the principle of decentralisation as an integral part of Somalia's governance structures.[195]

The genesis of Article 1 has not been elaborated upon and much still remains unknown concerning how it came about. Dedicated interviews conducted by the International Crisis Group seemingly revealed that several faction leaders who were present at the conference claimed to have signed the Declaration under significant pressure from the Technical Committee.[196] This version of the facts is in line with the account provided by two Somali scholars, Samatar and Samatar, concerning the later phases of the conference which they attended. In their detailed essay on the IGAD-led process, the two brothers claim that 'non-Somalis started to make the agenda' and that part of this agenda was to ensure the establishment of a system of federal governance – without Somalis having any say on the issue.[197]

The later phase of the Eldoret conference was indeed meant to tackle some of the substantial issues of the peace process, and saw the creation of a Leaders'

194 For an overview of early attempts at championing federalism in Somalia see Bryden, 'Somalia Redux' (n 128). For more recent discussion see Ayfare A Elmi, *Decentralization Options for Somalia* (2014) Heritage Institute for Policy Studies http://www.heritageinstitute.org/decentralization-options-somalia/ (last accessed 15 April 2018).

195 Eldoret Declaration (n 22).

196 ICG, 'Negotiating a Blueprint for Peace in Somalia' (n 21) and Mulugeta (n 15) 40. The Technical Committee was a body composed of representatives from the three IGAD 'frontline states' (Djibouti, Ethiopia and Kenya) mandated to manage the process at Eldoret.

197 Samatar and Samatar (n 16) 7.

Committee to work on a number of specific issues. The Leaders' Committee was a body comprising 22 members selected by the Technical Committee and mandated to approve the rules of procedure for the conference.[198] The creation of the Leaders' Committee was controversial and possibly ill-advised, as it had the effect of giving a veto power to faction leaders to decide about deeply contentious issues.[199] The International Crisis Group further reported that the work of the Committees was highly dysfunctional, with few participants and where none of the sessions managed to reach a quorum, so that 'the drafts tend to represent the views of a handful of like-minded delegates rather than a broad consensus'.[200]

Among the issues on which the Leaders were asked to work, one was the adoption of a federal Charter or Constitution. By mid-February 2003, the Leaders produced two possible charters. Samatar and Samatar report that Ethiopia and the warlords that it was supporting demanded their draft *alone*, which provided for a form of federal governance, should be debated in the plenary session and was to be adopted immediately.[201] Astonishingly, it is also reported that the Kenyan chair of the Technical Committee, Ambassador Kiplagat, seconded this request – much to the unhappiness of civil society and other actors, who were opposed to the warlords' plan. As a result (and with some additional protocol side-stepping in the plenary assembly), Ambassador Kiplagat simply announced to the plenary that the 'leaders' had agreed on a number of key issues, including the adoption of federalism and that the decision was final.[202]

It was at that moment that the seeds were planted for Somalia to have a new, transitional constitution to provide for the adoption of a federal state system. The state-building initiatives which followed-up the Eldoret peace talks, including the election of a Transitional *Federal* Parliament, the Transitional *Federal* Government and the promulgation of the Transitional *Federal* Charter (TFC), all stemmed from this commitment to establishing federalism. Specifically, Article 11 of the TFC provided that:

1. The Transitional Federal Government of the Somali Republic shall have a decentralised system of administration based on federalism.
2. The Somali Republic shall comprise of:
   (a) The Transitional Federal Government
   (b) State Governments (two or more regions federate, based on their free will)
   (c) Regional administrations.

198 ICG, 'Salvaging Somalia's Chance for Peace' (n 17) 3.

199 The International Crisis Group reported that 'by the end of the first phase, Leaders' Committee had emerged by default, rather than by design, as the supreme Somali decision-making body at the conference, and it is no longer apparent what purpose the remaining conference delegates actually serve'. ibid 4.

200 ICG, 'Negotiating a Blueprint for Peace in Somalia' (n 21) 4.

201 Samatar and Samatar (n 16) 10.

202 ibid 11.

In subsequent paragraphs, the TFC provided for the TFG to 'promote and develop' sub-state and regional forms of administration; and thereby mandated to appoint an independent Federal Constitution Commission to 'ensure that a Federation is achieved'.[203]

The TFC also gave a mandate to the TFG to implement the process of 'federating Somalia' within a certain timeframe and provided for an internationally supervised national referendum to be undertaken to approve the new Constitution.[204] By the end of the TFG's mandate, many steps were yet to be taken in order to turn the reality of the Somali state into a federal republic. According to Article 49 of the Provisional Constitution of 2012, federal member states need to be formed out of two or more of the 18 administrative regions as they existed before 1991.[205]

As a matter of fact, since the adoption of the TFC, the process of federating Somalia has been advancing. Today, the process of negotiation on the formation of state-level entities and delimitation of borders is ongoing, despite great challenges which at times threatened a relapse into violence and conflict. By late 2016, five entities have commenced the state building process at the regional level (the Interim Jubbaland, Galmudug and South West Administrations);[206] one does not want to take part in the federal government (Somaliland); and one would like to continue to govern their own region with a limited amount of power to the federal government (Puntland).[207] At the same time, the selection process for the Independent Boundaries and Federation Commission, responsible for determining the number and boundaries of federal states, had barely started by April 2015,[208] thus leaving interim administrations unsure of their legal status under the provisional constitution. This commission was meant to be appointed 60 days after the new government formed in following the passage of the draft constitution in 2012, but was instead established only in 2015.[209]

203 TFC art 11 paras 3 and 4.

204 ibid art 11 paras 8 and 3 respectively.

205 Article 49(5), *Provisional Constitution of the Federal Republic of Somalia*, adopted 1 August 2012 https://unpos.unmissions.org/provisional-constitution-federal-republic-somalia-0 (last accessed 15 April 2018).

206 See Report of the Secretary General on Somalia, UN Doc S/2016/27, 1–3 and Ken Menkhaus, 'Elections in the Hardest Places: The Case of Somalia' (2017) 28 *Journal of Democracy* 132.

207 Amina Adan, 'Is Federalism the Best Path for a State Like Somalia?' *Somalia Newsroom* (6 March 2015) http://somalianewsroom.com/is-federalism-the-best-path-for-a-state-like-somalia/ (last accessed 15 April 2018).

208 See Report of the Secretary General on Somalia, UN Doc S/2015/331, 1.

209 Provisional Constitution art 135(2.e); 'Can Federalism Work for Somalia?' *Irin News Briefing* (5 February 2014) http://www.irinnews.org/report/99600/briefing-can-federalism-work-in-somali (last accessed 15 April 2018). See also UN Press Release on the Communiqué on High Level Meeting in Somalia of 28 September 2015 in which the UN welcomes the creation of the Boundaries and Federation Commission http://www.un.org/press/en/2015/sg2218.doc.htm (last accessed 15 April 2018).

As things stand at present, Somalia is committed to becoming a federal republic. According to Article 1 (1) of the new Provisional Constitution Somalia is defined as a 'federal, sovereign, and democratic republic founded on inclusive representation of the people, a multiparty system advised by social justice'.[210] However, neither what precise shape the federal state shall take has been codified, nor the number and borders of the member states of the Federal Republic have yet been clearly defined. More than fifteen years on from Eldoret, the issue of federal *versus* unitarian constitutional model, is an issue on which Somalis are still divided. Federalists buy into the vision of a state arranged along clan-based blocks, whilst unitarians reject such a vision.

Supporters of federalism associate the unitary state system with authoritarianism and see a form of decentralisation as necessary.[211] The Unitarian model is favoured in particular by Islamists, who envisage a strong state where Islam is the main source of legislation, and also by secular national intellectuals.[212] The latter, in particular, look at federalism with suspicion, as they consider it an attempt to 'balkanise' Somalia, leaving the country divided into clan enclaves and thus weak and more subject to the influence of regional powers.[213] It is also argued that Somalia is unsuited to federalism as it lacks the characteristics of federal states: it is small and its people are largely homogeneous; it is also poor and cannot afford to pay for multiple levels of government.[214] An additional concern is the renewed sources of conflict that designing a federal structure would bring about, such as the potential to fuelling secessionist claims and to create unnecessary competition for power sharing struggles.

Somali activists and writers that are critical of the shift to federalism have also pointed out that Somalia already had a Constitution, and one that had been democratically accepted by the Somali population through a referendum in 1961. In view of this, they cannot accept as self-evident the immediate need to draft an alternative constitution, particularly at a time when no elected and representative government is in place.[215] Furthermore, critics' accusations point to the fact that the unitary model of governance adopted at Arta, which was in line with the model proposed by the 1960s Constitution, was substituted with a federal one at Eldoret because of external pressures. The accusation moved against the actors involved in the IGAD-sponsored process and against

210 Provisional Constitution (n 205) art 1(1).

211 Elmi, 'Decentralization Options for Somalia' (n 194).

212 Elmi, *Understanding the Somalia Conflagration* (n 12) 103.

213 ICG, 'Negotiating a Blueprint for Peace in Somalia' (n 21).

214 Elmi, *Understanding the Somalia Conflagration* (n 12).

215 See Abdi Dirshe, 'The New Somalia Roadmap: Perpetual conflict in the making' (17 October 2001) https://www.hiiraan.com/op2/2011/oct/the_new_somalia_roadmap_perpetual_conflict_in_the_making.aspx (last accessed 15 April 2018) and Ayfare A Elmi, 'In Search of a Somali Constitution' *Al Jazeera* (Doha, 25 January 2005) http://www.hiiraan.com/op4/2011/jan/17529/in_search_of_a_somali_constitution.aspx (last accessed 15 April 2018).

the Frontline States (Ethiopia in particular) is to have imposed, without a national debate or a referendum, an 'undefined and obscure form of federalism on Somalia'.[216]

There is indeed a strong view, among writers, that federalism is essentially a product of external intervention of actors involved in the engineering of the peace process. In particular, Ethiopia is believed to have strongly favoured a federal Somalia for three main reasons. First, as a way to weaken its neighbour (and discourage possible irredentist claims) by means of supporting internal divisions.[217] Secondly, because Ethiopia is a federal state itself, and as such it may have a political interest to have another federal state as a neighbour.[218] In this conception, the commitment to federalism – the basis of which were lied down at Eldoret – enshrined in the Transitional *Federal* Charter and Provisional Constitution of the *Federal* Republic, has essentially sought to impose a colonially political framework on Somalia.[219] Thirdly, supporting federal states inside Somalia could also be seen as a way to strengthen security, as these local authorities may be more effective in a limited area than an ineffective nationally organised security infrastructure.

In a recent field research conducted across five major cities in Somalia the Heritage institute for Policy Studies found that, today, a significant majority of Somalis (68%) support the idea of a federal system of governance.[220] The question thus turned from whether to adopt federalism in Somalia to how this should be done in a way which serves the interests of the country and of its people. An great majority (75%) of respondents from Southern Somalia, indeed, said that they were dissatisfied with the process of federation, which they see as a top-down, elite-driven process that systematically excludes communities from consultations and decision-making.[221] In the Provisional Constitution adopted in 2012 many issues were left still open to negotiation – such as the number of levels of administration that should be instituted; how they should be created (to reflect the situation on the ground or to be more uniformly distributed) and what criteria should be taken into consideration when establishing the sub-units.

216 Elmi, *Understanding the Somalia Conflagration* (n 12) 24. For more criticism see also Manuela Melandri and Mohmaed A Hassan, 'Somalia's Draft Constitution: Too Undemocratic?' *ThinkAfrica Press* (London, 3 July 2012) http://allafrica.com/stories/201207030981.html (last accessed 15 April 2018).

217 Markus Böckenförde, 'Beyond Federalism: Which Concept of Decentralization Reflects Best the Needs of Somalia?' Proceedings of the 9th Annual Conference on the Horn of Africa (Lund, Sweden, 4–6June 2010) 213–26; Ibrahim Farah and Sekou Touré, 'Engineering Peace in Somalia: A Call for a Re-examination of the Somali Peace Processes' *Development*, 6 March 2018; Samatar and Samatar (n 16) 11.

218 Mulugeta (n 15) 40.

219 Dirshe (n 215).

220 Heritage Institute for Policy Studies (n 191) 2.

221 ibid 3. On this issue see also Abubakar Mohamud Abubakar, 'The Patterns of State Rebuilding and Federalism in Somalia' (2016) 10 *African Journal of Political Science and International Relations* 88.

There remains, therefore, scope for debate and space for Somalis to design their constitutional structure on the basis of a truly representative process.

Today, the key question is whether this space is sufficient to ensure that in deciding the constitutional status of future Somalia the will of the people can be heard. So far, the impossibility to proceed with scheduled elections and national consultations have indeed brought to being governments that have been systematically selected rather than elected and national consultative exercises have systematically been impossible to conduct, because the governments that succeeded each other have systematically been unable to exercise control over the territory of Somalia. Overall, the details concerning the genesis of the current form and system of government in Somalia cannot lead us to establish that a meaningful connection has been made between the state-building process and popular will, and therefore that the shift to a federal Somalia, so far, does not embody an expression of the will of the Somali people.

5.5 The significance of a case study

State-building assistance has given Somalia a much-needed chance to achieve peace and reconciliation after many years of civil war. The transition process has also given the country a government, a parliament and a Provisional Constitution which laid down the principled foundations of the new Somali Republic. The creation of a federal state structure is now under way, and 'indirect elections' resulting in a new President, a new upper house of the Federal Parliament and a new lower house took place in late 2016 and early 2017.[222] International law gives a right to people of independent states freely to decide about their political status and to choose their form of government. In this chapter we discussed the significance and role that self-determination standards have played in the process of rebuilding a functioning state in Somalia. We looked in particular at three situations in which this right was at stake for the Somali people: the creation of a new government; the adoption of a constitution; and the decision to adopt a certain form of government and a certain constitutional model. The analysis has shown that practice in Somalia is in apparent contrast with what the legal right of self-determination mandates, but contrast was not always neat, and different degrees of 'accommodation' of legal standards to practice can be observed.

First, the chapter showed how, in relation to internal self-determination requirements, concerns regarding the representativeness of government and state institutions were present at all times. We have seen that the concept of representativeness

222 The Leaders of the SFG and Regional Administrations had, by December 2015, already convened that the 'one person, one vote' model for elections will not be applicable for 2016, but nonetheless they committed to the holding of voting procedures in 2016 as per constitutional mandate. See 'Report of the Secretary-General on Somalia' (n 206) 1. The 2016–17 elections used a scheme that involved 135 appointed clan elders, 275 separate clan-based elections in the lower house alone, and 14.025 electoral-college delegates. See Menkhaus, 'Elections in the Hardest Places' (n 206).

was translated into the 4.5 formula, a rule based on quotas assigned on the basis of lineage that was specifically created for the context under examination. Whilst the law provides clearer guidance in the case of racially or religiously divided states, it remains silent on what 'representative government' should mean in the case of a homogeneous society. The vague nature of the legal principle of self-determination and of its legal standards on this precise matter has allowed state-builders a wide degree of discretion when translating this concept into practice. Ultimately, the case of Somalia shows that, at least as far as ethnically and religiously homogeneous states are concerned, international law does not offer specific guidance, but is capable of providing space for the elaboration of context-specific rules to translate the concept of representativeness into concrete rules.

Secondly, as we saw in Chapters 3 and 4, the core essence of the right to self-determination mandates that any determination on the status of a people, including decisions on their form and system of government, must be attached to a free exercise of the will of that people. In relation to this, the present chapter has shown how, in the case under examination, the various steps through which new governments have been set up as part of the Somali National Reconciliation Process have never been able to show that the process was an effect of a free choice of the Somali people. This was the case because at no stage during the eleven years of transition was ever carried out a popular consultation which included the Somali people at large, but at maximum a small number of selected representatives. Indeed, the governmental authorities that guided the transition were neither created through an election process, nor were their mandates endorsed by any type of referendum or other established mechanism of popular consultation accepted as an established method to guarantee an expression of the will of the people.

For instance, here it was highlighted that the creation of an Elders' Committee – envisaged to guarantee that the selection of government representatives would reflect an attachment to the will of the people in a context where no consultation or popular mandate could be sought – is a mechanism that falls short of established self-determination standards. Despite the lack of precise definition concerning self-determination standards on popular consultation, I indeed argued that the extent to which the people at large are involved in an alleged exercise of the will of the people is an aspect which should be considered relevant in making an assessment of compliance with international law standards.[223] In the case in question, the small number of elders involved

223 It is interesting to note, in this respect, the words of the former President of Somalia Hassan Sheikh Mohamud ahead of the 2016–17 indirect elections: 'If today, Somalia is not possible with 'one-person, one-vote' ballot boxes all over the country. If this is not possible today, we should not stay where we are. We have to transition to something closer to that, so that next time we can reach that easily, . . . based on that now, anything other than extension and the 135 elders, or any number of elders, is an election for us'. Ty McCormic, 'Somalia's Incredible Shrinking Election' *Foreign Policy* (6 August 2015) http://foreignpolicy.com/2015/08/06/somalias-incredible-shrinking-election-hassan-sheikh-mohamud/ (last accessed 15 April 2018).

as well as the means for their appointment could by no means ensure that a meaningful connection between the establishment of the SFG and the will of the people was put in place. As a result, it is unsurprising that the institutions created as part of this process are perceived as unrepresentative and illegitimate in the eyes of many inside Somalia.

Thirdly, the external aspects of self-determination set out a requirement that decisions on status and governance issues are made freely by the people without the interference of external actors. In relation to this, analysis has shown that in Somalia external actors have consistently interfered with the process of decision-making in state-building activities, so that the decisions made were often the direct consequences of foreign interests rather than an expression of the free will of the Somali people. External interference in the state-building process was so pervasive that one can see the whole process, and with it its results, to be the direct consequence of external interference into Somalia's internal affairs. Most crucial decisions were indeed taken by, or with strong pressure from, neighboring states aiming to impose their agendas on the state-building process. External actors manipulated the process by supporting factions inside the country in order to turn them into important players at the national level; they organised the process and decided who should take part in crucial decision-making moments; they appointed figures and directed the agenda during meetings themselves. In addition, the Provisional Constitution adopted in 2012 provides a specific constitutional model that will form the basis of the new Somali state; a model that has not been endorsed by popular consultation and which has been perceived as an alien imposition by the Somali people.

Overall, the situation in Somalia has the capacity to illustrate how self-determination standards have been in many respects downplayed and disregarded in the process of reconstruction of a failed state. There is a discrepancy between what the law mandates and what practice shows about the role and significance of self-determination standards in the Somali state-building processes, and a number of consequences can be drawn from what this case study has revealed.

5.5.1 *The wider consequences of a case study: a new model of self-determination?*

There are two possible ways to explain the lack of correspondence between what the law mandates and what this study of practice shows. First, one could argue that Somalia is an example of bad practice, of how things can go wrong with the application of self-determination standards and of a lack of compliance on behalf of states with their obligation to ensure the realisation of the right. According to this approach, for over a decade the Somali people have been deprived of certain aspects of their right freely to decide on a number of issues related to the way in which their state was to be rebuilt. For instance, they have had imposed governments and governance agendas so that today they are subject to a relatively specific constitutional order not of their free choice. As a consequence, today the Somali people is also left with the mere possibility to choose which form of federalism to institute, rather than having the possibility to choose whether to have a Federal Republic at all. This is surely a limitation of their substantial right to choose, because as Cassese reminds us, since the right freely to decide is 'much more than choosing among what is on offer perhaps from one political or economic position only'.[224]

One problem with this first approach, as was highlighted in Chapter 2, is that using the law to assess practice does not help us to advance our understanding of the norm of self-determination. In an under-explored context such as state-building, where the contours of the right are not clearly established, it was submitted that state practice could be better used to make sense of how this complex norm is interpreted by states in this context and so to better understand its application. But there is also an additional reason why we should look at practice in Somalia through this wider lens. There is indeed a second problem with the use of an evaluative approach to interpret the findings of this case study. Namely, this problem is the striking silence of virtually all states in the international community in relation to an alleged violation of the law on self-determination in Somalia – or, at least, to a side-stepping and down-playing of self-determination standards in the process of reconstruction.

As we have seen above,[225] states' involvement in the reconstruction of Somalia happened in a climate of acquiescence, as there is no evidence of serious objections being raised by states, either those directly involved in the process or by the international community more generally. It must be mentioned a distinct exception: Eritrea. In a letter to the Security Council of May 2009 Eritrea used self-determination language to question the position of the international community on Somalia, but this letter cannot be used as strong evidence of *opinio juris* as Eritrea was directly involved in the conflict and was indeed being sanctioned by the UN for having provided military assistance to TFG opponents.[226] The letter reads:

> The Security Council statement (S/PRST/2009/15 issued on 15 May 2009) asserts that the 'Transitional Federal Government is the legitimate, internationally recognized Government of Somalia'. As my Government has underlined on many occasions, the highly complex and grave conflict in Somalia will not be resolved by arbitrary and ill-advised formulas that have no basis in international law and that do not reflect the wishes and sovereign political choices of the Somali people. 'Transitional Governments' that are periodically hatched in non-inclusive incubators outside Somalia have never survived the test of time in the past years in spite of the huge military and financial support extended to them by their external

224 Antonio Cassese, *Self-determination of Peoples: A Legal Reappraisal* (CUP 1995) 101.
225 See section 5.4.1.5.
226 Ambassador Araya Desta, Permanent Representative of Eritrea to the UN Security Council. UN Doc S/2009/256 of 20 May 2009.

> sponsors. ... The people of Somalia should not continue to be victims of ill-advised experiments and formulas worked out elsewhere. They deserve better. And above all, their sovereign rights to form their own Government thought their internal processes of peacebuilding and reconciliation should not be compromised.

Given the alleged *jus cogens* status attributed to self-determination in international law and the *erga omnes* character of its obligations,[227] one would expect states to be more keen to react to perceived violations of the right. The puzzling question, therefore, is what meaning should be attributed to silence. In view of a manifestation of state practice which sees the role and significance of the right to self-determination being severely reduced from what the principle allegedly mandates, it is important to make sense of this silence.

On the one hand, it can be suggested that the situation of Somalia is a case of tacitly tolerated exceptional illegality, an example of how things can go wrong in a severely problematic context moving out from a situation of chaos and anarchy. In such case, it would not be possible to draw conclusions suitable for generalisation from this single case study, but we could however use this example to illustrate a case of bad compliance in an extreme situation. At the same time, studying other cases could prove useful to find better examples of compliance and to see how, in other contexts, this norm has been interpreted as to turn into specific rules. On the other hand – and this is the position taken here – the situation of Somalia may not be an exception. An alternative approach to interpreting the findings of this study, indeed, is to think that Somalia is no exception, and that self-determination standards were only partially applied to the reconstruction of Somalia because states did think that no violation occurred. This interpretative framework values practice in-context as a means for developing obscure or vague aspects of the law, or to highlight developments and change in its conceptualisation which may occur through time.

In the case of Somalia, the contradiction between standards and practice could be explained because:

(i) states do not think that such standards fully apply in the context of post-conflict state-building
(ii) self-determination entitlements are suspended in certain circumstances, for instance when there is no state structure in place, until a state is able itself to allow its people to exercise their right through state institutions
(iii) states subordinate self-determination concerns to other considerations, such as security imperatives in certain contexts.

These are only three tentative justifications, but possibilities for their interpretation can be manifold. At first sight, a case can be made in favour of solutions

227 See discussion in chs 1 and 4.

(ii) and (iii) because in Somalia it was evident how, throughout the process of reconstruction, the holding of national elections, postponed for more than 10 years, was never called into question. Whilst it seemed acceptable for the international community that the various transitional governments could be set up by appointment, it would have not been acceptable for the international community to have a constitutional order that would see future governments normally being set up by appointment. Each single time in which the time-frame for transition has not been respected and elections postponed, a new time-frame for new elections was created. A republic based on the will of the people expressed through periodic, democratic elections has thus always been a firm objective of international engagement in Somalia. This is shown also by the fact that, being impossible to hold a constitutional referendum, the Constitution remained Provisional, pending an approval via referendum at a later stage, when security conditions will allow it.[228] This inclination towards a full application of self-determination standards seen as a long-term objective seems indeed to suggest that, although self-determination rights and obligations may need to be suspended or subordinated to other kind of concerns during the transitional phase, their relevance is never really called into question.

In relation to the second justification, it can be submitted that states might have not raised objections because decisions crucial to the state-building process in Somalia were taken through or pursuant to Security Council decisions or recommendations adopted under Chapter VII provisions. In this respect, silence could be telling with regard to the possible limits (and lack thereof) that self-determination poses upon the UN, and specifically upon the Security Council in the context of the exercise of its enforcement powers, and in relation to the normative status of this right. As was briefly explained in Chapter 1, the Security Council is indeed largely unconstrained by international law when acting under its Chapter VII powers, except when dealing with norms that have achieved peremptory status.[229]

Various authors submit that the UN, including the Security Council in the exercise of its enforcement powers, are somehow bound by self-determination and that, as a result of this, they cannot impose a particular form of government upon a population.[230] According to Gill,

228 Ainte (n 192).

229 See section 5.2.

230 See David Schweigman, *The Authority of the Security Council under Chapter VII of the UN Charter: Legal Limits and the Role of the International Court of Justice* (Kluwer Law 2001) 165 and Gregory Fox, *Humanitarian Occupation* (CUP 2008) 169. For instance, in the *Supplement* to *An Agenda for Peace*, Boutros-Ghali also reminded us that the UN cannot impose a new political structure or new state institutions, it can only help parties to the conflict to achieve peace. Report of the Secretary-General, 'Supplement to An Agenda for Peace: Position Paper of the Secretary-General on the Occasion of the Fiftieth Anniversary of the United Nations' (1995) UN Doc A/50/50-S/1995/1, para 15.

> 'whether or not "internal" self-determination implies some form of democratic governance as some contend and others dispute – there is no legal basis in the Charter, either in Chapter VII or elsewhere, to impose particular constitutional arrangements or forms of government upon a population. . . . This limitation on the UN and specifically upon the use by the Security Council of its enforcement powers to impose a particular political system or constitutional arrangement upon a population is based upon the fundamental principles of the independence of States and of respect for the self-determination of peoples'.[231]

Hence, whether silence could be explained because states believe that the principle of self-determination, as per Article 1(2), does not bind the Security Council in the exercise of its Chapter VII powers; or because the conduct of state-builders engaged in Somalia did not contravene to any aspect of self-determination that enjoys *jus cogens* status is therefore a matter open for discussion.

5.6 Conclusion

The history of the application of self-determination standards to the process of state-building in Somalia is a story of disappointment. This chapter offered an overview of how self-determination concerns were included in the process of reconstruction of state structure and governance institutions in the period from 2000 to 2012. Analysis has shown that, whilst certain aspects of the right have been included and interpreted throughout the process; others have been either discarded or downplayed when international actors designed, led and assisted with the implementation of state-building reforms. Indeed, it was shown how states and the international community have been supportive of a process aimed at rebuilding Somalia and its political status in a way which is characterised by a pervasive lack of attachment to the will of the people and by invasive external intervention in the country's internal affairs. This runs contrary to self-determination standards attached to the right as it applies to the people of an independent state.

The consequences of this practice have been spelled out, raising a number of questions concerning the meaning of the idiosyncrasies identified and the significance of the Somali experience for the wider discourse on international law and self-determination. Somalia can be seen to constitute an unpleasant negligence, or a stand-alone case of violation of the law, if one adopts an evaluative approach to the study of practice. If one adopts a different approach, more keen on seeing what practice reveals about the status of the law, Somalia can be seen either as a tolerated exception, dictated more by the lack of awareness of existing self-determination standards in relation to state-building; or as an example of

231 T D Gill, 'Legal and Some Political Limitations on the Power of the UN Security Council to Exercise its Enforcement Powers under Chapter VII of the Charter' (1995) 26 *Netherlands Yearbook of International Law* 33, 76.

practice that advances the elaboration of a specific model of self-determination for states which suffer from a protracted status of an authority vacuum.

Finally, should Somalia prove to be no exception in the state-building business, the findings of this study would open a complex array of questions that only a wider study to conduct a systematic review of substantial practice, thus aimed at analysing and comparing a significant number of cases, could begin to answer. This study should broaden its focus to include also less extreme cases of power vacuum, namely situations where the vacuum is left by the momentum of conflict rather than being the effect of a decade-long protracted situation. The lack of existing, extensive research on this matter makes this pilot study a path-opener in the research on self-determination, and it welcomes contributions by other scholars to open a debate on the significance of this norm in the domain of post-conflict reconstruction.[232] All in all, this study of the situation in Somalia should be seen only as the prelude to a bigger research project that includes and compares findings from a wide number of cases and situations. Such a conspicuous piece of research is necessary in order to understand fully how states think that self-determination ought to function in situations of transition.

232 A three-year research project that involves a group of scholars led by Professor Marc Weller at the Lauterpacht Centre for International Law, University of Cambridge, began to investigate the extent to which regulation of particular issue areas in peace agreements is consolidating towards the establishment of novel normative expectations. The project aims to explore whether practice is hardening from policy preference in individual instances of settlement into legal rules, and whether these rules are compatible with general international law. It would be useful to have a similar research to study practice on self-determination issues as understood in this thesis. See 'Legal Tools for Peace-Making Project' http://www.lcil.cam.ac.uk/legal_tools/about-legal-tools-peace-making-project (last accessed 15 April 2018).

Concluding remarks

State-building programmes are aimed at restoring governmental effectiveness in situations of protracted crisis that have determined the weakening or collapse of governance institutions. In almost the entirety of cases, state-builders do not set out to build new states: they engage with existing states for the purposes of rebuilding effective governance where government is missing or dysfunctional. This research has explored the role played by the legal principle of self-determination in this context. In so doing, this study has contributed to the existing debate on the role of international law in regulating state-building processes and opened new avenues for future research. The main argument set out is that international law on self-determination is not irrelevant in this area, but that its role and importance in the context of post-conflict state-building remains still largely unknown in legal scholarship. This is attributable to a lack of dedicated, systematic study of state practice on this matter. Having established this fact, the study uncovered some of the key questions concerning the way self-determination is used and applied in contemporary state-building practice, and proposed a new approach to study the relevance of the law on self-determination in this context.

This final chapter offers some concluding remarks and sets out ideas for future research arising from this project. It starts with an overview of the main findings of this study and then moves on to consider the implications of these findings, as well as the wider significance of this study for international law research. Original aspects of this project are also spelled out, and the contribution to scholarship made by the present research is outlined. In conclusion, some future challenges that can interest self-determination research are suggested.

1 Overview of key findings

Chapter 1 set out the need to introduce a discourse on self-determination in the area of state-building research. Starting with a conceptualisation of the phenomenon of state-building from the perspective of international law, the chapter set out to identify the overarching framework through which international law should understand state-building. It found that international law must deal with state-building using principles that regulate the friendly relations between states.

This means that failed states, like functioning states, are protected by international law, and are entitled to a number of rights and provisions that state-builders must consider when engaging in reconstruction programmes. It was argued that the key structure of this overarching protection framework, which also applies to states undergoing post-conflict reconstruction, is essentially threefold.

First, international law protects a failed state's territory, as it gives it a right to defend its territorial integrity and to maintain its territorial borders unchanged. Secondly, international law protects the independent status of a failed state and gives it a right to maintain its independence. In normal situations, this right is protected by the principle of non-intervention into a state's internal affairs. In situations of state-building, however, this right is limited. Whenever a failed state is deemed to constitute a threat to the maintenance of peace and security, its right to non-interference is indeed reduced and modified by international security concerns.

In this respect it was shown that, in legal scholarship, a debate exists concerning the extent to which the right to non-intervention can be reduced in favour of international state-builders. The exact nature of limits posed to international actors engaged in restoring governmental effectiveness in war-torn states is not clear-cut. Thirdly, international law protects the population of a failed state as it gives them a right to self-determination. In the colonial context, the relationship between self-determination and effectiveness granted primacy to the former, meaning that an effective government set up in violation of self-determination would be unlawful under international law. How the two relate in the context of state-building is an open question. Could self-determination act as a counter-balance against security interests in setting out the limits of action of international state-builders? In order to shed light on this issue, the chapter concluded by underlining the need to understand what we know about the role of self-determination in relation to state-building.

Chapter 2 was dedicated to a study of self-determination and state-building. It dug deep into this issue, offering a review of the literature that explored and explained what is known about the role played by self-determination in this context. The chapter found that there is a dominant narrative through which the study of self-determination in relation to state-building has been approached. This was called 'the evaluative approach', as it consists of a tendency on behalf of scholars to conceive and use self-determination as an evaluative yardstick through which to evaluate and assess state-building practice so as to find violations of the law. The chapter showed that there are problems in the way authors set up their evaluative frameworks and ultimately argued that this dominant approach does not, in fact, appreciate the way self-determination applies to state-building. Existing literature is as a result unhelpful in exploring the relevance and significance of this principle in the post-decolonisation phase of its development. In criticising the approach used so far by international law scholars, Chapter 2 suggested a map of action for new research to approach the study of self-determination. In the first place, the chapter recommended the new approach to include first a strong normative analysis.

Chapter 3 built on the conceptual map suggested above and provided an in-depth, first-hand analysis of one specific dimension of self-determination, namely of the right as it attaches to the people of independent states. This dimension of the right has often been overlooked in existing literature because it is considered essentially uncontroversial, owing to its strong overlap with the concept of state sovereignty. This chapter provided the first systemic account of this specific dimension, sub-norm or layer, of self-determination. The chapter examined its origins, development and conceptualisation, and found a core legal meaning attached to it. This is that the principle gives to the people of independent states a right to choose its form of government and to determine its economic, social and cultural development, free from internal domination and external interference.

Chapter 4 further explored the character of this norm and set out a conceptualisation of self-determination as a complex and multi-faceted norm. In addition, through a critique and a reinterpretation of the classic divide between internal and external self-determination it was argued that the sub-norm in question is a hybrid, indivisible norm which encompasses both internal and external aspects into a single, complex norm which retraces the contours of state sovereignty. However, a peculiarity of this norm, which strongly differentiates it from state sovereignty, is that it attaches to the people, and not to the state. Further, it was also argued that self-determination is neither simply a right nor simply a principle but it can be both, meaning a norm constituted of a bundle of rights, obligations and suggested standards to be adapted to various contexts. Whilst the rights are attached to the people, and to the people only, the chapter further highlighted how these obligations imposed by self-determination are distributed to several actors – including the territorial state, other states and peoples, and international actors.

Finally, Chapter 5 set out to test the application of the normative model elaborated in Chapters 3 and 4 through a study of practice. The chapter studied the state-building process in Somalia with the purpose of exploring whether practice reflects, expands, further details or possibly contradicts the interpretation of the norm set out earlier. Differently from the evaluative approach described in Chapter 2, this exercise did not seek to assess whether practice in Somalia complied with or violated the law. Instead, the research aimed to make sense of how this right had an impact on the reconstruction of Somalia. In so doing, the chapter aimed to provide a richer understanding of what the Somali state-building process can tell us more generally about the role and impact of self-determination in shaping the state-building process in a situation of power vacuum.

The analysis showed that, whilst selected aspects of self-determination were somewhat disregarded and marginalised in the process of rebuilding governance institutions, others were instead mainstreamed into the process. For instance, concerns on representativeness of bodies and institutions have been included into the process at all stages. A specific formula founded on the concepts of lineage and proportionality was elaborated to ensure the representative character of transitional institutions. Despite local criticism, the research found that this formula fits well within the discretion afforded by state-builders under the law of self-determination and is therefore an example of how the principle might turn into a rule in a specific context. On the contrary, the chapter showed that at crucial times when the future of the Somali people was being determined the core standards on self-determination, meant to guarantee an attachment of the process to the will of the people as well as the prohibition of external interference, were disregarded in practice. In relation to this, it was submitted that this phenomenon can in part be attributed to a lack of precise definition of what constitutes an expression of the will of the people in a given context, which makes it at times difficult to conceptualise legal standards in situations where neither a referendum nor national elections can be held. Nonetheless, the validity of mechanisms developed to select government representatives in Somalia was not considered to ensure respect for the standards imposed by the principle. In this respect, it was argued that the number of people consulted should be taken into account when seeking manifestations of compliance with the core requirement of self-determination – namely, that decisions concerning the status of a people should be an expression of the will of the people.

In addition, Chapter 5 also highlighted how the marginalisation of certain aspects of the right, including the prohibition of external interference on behalf of other states, was met with complete acquiescence in the international community. As Omozurike reminds us, states cannot be excluded from applying self-determination, because customary international law is binding on all states and also because they signed up to self-determination obligations under the UN Charter and other international human rights treaties.[1] The fact that states involved in the reconstruction of Somalia have not lived up to their obligation not to interfere in the process of determining Somalia's new form and system of government, together with their role in setting up a system of governance which did not reflect the will of the people, raised the question of how this was possible in practice. How can the complete lack of reaction on behalf of other states at the international level be justified in view of the evident disregard of basic standards of self-determination to which the Somali people are entitled? What meaning is to be attributed to silence is therefore an important question which has opened several avenues of interpretation. By providing an interpretation of the meaning of silence we can therefore make an assessment of whether the law of self-determination was simply neglected in this specific case or whether we are witnessing a process of interpretation of the law aimed at attributing a certain meaning to its application in the context of post-conflict state-building.

In conclusion, Chapter 5 raised significant questions about the wider relevance of the findings of a single case-study for our understanding of self-determination in international law. On the one hand, the situation in Somalia can indeed be seen as a case of tacitly tolerated exceptional illegality, possibly linked to the

1 U O Omozurike, *Self-determination in International Law* (Archon 1972) 196.

exceptional context of the power vacuum in which the country was left after the central government collapsed in 1991. On the other hand, the situation in Somalia may be seen as being no exception, but rather an example of practice that may also be seen elsewhere. If Somalia is not an isolated case, future research should be directed at making sense of how states, through practice, are attributing meaning to self-determination in the context of state-building, in order to understand whether and how their understanding of the law departs from the normative model that we have known so far.

2 Implications of the study and wider significance

The findings of this pilot study on the practice of state-building led to a number of implications for related issues in international law and policy. In the first place, the normative study on self-determination presented in Chapter 4 has delineated a model of self-determination which shows that the content and scope of this norm is complex, multi-faceted and multi-dimensional. In relation to the layer of self-determination examined here, the study of practice in Somalia has also shown that its application is a tricky business. Indeed, it was seen how, although the principle has a relatively defined legal content, the vague nature of its standards and the lack of defined rules for implementation led to a lack of enforcement mechanisms to ensure compliance. Similarly, there is also a lack of accountability mechanisms in the event of a violation, particularly in the event of a breach of the obligation to assist in the realisation of the right held by third party states. A classic limitation for the self-determination of sub-state groups is that 'a people cannot decide until somebody decides who are the people'.[2] For a people that is internationally recognised as a people entitled to self-determination, such as the people of an independent state, this absence of accountability mechanisms raises the issue of who determines whether the people have in fact freely determined their status when a determination is made.

Secondly, the study of practice in Somalia further evidenced that self-determination standards were applied selectively. In so doing, the study raised the question of why, and under what logic, self-determination standards were only partially mainstreamed into the process of state-building – namely in relation to representativeness criteria, and otherwise downplayed or simply ignored with the acquiescence of the international community. In Chapter 5, two possible explanations were offered to justify this behaviour. First, it was advanced that certain aspects of self-determination, in the process of state-building, could be suspended until a state is able to itself allow its people to exercise their right through state institutions. The second possibility, instead, would see self-determination standards being subordinated to other considerations – i.e.

2 Ivor Jennings in *The Approach to Self-government* 55 (1956), quoted by Pomerance in Michla Pomerance, 'Self-Determination Today: The Metamorphosis of an Ideal' (1984) 19 *Israel Law Review* 310, 311.

security concerns in the aftermath of conflict. We shall now see what are the implications of the two scenarios.

Surely, the idea that the sovereignty of failed and collapsed states may be suspended in certain circumstances is not entirely novel.[3] Some scholars found evidence that the international community, on the question of state-building intervention, now leans towards a policy of 'soft-sovereignty, one where state sovereignty can, in some instances, be penetrated – but the scope and extent of this doctrine is far from clear'.[4] As Chan further observes, in practice related to failed states such as Afghanistan, Somalia and Iraq,

> [t]here is perception that external sovereignty can be removed, withheld, transferred and returned contingent on the existence (and in arguably more controversial circumstances, the legitimacy) of a failing State's central government and public institutions. In other words, international recognition of external sovereignty has been, over the years, more frequently treated as dependent on the existence of *government*, rather than *Statehood*.[5]

Whether the concept of a temporary suspension, as has been advocated for sovereignty, may also be suitable to apply to self-determination is a question open to discussion. Examining the context of civil wars, Werner observed that in times of internal conflict, self-determination comes to play the role of state sovereignty, by equating the people with the entire population of a state, so that the two are considered interchangeably and often mentioned jointly to invoke the principle of non-intervention.[6] This dynamic raises some questions as to the independent function of the two. Alvarez, for instance, noticed that this dilemma was also raised by Security Council action in Iraq. In Resolutions 1483 (2003) and 1511 (2003) the Council effectively recognised the responsibilities and obligations of the United States and of the United Kingdom as occupiers, thus accepting that the sovereignty of Iraq was temporarily suspended.[7] However, at the same time, the Council also 'reserved the right of the Iraqi people

3 See Alexandros Yannis, 'The Concept of Suspended Sovereignty in International Law and Its Implications in International Politics' (2002) 13 *European Journal of International Law* 1037. See also Saira Mohamed, 'From Keeping Peace to Building Peace: A Proposal for a Revitalized United Nations Trusteeship Council' (2005) 105 *Columbia Law Review* 809.

4 Jan Wouters and Kenneth Chan, 'State-Building, Occupation and International Law: Friends or Foes?' (2012) Leuven Centre for Global Governance Studies, *Working Paper No 87* at 6 https://papers.ssrn.com/sol3/papers.cfm?abstract_id=2274806 (last accessed 15 April 2018).

5 Kenneth Chan, 'State Failure and the Changing Face of the *Jus ad Bellum*' (2013) 18 *Journal of Conflict and Security Law* 395, 407.

6 Wouter G Wener, 'Self-Determination and Civil War' (2011) 6 *Journal of Conflict and Security Law* 171, 188–89.

7 SC Res 1483 (2003) of 22 May 2003, preamble and SC Res 1511 (2003) of 16 October 2003, para 1. UN Doc S/Res/1483 and S/Res/1511.

to ultimately decide their own political future and type of government',[8] thus distinguishing between the two principles. A detailed study of the implementation of these resolutions – including an analysis of resolutions' provisions in view of the actions undertaken by the Coalition of Provisional Authority in Iraq to assist the Iraqi people in rebuilding effective governance – is necessary in order to shed light on whether and how this distinction had any repercussion in practice.

In relation to the possibility of subordinating self-determination to other concerns, things are no-less blurred. Amongst legal scholars there is indeed an ongoing debate on this matter. Looking at Article 1 of the human rights Covenants, Cassese observes that the Article, unlike other provisions of the Covenant, is couched in absolute terms – meaning that it does not include any 'escape clause' granting contracting states the power to restrict the exercise of the right to self-determination.[9] The impossibility to derogate from Article 1 is stressed also by Rosas, who highlights that derogation is not possible for Articles 1 to 4 of the Covenant on Civil and Political Rights (ICCPR), and that Article 1 in particular cannot be derogated, being also part of the Covenant on Economic, Social and Cultural Rights (ICESCR) and arguably a reaffirmation of customary international law.[10]

A contrary view is expressed by McCorquodale, who observes that common Article 1(3) 'implies a limitation on the right to self-determination as it provides that States have an obligation to respect the right in conformity with the provisions of the Charter of the United Nations'.[11] In the drafting process, the Committee responsible for Article 1 indeed stressed that the principle of self-determination should be considered 'in function of other provisions' and '*a basis* for the development of friendly relations, and in effect, *one of the appropriate measures* to strengthen universal peace'.[12] On this basis, Simpson argues that,

8 José E Alvarez, *International Organizations as Law-makers* (OUP 2006) 181. See also H J Richardson III, 'The Danger of the New Legal Colonialism' (2010) 104 *Proceedings of the Annual Meeting, American Society of International* 393, 396.

9 Cassese, however, notes that Art 1 is subject to the same limitations incorporated in the Covenant's other provisions. On this basis argues that the 'full' right to self-determination, to include the ability of individuals to exercise their political and civil rights, is not absolute and can be exceptionally curtailed in case of derogations made under art 4 of the Covenant. Antonio Cassese, *Self-determination of Peoples: A Legal Reappraisal* (CUP 1995) 53-54.

10 The same argument was made by Johnson, who argues that the right to self-determination is to some extent a right of customary international right, and so it is not affected by Art. 2(7), which limits only Charter rights. In this respect is also mentioned that Nicaragua had reported derogation from Art 1 to 5 in 1982, but because of doubts voiced by the Human Rights Commission it dropped the reference to Art. 1. See Allan Rosas, 'Internal Self-Determination' in Christian Tomuschat (ed), *Modern Law of Self-Determination* (Martinus Nijhoff 1993) 225 and CD Johnson, 'Toward Self-Determination: A Reappraisal as Reflected in the Declaration on Friendly Relations' (1973) 3 *Georgia Journal of international and Comparative Law Quarterly* 145, 160.

11 Robert McCorquodale, 'Self-Determination: A Human Rights Approach' (1994) 43 *International and Comparative Law Quarterly* 860, 878.

12 UNCIO, Vol VI, 704 (emphasis added).

in the Charter, self-determination is subordinated to the post-war system's fundamental norms, including Chapter VII measures and the general commitment to ensure peace and security.[13] Similarly, Thurer and Burri also argue that 'even though it is laid down in an unrestricted form, self-determination does not have an absolute character . . . it seems more productive to conceive self-determination in such a broad and functional fashion, than to lay much emphasis on neuralgic points, such as its possible dogmatic qualification as peremptory norm of international law'.[14] From a similar standpoint, Cassese writes:

> [i]n the UN Charter, self-determination was only considered as a means to further the development of friendly relations among states and to strengthen universal peace. It was not considered as an independent value but only as instrumental *vis a vis* that of peace, with the obvious consequence that it might and indeed should be set aside when its fulfilment would give rise to tension and conflict between states.[15]

All in all, according to McCorquodale the subordinate character of self-determination is justified in view of a general interest of international society in maintaining international peace and security. This general interest creates a limitation on the right of self-determination that is expressed in two ways: the territorial integrity of States and the maintenance of colonial boundaries *(uti possidetis juris)*.[16] The same is also argued by Summers, who observes that 'self-determination frequently takes a subordinate role in relation to principles such as *uti possidetis*, territorial integrity or the inviolability of frontiers'.[17]

In Chapter 2, we have seen that amongst scholars there is an unsubstantiated tendency to view the right to self-determination as a right for which limitation

13 Gerry J Simpson, 'The Diffusion of Sovereignty: Self-determination in the Post-colonial Era' (1996) 32 *Stanford Journal of International Law* 255, 266.

14 Daniel Thurer and Thomas Burri, 'Self-determination' (2010) *Max Planck Encyclopedia of Public International Law* www.mpepil.com (last accessed 15 April 2018).

15 Antonio Cassese, 'Political Self-determination: Old Concepts and New Developments' in A Cassese (ed), *UN Law, Fundamental Rights: Two Topics in International Law* (Sijthoff & Noordhoff 1979) 139. The same is argued by Prakash Sinha, 'Has Self-determination become a Principle of International Law today?' (1974) 14 Indian Journal *of International Law* 332, 336. See also Bruno Simma (ed), *The Charter of the United Nations: A Commentary* (OUP 1994) 44.

16 McCorquodale also admits that 'each of these limitations is applicable only to a few methods of exercise of the right of self-determination, and, even in those instances, they may not be appropriate in the particular circumstances of a claim'. McCorquodale (n 11) 879 and 883.

17 James Summers, *Peoples and International Law* (2nd edn, Brill 2014) 82. See also Kirgis for the concept of 'degrees of self-determination', outlining an inverse relationship between the degree of representative government, on one hand, and the extent of destabilization that the international community will tolerate in a self-determination claim. Frederic L Kirgis, 'The Degrees of Self-Determination in the United Nations Era' (1994) 4 *American Journal of International Law* 304, 308.

is permitted, or that can be set aside or suspended in certain circumstances.[18] Now, assuming that self-determination concerns can be subordinated to higher interests, and assuming also that self-determination can be subordinated to more general international security interests, the issue of how this limitation adapts to the rights of a self which does not question states' territorial integrity and international boundaries is a matter open for exploration. Again, this issue raises the question as to the relationship between state sovereignty, non-intervention and the independent functioning of self-determination. In this respect, also the role of the Security Council in administering the relationship between the fundamental interests of international peace and security and the implementation of the right to self-determination needs to be explored. As was highlighted by the UN Special Rapporteur Gros Espiell,

> The special nature of the powers granted to the Security Council under Article 24 of the Charter of the United Nations is indicative of the importance of the resolutions adopted by the Council and its potential role in ensuring the implementation of the right of self-determination, especially in cases where the Council acts under the provisions of Chapter VII of the Charter. The Council's ability to act is of course subject to the voting system applicable to the adoption of its resolutions (Art. 27, para. 3) and to the political considerations which that implies.[19]

A dedicated study of the relationship between self-determination and Chapter VII obligations in the context of state-building does not exist, and scattered information is particularly scant in relation to the layer of self-determination examined here. A study of how self-determination language (including paraphrased expressions citing the core aspects of the right) was used in Security Council resolutions is yet to appear.[20] New research that analyses whether and how this right was counter-balanced with other competing interests in Security Council resolutions adopted under Chapter VII would be a welcome contribution.[21] Such a study would necessarily have to consider in detail the question of whether the right to self-determination, or certain aspects of it, enjoy the status of *jus cogens*, because on this ultimately depends the answer to whether

18 See ch 2.2.1.

19 Hector Gros Espiell, 'The Right to Self-determination: Implementation of United Nations Resolutions' (1980) UN Doc E/CN.4/Sub.2/405/Rev.1 para 170.

20 In recent years, self-determination related language was used in Security Council resolutions in at least two situations: Afghanistan and Iraq. See Resolutions 1383 (2011), 1401 (2002), 1483 (2003), 1511(2003), 1546 (2004), 1637 (2005).

21 This topic was briefly touched upon in relation to the Security Council actions in Iraq. See eg Andrea Carcano, *The Transformation of Occupied Territory in International Law* (Brill Nijhoff 2015) 189–203 and Aristotle Constantinides, 'An Overview of Legal Restraints on Security Council Chapter VII Action with a Focus on Post-Conflict Iraq' www.esil-sedi.eu/sites/default/files/Constantinides_0.PD (last accessed 15 April 2018).

the Security Council is or is not limited by self-determination when acting under Chapter VII powers.

According to Article 53 of the Vienna Convention on the Law of Treaties, a peremptory norm of *jus cogens* is 'a norm accepted and recognised by the international community of States as a whole as a norm from which no derogation is permitted'.[22] A discussion on whether self-determination is an absolute right that carries *jus cogens* status or whether it is a norm that can be balanced against other fundamental norms and principles of international law will thus bear consequences on the debate over status of the norm. Scholarly discussion on this is ongoing, but the matter is not settled. Commentators remain divided about whether self-determination may be considered as a peremptory norm of *jus cogens*: whilst a majority seems to support this idea,[23] some remain more sceptical.[24]

According to the definition of *jus cogens* provided in the Vienna Convention, for Summers there are three tests that can be used to demonstrate that self-determination has achieved such a status.[25] First, there would need to be evidence of a consensus that self-determination has achieved *jus cogens* status on behalf of the international community of states as a whole. This formula entails that evidence of acceptance must be provided by an overwhelming majority of states, in a somewhat stricter criterion than the one resorted to when it must be determined whether a given practice has crystallised as customary law.[26] However, positive evidence that states are ready to accept self-determination as *jus cogens* is lacking. Statements in support of this position have been put forward by states in the drafting of treaties and in their submissions to the ICJ, but numbers fall short of general acceptance.[27]

22 Vienna Convention on the Law of Treaties (Vienna Convention) arts 53.

23 Hector Gros Espiell, 'Self-determination as *Jus Cogens*' in Antonio Cassese (ed), *UN Law, Fundamental Rights: Two Topics in International Law* (Sijthoff and Noordhoff International 1979) 167–74. See also 'Article 40: Commentary, Report of the International Law Commission', 56 GAOR (2001) Supplement No 10, (A/56/10) 284. More generally, see works cited in Summers (n 17) footnote 181 at 78 and Cassese (n 9) footnote 60 at 134.

24 See Aureliu Critescu, *The Right to Self-Determination: Historical and Current Development on the Basis of United Nations Instruments*, UN Doc E/CN.4/Sub.2/404/Rev.1 para 154 and Michla Pomerance, *Self-determination in Law and Practice: The New Doctrine in the United Nations* (Martinus Nijhoff 1982) 63.

25 Summers (n 17) 78-84 and 'The Status of Self-determination in International Law: A Question of Legal Significance or Political Importance?' (2003) 14 *Finnish Yearbook of International Law* 271.

26 Christian Tomuschat, 'The Security Council and *Jus Cogens*' in Enzo Cannizzaro (ed), *The Present and Future of Jus Cogens* (Sapienza Università 2015) 28.

27 On this point see Summers, *Peoples and International Law* (n 17) 80 and Matthew Saul, 'The Normative status of Self-Determination in International Law: A Formula for Uncertainty in the Scope and Content of the Right?' (2011) 11 *Human Rights Law Review* 609. See also Cassese, *Self-Determination of Peoples* (n 9) at 135–39, who affirms that authors who support the peremptory status of the norm do not provide any element of state practice or *opinio juris* in support of their view.

Secondly, Article 53 of the Vienna Convention indicates the consequence that 'a treaty is void if, at the time of its conclusion, it conflicts with a peremptory norm of international law'. In relation to this, Summers effectively enumerates a set of examples of treaties that appear to conflict with self-determination and which have not been treated as void in state practice – in particular the Australia–Indonesia Timor Gap Treaty of 1989, later upheld also by the United Nations Transitional Authority.[28] Thirdly, if self-determination was *jus cogens*, then by definition it would need to prevail over competing norms – unless they are peremptory too. As we have seen above, self-determination has normally been balanced against other principles such as territorial integrity and *uti possidetis*. The latter, in particular, is merely a pragmatic principle and certainly not a fundamental one that could be attributed *jus cogens* status. As the logic goes, for Summers the relationship of self-determination with other legal principles supports the idea that the former is not a peremptory norm of international law.[29]

From a similarly sceptical standpoint, in a recent article Saul has reorganised the debate on the normative status of self-determination and distinguished three ways in which scholars approach the issue.[30] He calls the 'entirety approach' the view according to which self-determination is taken to be *jus cogens* in its entirety; in the sense that all aspects of the norm, as soon as they are established as aspects of the norm, are elevated to *jus cogens* status.[31] Whilst this approach seems correct on purely moral grounds, from a positive law perspective Saul finds it difficult to accept this implication as valid, because *opinio juris* by an overwhelming majority of states would be needed to demonstrate that a certain aspect of the law has achieved peremptory status.

A more nuanced approach that he identifies in the literature elaborates on the possibility that self-determination is *jus cogens* in a qualified manner.[32] This is, for instance, the approach taken by the two United Nations Special Rapporteurs Critescu and Gros Espiell, though the two reach opposing views on the matter.[33] Finally, the third approach that Saul has identified is the 'possible approach', adopted by those who believe that self-determination only possibly has *jus cogens* status – or, better, only certain aspects of it and in certain contexts.[34] The major critique moved to these contributions is that, by remaining hesitant and inconclusive, they are in fact unhelpful in developing a clearer understanding of the normative status of the norm. In so doing, the discourse on the status of self-determination struggles to escape from the belief that no conclusion can be drawn until our knowledge on certain aspects of self-determination becomes more determinate.

Summing up, questions on the normative status of self-determination are unsettled and still leave room for debate amongst international law scholars.

28 Summers, *Peoples and International Law* (n 17) 81.
29 ibid.
30 Saul (n 27).
31 ibid 635-36.
32 ibid 637.
33 See nn 23 and 24 above.
34 Saul (n 27) 639-40.

From the positivist perspective, the qualified approach could be a useful tool to explore the status of self-determination as it applies outside of the context of decolonisation. A comprehensive study of the way the principle is systematically applied in the context of state-building, therefore, would certainly add substance to our current knowledge of the norm and, in this sense, it could also reveal important information concerning the principle's normative status.

2.1 *Local ownership as self-determination in disguise?*

Knowing more on self-determination can also contribute to the development of the policy debate in another key area of debate concerning peacebuilding: local ownership. This concept is used in the literature on peacebuilding and *jus post bellum* typically to deal with issues concerning the scope of action afforded by interveners, their relationship with local actors as well as questions on when and how to include local actors in decision-making.[35] In an article examining the concept of local ownership, Chesterman argued that the term is commonly used in the context of post-conflict reconstruction, but it is not clear whether it has consistency or substance.[36] Scholars indeed seem generally to agree that the term is mostly used in a rhetorical sense, with some suggesting that its fuzziness is actually the basis of its success.[37] Donais defines *local ownership* in post-conflict contexts as 'the extent to which domestic actors control both the design and implementation of political processes'.[38] More widely, scholarly literature accepts that ownership refers to the relationship among the various actors and stakeholders involved in the reconstruction of conflict-affected states – and in particular between the intervened and the recipients of an intervention.[39] This includes also the issue of who has the authority and responsibility for setting and implementing policy priorities during the transition period.[40]

35 See Annika S Hansen, 'From Intervention to Local Ownership: Rebuilding a Just and Sustainable Rule of Law after Conflict' in Carsten Stahn and Jan K Kleffner, *Jus Post Bellum: Towards a Law of Transition from Conflict to Peace* (TMC Asser 2008) and Matthew Saul, 'International Law and the Identification of an Interim Government to Lead Post-Conflict Reconstruction' in Matthew Saul and James Sweeney (eds), *International Law and Post-Conflict Reconstruction Policy* (Routledge 2015).

36 Simon Chesterman, Ownership in Theory and Practice: Transfer of Authority in UN Statebuilding Operations' (2007) 1 *Journal of Intervention and Statebuilding* 3, 4.

37 Chesterman (n 36) 10.

38 Timothy Donais, 'Empowerment or Local Imposition? Dilemmas of Local Ownership in Post-Conflict Peacebuilding Processes' (2009) 34 *Peace and Change* 3.

39 See Chesterman (n 36) 4; Timothy Donais, *Peacebuilding and Local Ownership: Post-Conflict Consensus Building* (Routledge 2012); and Sarah B K von Billerbeck, *Whose Peace? Local Ownership and United Nations Peacekeeping* (OUP 2016) 31.

40 See Timothy Donais, 'National Ownership and Post-Conflict Peacebuilding: from Principle to Practice' (2014) Centre for International Innovation, *Policy Brief No 43* https://www.cigionline.org/sites/default/files/cigi_pb_43.pdf (last accessed 15 April 2018) and Béatrice Pouligny, 'Supporting Local Ownership in Humanitarian Action' (2009) Global Public Policy Institute, *Humanitarian Policy Paper Series* https://www.alnap.org/system/files/content/. . ./gppippr-local-ownership-2009.pdf (last accessed 15 April 2018).

In the policy literature, ownership has been identified as the core issue around which two competing visions of peacebuilding diverge. On the one side there is a vision of liberal peacebuilding, which stresses the importance of international norms and values reflecting a belief that peace should be built through the application of liberal norms and standards. In this context, 'local ownership emerges out from a commitment by local actors to take ownership over a largely predetermined vision of peacebuilding'.[41] In such a top-down approach ownership is conceived merely as a buy-in of domestic elites into externally designed interventions.[42] This remains a minimalist vision of ownership, and one in which decision-making is gradually transferred back from interveners to local actors as the appropriate (liberal) institutional infrastructure becomes operational. In this perspective, ownership becomes an end to a means and therefore it also becomes acceptable to think of it in terms of levels or degrees, which depend on a number of factors and circumstances – such as capacities of local actors.[43]

On the other side, a communitarian approach to peacebuilding privileges the importance of local specificities, regardless of the degree of compliance with emerging international norms. To this view corresponds a more substantive, bottom-up approach to ownership and a more active role of local actors. In this scenario peacebuilding processes are to be designed, managed and implemented by local actors.[44] According to a communitarian understanding of ownership, indeed, 'national actors should own the entirety of the process of peacekeeping from its earliest stages and should not simply appropriate something that is externally designed and sanctioned'.[45] In essence, here ownership is a means to an end in designing transitions.

As we saw in Chapter 4, one of the functions of the legal principle of self-determination in the context of state-building is to regulate the relationship between the local populations and external actors that take part in the reconstruction – as well as to interpret the way conflicting obligations can and should be balanced.[46] It is therefore important to explore the relationship between the concept of ownership and the principle of self-determination, because it is clear that there is at least a conceptual correlation between the two. At the very minimum, as explained

41 Donais, 'Empowerment or Local Imposition?' (n 38) 5-6.

42 See von Billerbeck (n 39); Donais, 'National Ownership and Post-Conflict Peacebuilding' (n 40); Filip Edjus, "Here Is Your Mission, Now Own It!' The Rhetoric and Practice of Local Ownership in EU Interventions' (2017) 26 *European Security* 461.

43 Derick W Brinkerhoff, 'Where There's a Will, There's a Way? Untangling Local Ownership and Political Will in Post-Conflict Stability and Reconstruction Operations' (2007) 8 *The Whitehead Journal of Diplomacy and International Relations* 111, 114–15.

44 See von Billerbeck (n 39) and Donais, 'Empowerment or Local Imposition?' (n 38). Von Billerbeck (at 38) delineates also a third approach: a middle ground that calls for a local-international consensus, treating ownership as involving an ongoing consultation process with the population in the development of goals and activities.

45 See von Billerbeck (n 39) 66.

46 See ch 4, in particular section 4.2.

by Brinkerhoff, the two must be related because the notion of ownership – like self-determination – has to do with people.[47]

The conceptual link between the two terms is made indeed by a number of writers.[48] Donais argues that in dealing with the relationship between insiders and outsiders in the reconstruction, local ownership ends up being linked to the concept of state self-determination, because it is about 'the freedom to choose among alternate sociopolitical and economic organizing principles'.[49] Von Billerbeck, in her recent book on local ownership in United Nations peacekeeping, convincingly argues that the two conceptions of ownership, liberal and communitarian, correspond to two different conceptions of self-determination. In her view, in communitarian understandings of ownership self-determination is an open concept, 'one in which people have the option to choose any form of government, liberal or illiberal, which cannot be sanctioned or rejected by the broader international community'.[50] Contrarily, the liberal conception of ownership affects the degree of self-determination that exists in post-conflict countries because it entails policies that do not leave local actors the space and possibility to determine a plan for peace by themselves.[51] In the reality of peacekeeping operations, however, von Billerbeck accepts that it is sensible to envisage how a balance needs to be struck between the normative principles of self-determination – with their more open-ended models of peacemaking – and the operational duties of interveners who aim to build effective and long-lasting peace.

Overall, the normative dilemmas that permeate the policy debate on local ownership seem to present the same overarching questions that arise in the same context in relation to the role of self-determination as a legal principle. How much space should interveners afford in decision-making in post-conflict settings? How and when to include the local population in decision-making processes related to the transition? Other than being at the very core of the policy debate, these issues are also of direct relevance to discourse on the role of the legal principle of self-determination. In addition, there are, once again, issues of hierarchy and prioritisation. As Donais put it:

> the normative core of the debate regarding the meaning of ownership hinges on whether national ownership is an absolute right, consisted with

47 See Brinkerhoff (n 43) 112.

48 According to Richmond, the link is clear, but state-builders 'studiously avoid mentioning the term self-determination', using local ownership as a compromise term perhaps because of the echoes of words such as national liberation from a past colonial era. Oliver P Richmond, 'Beyond Local Ownership in the Architecture of Peacebuilding' (2012) 11 *Ethnopolitics* 354, 358.

49 Donais, 'Empowerment or Local Imposition?' (n 38) 7.

50 See von Billerbeck (n 39) 73. Interestingly, in ch 2 we have already seen how a similar dualism between self-determination as a means versus self-determination as an end to a means plays out in relation to the place that self-determination should occupy in the modern law of occupation. See ch 2.2.1.1.2.

51 ibid 74-75.

> internationally recognized principles of sovereignty and self-determination, or a conditional right, contingent on the acceptance of key international norms such as respect for democracy, human rights and the rule of law.[52]

To conclude, there is reason to believe that the policy debates on local ownership would benefit from the development of better knowledge on self-determination. Whilst the two remain separate concepts – one pertaining to the realm of law and the other to the policy discourse – self-determination and ownership share at least a common purpose in post-conflict situations. Introducing a conception of ownership that is supported by legal standards and definitions of self-determination could indeed facilitate the process of defining the strategic roles of local and international actors involved in peacebuilding, as well as suggest strategies for the allocation of authority during transitions. A more developed notion of ownership, in its turn, could offer precious and concrete guidance in transitional contexts to help in determining whose voices should be heard when priorities need to be set.

2.2 *Contribution to scholarship and originality of the study*

This research invoked the application of self-determination in the context of state-building and identified a particular layer of the concept, mostly overlooked in existing literature, which enters into play in situations of state-building. A study to dissect the concept of self-determination and analyse a particular dimension of it, with a view to singling out the character, scope and content of the norm as it applies to the people of a state as a whole was missing. Aiming to fill this gap, in Chapters 3 and 4 this study presented an original account of the scope, content and character of this specific layer of the norm, which served to shed light on this relatively unknown dimension of self-determination. In contrast with existing studies, the analysis dealt with both internal and external aspects of self-determination, aiming to offer a full picture of what the right entails in terms of rights and obligations. In addition, this study provided an original account of the Somali National Reconciliation Process from the perspective of international law on self-determination.

This research is the first full-length studies to analyse the role and significance of the law on self-determination in the context of post-conflict state-building. The study partly overlaps in focus with Saul's recent book *Popular Governance of Post-conflict Reconstruction*,[53] as the two books set each other off to answer similar research questions. They differ, however, in the way they answer these questions. Saul's study has two main objectives. First, it sets out to identify the scope and content of the law that applies to post-conflict reconstruction, to include the law

52 Donais, 'National Ownership and Post-Conflict Peacebuilding' (n 40) 4.

53 Matthew Saul, *Popular Governance of Post-Conflict Reconstruction: The Role of International Law* (CUP 2014).

on self-determination, state sovereignty and the right to political participation. Secondly, the book aims to evaluate the appropriateness of the extant international law on popular governance for regulating transitions from conflict to peace.[54] In doing so, Saul focuses on two case studies of post-conflict situations in which control of the territory and the capacity to reconstruct was dependent on international actors, whilst the formal responsibility for decision-making rested with domestic governments. The two cases analysed are Sierra Leone and Afghanistan.[55]

Coming from different directions, the present study and Saul's book share some common findings, namely that self-determination standards tend to be vague, under-defined and light-touch in nature. Despite this common vision, the two studies reach different conclusions on the meaning and significance of such vagueness. For Saul, the lack of defined criteria for what constitutes self-government in situations where there is no effective control can legitimately be resolved by the political preferences of international actors involved in the reconstruction, given the lack of a principled basis to determine which actors should enjoy governmental status.[56] In fact, Saul argues that the law leaves open the possibility that international actors prioritise self-interest over the best interests of the population, but that, overall, the wide degree of discretion afforded by international actors under current international law is useful in this context because it serves the purposes of successful state-building.[57]

On the contrary, this study has shown that indeterminacy does not necessarily mean that the law does or should remain silent on certain matters, because there are additional aspects of the law which apply to the self in question. Benefitting from a more in-depth analysis of the content and scope of a single layer of self-determination, this research has expanded the discussion on the application and significance of the norm. In particular, by exploring and revisiting the classic internal/external divide that has so far monopolised self-determination discourse in international law, the present study contributed to round up the discourse on self-determination by including also the external aspects of the right. As a result, the indeterminacy of 'internal' self-determination standards constitutes only a part of the picture in determining the significance of the norm in the context of state-building. In Chapters 4 and 5, indeed, it was shown how external aspects of self-determination – such as the prohibition of external interference in the process through which the people choose their form of government – hold their legal weight in the context of state-building. In so doing, external aspects work to reduce the scope of action available to international actors in restoring effective governance. The precise contour of these limits and the extent to which the scope of action of state-builders is reduced is now a question for future research to answer in detail.

54 ibid 4.
55 ibid. See, respectively, chs 5 and 6.
56 ibid ch 3.
57 ibid 80 and 230–33.

In spite of differences, it is nonetheless important that dedicated discussion on self-determination issues has now started to appear in this ever-growing field of practice, so that a rich debate can be opened on this matter. In view of the ongoing discourse on the potential of developing a *jus post bellum*,[58] the importance of discussing the role of self-determination in post-conflict reconstruction is self-evident. If a *jus post bellum* is to be elaborated, the importance of discussing the place of the right to self-determination within this body of law cannot be understated.

3 Future challenges for legal research on self-determination

The present study opened the floor to discussion about the potential and challenges for new research on the development of self-determination in the post-colonial world. In particular, three main avenues have been exposed to the need for further research. First, the study highlighted the need to carry out a bigger research project to investigate the role played by self-determination standards in various state-building settings. This project should include a significant number of countries, as a way of identifying potential patterns and recurrent situations. Cases should be selected on certain principled grounds. The analysis should look into situations where, owing to a military intervention there is no government in place to start the reconstruction. The case of Somalia was an extreme example because the situation of a power vacuum had lasted for many years, instead of being the direct consequence of a government ousted as a result of a military intervention. Other cases in which the situation of governmental collapse was more short-lived should be identified. Secondly, it would be useful to prioritise analysis of situations where the state-building process has radically transformed the economic and political system in place in the country. Some possibilities would be the situation in Afghanistan and Iraq after the 2001 and 2003 invasions, and to some extent also the situation in Libya after the NATO bombing of 2011. Research must also be directed at the role of self-determination language in Security Council resolutions, in particular in places where a Chapter VII mandate has been used (Iraq).

Secondly, a challenge that has opened up for self-determination research concerns its ability to understand whether current practice leans towards a concept of the right which tolerates balance and derogation. Understanding whether state practice is inclined to set out a conception of self-determination that aims to balance the principle and derogate the right is an important question that future research could help to answer. Thirdly, should it be found that self-determination is in fact a right that can be subjected to derogation in the context of state-building, future studies should aim to develop a derogation regime if the qualified application of self-determination standards is to be taken

58 See ch 1.2.

seriously and not happen in an arbitrary manner. At present, there is a lack of guidance concerning how derogation for self-determination could take place; without such a regime in place, the risk of abuses and, with it, violations of this fundamental principle are concrete. According to Summers, the representativeness clause inserted in Principle 5, paragraph 7 of the Friendly Relations Declaration made the balance between national self-determination ambitions and territorial integrity less arbitrary, because it linked territorial integrity to representative, non-discriminatory government.[59] In so doing, the right was restricted by satisfaction rather than by arbitrariness, and by appealing to certain standards of liberalism.[60] A future challenge, therefore, is to understand what restrictions could be imposed on the right of the population of an entire state, where territorial integrity is not at stake.

This is a particularly arduous question, given the crucial role of the state in exercising the balancing function between the right of self-determination and other rights and interests within the human rights system. Derogation indeed needs conscious statements, but in the absence of a local government, who would have the authority to make this statement? Moreover, would the derogation of rights concern also the obligations held by third party states participating in the reconstruction, given that the obligations imposed by self-determination have an *erga omnes* character?[61] As has been highlighted, the importance of the rule of law in peacebuilding processes calls for strict adherence to rather than derogation from existing obligations.[62] Should exemptions become necessary in a state of emergency, 'these should be tailored to existing needs and long-term goals. Any such exemption should be introduced under transparent procedures and be open for independent control …'.[63] Without a derogation regime in place, the risks of non-compliance are self-evident. Future research on self-determination should take this issue seriously, given the centrality of state-building as a policy to re-establishing governmental effectiveness after conflict.

4 A right in abeyance?

This study has contributed to existing scholarship by opening up new streams of analysis for future research to establish what is the impact and significance of self-determination in international law. It has shown that the way self-determination

59 Summers, *Peoples and International Law* (n 17) 570.

60 ibid.

61 On this point see Cassese, *Self-determination of Peoples* (n 9); Saul, 'The Normative status of Self-Determination' (n 27) 632; *East Timor (Portugal v. Australia)* [1995] ICJ Rep 90 and *Legal Consequences of the Construction of a Wall in the Occupied Palestinian Territory* (Advisory Opinion) [2004] ICJ Rep 136 at paras 155–56.

62 Dieter Fleck, '*Jus Post Bellum* as a Partly Independent Legal Framework' in Carsten Stahn, Jennifer S Easterday and Jan Iverson (eds), *Jus Post Bellum: Mapping the Normative Foundations* (OUP 2014) 55.

63 ibid.

concerns have been mainstreamed into the process of reconstruction of Somalia has been disappointing to say the least. Disregard of the legal standards of self-determination, coupled with procrastinating promises of democratic governance and silent reaction on behalf of the international community all together seem to suggest that the law on self-determination was not perceived to have been blatantly violated, or purposely ignored, or carefully derogated by the actors engaged in rebuilding state structures in Somalia. Rather, it appears that self-determination standards have been used selectively at different stages of the process, leaving the right applied more in the sense of an overall purpose for future realisation than as a process.[64]

In 1921, for the Committee of Jurists the political principle of national self-determination was something that was normally dormant and enclosed within sovereignty.[65] It is during periods of political transformation, when the existence of States becomes uncertain, that the principle becomes applicable to reconstitute the political normality of statehood.[66] As Koskenniemi reminds us, this distinction between 'normal' and 'abnormal' situations has since been at the core of discussion about the legal significance of the right.[67] In practice, the compromise position adopted by the international community was to associate abnormality almost exclusively with colonialism.[68] In contemporary practice, situations of state-building are situated at the intersection between normality and abnormality. For the people of a failed state, statehood and independence are not challenged, but their future is nonetheless at stake when state structures have collapsed and international state-builders step in to rebuild governance institutions, often from scratch. In such moments, sovereignty and non-intervention rights can be suspended in view of higher interests, but exactly what happens to self-determination is yet to be established.

It seems reasonable to conclude this research with a warning. The model of self-determination that was applied in Somalia is not encouraging from the perspective of people's rights. The Somali people have been deprived of their entitlements to self-determination for many years during the transition and, to some extent, also after the transition was officially completed. This book argued that, if Somalia was not an exception, then we must understand how this was possible and what role is left for self-determination standards in such context.

64 For instance, Summers notes that the wording of common Article 1 of the Covenants conceptualizes states' obligations as a duty to 'promote the realization of the right of self-determination', thus seemingly being orientated towards a progressive realization of the right. Summers, *Peoples and International Law* (n 17) 330.

65 *Aaland Islands Case* (1920) *League of Nations Official Journal Spec Supp* 3.

66 Martti Koskenniemi, 'National Self-Determination Today: Problems of Legal Theory and Practice' (1994) 43 *International and Comparative Law Quarterly* 241, 246. See also Nathaniel Berman, 'Sovereignty in Abeyance: Self-Determination and International Law' (1988) 7 *Wisconsin International Law Journal* 51.

67 Koskenniemi (n 66) 254.

68 ibid.

In Somalia self-determination worked more as a promise for the future rather than as a *modus operandi* followed by state-builders in orchestrating transition. Whether this was done as a result of a specific understanding of the meaning and significance of this right in this context, or whether this was due to an arbitrary application of the right remains an open question.

In order to avoid future situations where self-determination is applied selectively and in an arbitrary manner, a derogation regime could be elaborated, so that it becomes clear in what circumstances, how and legitimately by whom the people of a state can be deprived of certain aspects of their right to self-determination. As things stand at present, state-building practice has shown that in times of political transition self-determination, one of the most important normative developments of the 20th century, is in many respects a right in abeyance.

Annex 1

Table A.1 List of General Assembly resolutions and voting records

Enhancing the effectiveness of the principle of periodic and genuine elections			*Respect for the principles of national sovereignty and non-interference in the internal affairs of states in their electoral processes*		
Year	*Res number*	*Voting*	*Year*	*Resolution no*	*Voting*
1988	43/157	without a vote	–	–	–
1989	44/146	without a vote	1989	44/147	113-23-11
1990	45/150	129-8-9	1990	45/151	111-29-11
1991	46/137	134-4-13	1991	46/130	102-40-13
1992	47/138	141-0-20	1992	47/130	99-45-16
1993	48/131	151-0-13	1993	48/124	101-51-17
1994	49/190[1]	155-1-12	1994	49/180	97-57-14
1995	50/185	156-0-15	1995	50/172	91-57-21
1997	52/129[2]	157-0-15	1997	52/119	98-58-12
1999	54/173	153-0-11	2000	54/168	91-59-10
2001	56/159	162-0-8	2001	56/154[3]	99-10-59
2003	58/180	169-0-8	2003	58/189	111-10-55
2004	59/201[4]	172-0-15	2004	–	–
2005	60/162	173-0-1	2005	60/164	110-6-61
2007	62/150	182-0-2	2007	–	–
2009	64/155	without a vote	2009	–	–
2011	66/163	without a vote	2011	–	–
2013	68/164	without a vote	2013	–	–
2015	70/168[5]	168-0-15			
2017	72/164	175-0-13			

1 From this year the resolution title was changed to *Strengthening the Role of the UN in Enhancing the Effectiveness of the Principle of Periodic and Genuine Elections.*
2 From this year the resolution title was changed to *UN Role in Enhancing Elections and Promoting Democratization.*
3 Title was changed to *Respect for the principles of national sovereignty and non-interference in the internal affairs of States in electoral processes as an important element for the promotion and protection of human rights.*
4 The title of this resolution is *Enhancing the role of regional, sub-regional and other organizations and arrangements in promoting and consolidating democracy.*
5 From this year the resolution title changed to *Strengthening the Role of the UN in Enhancing Periodic and Genuine Elections and the Promotion of Democratization.*

Sources

Books and articles

Abubakar AM, 'The Patterns of State Rebuilding and Federalism in Somalia' (2016) 10(6) *African Journal of Political Science and International Relations* 88

Adan A, 'Is Federalism the Best Path for a State Like Somalia?' *Somalia Newsroom* (6 March 2015) http://somalianewsroom.com/is-federalism-the-best-path-for-a-state-like-somalia/ (last accessed 15 April 2018)

Addo MK, 'Political Self-Determination within the Context of the African Charter on Human and People's Rights' (1988) 32 *Journal of African Law* 182

Ainte A, 'Somalia: Legitimacy of the Provisional Constitution' (2014) 25 *Conciliation Resources, ACCORD* 60 http://www.c-r.org/accord/legitimacy-and-peace-processes/somalia-legitimacy-provisional-constitution (last accessed 15 April 2018)

Akpinarli N, *The Fragility of the "Failed State" Paradigm: A Different International Law Perception of the Absence of Effective Government* (Martinus Nijhoff 2010)

Alvarez JE, *International Organizations as Law-makers* (OUP 2006)

Apuuli KP, 'Somalia After the United Nations-Led Djibouti Peace Process' (2011) 20 *African Security Review* 45

d'Aspremont J, '1989-2010: The Rise and Fall of Democratic Governance in International Law' in Crawford J and Nouwen S (eds), *Select Proceedings of the European Society of International Law, vol 3* (Hart Publishing 2011)

Atta-Asamoah A, 'Long way to restoration: Lessons from Somalia's transition process' (2013) *ISS Situation Report*, 7 https://www.issafrica.org/uploads/SitRep2013_9July-Asamoah.pdf (last accessed 15 April 2018)

Barnes C and Hassan H, 'The Rise and Fall of Mogadishu's Islamic Courts' (2007) 1 *Journal of Eastern African Studies* 151

Barten U, *Minorities, Minority Rights and Self-Determination* (Springer 2014)

Bass GJ, 'Jus Post Bellum' (2004) 32 *Philosophy & Public Affairs* 384

Batalla A, 'The Right to Self-Determination: ICCPR and the Jurisprudence of the Human Rights Committee' (2006) *Symposium on the Right to Self-Determination in International Law* http://unpo.org/downloads/AnnaBatalla.pdf (last accessed 15 April 2018)

Baxter R, 'Official Documents: United Nations Draft International Covenants on Human Rights' (1964) 58 *American Journal of International Law* 857

Bayefsky AF, *Self-determination in International Law: Quebec and Lessons Learned, Legal Opinions / selected and introduced by Anne F. Bayefsky* (Kluwer 2000)

Beauvais JC, 'Benevolent Despotism: A Critique of UN State-Building in East-Timor' (2001) 33 *New York University Journal of International Law and Politics* 1101

Bell C, *On the Law of Peace: Peace Agreements and the Lex Pacificatoria* (OUP 2008)

——— 'Peace Settlements and International Law: From *Lex Pacificatoria* to *Jus Post Bellum*' in White ND and Henderson C (eds), *Research Handbook on International Conflict and Security Law: Jus ad Bellum, Jus in Bello and Jus Post Bellum* (Edward Elgar Publishing 2013)

Bellamy AJ, 'The Responsibilities of Victory: Jus Post Bellum and the Just War' (2008) 34 *Review of International Studies* 601

Benvenisti E and Keinan G, 'The Occupation of Iraq: A Reassessment' in Pedrozo RA (ed), *International Law Studies: The War in Iraq: A Legal Analysis* (Naval War College 2010)

Berman N, 'Sovereignty in Abeyance: Self-Determination and International Law' (1988) 7 *Wisconsin International Law Journal* 51

Bhuta N, 'The Antinomies of Transformative Occupation' (2005) 16 *European Journal of International Law* 721

——— 'Against State-Building' (2008) 15 *Constellations* 517

——— 'Democratization, Statebuilding and Politics as Technology' in Bowden B, Charlesworth H and Farrall J (eds), *The Role of International Law in Rebuilding Societies after Conflict: Great Expectations* (CUP 2009)

——— 'New Modes and Orders: The Difficulties of a *Jus Post Bellum* of Constitutional Transformation' (2010) 60 *University of Toronto Law Journal* 799

von Billerbeck SBK, *Whose Peace? Local Ownership and United Nations Peacekeeping* (OUP 2016)

Blay SKN, 'Changing African Perspectives on the Right of Self-Determination in the Wake of the Banjul Charter on Human and People's Rights' (1985) 29 *Journal of African Law* 147

Blum Y, 'Reflections on the Changing Concept of Self-determination' (1975) 10 *Israel Law Review* 509

Bockenforde M, 'Beyond Federalism: Which Concept of Decentralization Reflects Best the Needs of Somalia?' in *Horn of Africa and Peace: The Role of Democratic Governance versus Sectarian Politics in Somalia*, Report of the 9th Annual Conference on the Horn of Africa (4-6 June 2010 Lund, Sweden) (Lund University Press 2010)

Boon K, 'Obligations of the New Occupier: The Contours of a *Jus Post Bellum*' (2005) 31 *Loyola of Los Angeles International and Comparative Law Review* 101

Bossuyt MJ, *Guide to the "Travaux Préparatoires" of the International Covenant on Civil and Political Rights* (Martinus Nijhoff 1987)

Bowden B, Charlesworth H and Farrall J (eds), *The Role of International Law in Rebuilding Societies after Conflict: Great Expectations* (CUP 2009)

Bowring B, 'Positivism *versus* Self-determination: The Contradictions of Soviet International Law' in Marks S (ed), *International Law on the Left: Re-examining Marxist Legacies* (CUP 2008)

Bradbury M, *Becoming Somaliland* (Progressio 2008)

Brinkerhoff DW, 'Where There's a Will, There's a Way? Untangling Local Ownership and Political Will in Post-Conflict Stability and Reconstruction Operations' (2007) 8 *The Whitehead Journal of Diplomacy and International Relations* 111

Brooks RE, 'Failed States, or the State as Failure?' (2005) 72 *The University of Chicago Law Review* 1159

Brown B, 'Intervention, Self-Determination, Democracy and The Residual Responsibilities of the Occupying Power in Iraq' (2004) 11 *UC Davis Journal of International Law and Policy* 23

Brown PM, 'The Aaland Islands Question' (1921) 15 *American Journal of International Law* 268

Brownlie I, 'An Essay in the History of the Principle of Self-Determination' in Alexandrowicz CH (ed), *Grotian Society Papers 1968. Studies in the History of the Law of Nations* (Martinus Nijhoff 1970)

——— *Principles of Public International Law* (7th edn, OUP 2008)

Bryden M, 'Storm Clouds over Somalia as Rivals Prepare for Battle' *The Nation (Kenya)* (8 December 2006) http://old.crisisgroup.org/ar/Regions%20Countries/Africa/Horn%20of%20Africa/Somalia/op-eds/storm-clouds-over-somalia-as-rivals-prepare-for-battle.html (last accessed 15 April 2018)

——— 'Somalia Redux: Assessing the New Somali Federal Government'(2013) *Report of the Center for Strategic and International Studies* http://csis.org/publication/somalia-redux (last accessed 15 April 2018)

——— and Tres T, Somalia's troubled transition: Vision 2016 revisited, Marsh E (ed), *Sahan, Path Finders in Policy and Practice* (May 2015)

Buchan R, 'International Community and the Occupation of Iraq' (2007) 12 *Journal of Conflict & Security Law* 37

——— *International Law and the Construction of the Liberal Peace* (Hart Publishing 2013) 220

Burke J, 'Mogadishu truck bomb: 500 casualties in Somalia's worst terrorist attack' *The Guardian* (London, 16 October 2017) https://www.theguardian.com/world/2017/oct/15/truck-bomb-mogadishu-kills-people-somalia (last accessed 15 April 2018)

Butler S, Separating Protection from Politics: The UN Security Council, the 2011 Ivorian Political Crisis and the Legality of Regime Change' (2015) 20 *Journal of Conflict and Security Law* 251

Cameron L and Everly R, 'Conceptualizing the Administration of Territory by International Actors' (2010) 21 *European Journal of International Law* 221

Caplan R, *A New Trusteeship? The International Administration of War-torn Territories*, Adelphi Paper No 341 (OUP/International Institute for Strategic Studies 2002)

Carcano A, 'End of the Occupation in 2004? The Status of the Multinational Force in Iraq after the Transfer of Sovereignty to the Interim Iraqi Government' (2006) 11 *Journal of Conflict and Security Law* 41

——— *Transformation of Occupied Territory in International Law* (Brill Nijhoff 2015)

von Carlowitz L, 'UNMIK Lawmaking between Effective Peace Support and Internal Self-Determination' (2003) 41 *Archiv des Völkerrecht* 336

Cassese A, 'Political Self-determination: Old Concepts and New Developments' in Cassese A (ed), *UN Law and Fundamental Rights: Two Topics in International Law* (Sijthoff & Noordhoff 1979)

——— *Self-determination of Peoples: A Legal Reappraisal* (CUP 1995)

——— 'The International Court of Justice and the Right of Peoples to Self-determination' in Lowe V and Fitzmaurice M (eds), *Fifty Years of the International Court of Justice: Essays in Honour of Sir Robert Jennings* (CUP 1996)

Chan K, 'State Failure and the Changing Face of the *Jus ad Bellum*' (2013) 18 *Journal of Conflict and Security Law* 395

Chandler D, *Bosnia: Faking Democracy After Dayton* (Pluto 2000)

——— *Empire in Denial: The Politics of State-Building* (Pluto 2006)

——— 'The Uncritical Critique of "Liberal Peace"' (2010) 36 *Review of International Studies* 137

Charlesworth H, 'Law After War' (2007) 8 *Melbourne Journal of International Law* 233

Chayes A, 'Chapter VII ½: Is *Jus Post Bellum* Possible?' (2013) 24 *European Journal of International Law* 291

Chen L, 'Self-Determination: An Important Dimension of the Demand for Freedom' (1981) 75 *Proceedings of the American Society of International Law* 88

Chesterman S, 'Occupation as Liberation: International Humanitarian Law and Regime Change' (2004) 18 *Ethics & International Affairs* 51

——— *You, the People: The United Nations, Transitional Administration, and State-Building* (OUP 2004)

——— 'From State Failure to State-Building: Problems and Prospects for a United Nations Peacebuilding Commission' (2007) 2 *Journal of International Law and International Relations* 155

——— 'Ownership in Theory and Practice: Transfer of Authority in UN Statebuilding Operations' (2007) *1 Journal of Intervention and Statebuilding* 3

——— 'International Territorial Administration and the Limits of Law' (2010) 23 *Leiden Journal of International Law* 437

Chetail V, 'Introduction: Post-Conflict Peacebuilding – Ambiguity and Identity' in Chetail V (ed), *Post-conflict Peacebuilding: A Lexicon* (OUP 2009)

Chopra J, 'Introducing Peace Maintenance' in Chopra J (ed), *The Politics of Peace-Maintenance* (Boulder 1998)

——— 'Building State Failure in East Timor' (2002) 33 *Development and Change* 979

Cobban A, *National Self-determination* (OUP 1947)

Cohen JL, 'The Role of International Law in Post-Conflict Constitution-Making: Toward a *Jus Post Bellum* for "Interim Occupations"' (2006) 51 *New York Law School Law Review* 497

Coleman AK, *Resolving Claims to Self-Determination: Is there a Role for the International Court of Justice?* (Routledge 2014)

Constantinides A, 'An Overview of Legal Restraints on Security Council Chapter VII Action with a Focus on Post-Conflict Iraq' www.esil-sedi.eu/sites/default/files/Constantinides_0.PD (last accessed 15 April 2018)

Craven M, *The International Covenant on Economic, Social, and Cultural Rights: A Perspective on its Development* (Clarendon Press 1998)

Crawford J, 'The Rights of Peoples: "Peoples" or "Governments"?' in Crawford J (ed), *The Rights of Peoples* (Clarendon Press 1988)

——— 'Book Review of Antonio Cassese, *Self-determination of Peoples*: A Legal Reappraisal' (1996) 90 *American Journal of International Law* 331

——— 'The General Assembly, the ICJ, and Self-determination' in Lowe V and Fitzmaurice M (eds), *Fifty Years of the International Court of Justice: Essays in Honour of Sir Robert Jennings* (CUP 1996)

——— 'The Right to Self-Determination in International Law: Its Development and Future' in Alston P (ed), *People's Rights* (OUP 2001)

——— *The Creation of States in International Law* (2nd edn, OUP 2006)

Critescu A, *The Right to Self-Determination: Historical and Current Development on the Basis of United Nations Instruments* UN Doc E/CN.4/Sub.2/404/Rev.1 (United Nations 1981)

Cryer R, 'Law and the *Jus Post Bellum*: Counselling Caution' in May L and Forcehimes AT (eds), *Morality, Jus Post Bellum and International Law* (CUP 2012)

Cuyckens H, *Revisiting the Law of Occupation* (Brill Nijhoff 2018)
Daase C, 'The Redistribution of Resources in Internationalized Intra-State Peace Processes by Comprehensive Peace Agreements and Security Council Resolutions' (2011) 3 *Goettingen International Law Journal* 23
——— 'The Law of the Peacemaker: The Role of Mediators in Peace Negotiations and Law-Making' (2012) 1 *Cambridge Journal of International and Comparative Law* 107
Dam-de Jong D, *International Law and Governance of Natural Resources in Conflict and Post-Conflict Situations* (CUP 2015)
Daglish K and Nasu H, 'Towards a True Incarnation of the Rule of Law in War-Torn Territories: Centring Peacebuilding in the Will of the People' (2007) 54 *Netherlands International Law Review* 81
De Brabandere E, *Post-conflict Administrations in International Law: International Territorial Administration, Transitional Authority and Foreign Occupation in Theory and Practice* (Martinus Nijhoff 2009)
——— 'Responsibility for Post-Conflict Reforms: A Critical Assessment of Jus Post Bellum as a Legal Concept' (2010) 43 *Vanderbilt Journal of Transnational Law* 119
——— 'The Concept of Jus Post Bellum in International Law: A Normative Critique' in Stahn C, Easterday JS and Iverson J (eds), *Jus Post Bellum: Mapping the Normative Foundations* (OUP 2014)
De Wet E, *The Chapter VII Powers of the United Nations Security Council* (Hart Publishing 2004)
DiMeglio RP, 'The Evolution of the Just War Tradition: Defining Jus Post Bellum' (2005) 186 *Military Law Review* 140
Dirshe A, 'The New Somalia Roadmap: Perpetual conflict in the making' (17 October 2001) https://www.hiiraan.com/op2/2011/oct/the_new_somalia_roadmap_perpetual_conflict_in_the_making.aspx (last accessed 15 April 2018)
Doehring K, 'Self-determination' in Simma B and others (eds), *The Charter of the United Nations: A Commentary, Vol I* (2nd edn, OUP 2002)
Donais T, 'Empowerment or Local Imposition? Dilemmas of Local Ownership in Post-Conflict Peacebuilding Processes' (2009) 34 *Peace and Change* 3
——— *Peacebuilding and Local Ownership: Post-Conflict Consensus Building* (Routledge 2012)
——— 'National Ownership and Post-Conflict Peacebuilding: from Principle to Practice' (2014) Centre for International Innovation, *Policy Brief No 43* https://www.cigionline.org/sites/default/files/cigi_pb_43.pdf (last accessed 15 April 2018)
Drew C, 'The East Timor Story: International Law on Trial' (2001) *European Journal of International Law* 651
van den Driest S, "Pro-Democratic' Intervention and The Right to Political Self-Determination: The Case of Operation Iraqi Freedom' (2010) LIV *Netherlands International Law Review* 29
——— *Remedial Secession: A Right to External Self-Determination as a Remedy to Serious Injustices?* (Intersentia 2013)
Duale AY, 'Less and more than the sum of its parts: The failed merger of Somaliland and Somalia and the tragic quest for 'Greater Somalia'' in Bereketeab R (ed), *Self-Determination and Secession in Africa: The Post-colonial State* (Routledge 2015)

Duffield M, *Development, Security and Unending War: Governing the World of Peoples* (Polity 2007)

Dworkin R, *Taking Rights Seriously* (Bloomsbury 2013)

Eagleton C, 'Self-Determination in the United Nations' (1953) 47 *American Journal of International Law* 88

Edjus F, "Here Is Your Mission, Now Own it!' The Rhetoric and Practice of Local Ownership in EU Interventions' (2017) 26 *European Security* 461

Elmi AA, 'In Search of a Somali Constitution' *Al Jazeera* (Doha, 25 January 2005) http://www.hiiraan.com/op4/2011/jan/17529/in_search_of_a_somali_constitution.aspx (last accessed 15 April 2018)

——— *Understanding the Somalia Conflagration: Identity, Political Islam and Peacebuilding* (Pluto Press 2010)

——— *Decentralization Options for Somalia* (2014) Heritage Institute for Policy Studies http://www.heritageinstitute.org/decentralization-options-somalia/ (last accessed 15 April 2018)

Emerson R, 'Self-determination' (1971) 65 *American Journal of International Law* 459

Eno MA, 'Inclusive but unequal: the enigma of the 14th SRNC and the four-point-five (4.5) factor' in Osman AA and Souarè IK (eds), *Somalia at the Crossroads: Challenges and Perspectives on Reconstructing a Failed State* (Adonis & Abbey 2007)

Fan H, 'The Missing Link between Self-Determination and Democracy: The Case of East Timor' (2007) 6 *Northwestern Journal of International Human Rights* 176

Farah I and Touré S, 'Engineering Peace in Somalia: A Call for the Re-examination of the Somali Peace Processes' *Development* (2018) https://doi.org/10.1057/s41301-018-0153-x (last accessed 15 April 2018)

Farmer A, 'Towards a Meaningful Rebirth of Economic Self-determination: Human Rights Realization in Resource-Rich Countries' (2006) 39 *New York University Journal of International Law and Policy* 417

Fassbender B and Bleckmann A, 'Article 2(1)' in Simma and others (eds), *The Charter of the United Nations: A Commentary, Vol II* (2nd edn, OUP 2002)

Felbab-Brown V, 'Why are Efforts to Counter Al-Shabaab Falling so Flat?' *Brookings* (Washington, 5 April 2016) http://www.brookings.edu/blogs/order-from-chaos/posts/2016/04/05-counterterrorism-state-building-somalia-felbabbrown (last accessed 15 April 2018)

di Felice B, 'International Transitional Administration: The United Nations in East Timor, Bosnia-Herzegovina, Eastern Slavonia, and Kosovo – a Bibliography' (2007) 35 *International Journal of Legal Information* 63

Fischer R, 'The Participation of Microstates in International Affairs' (1968) 62 *Proceedings of the American Society of International Law* 166

Fleck D, '*Jus Post Bellum* as a Partly Independent Legal Framework' in Stahn C, Easterday JS and Iverson J (eds), *Jus Post Bellum: Mapping the Normative Foundations* (OUP 2014)

Fox GH, 'The Right to Political Participation in International Law' (1992) 17 *Yale Journal of International Law* 539

——— 'The Occupation of Iraq' (2005) 36 *Georgetown Journal of International Law* 195

——— *Humanitarian occupation* (CUP 2008)

Franck TM, 'The Emerging Right to Democratic Governance' (1992) 86 *American Journal of International Law* 46

Fukuyama F, *State Building: Governance and World Order in the Twenty-First Century* (Cornell University Press 2004)
The Fund For Peace Country Analysis Indicators and Their Measures (2011) The Fund for Peace Publication CR-10-97-CA (11-05C) 20 https://issuu.com/fundforpeace/docs/cr-10-97-ca-conflictassessmentindicators-1105c (last accessed 15 April 2018)
Gareau JF, 'Shouting at the Wall: Self-determination and the Legal Consequences of the Construction of a Wall in the Occupied Palestinian Territory' (2005) 18 *Leiden Journal of International Law* 489
Gettleman J, 'Ethiopia Hits Somali Targets, Declaring War' *New York Times* (25 December 2005)
Ghani A and Lockhart C, *Fixing Failed States: A Framework for Rebuilding a Fractured World* (OUP 2009)
Gill TD, 'Legal and Some Political Limitations on the Power of the UN Security Council to Exercise Its Enforcement Powers under Chapter VII of the Charter' (1995) 26 *Netherlands Yearbook of International Law* 33
Ginsburg T, Chibub J and Frosini J, *Analytic Report on the Consultation Draft Constitution of the Somali Republic* (2012) International Development Law Organization
Ginsburgs G, '"Wars of National Liberation" and the Modern Law of Nations: The Soviet Thesis' in Baade HW (ed), *The Soviet Impact on International Law* (Oceana 1965)
Giorgetti C, 'Why Should International Law Be Concerned about State Failure?' (2009–10) 16 *ILSA Journal of International & Comparative Law* 469
——— *A Principled Approach to State Failure: International Community Actions in Emergency Situations* (Martinus Nijhoff 2010)
——— 'Using International Law in Somalia's Post-conflict Reconstruction' (2014) 53 *Columbia Journal of Transnational Law* 48
Gowlland-Debbas V, 'The Relationship between the International Court of Justice and the Security Council in the Light of the *Lockerbie* Case' (1994) 88 *American Journal of International Law* 643
Gros Espiell E, 'Self-Determination as Jus Cogens' in Cassese A (ed), *United Nations, Fundamental Rights: Two Topics in International Law* (Sijthoff and Noordhoff 1979)
——— *The Right to Self-determination: Implementation of United Nations Resolutions*, UN Doc E/CN.4/Sub.2/405/Rev.1 (United Nations 1980)
Guilfoyle D, 'Piracy Off Somalia: A Sketch of the Legal Argument' *EJIL: Talk!* (20 April 2009) http://www.ejiltalk.org/piracy-off-somalia-a-sketch-of-the-legal-framework/ (last accessed 15 April 2018)
——— 'Counter-piracy Law Enforcement and Human Rights' (2010) 59 *International and Comparative Law Quarterly* 141
Hagmann T, 'Stabilization, Extraversion and Political Settlement in Somalia' The Rift Valley Institute and Political Settlements Research Programme (2016) http://riftvalley.net/download/file/fid/4139 (last accessed 15 April 2018)
Hameiri S, 'Failed States or a Failed Paradigm? State Capacity and the Limits of Institutionalism' (2007) 10 *Journal of International Relations and Development* 122
——— 'Capacity and its Fallacies: International State Building as State Transformation' (2009) 38 *Millennium* 55

Hannum H, 'Legal Aspects of Self-Determination' *The Princeton Encyclopedia of Self-Determination* https://pesd.princeton.edu/?q=node/254 (last accessed 15 April 2018)

——— *Autonomy, Sovereignty and Self-Determination: The Accommodation of Conflicting Rights* (University of Pennsylvania Press 1990)

——— 'Rethinking Self-Determination' (1993) 34 *Virginia Journal of International Law* 1

——— *Autonomy, Sovereignty and Self-Determination: The Accommodation of Conflicting Rights, Revised Edition* (University of Pennsylvania Press 1996)

Hansen AS, 'From Intervention to Local Ownership: Rebuilding a Just and Sustainable Rule of Law after Conflict' in Stahn C and Kleffner JK, *Jus Post Bellum: Towards a Law of Transition from Conflict to Peace* (TMC Asser Press 2008)

Harper M, *Getting Somalia Wrong? Faith, War and Hope in a Shattered State* (Zed Books 2012)

——— 'Somalia: Whose Country Is It, Anyway?' (2013) 37 *Fletcher Forum of World Affairs* 161

Hassan MO, 'EU Delegation Pushes Somalia Peace Talks' *The Washington Post* (12 December 2006)

Hay E, 'International(ized) Constitutions and Peacebuilding' (2014) 27 *Leiden Journal of International Law* 141

Helman GB and Ratner SR, 'Saving Failed States' (1992–93) 89 *Foreign Policy* 3

Heritage Institute for Policy Studies, 'Federal Somalia: Not If but How' (2015) Policy Brief http://www.heritageinstitute.org/federal-somalia-not/ (last accessed 15 April 2018)

——— 'Survey of Public Opinion on Somalia's Provisional Constitution' (2017) Policy Brief http://www.heritageinstitute.org/survey-public-opinion-somalias-provisional-constitution/ (last accessed 15 April 2018)

Hersi AM, 'Application of Power-Sharing Models in Managing Intractable Clan Conflict in Somalia' (2015) 2 *International Journal of Political Science* 7

Higgins R, 'The United Nations and Lawmaking: The Political Organs' (1970) 64 *American Journal of International Law* 43

——— *Problems and Process: International Law and How We Use It* (Clarendon Press 1994)

——— 'Postmodern Tribalism and the Right to Secession, Comments' in C Brölmann and others (eds), *Peoples and Minorities in International Law* (Springer 1993)

Houben PH, 'Principles of International Law Concerning Friendly Relations and Co-Operation among States' (1967) 61 *American Journal of International Law* 703

Howden D, 'UN-Backed Invasion of Somalia Spirals Into Chaos' *The Independent* (London, 15 December 2011) http://www.independent.co.uk/news/world/africa/un-backed-invasion-of-somalia-spirals-into-chaos-6276959.html (last accessed 15 April 2018)

Human Rights Watch, 'Shell-Shocked: Civilians Under Attack in Mogadishu' (2007) Vol 19, No 12(A) www.hrw.org/sites/default/files/reports/somalia0807webwcover.pdf (last accessed 15 April 2018)

Ibrahim M, 'Somalia Selects Activist as Leader' *New York Times* (10 September 2012) http://www.nytimes.com/2012/09/11/world/africa/parliament-selects-mohamud-as-somalias-president.html?_r=0 (last accessed 15 April 2018)

Ignatieff M, *Empire Lite: Nation-Building in Bosnia, Kosovo and Afghanistan* (Vintage 2003)

International Crisis Group (ICG) 'Salvaging Somalia's Chance for Peace' (2002) Africa Brief n° 11 https://www.crisisgroup.org/africa/horn-africa/somalia/salvaging-somalias-chance-peace (last accessed 15 April 2018)

——— 'Negotiating a Blueprint for Peace in Somalia' (2003) Africa Report n° 59 https://www.crisisgroup.org/africa/horn-africa/somalia/negotiating-blueprint-peace-somalia (last accessed 15 April 2018)

——— 'The Kenyan Military Intervention in Somalia' (2012) Africa Report no 184 https://www.crisisgroup.org/africa/horn-africa/kenya/kenyan-military-intervention-somalia (last accessed 15 April 2018)

——— 'Somalia: from troubled transition to a tarnished transition?'(2012) *Media Release* https://www.crisisgroup.org/africa/horn-africa/somalia/somalia-troubled-transition-tarnished-transition (last accessed 15 April 2018)

Iverson J, 'Transitional Justice, *Jus Post Bellum* and International Criminal Law: Differentiating the Usages, History and Dynamics' (2013) 7 *International Journal of Transitional Justice* 413

Jamnejad M and Wood M, 'The Principle of Non-intervention' (2009) 22 *Leiden Journal of International Law* 345

Jeng A, *Peacebuilding in the African Union* (CUP 2012)

Johnson CD, 'Toward Self-Determination: A Reappraisal as Reflected in the Declaration on Friendly Relations' (1973) 3 *Georgia Journal of International and Comparative Law Quarterly* 145

Joselow G, 'Drafting Somalia's constitution opens debate on religion, law' *Voice of America* (Washington, 29 March 2012) http://www.voanews.com/english/news/Drafting-Somalias-Constitution-Opens-Debate-on-Religion-Law-144862645.html (last accessed 15 April 2018)

Kaplan S, 'The Remarkable Story of Somaliland' (2008) 19 *Journal of Democracy* 143

Kasaija AP, 'The UN-led Djibouti Peace Process for Somalia 2008–2009: Results and Problems' (2010) 28 *Journal of Contemporary African Studies* 261

——— 'Somalia after the United Nations-led Djibouti peace process' (2011) 20 *African Security Review* 45

Kaur S, 'Self-determination in International Law' (1972) 10 *Indian Journal of International Law* 479

Kelsen H, *The Law of the United Nations: A Critical Analysis of its Fundamental Problems* (Praeger 1964) 53

Khayre AAM, 'Self-Defence, Intervention by Invitation, or Proxy War? The Legality of the 2006 Ethiopian Invasion of Somalia' (2014) 22 *International and Comparative Law Quarterly* 208

Kilangi A, 'Permanent Sovereignty Over Natural Resources, General Assembly Resolution 1803 (XVII) of 14 December 1962' Introductory Note http://legal.un.org/avl/ha/ga_1803/ga_1803.html (last accessed 15 April 2018)

Kinderlen HF, *From Trieste to East Timor: The Legal Framework for the Administration of Areas of Conflict by the United Nations – Von Triest nach Osttimor. Der völkerrechtliche Rahmen für die Verwaltung von Krisengebieten durch die Vereinten Nationen* (Springer 2008)

Kiss A, 'The People's Right to Self-Determination' (1986) 7 *Human Rights Law Journal* 165

Kiwanuka RN, 'The Meaning of "People" in the African Charter on Human and People's Rights' (1988) 82 *American Journal of International Law* 80

Klabbers J, 'The Right to Be Taken Seriously: Self-Determination in International Law' (2006) 28 *Human Rights Quarterly* 186

Knoll B, *The Legal Status of Territories Subject to Administration by International Organizations* (CUP 2008)

Knop K, *Diversity and Self-Determination in International Law* (CUP 2002)

Kohen MG (ed), *Secession: International Law Perspectives* (CUP 2006)

Kokott J, 'States, Sovereign Equality' (August 2007) *Max Planck Encyclopedia of Public International Law* http://opil.ouplaw.com/home/epil (last accessed 15 April 2018)

Kondoch B, 'The United Nations Administration of East Timor' (2001) 6 *Journal of Conflict and Security Law* 245

Korhonen O, 'The "State-Building Enterprise": Legal Doctrine, Progress Narratives and Managerial Governance' in Bowden B, Charlesworth H and Farrall J (eds), *The Role of International Law in Rebuilding Societies after Conflict: Great Expectations* (CUP 2009)

Koskenmaki R, 'Legal Implications Resulting from State Failure in Light of the Case of Somalia' (2004) 73 *Nordic Journal of International Law* 1

Koskenniemi M, 'National Self-Determination Today: Problems of Legal Theory and Practice' (1994) 43 *International and Comparative Human Rights Quarterly* 241

Kouroutakis A, 'The Provisional Constitution of the Federal Republic of Somalia: Process, Architecture, and Perspectives' (2014) 3 *Cambridge Journal of International and Comparative Law* 1

Kreijen G, *State Failure, Sovereignty and Effectiveness* (Nijhoff 2004)

Kreuter AC, 'Self-determination, Sovereignty and the Failure of States: Somaliland and the Case for Justified Secession' (2010) 19 *Minnesota Journal of International Law* 363

Lachs M, 'The Law in and of the United Nations (Some Reflections on the Principle of Self-Determination)' (1961) 1 *Indian Journal of International Law* 429

Laing EA, 'The Norm of Self-Determination, 1941–1991' (1991–1992) 22 *California Western International Law Journal* 209

Lansing R, *The Peace Negotiations: A Personal Narrative* (Houghton Mifflin 1921)

Lemay-Hérbert N, 'Statebuilding without Nationbuilding? Legitimacy, State Failure and the Limits of the Institutionalist Approach' (2009) 3 *Journal of Intervention and Statebuilding* 21

——— 'The Semantics of Statebuilding and Nationbuilding: Looking beyond neo-Weberian Approaches' in Lemay-Hérbert N, Onuf N, Rakic V and Bojanic P (eds), *Semantics of Statebuilding: Language, Meanings and Sovereignty* (Routledge 2013)

Lenin VI, 'The Question of National Policy' in *Lenin, Collected Works, Vol 20* (first published 1914, Progress Publishers 1967)

——— 'The Right of Nations to Self-Determination' in *Lenin, Collected Works, Vol 20* (first published 1914, Progress Publishers 1967)

Levitt JI, 'Illegal Peace? An Inquiry into The Legality of Power-Sharing with Warlords and Rebels in Africa' (2006) 27 *Michigan Journal of International Law* 495

——— *Illegal Peace in Africa: An Inquiry into the Legality of Power Sharing with Warlords, Rebels and Junta* (CUP 2012)

Lewis I, *Understanding Somalia and Somaliland* (Hurst & Company 2008)

Lotz C, 'International Norms in Statebuilding: Finding a Pragmatic Approach' (2010) 16 *Global Governance* 219

Maguire A, 'Law Protecting Rights: Restoring the Law of Self-determination in the Neo-colonial World' (2008) 12 *Law Text Culture* 12

Maley W, 'Democracy and Legitimation: Challenges in the Reconstitution of Political Processes in Afghanistan' in Bowden B, Charlesworth H and Farrall J (eds), *The Role of International Law in Rebuilding Societies after Conflict: Great Expectations* (CUP 2009)

Mardikian L, 'Economic Self-determination in Post-conflict Reconstruction: The Case Study of Timor-Leste' in Saul M and Sweeney JA (eds), *International Law and Post-Conflict Reconstruction Policy* (Routledge 2015)

Marxsen C, 'The Concept of Territorial Integrity in International Law: What are the Implications for Crimea?' (*Zeitschrift für ausländisches öffentliches Recht und Völkerrecht, Heidelberg Journal of International Law, 2015, Forthcoming)* http://ssrn.com/abstract=2515911 (last accessed 15 April 2018)

Matheson MJ, 'United Nations Governance of Post-Conflict Societies' (2001) 95 *American Journal of International Law* 76

McCormic T, 'Somalia's Incredible Shrinking Election' *Foreign Policy* (6 August 2015) http://foreignpolicy.com/2015/08/06/somalias-incredible-shrinking-election-hassan-sheikh-mohamud/ (last accessed 15 April 2018)

McCorquodale R, 'Self-Determination: A Human Rights Approach' (1994) 43 *International and Comparative Law Quarterly* 860

McWhinney E, 'Friendly Relations and Cooperation among States: Debate at the Twentieth General Assembly, United Nations' (1966) 60 *American Journal of International* Law 356

——— *Self-determination of Peoples and Plural-Ethnic States in Contemporary International Law: Failed States, Nation-building and the Alternative, Federal Option* (Brill 2007)

Melandri M, 'The State, Human Rights and the Ethics of War Termination: A Critical Appraisal' (2011) 7 *Global Ethics* 241

——— 'Self-determination and State-building in International Law: The Need for a New Research Approach' (2015) 20 *Journal of Conflict and Security Law* 75

——— and Hassan MA, 'Somalia's Draft Constitution: Too Undemocratic?' *Think Africa Press* (3 July 2012) http://allafrica.com/stories/201207030981.html (last accessed 15 April 2018)

Menkhaus K, 'The Crisis in Somalia, Tragedy in Five Acts' (2007) 106 *African Affairs* 357

——— *Somalia: A Country in Peril, a Policy Nightmare* (September 2008) ENOUGH Strategy Paper http://www.enoughproject.org/publications/somalia-country-peril-policy-nightmare (last accessed 15 April 2018)

——— 'If Mayors Ruled Somalia: Beyond the State-building Impasse' (2014) The Nordic Africa Institute, Policy Note http://www.nai.uu.se/news/articles/2014/04/29/154351/index.xml (last accessed 15 April 2018)

——— 'Elections in the Hardest Places: The Case of Somalia' (2017) 28 *Journal of Democracy* 132

Mhango M, 'Governance, Peace and Human Rights Violations in Africa: Addressing the Application of the Right to Self-Determination in Post-Independence Africa' (2012) 5 *African Journal of Legal Studies* 199

Miti K, 'Somalia: The Endless Search for Peace' (2010) AISA Briefing No 25 http://www.ai.org.za/wp-content/uploads/downloads/2011/11/No-25.-Somalia-The-Endless-search-for-Peace.pdf (last accessed 15 April 2018)

Mohamed S, 'From Keeping Peace to Building Peace: A Proposal for a Revitalized United Nations Trusteeship Council' (2005) 105 *Columbia Law Review* 809

Møller B, 'The Somali Conflict: The Role of External Actors' (2009) *Danish Institute for International Studies*, Report No 3 https://www.econstor.eu/bitstream/10419/59871/1/592906116.pdf (last accessed 15 April 2018)

Moore M (ed), *National Self-Determination and Secession* (OUP 1998)

de Moral I, 'An Approach to the Democratic Debate in International Law' (in Spanish) (2010) 10 *Anuario Mexicano de Derecho Internacional* 97

Mukhtar MH, 'Somali Reconciliation Conferences: The Unbeaten Track' in Osman AA and Souaré IK (eds), *Somalia at the Crossroads: Challenges and Perspectives on Reconstituting a Failed State* (Adonis & Abbey 2007)

Mulugeta K, *The Role of Regional and International Organizations in Resolving the Somali Conflict: The Case of IGAD* (Friederich Ebert-Stiftung 2009) http://library.fes.de/pdf-files/bueros/aethiopien/07937-book.pdf (last accessed 15 April 2018)

Murithi T, 'Inter-Governmental Authority on Development on the Ground: Comparing Interventions in Sudan and Somalia' in F Soderbaum and R Tavares, *Regional Organizations in African Security* (Routledge 2011)

Murphy R (ed), *Post-Conflict Rebuilding and International Law* (Routledge 2016)

Murray G, 'Self-Determination of Nationalities' (1922) 1 *Journal of the British Institute of International Affairs* 6

Musgrave TD, *Self-Determination and National Minorities* (Clarendon Press 1997)

Nowak M, *UN Covenant on Civil and Political Rights: CCPR Commentary* (2nd rev edn, Engel Verlag 2005)

O'Connor V, 'Traversing the Rocky Road of Law Reform in Conflict and Post-Conflict States: Model Codes for Post Conflict Criminal Justice as a Tool of Assistance' (2005) 16 *Criminal Law Forum* 231

Office of the United Nations High Commissioner for Human Rights, *Rule-of-Law Tools for Post-Conflict States* (9 vols OHCHR 2006)

Orakhelashvili A, 'The Post-War Settlement in Iraq: The UN Security Council Resolution 1483 (2003) and General International Law' (2003) 8 *Journal of Conflict and Security Law* 307

——— *Peremptory Norms in International Law* (OUP 2006)

Orend B, 'Just Post Bellum: The Perspective of a Just-War Theorist' (2007) 20 *Leiden Journal of International Law* 573

Orford A, *Reading Humanitarian Intervention: Human Rights and the Use of Force in International Law* (CUP 2003)

——— 'International Territorial Administration and The Management of Decolonization' (2010) 59 *International and Comparative Law Quarterly* 227

Osinbajo Y, 'Legality in a Collapsed State: The Somali Experience' (1996) 45 *International and Comparative Law Quarterly* 910

Osterdahl I and van Zadel E, 'What Will Jus Post Bellum Mean? Of New Wine and Old Bottles' (2009) 14 *Journal of Conflict and Security Law* 175

Ottolenghi M, 'The Stars and Stripes in Al-Fardos Square: The Implications for International Law of Belligerent Occupation' (2007) 72 *Fordham Law Review* 2177

Padeldorf NJ and Andersson KG, 'The Aaland Islands Question' (1939) 22 *American Journal of International Law* 465

Paris R, 'International Peacebuilding and the "*Mission Civilisatrice*"' (2002) 28 *Review of International Studies* 637

——— *At War's End: Building Peace after Civil Conflict* (CUP 2004)

Pattison J, '*Jus post Bellum* and the Responsibility to Rebuild' (2015) 45 *British Journal of Political Science* 635

Peters N, 'The Principle of Democratic Teleology in International Law' (2008) 34 *Brooklyn Journal of International Law* 33

Pomerance M, 'The United States and Self-Determination: Perspectives on the Wilsonian Conception' (1976) 70 *American Journal of International Law* 1

——— *Self-determination in Law and Practice: The New Doctrine in the United Nations* (Martinus Nijhoff 1982)

——— 'Self-Determination Today: The Metamorphosis of an Ideal' (1984) 19 *Israel Law Review* 310

Pouligny B, 'Supporting Local Ownership in Humanitarian Action' (2009) Global Public Policy Institute, *Humanitarian Policy Paper Series* https://www.alnap.org/system/files/content/resource/files/main/gppippr-local-ownership-2009.pdf (last accessed 15 April 2018)

Primoratz I and Pavković A (eds), *Identity, Self-Determination and Secession* (Ashgate 2006)

Prunier G and Wilson B, 'A World of Conflict Since 9/11: The CIA coup in Somalia' (2006) 33 *Review of African Political Economy* 749

Pugh M, 'Peacekeeping and Critical Theory' (2004) 11 *International Peacekeeping* 39

——— 'Reflections on Aggressive Peace' (2014) 19 *International Peacekeeping* 410

Quane H, 'The United Nations and the Evolving Right to Self-determination' (1998) 47 *International and Comparative Law Quarterly* 537

Radan P, 'Secessionist Referendum in International and Domestic Law' (2012) 18 *Nationalism and Ethnic Politics* 8

Raic D, *Statehood and the Law of Self Determination* (Kluwer Law 2002)

Ratner S, 'Drawing a Better Line: *Uti possidetis* and the Borders of New States' (1996) 90 *American Journal of International Law* 590

Richardson III HJ, 'The Danger of the New Legal Colonialism' (2010) 104 *Proceedings of the Annual Meeting, American Society of International* 393

Richmond OP, 'UN Peace Operations and the Dilemmas of the Peacebuilding Consensus' (2004) 11 *International Peacekeeping* 83

'The Problem of Peace: Understanding the "Liberal Peace"' (2006) 6 *Conflict, Security & Development* 291

——— 'Beyond Local Ownership in the Architecture of Peacebuilding' (2012) 11 *Ethnopolitics* 354

Rigo-Sureda A, *The Evolution of the Right to Self-determination: A Study of United Nations Practice* (Sijthoff 1973)

Roberts A, 'The End of Occupation: Iraq 2004' (2005) 54 *International and Comparative Law Quarterly* 27

——— 'Transformative Military Occupation: Applying the Laws of War and Human Rights' (2006) 100 *American Journal of International Law* 580

Rosas A, 'Internal Self-Determination' in Tomuschat C (ed), *Modern Law of Self-Determination* (Brill 1993)

Rosenstock R, 'The Declaration of Principles of International Law Concerning Friendly Relations: A Survey' (1971) 65 *American Journal of International Law* 713

Rotberg RI, *When States Fail: Causes and Consequences* (Princeton University Press 2004)

Roth BR, *Governmental Illegitimacy in International Law* (OUP 1999)

Roth-Arriaza N and Mariezcurrena J (eds), *Transitional Justice in the Twenty-First Century: Beyond Truth versus Justice* (CUP 2006)

Russell HS, 'The Helsinki Declaration: Brobdingnag or Lilliput?' (1976) 70 *American Journal of International Law* 242

Sahovic M, *Principles of International Law Concerning Friendly Relations and Cooperation* (Belgrade Institute of International Politics and Economics 1972)

Samatar AI, 'The Miracle of Mogadishu' (2006) 33 *Review of African Political Economy* 581

——— 'Ethiopian Invasion of Somalia: US Warlordism and AU Shame' (2007) 34 *African Review of Political Economy* 153

——— 'The Porcupine Dilemma: Governance and Transition in Somalia' (2007) 7 *Bildhaan: An International Journal of Somali Studies* 39

——— 'Debating Somali Identity in a British Tribunal: The Case of The BBC Somali Service' (2010) 10 *Bildhaan: An International Journal of Somali Studies* 36

——— 'Somalia's fleeting opportunity for hopeful change?' *Al-Jazeera* (Doha, 18 September 2012) http://www.aljazeera.com/indepth/opinion/2012/09/2012 91612255832176.html (last accessed 15 April 2018)

——— and Samatar AI, 'Somali Reconciliation: Editorial Note' (2008) 3 *Bildhaan: An International Journal of Somali Studies* 1

Samuels K, 'State-building and the Political Transition after Conflict' (2005) 99 *Proceedings of the American Society of International Law Annual Meeting* 171

——— 'Post-Conflict Constitutions and Constitution-Making' (2006) 6 *Chicago Journal of International Law* 663

——— 'Constitution-building During the War on Terror: The Challenge of Somalia' (2008) 40 *New York University Journal of International Law and Politics* 597

Sassòli M, 'Legislation and Maintenance of Public Order and Civil Life by Occupying Powers' (2005) 16 *European Journal of International Law* 661

Saul M, 'From Haiti to Somalia: The Assistance Model and the Paradox of State Reconstruction in International Law' (2009) 11 *International Community Law Review* 119

——— 'The Impact of the Legal Right to Self-Determination on the Law of Occupation as a Framework for Post-Conflict State Reconstruction' in Quenivet N and Shah S (eds), *International Law and Armed Conflict: Challenges in the 21st Century* (TMC Asser Press 2010)

——— 'Local Ownership of Post-Conflict Reconstruction in International Law: The Initiation of International Involvement' (2011) 16 *Journal of Conflict and Security Law* 165

——— 'The Normative Status of Self-Determination in International Law: A Formula for Uncertainty in the Scope and Content of the Right?' (2011) 11 *Human Rights Law Review* 609

——— 'The Search for an International Legal Concept of Democracy: Lessons from the Post-Conflict Reconstruction of Sierra Leone' (2012) 13 *Melbourne Journal of International Law* 1

——— 'Creating Popular Governments in Post-Conflict Situations: The Role of International Law' in Stahn C, Easterday JS and Iverson J (eds), *Jus Post Bellum* (OUP 2014)

——— *Popular Governance of Post-Conflict Reconstruction: The Role of International Law* (CUP 2014)

——— 'International Law and the Identification of an Interim Government to Lead Post-Conflict Reconstruction' in Saul M and Sweeney J (eds), *International Law and Post-Conflict Reconstruction Policy* (Routledge 2015)

——— and Sweeney JA, 'Introduction' in Saul M and Sweeney JA (eds), *International Law and Post-Conflict Reconstruction Policy* (Routledge 2015)

Scheffer D, 'Beyond Occupation Law' (2003) 97 *American Journal of International Law* 842

Scheining M and Aikio P (eds), *Operationalizing the Right of Indigenous Peoples to Self-Determination* (Abo Akademi University 2000)

Schuck M, 'When the Shooting Stops: Missing Elements in Just War Theory' (1994) 111 *Christian Century* 982

Schweigman D, *The Authority of the Security Council under Chapter VII of the UN Charter: Legal Limits and the Role of the International Court of Justice* (Kluwer Law 2001)

Shaw MN, 'The Western Sahara Case' (1978) 49 *British Yearbook of International Law* 119

——— 'Peoples, Territorialism and Boundaries' (1997) 3 *European Journal of International Law* 478

Sheikh A and Omar F, 'Al-Shabaab militants attack Government building, at least 10 dead' *Reuters* (New York, 14 April 2015) http://www.reuters.com/article/2015/04/14/us-somalia-blast-attacks-idUSKBN0N50T520150414 (last accessed 15 April 2018)

Sheeran SP, 'International Law, Peace Agreements and Self-Determination: The Case of The Sudan' (2011) 60 *International and Comparative Law Review* 423

Silva M, *State Legitimacy and Failure in International Law* (Brill 2014)

Simma B and others (eds), *The Charter of the United Nations: A Commentary* (OUP 1994)

Simpson GJ, 'The Diffusion of Sovereignty: Self-Determination in the Post-Colonial Age' (1996) 32 *Stanford Journal of International Law* 255

Sinha P, 'Is Self-Determination Passé?' (1973) 12 *Columbia Journal of Transnational Law* 260

——— 'Has Self-determination Become a Principle of International Law Today?' (1974) 14 *Indian Journal of International Law* 332

de Sousa RRP, 'External Interventions and Civil War Intensity in South-Central Somalia (1991–2010)' (2014) 29 *Cuadernos de Estudios Africanos* 57

Spijkers O, *The United Nations, the Evolution of Global Values and International Law* (Intersentia 2011)

Stahn C, 'Governance beyond the State: Issues of Legitimacy in International Territorial Administration' (2005) 2 *International Organizations Law Review* 9

——— '"Jus ad Bellum', "Jus in Bello" … "Jus Post Bellum"? Rethinking the Conception of the Law of Armed Force' (2006) 17 *European Journal of International Law* 921

——— *The Law and Practice of International Territorial Administration: Versailles to Iraq and Beyond* (CUP 2008)

——— 'Jus Post Bellum: Mapping the Discipline(s)' in Stahn C and Kleffner JK, *Jus Post Bellum: Towards a Law of Transition from Conflict to Peace* (TMC Asser Press 2008)

——— and Kleffner JK, *Jus Post Bellum: Towards a Law of Transition from Conflict to Peace* (TMC Asser Press 2008)

——— Easterday JS and Iverson J, *Jus Post Bellum: Mapping the Normative Foundations* (OUP 2014)

Stathpoulou K, 'Self-Determination, Peace-Making and Peace-Building: Recent Trends in African Intra-State Peace Agreements' in French D (ed), *Statehood and Self-Determination: Reconciling Tradition and Modernity in International Law* (CUP 2013)

Sterio M, *The Right to Self-Determination under International Law: "Selfistans", Secession and the Rule of the Great Powers* (Routledge 2013)

Stromseth JE, Wippman D and Brooks R, *Can Might Make Rights? Building the Rule of Law after Military Interventions* (CUP 2006)

Summers J, 'The Status of Self-determination in International Law: A Question of Legal Significance or Political Importance?' (2003) 14 *Finnish Yearbook of International Law* 271

——— 'The Rhetoric and Practice of Self-Determination: A Right of All Peoples or Political Institutions?' (2004) 73 *Nordic Journal of International Law* 325

——— 'The Right to Self-Determination and Nationalism in International Law' (2005) 12 *International Journal on Minority Rights* 325

——— (ed), *Kosovo: A Precedent? The Declaration of Independence, the Advisory Opinion and Implications for Statehood, Self-determination and Minority Rights* (Martinus Nijhoff 2011)

——— 'The Concept of Internal and External Self-Determination Reconsidered' in French D (ed), *Statehood and Self-Determination: Reconciling Tradition and Modernity in International Law* (CUP 2013)

——— *Peoples and International Law: How the Right of Self-Determination and Nationalism Shape a Contemporary Law of Nations* (2nd edn, Martinus Nijhoff 2014)

Talmon S, 'Who is a legitimate government in exile? Towards normative criteria for governmental legitimacy in international law' in Goodwin-Gill G and Talmon S (eds), *The Reality of International Law. Essays in Honour of Ian Brownlie* (OUP 1999)

Tay N and Smith D, 'Somalia's first Parliament since 1991 inaugurated in Mogadishu' *The Guardian* (London, 20 August 2012) http://www.theguardian.com/world/2012/aug/20/somalia-first-parliament-inaugurated (last accessed 15 April 2018)

Teitel R, 'Rethinking *Jus Post Bellum* in an Age of Global Transitional Justice: Engaging with Michael Walzer and Terry May' (2013) 24 *European Journal of International Law* 335

Thornberry P, 'The Democratic or Internal Aspect of Self-determination with Some Remarks on Federalism' in Tomuschat C (ed), *Modern Law of Self-Determination* (Martinus Nijhoff 1993)

Thürer D, 'The "Failed State" in International Law' (1999) *81 International Review of the Red Cross* 731

——— 'Self-determination' in *Max Planck Encyclopedia of Public International Law, Vol IV* (OUP 2008)

——— and Burri T, 'Self-determination' (2010) *Max Planck Encyclopedia of Public International Law* http://opil.ouplaw.com/home/epil (last accessed 15 April 2018)

Tomuschat C, 'Self-Determination in a Post-Colonial World' in Tomuschat C (ed), *Modern Law of Self-Determination* (Martinus Nijhoff 1993)

——— 'The Security Council and *Jus Cogens*' in Cannizzaro E (ed), *The Present and Future of Jus Cogens* (Sapienza Università 2015)

Toone JE, 'Occupation Law During and After Iraq: The Expedience of Conservationism Evidenced in the Minutes and Resolutions of the Iraqi Governing Council' (2012) 24 *Florida Journal of International Law* 469

Tzakanopoulos A, 'Human Rights and United Nations Security Council Measures' in de Wet E and Vidmar J (eds), *Norm Conflicts in Public International Law: The Place of Human Rights* (OUP 2012).

Umozurike UO, *Self-determination in International Law* (Archon 1972)

United Nations, UNDP/UNPOS Joint Constitution Unit, *Guidebook on the Provisional Constitution of Somalia* (2012) http://docplayer.net/29951376-Guidebook-on-the-provisional-constitution-of-somalia.html (last accessed 15 April 2018)

United Nations Development Programme, Country Office for Somalia (2012) *Gender in Somalia Brief*, 3 http://www.undp.org/content/dam/rbas/doc/Women's%20 Empowerment/Gender_Somalia.pdf (last accessed 15 April 2018)

United Nations Department of Peacekeeping Operations (UNDPKO), *Handbook on United Nations Multidimensional Peacekeeping Operations* (UNDPKO Best Practices Unit 2003)

Vidmar J, 'The Right of Self-Determination and Multiparty Democracy: Two Sides of the Same Coin?' (2010) 10 *Human Rights Law Review* 239

——— *Democratic Statehood in International Law: The Emergence of New States in Post-Cold War Practice* (Hart Publishing 2013)

Waldron J, 'Two Conceptions of Self-determination' in Besson S and Tasioulas J (eds), *The Philosophy of International Law* (OUP 2010)

Walter C, von Ungern-Sternberg A and Abushov K (eds), *Self-Determination and Secession in International Law* (OUP 2014)

Weller M, *Escaping the Self-determination Trap* (Martinus Nijhoff 2009)

——— 'Settling Self-Determination Conflicts: Recent Developments' (2009) 20 *European Journal of International Law* 111

——— and Wolff S (eds), *Autonomy, Self-Governance and Conflict Resolution: Innovative Approaches to Institutional Design in Divided Societies* (Routledge 2005)

Wener WG, 'Self-Determination and Civil War' (2011) 6 *Journal of Conflict and Security Law* 171

Wengler W, 'Le Droit à la Libre Disposition des Peuples Comme Principe de Droit International' (1957) 10 *Revue Hellenique de Droit International* 27

Wheatley S, *Democracy, Minorities and International Law* (CUP 2005)

——— 'The Security Council, Democratic Legitimacy and Regime Change in Iraq' (2006) 17 *European Journal of International Law* 531

Whelan A, 'Wilsonian Self-Determination and the Versailles Settlement' (1994) 43 *International and Comparative Law Quarterly* 99

White ND, 'The Will and Authority of the Security Council after Iraq' (2004) 17 *Leiden Journal of International Law* 645

——— *Advanced Introduction to International Conflict and Security Law* (Edward Elgar Publishing 2014)

White RA, 'Self-Determination: Time for a Re-Assessment' (1981) XXVIII *Netherlands International Law Review* 147

Wilde R, 'The Skewed Responsibility Narrative of the "Failed States" Concept' (2002–2003) 9 *ILSA Journal of International and Comparative Law* 425
——— *International Territorial Administration: How Trusteeship and the Civilizing Mission Never Went Away* (OUP 2008)
——— 'From Trusteeship to Self-Determination and Back Again: The Role of the Hague Regulations in the Evolution of International Trusteeship, and the Framework of Rights and Duties of Occupying Powers' (2010) 31 *Loyola of Los Angeles International and Comparative Law Review* 75
Williams PD, 'Into the Mogadishu Maelstrom: The African Union Mission in Somalia' (2009) 16 *International Peacekeeping* 514
Wilson W, 'Address to the United States Senate, 22 January 1917' in Link AS (ed), *The Papers of Woodrow Wilson, Vol 40* (Princeton University Press 1982)
Witten RM, 'The Declaration on Friendly Relations' (1971) 12 *Harvard International Law Journal* 509
Wolfrum R, 'Chapter 1: Purposes and Principles' in Simma B and others (eds), *The Charter of the United Nations: A Commentary* (OUP 1994)
——— 'International Administrations in Post-conflict Situations by the United Nations and Other International Actors' (2005) 9 *Max Planck Yearbook of United Nations Law* 649
——— 'Iraq – From Belligerent Occupation to Iraqi Exercise of Sovereignty: Foreign Power versus International Community Interference' (2005) 9 *Max Planck Yearbook of United Nations Law* 1
Woolsey TS, 'Self-Determination' (1919) 13 *American Journal of International Law* 302
Wouters J and Chan K, 'State-Building, Occupation and International Law: Friends or Foes?' (2012) Leuven Centre for Global Governance Studies, *Working Paper No 87* http://papers.ssrn.com/sol3/papers.cfm?abstract_id=2274806 (last accessed 15 April 2018)
Wright Q, 'Recognition and Self-determination' (1954) 48 *American Society of International Law Proceedings* 23
Xanthaki A, 'The Right to Self-Determination: Meaning and Scope' in Ghanea N and Xanthaki A (eds), *Minorities, Peoples and Self-determination* (Martinus Nijhoff 2004)
——— *Indigenous Rights and United Nations Standards: Self-Determination, Culture and Land* (CUP 2007)
Yannis A, 'State Collapse and Prospects for Political Reconstruction and Democratic Governance in Somalia' (1997) 5 *African Yearbook of International Law* 23
——— 'State Collapse and its Implications for Peacebuilding and Reconstruction' (2002) 33 *Development and Change* 817
Yihdego ZW, 'Ethiopia's Military Action Against the Union of Islamic Courts and Others in Somalia: Some Legal Implications' (2007) 56 *International and Comparative Law Quarterly* 666
Youngjin J, 'In Pursuit of Reconstructing Iraq: Does Self-Determination Matter?' (2005) 33 *Denver Journal of International Law and Policy* 391
Yusuf AA, 'Government Collapse and State Continuity: The Case of Somalia' (2003) 13 *Italian Yearbook of International Law* 11
Yusuf M, 'More Than 200 Approved for New Somali Parliament' *Voice of America* (Washington, 19 August 2012) http://www.voanews.com/content/more-than-200-approved-for-new-somali-parliament/1491225.html (last accessed 15 April 2018)

Zartman IW (ed), *Collapsed States: the Disintegration and Restoration of Legitimate Authority* (Lynne Rienner 1995)
Zimmerman A and Stahn C, 'Yugoslav Territory, United Nations Trusteeship or Sovereign State? Reflections on the Current and Future Legal Status of Kosovo' (2001) 70 *Nordic Journal of International Law* 423
Zyberi G, 'Self-determination through the Lens of the International Court of Justice' (2009) 56 *Netherlands International Law Review* 429

Unattributed press articles

'Can Federalism Work for Somalia?' *Irin News Briefing* (Nairobi, 5 February 2014) http://www.irinnews.org/report/99600/briefing-can-federalism-work-in-somali (last accessed 15 April 2018)
'Communiqué on High Level Meeting in Somalia' *UN Press Release* (New York, 28 September 2015) http://www.un.org/press/En/2015/sg2218.doc.htm (last accessed 15 April 2018)
'Communiqué on the Electoral Model for 2016' *Somaliland Press* (27 January 2016) http://www.somalilandpress.com/somaliacommunique-on-the-electoral-model-for-2016/ (last accessed 15 April 2018)
'Kenya attack: 147 dead in Garissa University assault' *BBC News* (London, 3 April 2015) http://www.bbc.com/news/world-africa-32169080 (last accessed 15 April 2018)
'New Somali Alliance Threatens War' *BBC News* (12 September 2007) http://news.bbc.co.uk/2/hi/africa/6990928.stm (last accessed 15 April 2018)
'Somali Leaders Back New Constitution' *BBC News Africa* (Nairobi, 1 August 2012) http://www.bbc.com/news/world-africa-19075685 (last accessed 15 April 2018)
'Somali Leaders Launch Reconciliation Bid' *Al-Jazeera* (Doha, 4 September 2011) http://www.aljazeera.com/news/africa/2011/09/201194153630941320.html (last accessed 15 April 2018)5
'Somalia National Peace Conference' *SN News* (6 April 2000) http://www.banadir.com/whatisthere.htm (last accessed 15 April 2018)
'Somalia: Parliament will meet in Baidoa, confirms President' *Irin News* (14 February 2006) http://www.irinnews.org/printreport.aspx?reportid=58133 (last accessed 15 April 2018)
'Somalia Swears in Historic New Parliament' *Al-Jazeera* (Doha, 23 August 2012) http://www.aljazeera.com/news/africa/2012/08/2012818183718864689.html (last accessed 15 April 2018)
'Somalis Vow a Holy War Against Ethiopia' *BBC News* (9 October 2006) http://news.bbc.co.uk/1/hi/world/africa/6032907.stm (last accessed 15 April 2018)
'The Rise of the Shabaab' *The Economist* (18 December 2008) http://www.economist.com/node/12815670 (last accessed 15 April 2018)

Other sources

African Union

Report of OAU Secretary-General on Draft African Charter on Human and People's Rights, OAU Doc C.M./1149 (XXXVII) 1981

African Union, Peace and Security Council, 29th Meeting, Addis Ababa, Ethiopia, Doc PSC/PR/2(XXIX) 12 May 2005

African Union, Peace and Security Council, Communiqué of the 163th Meeting, Addis Ababa, Ethiopia, Doc PSC/MIN/Comm.4 (CLXIII) 22 December 2008

African Union, Communiqué of the 306th Peace and Security Council Meeting on the Situation in Somalia, Addis Ababa, Ethiopia, 5 January 2012 http://amisom-au.org/2012/01/commuique-of-the-306th-psc-meeting-on-the-situation-in-somalia/ (last accessed 15 April 2018)

Council of Europe

Council of Europe, 2748th General Affairs Council Meeting, 15 September 2015, ref CL06-182EN http://europa.eu/rapid/press-release_PRES-06-241_en.doc (last accessed 15 April 2018)

IGAD

Communiqué of the 30th Extraordinary Session of the IGAD Council of Ministers on the Prevailing Political and Security Situation in Somalia, Addis Ababa, Ethiopia, 18 November 2008 http://www.operationspaix.net/DATA/DOCUMENT/3105~v~Communique_of_the_30th_Extra-ordinary_Session_of_the_IGAD_Council_of_Ministers_on_the_Security_and_Political_Situation_in_Somalia.pdf (last accessed 15 April 2018)

United Nations Conference on International Organization

1 Doc UN Conf. on Int'l Org., Committee I/1 (1945)

6 Doc UN Conf. on Int'l Org., Committee I/1 (1945)

17 Doc UN Conf. on Int'l Org., Committee I/1(1945)

18 Doc UN Conf. On Int'l Org., Committee I/1 (1945)

United Nations General Assembly Official Records (GAOR)

GAOR, 5th Session, Draft Decision, UN Doc A/C.3/L.96, 6 November 1950

GAOR, 5th Session, Report of the Third Committee, UN Doc A/1559, 29 November 1950

GAOR, 7th Session, Summary Records of the 447th Meeting, UN Doc A/C.3/SR.447, 18 November 1952

GAOR, 7th Session, Summary Records of the 447th Meeting, UN Doc A/C.3/SR.454, 24 November 1952

GAOR, 10th Session, Report of the Third Committee, Summary Records of the 641st Meeting, UN Doc A/C.3/SR.641, 21 October 1955

GAOR, 10th Session, Report of the Third Committee, UN Doc A/3077, 8 December 1955

GAOR, 24th Session, Report of the Special Committee on Principles of International Law Concerning Friendly Relations and Co-operation Among States, Supp. 19, UN Doc A/7619 (1969)

GAOR 25th Session, 6th Committee, Summary Records of the 1178th Meeting, UN Doc A/C.6/SR.1178, 23 September 1970
GAOR, 25th Session, Draft Amendment, UN Doc A/AC.125/L.80 (1970)
GAOR 25th Session, Report of the Drafting Committee, UN Doc A/AC.125/L.86, 1 May 1970
GAOR, 25th Session, Report of the Special Committee on Principles of International Law Concerning Friendly Relations and Co-operation Among States, Supp. 18, UN Doc A/8018 (1970)
GAOR, 43rd Session, Amendments to Draft Resolution, UN Doc A/C.3/43/L.80, 29 November 1988
GAOR, 43rd Session, Summary Records of the 57th Meeting, UN Doc A/C.3/43/SR.57, 30 November 1988
GAOR, 56th Session, Article 40: Commentary, Report of the International Law Commission, Supplement No 10, UN Doc A/56/10 (2001)
General Assembly, 58th Session, Report of the Study Group of the International Law Commission, 'Fragmentation of International Law: Difficulties Arising from the Diversification and Expansion of International Law' (2006) UN Doc A/CN.4/L.682/Add.1, 2 May 2006
General Assembly, 59th Session, Report of the High-level Panel of Threats, Challenges, and Change: *A More Secure World: Our Shared Responsibility* (2004) UN Doc A/59/565, 2 December 2004

United Nations General Assembly Resolutions

GA Resolution 545 (VI), 5 February 1952
GA Resolution 1314 (XIII), 12 December 1958
GA Resolution 1514 (XV), 14 December 1960
GA Resolution 1541 (XV), 15 December 1960
GA Resolution 1803 (XVII), 14 December 1962
GA Resolution 2131 (XX), 21 December 1965
GA Resolution 2625 (XXV), 24 October 1970
GA Resolution 43/157, UN Doc A/Res/43/157, 8 December 1988
GA Resolution 44/146, UN Doc A/Res/44/146, 15 December 1989
GA Resolution 44/147, UN Doc A/Res/44/147, 15 December 1989
GA Resolution 45/150, UN Doc A/Res/45/150, 18 December 1990
GA Resolution 45/151, UN Doc A/Res/45/151, 18 December 1990
GA Resolution 46/130, UN Doc A/Res/46/130, 17 December 1991
GA Resolution 46/137, UN Doc A/Res/46/137, 17 December 1991
GA Resolution 47/130, UN Doc A/Res/47/130, 18 December 1992
GA Resolution 47/138, UN Doc A/Res/47/138, 18 December 1992
GA Resolution 48/124, UN Doc A/Res/48/124, 20 December 1993
GA Resolution 48/131, UN Doc A/Res/48/131, 20 December 1993
GA Resolution 49/180, UN Doc A/Res/49/180, 23 December 1994
GA Resolution 49/190, UN Doc A/Res/49/190, 23 December 1994
GA Resolution 50/6, UN Doc A/Res/50/6, 24 October 1995
GA Resolution 50/172, UN Doc A/Res/50/172, 22 December 1995
GA Resolution 50/185, UN Doc A/Res/50/185, 22 December 1995
GA Resolution 52/119, UN Doc A/Res/52/119, 12 December 1997

GA Resolution 52/129, UN Doc A/Res/52/129, 12 December 1997
GA Resolution 54/168, UN Doc A/Res/54/168, 17 December 1999
GA Resolution 54/173, UN Doc A/Res/54/173, 17 December 1999
GA Resolution 56/154, UN Doc A/Res/56/154, 19 December 2001
GA Resolution 56/159, UN Doc A/Res/56/159, 19 December 2001
GA Resolution 58/180, UN Doc A/Res/58/180, 22 December 2003
GA Resolution 58/189, UN Doc A/Res/58/189, 22 December 2003
GA Resolution 59/201, UN Doc A/Res/59/201, 20 December 2004
GA Resolution 60/162, UN Doc A/Res/60/162, 16 December 2005
GA Resolution 60/164, UN Doc A/Res/60/164, 16 December 2005
GA Resolution 62/150, UN Doc A/Res/62/150, 18 December 2007
GA Resolution 64/155, UN Doc A/Res/64/155, 18 December 2009
GA Resolution 66/163, UN Doc A/Res/66/163, 19 December 2011
GA Resolution 68/164, UN Doc A/Res/68/164, 18 December 2013

United Nations Security Council Meeting Records, Letters and Statements

Meeting Records, UN Doc S/PV.4392, 19 October 2001
Meeting Records, UN Doc S/PV.4487 (Resumption 1), 11 March 2002
Meeting Records, UN Doc S/PV.5579, 6 December 2006
Meeting Records, UN Doc S/PV.5614, 26 December 2006
Meeting Records, UN Doc S/PV.6718, 22 February 2012
Letter dated 19 May 2009 from the Permanent Representative of Eritrea to the United Nations addressed to the President of the Security Council, UN Doc S/2009/256, 20 May 2009
Statement by the President of the Security Council, UN Doc S/PRST/2001/30, 31 October 2001
Statement by the President of the Security Council, UN Doc S/PRST/2004/43, 19 November 2004
Statement by the President of the Security Council, UN Doc S/PRST/2006/11, 15 March 2006

United Nations Security Council Reports

Report of the Monitoring Group on Somalia, submitted in accordance with Resolution 1724 (2006), UN Doc S/2007/436, 18 July 2007
Report of the Monitoring Group on Somalia pursuant to Security Council resolution 1676 (2006), S/2006/913, 22 November 2006
Report of the Panel of Experts on Somalia pursuant to Security Council Resolution 1425 (2002), UN Doc S/2003/223, 25 March 2003
Report of the Team of Experts appointed pursuant to Security Council Resolution 1407 (2002) paragraph 1, concerning Somalia, UN Doc S/2002/722, 3 July 2002
Report of the Secretary-General, 'An Agenda for Peace' UN Doc A/47/277-S24111, 17 June 1992
Report of the Secretary-General, 'Supplement to An Agenda for Peace: Position Paper of the Secretary-General on the Occasion of the Fiftieth Anniversary of the United Nations' UN Doc A/50/60-S/1995/1, 3 January 1995

Report of the Secretary-General on the Situation in Somalia, UN Doc S/2000/1211, 19 December 2000
Report of the Secretary-General on the Situation in Somalia, UN Doc S/2001/963, 11 October 2001
Report of the Secretary-General on the Situation in Somalia, UN Doc S/2009/709, 27 June 2002
Report of the Secretary-General on the Situation in Somalia, UN Doc S/2002/1201, 25 October 2002
Report of the Secretary-General on the Situation in Somalia, UN Doc S/2003/231, 26 February 2003
Report of the Secretary-General on the Situation in Somalia, UN Doc S/2003/987, 13 October 2003
Report of the Secretary-General on the Situation in Somalia, UN Doc S/2004/469, 9 June 2004
Report of the Secretary-General on the situation in Somalia, UN Doc S/2007/381 of 25 June 2007
Report of the Secretary-General on the situation in Somalia, UN Doc S/2007/658 of 7 November 2007
Report of the Secretary-General on Somalia, UN Doc S/2011/759, 9 December 2011
Report of the Secretary-General on Somalia, UN Doc S/2012/283, 1 May 2012
Report of the Secretary General on Somalia, UN Doc S/2012/643, 22 August 2012
Report of the Secretary-General on Somalia, UN Doc S/2015/331, 12 May 2015
Report of the Secretary-General on Somalia, UN Doc S/2016/27, 8 January 2016
Special Report of the Secretary-General on the Situation in Somalia, UN Doc SC/2012/74, 31 January 2012

United Nations Security Council Resolutions

SC Res 216 (1965), UN Doc S/Res/216, 12 November 1965
SC Res 733 (1992), UN Doc S/Res/733, 23 January 1992
SC Res 1244 (1999), UN Doc S/Res/1244, 10 June 1999
SC Res 1483 (2003), UN Doc S/Res/1483, 22 May 2003
SC Res 1500 (2003), UN Doc S/Res/1500, 14 August 2003
SC Res 1511 (2003), UN Doc S/Res/1511, 16 October 2003
SC Res 1645 (2005), UN Doc S/Res/1645, 20 December 2005
SC Res 1676 (2006), UN Doc S/RES/1676, 10 May 2006
SC Res 1725 (2006), UN Doc S/Res/1725, 7 December 2006
SC Res 1744 (2007), UN Doc S/Res/1744, 20 February 2007
SC Res 1844 (2008), UN Doc S/Res/1844, 20 November 2008
SC Res 2010 (2011), UN Doc S/Res/2010, 30 September 2011
SC Res 2036 (2012), UN Doc S/Res/2036, 22 February 2012

United Nations Treaty Bodies

Commission on Human Rights, 7th Session, Draft First International Covenant on Human Rights and Measures of Implementation, UN Doc E/CN.4/514, 29 March 1951
Commission on Human Rights, 8th Session, Summary Record of the 253rd Meeting, UN. Doc E/CN.4/SR.253, 15 April 1952

Commission on Human Rights, 8th Session, Summary Record of the 257th Meeting, UN Doc E/CN.4/SR.257, 17 April 1952.

Committee on the Elimination of Racial Discrimination, General Recommendation XXI (48) UN Doc CERD/C/365/Rev.1 (2000)

Human Rights Committee, General Comment No 12, CCPR/C/21/Add.3, 12 April 1984

Human Rights Committee, General Comment No 25, CCPR/C/21/Rev.1/Add.7, 27 August 1996

Human Rights Committee, Consideration of Reports Submitted by State Parties under Article 40 of the Covenant: Comments of the Human Rights Committee, UN Doc CCPR/C/79/Add.38, 3 August 1994

Reports by Somali Transitional Institutions

The Main Report of the Federal Constitution Commission on Consultation Draft Constitution, 30th July 2010, http://www.tandemproject.com/pdf/final_main.pdf (last accessed 15 April 2018)

Progress Report of the Independent Federal Constitution Commission on the Consultation Draft Constitution, July 2011 http://www.dastuur.org (last accessed 2 July 2012)

Speeches and Interviews

Address delivered by President Woodrow Wilson at the First Annual Assemblage of the League to Enforce Peace: *American Principles*, 27 May 1916 http://www.presidency.ucsb.edu/ws/?pid=65391 (last accessed 15 April 2018)

Speech delivered by Abdiweli Mohamed Ali, Prime Minister of Somalia, Chatham House (London, UK, 20 February 2012)

Interview with Mario Raffaelli, Trento, Italy, 4 May 2015

Websites

African Elections Database, 'Elections in Somalia' http://africanelections.tripod.com/so.html#1961_Constitutional_Referendum (last accessed 15 April 2018)

BBC News, 'Somalia Profile: Timeline' http://www.bbc.com/news/world-africa-14094632 (last accessed 15 April 2018)

Intergovernmental Authority on Development (IGAD) http://www.igad.int/ (last accessed 15 April 2018)

The Princeton Encyclopedia of Self-Determination, https://pesd.princeton.edu/?q=node/254 (last accessed 15 April 2018)

United States Department of State Bureau of African Affairs, *U.S. Relations with Somalia*, (16 August 2013) http://www.state.gov/r/pa/ei/bgn/2863.htm (last accessed 15 April 2018)

United States Government, Department of State, 'Designation of Al-Shabaab' 18 March 2008 https://web.archive.org/web/20080319184009/http://www.state.gov/r/pa/prs/ps/2008/mar/102338.htm (last accessed 15 April 2018)

Wikileaks, Cable ID: 06ADDISABABA2901_a of 31 October 2006; original classification: SECRET https://search.wikileaks.org/plusd/cables/06ADDISABABA2901_a.html (last accessed 15 April 2018)

Index

For Product Safety Concerns and Information please contact our EU representative GPSR@taylorandfrancis.com Taylor & Francis Verlag GmbH, Kaufingerstraße 24, 80331 München, Germany

Batch number: 10725973

Printed by Printforce, the Netherlands